I0161547

Phil's 3rd Favorite 500

Still More Loves of a Moviegoing Lifetime

Phil Berardelli

Mountain Lake Press
Mountain Lake Park, Maryland

Also by Phil Berardelli:

Phil's Favorite 500: Loves of a Moviegoing Lifetime

Phil's 2nd Favorite 500: More Loves of a Moviegoing Lifetime

Phil's 1001 Nights at the Movies: Quick Takes for Your Consideration

Phil's 3ʳᵈ Favorite 500
Still More Loves of a Moviegoing Lifetime
By Phil Berardelli

Copyright © 2022 Phil Berardelli
All Rights Reserved

ISBN: 978-1-959307-18-1

Published in the United States of America
By Mountain Lake Press

Printed in the United States of America

Cover design by Jutta Medina

No part of this book may be reproduced, stored in a data base or other retrieval system, or transmitted in any form by any means, including mechanical, electronic, photocopying, recording or otherwise, without the prior written permission of the author.

1

*To Gary Arnold, my dear friend and former co-host,
one of the finest film critics
America has ever produced,
whose affection for the movies is unsurpassed*

CONTENTS

3. Arthouse Attractions

4. Art, Imitating Artists

Five Before the Code 63

6. Biblical Proportions

7. Coming of Age

5

12. Disorder in the Court

13. The Electrician's Son

14. Father Figures

17. Hillwilla Heaven

18. Loves Won, Lost or Regained

9

10

27. (Mostly) British Capers

28. My Home Town

29. Another Pittsburgh Boy

13

14

15

45. They're History

46. Tragedy Tomorrow...

19

Epilogue: What Went Wrong?

Introduction to the 3rd Compilation

When I began writing Phil's Favorite 500 over a decade ago, I quickly ran into a surprising problem: My favorites numbered many more than my intended title. In fact, I had so large an excess that, six years later, I easily pulled an equal number of titles into Phil's 2nd Favorite 500, again with a bunch left over. As you can see, I've pulled together 500 more for this third compilation – plus an Epilogue covering 20 more, for reasons I'll explain there. Now, I think I need to relate why I attempted this ambitious undertaking in the first place. It has to do with the word "favorites."

As I mentioned in my original Introduction, over my lifetime of watching movies – now approaching its eighth decade – I've seen well more than 5,000, encompassing all genres, lengths, formats and, most pertinent, levels of quality. From that total, I've culled the 1500 entrées featured in my books because they brought me significant entertainment value. In the best cases, the movies became unforgettable memories for me; in others, at the least, I regarded them as enjoyable experiences. But in every case, I have tried to describe what attracted me not only to that particular title but also to the medium of cinema: its power to amaze, amuse, frighten and even shock.

In human history, and the world over, the cinema experience is unique, in that few other forms of communication can connect so quickly an audience. It's been said that music, art and mathematics represent universal languages, phenomena that can be appreciated by any person on the planet. Yes, all three can serve as means of breaking down cultural differences. But I would argue that movies are the most irresistible cultural bridge.

I recall two convincing examples. In the 1964 British movie *Zulu* (not here), the production company shot on location in Africa and employed real Zulus as extras. As a treat for the tribe, the crew brought in reels of movies to show in the evenings. Did the Zulus express confusion or indifference to the images projected on a screen? No. They became instantly enthralled; laughing, gasping and applauding at a medium they had never witnessed before.

A decade later, director John Huston found 103-year-old Karroom Ben Bouih working as a night watchman near the Morocco location of his movie, *The Man Who Would Be King* (PF5). Huston hired him to play the chief of a mythical tribe living somewhere in remote 19th-century Pakistan. Despite his age, the man had never seen a movie. When Huston showed Ben Bouih footage of himself on the screen, he immediately declared that he would now live forever – an insight that can escape even the most sophisticated moviegoers. Yes, as long as there is a human race, those who have appeared on film will live.

Getting back to my third bunch of favorites, I like most of these 500 movies – and I love some of them – for various reasons. I also respect their value as art, being as they are the product of the efforts of thousands of talented professionals. Incidentally, I placed some of the titles here, instead of in the second compilation, not because I thought less of them but because they fit better into the categories I've established. Some, however, veer into marginal territory. I have seen them at various stages in my life, and I like at least parts of them. But I'm not sure I'll want to see them again. Nevertheless, I think each is worth your consideration.

You might have noticed I dedicated this third volume to my dear friend Gary Arnold. Wherever appropriate and available, I've also included brief excerpts from his reviews. I could never match Gary's erudition on this subject or his impressive personal connections to people in the movie business. But I hope you'll find my enthusiasm contagious. I also hope, as I expressed in Phil's Favorite 500, that you'll discover among these titles some that will become both favorites and your own treasured memories.

Once more, enjoy!

Reading Notes

[B&W] = Shown in black & white

[W] = Shown in a widescreen (also known as "letterbox") format, so look for that version

[3D] = Shown in 3D format (in selected theaters, usually at a premium price)

[PF5] = Reviewed in Phil's Favorite 500

[P25] = Reviewed in Phil's 2nd Favorite 500]

In the 10 years since I first published Phil's Favorite 500, as an ebook only, I've continually had to adjust the formatting to accommodate all of the rapid changes and exploding variety of online video content. For example, I originally included an "[N]" notation with selected titles, signifying that Netflix carried them. But as I quickly found out, Netflix offerings tended to come and go – or they shifted between DVD and instant video – on a regular basis. The same with Amazon's online titles available via its Prime® service. Even the vast Internet Movie Data Base, which once offered a wide variety of easily accessible movie clips, has become more problematic because almost all of them are preceded by ads – most of them lengthy – and even IMDB sometimes shuffles what's available. In short, the changes are happening too rapidly to track. So, for now I'm leaving it to you to search Netflix, Amazon and the other streaming and DVD/Blu-ray services for available titles. For a while, an Internet search engine called Can I Stream It? and designed specifically to help you with this process was available. But they seem to have been bought by Apple, which integrated the service into one of its apps. Your best bet now is to search the phrase "can I stream it" online.

Finding Clips and Featurettes

In my ebook edition – which I hope you will consider as a supplement to this volume – I tried to make it easy to sample clips and short features associated with each title by providing hotlinks to YouTube search pages. At the end of each capsule comment in the ebook, if you'd like to see what is available on YouTube, you can just click on the link marked "YouTube clips," and from there you can jump to whatever is available on that particular day. It's the simplest solution I could manage, though it often will require you to do some scrolling to find the best video sample of a particular title. The same for selected movie music soundtracks and related featurettes, which I embedded within the ebook text of some of the capsules. If you purchased one of the older versions of the book, you probably experienced trouble linking to some of the specific videos. The problem was, and still is, that links can be removed at any time, whether because of copyright issues or other reasons. So, the YouTube-search approach remains the best available option. It won't guarantee you'll get to see a clip based on a particular recommendation, but if it's anywhere on YouTube you'll at least have a chance of finding it.

One caution, however. Though the practice has diminished considerably over the past couple of years, YouTube remains besieged with what can only be called video spam where movie titles are concerned. When you use the search links I've provided, you'll frequently see listings purporting to show you, for free, full-length versions. In reality, they're what has come to be known as "click bait," or invitations to go to other websites or pages, many of which are probably illegitimate. Don't fall for it. You can spot the faux sites by noting the number of views they've received (usually fewer than 1,000) and by their recent posting dates, because YouTube constantly tries to scrub them from its roster. Instead, rent or buy your movie choices from legitimate online retailers – indeed, YouTube and Amazon offer many of my titles for a small fee or a modest price, and YouTube recently began posting many popular movies at full length, for free but with embedded ads. Likewise, on IMDB, you can find many titles to rent. There are other good services as well, and the rates are almost always reasonable.

Titles Included and Not Included

With 500 movies to keep track of, and with lots of cross references, I continually risk making things confusing. In this third compilation, there are many times when I mention titles already covered in Phil's Favorite 500 or Phil's 2nd Favorite 500. As I did in those two books, when I mention a movie not included, I parenthetically note its absence. Otherwise, you can assume you'll find it elsewhere in the text. And for titles I encapsulated in the first two books, I include here the references "(PF5)" and "(P25)." Shameless self-promotion, I admit, but it also tells you where to find a more detailed recommendation. Please indulge my intrusion.

Meanwhile, I've carried over a style rule for making movie titles within the list easy to spot: I've italicized them. In cases where I mention stage plays or songs, I've enclosed them in quotes. If it's books, they're underlined. And for TV shows, newspapers and related names, I've just capitalized them.

1. Adult, in the Best Sense

From years ago to this day, anytime someone uses the term "adult" to describe a movie it's often meant that the content is considered inappropriate for younger audiences, usually because of a sexually explicit nature. Not here, with this beginning section. I chose these 15 dramas because they treat their themes with maturity, subtlety, seriousness and skill. They are all fine films and worth your consideration._Unless otherwise specified, the name associated with each of the listed titles is the director.

The Apostle
1997 – written and directed by Robert Duvall

The venerable Duvall also stars in this portrait of a Euwliss F. "Sonny" Dewley, a passionate fundamentalist preacher who suffers from a terrible temper, a deep character flaw that causes him to beat a man to death at a youth baseball game, rendering him a fugitive. But his self-recognized grievous sin also sets him on a path to redemption, so that when the law finally catches up with him, he faces the consequences with humility. Duvall, in an Oscar-nominated performance, completely humanizes Sonny, to the point where you ache for him when, despite his acts of atonement, he still must pay for his crime. The movie also features a rare dramatic role for Farrah Fawcett, well known in the 1980s for as one of the three principals in the popular TV series Charlie's Angels. A small movie but a gripping one, and a personal triumph for Duvall, who partially financed the production. [Trivia note: Duvall's own religious roots follow the beliefs portrayed in the movie] [Caution: violence] **[W]**

Clean and Sober
1988 – Glenn Gordon Caron

Another actor (like Fawcett) who began primarily in light-comedy roles, Michael Keaton turns in an effective and affecting performance in this disturbing tale about a man's descent into drug abuse. Keaton plays Daryl Pointer, a real estate agent whose cocaine habit has landed him in a heap of trouble – even for substance abusers. Out of options, he enrolls in a rehabilitation program run by a man going only by the name of Craig (Morgan Freeman, in an excellent early role). It's a grueling ordeal from then on, but Keaton and Freeman are both riveting, and they're ably supported by Kathy Baker as a fellow enrollee with a physically abusive boyfriend (Luca Bercovici, one of my favorite little-known character actors), and the versatile M. Emmett Walsh as a recovering addict. [Caution: rough language and adult themes] [W]

Days of Wine and Roses
1962 – Blake Edwards
Continuing the theme of substance abuse, Jack Lemmon and Lee Remick co-star in this shattering drama about alcoholism. They play Joe and Kristen Clay, a married couple who fall completely under the grip of frequent drinking to excess and – here's the shocking aspect – the affliction affects Remick's character more than Lemmon's. This one requires a bit of fortitude because it's heavy going from beginning to end. Yet it's among the finest roles for the two lead actors, both of whom were nominated for Oscars, and it's one of the best films Edwards ever directed. The great Henry Mancini did the moving, melancholy score, including the popular title song, with lyrics by Johnny Mercer. [Trivia notes: 1) The movie was credited with promoting and popularizing Alcoholics Anonymous. 2) Lemmon's performance and Edwards's directing no doubt stemmed from the fact that both men had suffered bouts of alcoholism – not only in their respective pasts but also during the movie's production. Both later confessed to seeking help for their addictions from AA] [Caution: adult themes] [B&W] [W]

Fate Is the Hunter
1964 – Ralph Nelson
A commercial airliner flying in a clear sky suddenly suffers catastrophic engine failure and must make an emergency landing

28

on a beach, where it hits an obstacle and explodes, killing almost everyone aboard. The investigative team, led by Sam McBane (Glenn Ford) and assisted by a surviving flight attendant (Suzanne Pleshette), must unravel the frightening mystery. It's an immersive, straightforward drama, though not based on any real incident. Also, the airliner depicted in the story is a deliberately artificial concoction meant to avoid any legal challenges by aircraft manufacturers. [Trivia note: *Fate Is the Hunter* is derived from a memoir of the same name by Ernest K. Gann (who also wrote the source novel and screenplay for *The High and the Mighty* – see PF5). Except that the book contains no episodes related to the movie's scenario] **[B&W] [W]**

The Flight of the Phoenix
1965 – Robert Aldrich
Another air-disaster story but with a gripping twist. A "Phoenix," as you might know from legend, is a fabulous bird resurrected from the ashes of its former life. In this case, it's a bare-bones aircraft constructed from the remains of a much-larger cargo and passenger plane that has crashed deep in the Libyan desert, stranding eight men. James Stewart (pilot of both the ill-fated mothership and the Phoenix, and a veteran military pilot in real life) heads the cast that includes Richard Attenborough, Ernest Borgnine, George Kennedy and Peter Finch – Oscar winners all – as well as Ian Bannen and Hardy Krüger. It's a raw, gripping adventure tale. [Trivia note: Famed stunt pilot Paul Mantz died while performing the escape … flight of the Phoenix] **[W]**

The Harder They Fall
1956 – Mark Robson
Here's one you've possibly never heard of but trust me; it's well worth finding. Not to be confused with the violent and distasteful 2021 Netflix production, it's a … excuse the expression, hard-hitting drama about corruption in professional boxing. Based on a 1948 novel by the legendary Budd Schulberg that closely mirrors the real careers of several professional boxers, it was also Humphrey Bogart's last role. He died early the following year of lung cancer. Bogie plays Eddie Willis, a former newspaper

29

sportswriter turned boxing promoter who's been drawn into the web of corruption in the fight game in his city. Eventually he recovers his courage and self-respect, leading to an inevitable confrontation with the crooked powers that be. The cast includes former heavyweight champions Max Baer and Jersey Joe Walcott, as well as Rod Steiger as the head bad guy. [Trivia notes: 1) Two years earlier, Schulberg had written the Oscar-winning script for *On the Waterfront* (P25), another story about corruption in the fight game, featuring Marlon Brando as failed fighter Terry Malloy – with Steiger playing his brother and promoter. Schulberg was then hired to adapt his novel for *The Harder They Fall*, but Columbia Pictures head Harry Cohn vetoed the decision. Cohn and Schulberg's father, the former head of Paramount, nursed longstanding animosities. 2) The source novel parallels real events in New York's boxing world over the previous decades, and the movie adds to those parallels in intriguing ways. For example, the character of Toro Moreno (Mike Lane) closely resembles former champion Primo Carnera, who lost his title to Max Baer. Here, Baer plays Buddy Brannen, the fighter who defeats Moreno. 3) Carnera thought the movie disparaged him so much that he sued the producers for defamation – though he lost the case] [Caution: ring violence and adult themes] **[B&W]**

In Her Shoes
2005 – Curtis Hanson
Toni Collette and Cameron Diaz in a slow-starting, often grating but ultimately affecting drama about family alienation – with Diaz in her best role as a wayward sibling. Rose (Collette) is strait-laced and hardworking, while Maggie (Diaz) is promiscuous, unreliable and a substance abuser. Maggie often seeks Rose's help for cash and a place to stay, which Rose usually grants, even though each time the outcome costs her more than she bargained for. But Maggie pushes things too far when, during one of her stays, she sleeps with Rose's fiancé Jim (veteran TV actor Richard Burgi). Understandably furious, Rose ejects Maggie from her apartment and, presumably, her life. The crisis throws the story in a new and unexpected direction when the now-desperate

Maggie seeks out Ella (Shirley MacLaine in a strong supporting role), the girls' grandmother who lives in a Florida retirement community. Ella takes Maggie under her wing but with toughness and wisdom, enough to set Maggie on a difficult path to self-renewal and, eventually, reconciliation. As mentioned, slow-starting and often grating, but in the end a worthwhile and mature viewing experience. [Trivia note: The girls' mother, seen only in photos, is Croatian model–actress Ivana Miličević who, the following year, appeared as one of the Bond girls in *Casino Royale* (PF5)] [Caution: language and sexuality] **[W]**

Iris
2001 – co-written and directed by Richard Eyre
Based on the true story of author Iris Murdoch, who slowly but irrevocably slid into dementia caused by Alzheimer's disease, Judi Dench performs the title role as the elderly Iris, with Jim Broadbent in an Oscar-winning role as her husband John Bayley. In a parallel storyline, Kate Winslet portrays Iris in her younger years, with Hugh Bonneville (now immortal as Lord Grantham in the smash British TV series Downton Abbey) as the younger Bayley. It's a heartrending drama, as we watch Iris's frightening but inevitable decline, made even more poignant by Dench's superb portrayal of the author facing her fate as well as flashbacks of Iris in her prime, and Winslet's free-spirited romp as Iris in her youth. [Trivia note: Winslet holds a unique distinction among all actresses. She was twice nominated for playing the same person as another actress in the same movie. Here, both she and Dench were nominated for their respective roles as the younger and older Iris. Four years earlier, she and Gloria Stuart were nominated for playing the young and old Rose DeWitt Bukater in *Titanic* (PF5). None of them won, though to my dying day I'll argue that Stuart should have been awarded Best Actress by acclamation] [Caution: sexuality and adult themes] **[W]**

Jacknife
1989 – David Jones
"Every once in a while, someone special comes along, and your life will never be the same again," says the narrator describing this

31

story in the movie's trailer. Maybe that's a bit of exaggeration, but Joseph "Megs" Megessey (Robert De Niro) does fit that definition. The story, within its classic man-rides-into-town plot, does indeed change the lives of David and Martha (Ed Harris and Kathy Baker), a brother and sister living a quiet but uneasy existence. Megs and David served in the Army together in Vietnam, and both carry the scars of their experiences. Megs exhibits friendliness and good humor, but both can vanish instantly when he feels threatened or provoked. David, though quiet, sullen and reserved, always seems to be within an inch of losing control. Given the men's dispositions and common history, there's bound to be a confrontation, particularly when Megs begins to show romantic interest in the shy Martha. Another heavy-going drama, it presents a faint but constant flicker of redemption and rebirth that should keep you involved. [Caution: sexuality and adult themes] **[W]**

Julia
1977 – Fred Zinnemann
Based on a section of playwright Lillian Hellman's memoir Pentimento, it's the story of her relationship with a close childhood friend, the eponymous Julia (Vanessa Redgrave in an Oscar-winning role), who becomes a target of the Nazis for her efforts to protect Jews in Austria in the 1930s. The movie follows the harrowing attempt by Hellman (Jane Fonda) to rescue Julia from impending capture and, subsequently, to locate and adopt Julia's young daughter Lily. Beautifully shot by cinematographer Douglas Slocombe, it's another extraordinary film by Zinnemann, who had previously won Best Picture Oscars for *From Here to Eternity* and *A Man for All Seasons* (both in PF5). Also starring Jason Robards (likewise in an Oscar-winning role) as famed detective writer Dashiell Hammett, with whom Hellman lived for the rest of his life. [Trivia notes: 1) Screenwriter Alvin Sargent had appeared in a minor role in *From Here to Eternity*, though Zinnemann wasn't aware of the connection when he hired Sargent to write the Oscar-winning adaptation for *Julia*. 2) The movie marked the beginning of Meryl Streep's extraordinary

32

career as a film actress, though she would first rise to prominence the following year in the powerhouse TV miniseries Holocaust] **[W]**

The Lost Weekend
1945 – co-written and directed by Billy Wilder
Ray Milland, in the performance of his career, plays Don Birnam, an alcoholic writer, in Wilder's first Best Picture winner. Like *Days of Wine and Roses*, above, this is no one's idea of a good time. Yet it's a compelling look at one man's inability to control his appetite for booze. Unlike Jack Lemmon's character in the later movie, we meet Birnam already at the peak of his addiction. He's a man who will literally say or do anything to perpetuate his habit. Nothing seems beneath him, including outright theft. And despite the best efforts of those close to him, Birnam will not stop doing whatever he must to gain that next drink. That is, until… Well, better to let the resolution unfold on its own. As Wilder, again with his co-writer Charles Brackett, showed five years later with *Sunset Boulevard*, he wasn't only adept at classic comedy; he could create pretty damned good adult dramas as well. In this case he fashioned Birnam's character based on his work with detective story writer Raymond Chandler, whose real alcoholism apparently rivaled what Milland portrayed as Birnam. [<u>Trivia</u> <u>notes</u>: 1) As serious as the drama was, it produced a bright spot in Wilder's life. He met his wife Audrey on the set when she was cast as an extra in one scene. 2) *The Lost Weekend* is one of only three films to win both Best Picture and the coveted *Palme d'Or* at the Cannes Film Festival. The other two were *Marty* (<u>P25</u>) a decade later and the decidedly unpleasant Korean feature *Parasite* (not on my lists) in 2019] [<u>Caution</u>: adult themes and intense scenes involving delirium tremens] **[B&W]**

The Man in the Gray Flannel Suit
1956 – written and directed by Nunnally Johnson
Call this the dark side of *The Best Years of Our Lives* (<u>PF5</u>), William Wyler's masterful portrait of returning World War II veterans and their struggles to return to normalcy. Here, Gregory Peck stars as Tom Rath, a 1950s middle-class executive harboring two secrets.

A former Army officer who served in the war in both Europe and the Pacific, Rath continues to suffer from what we now call post-traumatic stress, which manifests itself in vivid but frightening flashbacks from the battles he fought and survived, including of the enemy soldiers he killed plus one horrible accident. PTS was – and still is – a condition befalling many of the men who experienced combat. In addition, while overseas Rath engaged in an affair with a young Italian woman, an affair that produced a child. All of this, plus several other issues, produces almost unbearable strains on both Rath and his wife Betsy (Jennifer Jones). What happens as a result, however, seems less important than writer–director Johnson's effort to probe the lingering inner turmoil of men who fought in the biggest conflict in history. You might quibble at the ending, but my guess is you'll appreciate the mature portrait of '50s America it presents. [Trivia notes: 1) This second pairing of Peck and Jones was far less dramatic than their first, as ill-fated lovers in David O. Selznick's colossal bomb of a western, *Duel in the Sun* (P25). 2) Watch for a brief appearance by DeForest Kelly, now and forever known as Dr. Leonard "Bones" McCoy in the original Star Trek TV series.] [Caution: adult themes] **[W]**

Nell
1994 – Michael Apted
In the woods outside a small North Carolina town lives what appears to be a wild child named Nell (Jodie Foster). Unknown to most of the local population, and existing without contact with anyone except her mother, she is discovered by Jerry Lovell (Liam Neeson), a doctor who has arrived to certify her mother's death. Lovell finds that Nell, who has never experienced human contact outside her home, speaks in an almost unrecognizable version of English. Seeking help to learn more about her and help her integrate into adult society, he enlists Paula Olsen and Al Paley (Natasha Richardson and Richard Libertini, in a rare dramatic role), both of whom specialize in childhood autism, a disorder with similar symptoms. The move quickly backfires because the researchers conclude that Nell should be institutionalized.

Therein begins a struggle between Lovell and Olsen, and particularly Paley, who sees no alternative. But Lovell, as he learns more about Nell's unique nature, persists, eventually drawing Olsen to agreement. The story leads, somewhat predictably, to a court hearing about Nell's fate. It's a moving, thought-provoking story, graced by two fine performances by Leeson and Richardson, and above all by Foster, who garnered a Best Actress Oscar nomination and a win by her peers in the Screen Actors Guild. [Trivia notes: 1) Foster had originally planned to direct the movie but then declined when she realized performing the role presented challenges enough. 2) Neeson and Richardson fell in love during the production and were married that same year. 3) Nick Searcy, playing the local sheriff here, likewise briefly played a sheriff named Rawlins the previous year in *The Fugitive* (PF5)] [Caution: non-sexual nudity and adult themes] **[W]**

An Unmarried Woman
1978 – written and directed Paul Mazursky
Later in this list I've included a chapter about movies in the 1960s. I mention it because I doubt this one could have been made then, only a decade earlier. But by the late '70s, with the women's liberation movement gaining momentum, Jill Clayburgh plays a role that many of her peers found identifiable, and maybe defiantly so. She's Erica Benton, a woman attempting to find life and love again after her marriage to Martin Benton (Michael Murphy) suddenly dissolves. And I mean "suddenly." The couple is walking along a street on the upper West Side of Manhattan, near their apartment, when Martin abruptly announces he wants a divorce and then quickly walks away. Erica reacts with disbelief followed by vomiting on the sidewalk. That's the low and starting point. From there, it's an often-excruciating process to rebuild her life and self-esteem. And it's a tribute to Clayburgh's talent and appeal (she was nominated for an Oscar, and she won Best Actress at Cannes) that she makes you ache for everything she endures and feel satisfied with what she manages to accomplish.

With Cliff Gorman and Alan Bates as her potential suitors. [Caution: explicit sexuality] **[W]**

Without a Trace
1983 – produced and directed by Stanley R. Jaffe

Based on an amalgam of true incidents, the story represents every parent's nightmare. Susan Selky (the always appealing Kate Nelligan) lives in Brooklyn and teaches English at Columbia University. She's also a single mother, raising Alex (Danny Corkill), her six-year-old son. One morning, she sends Alex off to his nearby neighborhood school. Later that day, she discovers to her horror that not only did Alex not arrive at school, but he has also disappeared … without a trace. The revelation leads to a frantic search, led by NYPD Lieutenant Al Minetti (Judd Hirsch, in his best role), watched by the whole city via the news media and relentlessly destroying Susan emotionally. It's riveting drama, skillfully helmed by Jaffe in a departure from his usual solitary role as a producer. [Personal note: Joan McMonagle, who plays a TV reporter, was a college classmate of mine. Back then, she was a popular personality on campus, and I only knew of her. We became acquainted three decades later when I paid tribute to her in an essay for The Washington Post] [Caution: language and adult themes] **[W]**

2. Arrested Development

From the mature to the ridiculous. Movies can go mighty lowbrow and still entertain, such as this raunchy quintet and two entrées of relatively innocent silliness.

Animal House

1978 – John Landis

Formally known as *National Lampoon's Animal House*, lots of movie buffs consider this one a comedy classic, but I can't agree because 1) it's as crude and cynical as can be and 2) it's got plenty of awkward stretches. But when it's funny, it's really funny. The year is 1962, and Delta House, the outlaw fraternity at fictional Faber College, has become a haven for the dregs of the student body: schemers, slackers, heavy drinkers and flunkers. In other words, compared to the snobs and stiffs populating the other fraternities and the sororities, they're the most fun on campus. And no one is more fun, because no one is less inhibited, than Bluto (Saturday Night Live's John Belushi in his debut movie role), for whom nothing is off limits. It all leads to a witty takeoff on the epilogue of *American Graffiti*, and wait 'til you find out what happens to Bluto. No point in describing the plot because it's only a libretto for the crudity and mayhem. You'll either put aside your good taste to dig in for the duration, or you'll tune out quickly. Watch for veteran character (and dramatic) actor Bruce McGill in his debut as Bluto's co-slacker, Daniel Simpson "D" Day. [Caution: un-PC humor and naughty sexuality galore] **[W]**

Artists and Models

1955 – co-written and directed by Frank Tashlin

Years ago, National Lampoon magazine annually gave out what it called its "Arrested Development Award," and the joke was, as

37

the magazine declared, it "always [went] to Jerry Lewis." I'd add, with good reason. Lewis, who was not without talent, particularly in his later years, spent most of his movie career acting in a most juvenile way. *Artists and Models* is no exception. Here, Lewis is Eugene Fullstack, who would be called a nerd in later years. Fullstack is a devotee of comic books, particularly the adventures of a character called Bat Lady (the model for whom is eventually revealed as Shirley MacLaine, in an early role). Dean Martin, Lewis's co-star and comedy partner, plays Rick Todd, a struggling artist who acts as Eugene's straight man – something Martin did in all 17 movies the team made together in the 1940s and '50s. This being a musical, Martin also sings, including "*Inamorata*" ("Sweetheart"), which became a hit that year. The rest of the plot? Pure nonsense, all of it, but innocuous and entertaining for its time, with Dorothy Malone, Eva Gabor and the voluptuous Anita Ekberg joining MacLaine as the "models" in the title. [Trivia notes: 1) Martin and Lewis's eventual break-up, one of the most famous and notorious in show business, occurred 10 years to the day after their first appearance together, in an Atlantic City nightclub. 2) This marked the first of seven times Martin and MacLaine appeared together in a movie, including *Ocean's 11* (PF5), the mid-sixties comedy *What a Way to Go!* and the dark drama *Some Came Running* (neither on my lists)] **[W]**

Cheech & Chong's Next Movie
1980 – co-written and directed by Thomas Chong
Call them the Laurel & Hardy of the stoner age – for reasons I'll explain momentarily. The partnership of Richard "Cheech" Marin and Thomas Chong made nine movies together (this was their second – hence their "next" movie) as well as 11 albums of their comedy routines and countless standup appearances. In all of them, Marin – co-writer of this movie – plays a vaguely Mexican-American persona, while Chong … well, his ethnic origins are indefinite and his main characteristic is his perpetual, marijuana-induced haze. But I consider the comparison to the immortal Stan & Ollie appropriate. Like their predecessors, they get themselves into perpetual trouble. Also like Laurel & Hardy, fate and/or

providence always seems to bail them out before things disintegrate into total disaster. In fact, if you can check your senses of good taste, decorum and maturity at the door, you might find the boys rather endearing. Oh, the plot? It's uneven at best, but no worries; you'll either go with it, as I did, or you won't. [Caution: language, explicit sexuality and profligate drug use] **[W]**

The Groove Tube
1974 – co-written and directed by Ken Shapiro
I readily admit this title is offensive, almost continuously so. But *The Groove Tube* for some brave souls might be worth a look. Trust me on this – it contains some of the most tasteless material ever presented. In structure it's sort of an episodic parody of television, but even that's too tight a description. It's more accurate to call the movie a string of unrelated bits of varying lengths, which range from painfully funny to totally unfunny, with one really cute and innocuous musical segment coming at the very end and starring Shapiro – who also appears elsewhere. This is not for the squeamish or the dainty. It's graphic in places but also raunchily funny. There are lots of laughs – if you're willing to set aside your sense of good taste for an hour and a half. Also, watch for Saturday Night Live's Chevy Chase at the beginning of his career in two of the segments; one silly and cute, and the other as crude as can be. [Repeating my caution: not for the kids or those with delicate sensibilities – offense material pervades] **[W]**

Saving Silverman
2001 – Dennis Dugan
Reverting back to utter tastelessness, once again you should consider putting your sensibilities on hold. If you do you might find yourself laughing your head off at times. The story concerns the friendship among three young men that's threatened when one of them (Jason Biggs) becomes engaged to a, let's say, very forceful woman (Amanda Peet, proving once again, as she has in several mediocre titles, that she's a first-rate screen comedienne). So, to save him from himself, his buddies (Steve Zahn and Jack Black) kidnap the woman and try to persuade him that she's

39

deserted him. It's pointless to reveal more, because the more you know, the more you might be repelled. But if you're adventurous enough to sample something purely for laughs regardless of its crudity, you might want to give this one a try. It's as raunchy as can be but all in good fun, no one is really harmed, and there's a nice concert performance at the end featuring the cast and a surprise guest. [Caution: sexuality and language] **[W]**

Team America: World Police
2004 – written and directed by Trey Parker and Matt Stone

Animal House, Cheech & Chong's Next Movie, The Groove Tube and *Saving Silverman* are positively demure compared to this one, even though it's done entirely with marionettes (though it cost more to produce -- $32 million – than the four others combined). If you're unfamiliar with the crudely animated but wickedly funny TV show South Park, which Parker and Stone also produced, then you'll want to exercise a great deal of caution here. How much caution? Does the idea of graphic sex performed by those aforementioned marionettes intrigue or repel you? Or, how about the fact that even the movie's theme song contains obscene lyrics? Just know, with Parker and his team, nothing – repeat, *nothing* – is sacred. On the other hand, *Team America* presents, by far, the most elaborate use of real marionettes ever filmed – hence the huge production cost. [Trivia note: In the movie's spectacular opening scene, what momentarily looks like a crude puppet show was originally staged as a prank by Parker and Stone on the executives at Paramount, *Team America*'s distributor] [Caution: very rough language, disgusting bodily functions and, as mentioned, graphic sex] **[W]**

Weekend at Bernie's
1989 – Ted Kotcheff

Lots of needless complications in this caper about two young insurance company employees (Andrew McCarthy and Jonathan Silverman) who discover that their boss (Terry Kiser, the "Bernie" in the title) is not only crooked but also has taken out a contract on their lives. Instead, the aspect you need to know, going in, is that Bernie dies suddenly, and to preserve their lives and livelihoods the young men conspire to portray Bernie as still living, at least through the ... weekend. Therein begins a nonsensical but hilarious series of events in which the newly dead Bernie continues to interact with visitors, partygoers and passersby – none of whom seems to notice his ... um, condition. McCarthy and Silverman play pretty good straight men to Kiser, but he owns the movie, in a role he seemed born to play. His face, frozen in a vague smirk, gets funnier each time you see it. [Trivia notes: 1) Not much more can happen to a dead guy, but the Bernie character did present certain hazards to Rock Walker, the stunt double for Kiser in certain scenes. Walker broke several ribs during filming. 2) His unique and memorable performance as the stiff in *Weekend at Bernie's* became Kiser's signature role, along with its sequel, *Weekend at Bernie's II* (not here). But he has been a journeyman actor for over half a century with well more than 100 movie and TV credits to his name] [Caution: language, violence and sexuality] **[W]**

3. Arthouse Attractions

Back in the 1950s, '60s and into the '70s many cities – and even a few small towns – featured movie theaters that catered to serious moviegoers. They showed attractions, mostly foreign, that required a degree of patience and sophistication. Most were presented in their original languages with subtitles. They generally dealt more deeply, and sometimes explicitly, with the human condition than the features Hollywood was distributing. I spent many, many happy hours in my college years and young adulthood, sitting in such auditoriums surrounded by enthusiastic cinephiles who likewise sought the latest creations that foreign filmmakers – *auteurs*, as they were called – could offer. Many garnered honors in Hollywood, in the form of Oscars for Best Foreign Film or Best Director. Or, at the world's foremost gathering, they competed for the *Palme d'Or* (Grand Prize) at the Cannes Film Festival. Returning to the theme of adult drama, with a comedy and a musical mixed in, this baker's dozen follows or continues the arthouse tradition, either in portraying (for mature audiences) the many facets of the human condition or in presenting the unique cinematic sensibilities and creativity of their *auteurs*.

All About My Mother
1999 – Spain – written and directed by Pedro Almodóvar

Almodóvar's most serious work – though it's still partly a comedy – *Todo Sobre Mi Madre* covers such adult topics as death, religious faith, diseases, family relationships and gender identification. In the central story, Manuela (Cecilia Roth), a nurse, attempts to find a recipient for the heart of her son, killed in a pedestrian accident. The search leads her on a journey and a series of experiences you'll probably find a bit excessive in their complexity.

Almodóvar is Spain's equivalent of Bertrand Blier, the French *auteur* whose movies frequently pushed their themes to outrageousness but with hilarious results. There's outrageousness here as well, but in some ways it's less jarring because it's tempered by Almodóvar's basic humanity and his affection for his characters. The movie won him his only Best Foreign Film Oscar. [Caution: sexuality and adult themes] **[W]**

Amnesia
2015 – Switzerland and France – co-written and directed by Barbet Schroeder
Marthe Keller, in her best role, stars as ... Martha, a German woman living alone on the beguiling Spanish island of Ibezia who stays in denial of her country's sordid past in World War II. She becomes platonically involved with Jo, another German, a young man who composes and records electronic music. The late, great Bruno Ganz co-stars as a visitor who recalls Germany's history most vividly, and his admitted role in Nazi atrocities creates a climactic, though nonviolent, confrontation between him and Martha. Unusual roles for both Keller and Ganz, but a satisfying drama. The title? It refers to the name of a nightclub on the island. [Trivia note: Jo's house in the movie has belonged to director Schroeder's family since the early 1950s] [Caution: sexuality and adult themes] **[W]**

Antonia's Line
1995 – The Netherlands – written and directed by Marleen Gorris
Like *All About My Mother*, Gorris's Oscar-winner displays some extremely strange characters and takes on a host of human topics, particularly sexual relationships. But what it really resembles is *The World According to Garp* (PF5). Like Jenny Fields (Glenn Close), who gathers a group of sympathetic outcasts and misfits on her family's seaside estate, Antonia (Willeke van Ammelrooy) brings a similar bunch to her farm in Holland in the years following World War II. Also like Jenny Fields, Antonia's daughter Danielle (Els Dottermans) wants to have a child but without the obligation

43

of marriage – except that Danielle's … ahem, quest is on explicit view, whereas Jenny merely described her accomplishment. Like Garp (Robin Williams), Danielle often indulges in flights of fancy. And both movies fixate a bit on the subject of death. The parallels aren't exact, however. For one thing, some of the male denizens of Antonia's village are much more prone to unrestrained earthiness, flashes of temper and outright sexual assault, while others happily and eagerly procreate with their occasional partners. For another, this story is told in flashbacks, using a narrator; Sarah (Thyrza Ravesteijn), the daughter of Thérèse (Veerle van Overloop), who is Danielle's offspring. It's complicated, but the characters are distinct, and Gorris keeps things moving without confusion. Some of the plotlines end happily; others don't. It's a tale both bitter and sweet, with some lovely scenery (though the movie was filmed in Belgium, not The Netherlands). [Caution: explicit sexuality] **[W]**

Belle Époque
1992 — Spain – co-written and directed by Fernando Trueba
The movie takes the basic plotline of Jean Cocteau's classic *Beauty and the Beast* (elsewhere), turns the concept on its head and multiplies the number of participants. Here, a father offers *four* of his daughters to a prospective mate, not because his life is in danger but because he's looking for an heir. Another Best Foreign Film winner, Trueba's romantic comedy tracks the love exploits of Clara, Violeta, Rocio and Luz (Oscar-winner Penélope Cruz), the four nubile daughters of Manolo (actor–director Fernando Fernán Gómez), a wealthy landowner in pre-Civil War Spain. One by one, the girls receive the tentative courtship of Fernando (Jorge Sanz), a handsome soldier who has secretly deserted. One by one – at least, for the first three times and for various reasons – the couples don't click. But this being a comedy, it eventually ends happily. [Viewing note: Maybe skip the movie's first few minutes. It contains one of the most jarring and unpleasant (both visually and musically) openings I've ever seen] [Trivia notes: 1) The term *Belle Époque* traditionally refers to a period of French history in the late decades of the 19th century. Here, it describes Manolo's

idyllic estate and the breezy romances of his daughters. 2) Although the story is set in Spain, Trueba (pronounced Tru-AY-bah) shot the movie in Portugal, which he said provided better scenic representations of the story he wanted to tell] [Caution: sexuality, often in a humorous context] **[W]**

Black Orpheus
1959 – Brazil and France – co-written and directed by Marcel Camus

At the time called one of the most colorful films ever made, it's also a hip musical based on the Greek myth of Orpheus and Eurydice, involving the brief but fiery affair between a pair of immortals of surpassing physical beauty. Except here, the movie is set in the Leme neighborhood of Rio de Janeiro at the time of *carnaval*, the city's enormous, world-famous festival, and the affair takes place between a French tourist named Eurydice (Marpessa Dawn) and Orpheu (Breno Mello), a local trolley driver. The *bossa nova* music, by Antonio Carlos Jobim and Luis Bonfa, imbues the story with an irresistible energy that, aside from its tragic aspects (it *is* based on mythology, after all), has made the movie a popular diversion among its international fans for over six decades. It's also one of the few titles to win both Best Foreign Film and the *Palme d'Or*. [Personal note: Marpessa Dawn was not born in France or Brazil but in the United States. In fact, she was raised on a farm near Pittsburgh – the same background as yours truly] [Caution: mild sexuality and one vertiginous scene of shocking violence]

Breathless
1959 – France – written and directed by Jean-Luc Godard

In the 1950s, three stars with bold on-screen personalities electrified audiences in tales of young punks gone astray. They included Marlon Brando as a motorcycle gang member in *The Wild One*, James Dean as a delinquent in *Rebel Without a Cause* (neither on my lists) and, arguably the most wayward and dangerous of the trio, Jean-Paul Belmondo as a thief and murderer in *À Bout de Souffle (Out of Breath)*. Shot in a jumpy style called *cinéma-vérité*, to resemble a documentary, *Breathless* (its English

45

title) became an immediate hit among young French audiences, and its popularity spread globally, making Belmondo an international sensation. His co-star, the waiflike Jean Seberg, an Iowa native, was just as impressive (after seeing the film, François Truffaut called Seberg "the best actress in Europe") though for some reason her appeal never matched Belmondo's iconic status, which for a time rivaled Brando's. [Trivia note: Other than Francis Ford Coppola's Vietnam epic *Apocalypse Now* (P25), this is the only mainstream film I can recall that offers no opening or closing credits] **[B&W]**

César and Rosalie
1972 – France – co-written and directed by Claude Sautet
An unusual love triangle – actually, more of a friendship triangle – involving a divorcée (Romy Schneider), her new suitor (Yves Montand), her former lover (Sami Frey) and the subsequent coupling, recoupling, uncoupling and (unexpected) reconciliation involved. It's a gentle and sophisticated romantic tale enhanced by the star power and appeal of its two leads. [Caution: mild sexuality] **[W]**

Cousin Cousine
1975 – France – co-written and directed by Jean-Charles Tacchella
As the title describes, it's about two cousins – though they're related only by marriage, and a recent one at that. Ludovic and Marthe (Victor Lanoux and the luminous Marie-Christine Barrault) meet at a family wedding and quickly become attracted to each other. When they discover that their respective spouses have been engaging in an affair, they seek solace in each other; platonically at first but soon via their own passionate affair. Audiences seemed to crave and embrace the uninhibited, playful, guilt-free nature of the relationship as it unfolds, thereby making *Cousin Cousine* the most popular foreign film of the year. [Trivia note: Hollywood made a pale imitation called *Cousins* in 1989, starring Ted Danson and Isabella Rossellini (not on my lists)] [Caution: sexuality, sophisticated as it might be] **[W]**

A Fortunate Man
2018 – Denmark – co-written and directed by Bille August

In the Ingmar Bergman tradition, this dark and brooding but exquisitely photographed and meticulously paced story follows the adult life of Peter Andreas Sidenius (Esben Smed). He's a struggling engineering student from the Danish countryside who moves to Copenhagen in the late 19th century to seek his fortune. Peter dreams of building vast public-works projects to aid the people of his country. Early in his struggles, he meets and is seduced by Lisbeth (Sophie-Marie Jeppesen), a friendly waitress who quickly proposes cohabitation and marriage. But that destiny just as quickly subsides as Peter meets Ivan Salomon (Benjamin Kitter), scion of a wealthy Jewish family, who becomes Peter's benefactor. Ivan introduces him to his sisters, Nanny (beautiful and vivacious Julie Christiansen) and Jakobe (Katrine Greis Rosenthal, who resembles Cher in her younger days). Though Nanny is attracted to Peter, Jakobe falls in love with – and is impregnated by – him. Therein continues a slow but enthralling drama that eventually overwhelms and crushes Peter's ambitions, almost all of it due to his own obstinate behavior and misjudgments. Based on Danish author Henrik Pontoppodian's Nobel Prize-winning, multi-volume novel *Lykke-Per*, commonly translated as "Lucky Person," the story moves along abruptly at times, with certain prominent characters suddenly disappearing from the narrative. But the script and performances never display a wrong note. As with the titles in my first chapter, *A Fortunate Man* is an adult drama in the best sense. And, as mentioned, the cinematography by Dirk Brüel is gorgeous. [Caution: adult themes and sexuality] **[W]**

Gemma Bovery
2014 – France – co-written and directed by Anne Fontaine

The coincidentally named Gemma Arterton plays the misspelled version of the ill-fated Madame in a weird adaptation of the Flaubert novel. The story takes place in Normandy, where a baker named Martin (Fabrice Luchini) develops a fixation on an expatriate British woman, the aforementioned Gemma, who is married to Charles Bovery and living across the road from Martin. Instantly fascinated, Martin begins furtively following and studying her, and he comes to believe that Gemma's life is paralleling that of the literary Jemma Bovery, with the same ominous possibilities. That is what ultimately happens, though in a sudden, shocking and unexpected way. [Trivia note: Madame Bovary is one of the most adapted works of French literature. Other than *Gemma Bovery*, which is a rather unusual take, nine movies have been based on the novel, beginning in the 1930s, along with two TV miniseries] [Caution: sexuality] **[W]**

Like Water for Chocolate
1992 – Mexico – Alfonso Arau

Romance, sex and magical cooking in early 20th-century Mexico. They're the main ingredients in the story featuring Tita (Lumi Cavasos), a lovely young woman charged with caring for her newly widowed mother for life at the expense of her own prospects for marriage and motherhood. Tita seems to have inherited the ability to transform food by adding ingredients such as her own tears, resulting in anyone who consumes her cooking becoming filled with Tita's contributing emotions: deep sadness, sexual satisfaction and so forth. The mystical trait also allows Tita to, literally, cast spells onto anyone – including herself. That's the basic story, but I'm leaving for you to discover the complex and convoluted relationships involving everyone surrounding Tita. Fear not; you'll enjoy the ride, as did the millions of moviegoers who made *Like Water for Chocolate* one of the most popular attractions of that year. As in *Fiddler on the Roof* (PF5), social traditions – and the struggles against them – figure prominently. And as in *Antonia's Line*, we hear the story via a narrator from a succeeding generation. [Trivia note: The movie's title refers to the fact that … like water must reach a boil before being added to create hot chocolate; so, too, must emotions sometimes boil to resolve conflicts plaguing the human condition] [Caution: explicit sexuality] **[W]**

The Red Shoes
1948 – England – Michael Powell and Emeric Pressburger

Like *Black Orpheus*, this one's based on mythology, though it's more lavishly produced, among the last films to be shot in the original three-strip Technicolor process. Based on "The Ballet of the Red Shoes" by Hans Christian Andersen, it's the tragic story of Victoria (Moira Shearer, a real *prima ballerina*), a dancer struggling within a love triangle while striving to excel at her craft. The movie's centerpiece is its extraordinary 15-minute ballet, which presages the better-known centerpiece in *An American Paris* (PF5). Taking six weeks to shoot, it involved more than 50 other dancers and more than 100 large-scale backgrounds by German artist Hein Heckroth. The result is arguably the most beautiful ballet sequence ever presented in a movie. It's distinctive not because of the dancing, which is ordinary, but for its colorful settings, lively music and staging – involving frequent rapid cutting, camera movement and special effects – and for Shearer's surpassing beauty. [Trivia notes: 1) Powell and Pressburger apparently were thrilled when, after a year of trying, Shearer agreed to do the movie because they had been seeking a fine dancer who was also a beautiful woman. They had been considering actresses such as Lauren Bacall and, years earlier, Merle Oberon, figuring to substitute a professional for the dance scenes. 2) Shearer might have regretted the decision, however, when her performance of "The Ballet of the Red Shoes," on a concrete studio floor instead of the wooden boards of a stage, caused a great deal of pain and injury to her feet. And the times when she had to be suspended from wires in a harness damaged her skin. 3) "The Ballet of the Red Shoes" in this movie indeed inspired Gene Kelly and Vincente Minnelli when they planned their ballet sequence for *An American in Paris*, staged to the immortal George Gershwin tune. 4) As with *The Leopard*, Martin Scorsese greatly admired *The Red Shoes*, to the point where he collected memorabilia from the production – including, of course, a pair of the shoes – and he helped fund the film's restoration for its 60th anniversary]

The Umbrellas of Cherbourg
1964 – France – written and directed by Jacques Demy

Coincidentally, the year 1964 offered two musicals in which *parapluies* featured prominently; Disney's sublime *Mary Poppins* (PF5) and the *Palme d'Or* winner, Demy's bittersweet love story, in which all of the dialogue is sung, opera-style. The movie captivated audiences, whether couples in love, couples potentially getting together or longing singles, with Jean Rabier's moody cinematography, the exquisite beauty of 19-year-old Catherine Deneuve in her first starring role, and Michel Legrand's liltingly romantic score, including the centerpiece song, "I Will Wait for You," which became an international hit. [Trivia notes: 1) O.N.M. of Paris, the umbrella supplier for the movie, earned an unprecedented mention in the opening credits. 2) *Les Parapluies des Cherbourg* is actually the middle installment in a trilogy of musicals by Demy, all three featuring the same leads. The other two, *Lola* in 1961 and *The Young Girls of Rochefort* in '67, never achieved similar popularity (and neither is on my lists)] [Caution: mild sexuality] **[W]**

4. Art, Imitating Artists

Surprising, but quite a few good movies deal with the lives, careers and proclivities of painters and sculptors. Perhaps it's because attempts to dramatize the writing process on film have, with few exceptions, fallen flat. I also suspect that because biographies of artists tend to contain a certain amount of sexual content, involving models, lovers, partners and spouses; no doubt it's a strong attraction to the imaginations of moviemakers – and sometimes, as you'll note below, their inappropriate imaginations. But most of all, I think, it's because of the ability of great artists, using only lines and colors, or lumps of clay or stone, to create works that can take your breath away. There's also the frequent connection between genius and madness. You'll see examples of both among these 18 dramas, 12 of them based on true stories or real characters.

Age of Consent
1969 – Australia – Michael Powell
From the world of ballet in *The Red Shoes*, 21 years earlier, Powell in his last directorial effort chose this sexy story about Bradley Morahan, a temperamental painter (James Mason), and Cora, a young and free-spirited Aussie girl who attracts his attention (the great and versatile Helen Mirren at her start). Ostensibly, this is about an artist and his model – though Mason's character, as we're shown early on, is not without a bit o' manly lust. But Powell and screenwriter Peter Yeldham apparently couldn't resist adding the possibility of an eventual romantic involvement between the two. It's more of a distraction and an unnecessary complication. The real interest is in the professional relationship and its liberating effect on a young woman on the cusp of adulthood and freedom. [Trivia notes: 1) Ron and Valerie Taylor,

51

who compiled the live shark footage for *Jaws* (PF5), photographed Mirren's underwater scenes. 2) Mason's interactions with Mirren were, by all accounts, respectful and professional. But his character's brief dalliance with an old girlfriend (Clarissa Kaye) produced a real romance for the two actors that later turned into an enduring marriage. 3) Mason's character is based on Australian artist Norman Lindsey, the subject of *Sirens* (below); indeed, the story derives from Lindsey's autobiographical novel] [Caution: sexuality and prolonged nudity] **[W]**

The Agony and the Ecstasy
1965 – produced and directed by Carol Reed

Yes, Mad Magazine once published a sendup of this movie titled "The Agony and the Agony," and yes, it does get a bit overblown at times – I even considered including it in my section on big-budget fiascos. Nevertheless, Charlton Heston as Michelangelo, and Rex Harrison as Pope Julius II, go at each other in entertaining ways as the immortal artist, under the pontiff's patronage, attempts to paint the ceiling of the Sistine Chapel in the Vatican over the four-year period beginning in 1508. Based on a chapter of Irving Stone's best-seller of the same name, it's a lavish re-creation of the artistic process that led to probably the most famous fresco of all time. It's also a full-blooded conflict of personalities, both onscreen and off. When the narrator of the movie's trailer declares, "Two great stars clash," he wasn't exaggerating. Heston and Harrison apparently never liked each other, and their mutual disdain shows up clearly. But given the enmity between the artist and his patron, director–producer Reed couldn't have chosen better-suited actors if he tried. [Trivia note: Two cast members were connected to the James Bond thriller *Thunderball* (PF5), made that same year: Adolfo Celi, here playing a cardinal, was the villainous Emilio Largo; and Diane Cilento, as Michelangelo's lover, was Sean Connery's first wife] **[W]**

The Best Offer
2013 – Italy and England – written and directed by Giuseppe Tornatore

The director, who gave us the sublime *Cinema Paradiso* (PF5), here presents Geoffrey Rush in a deeply complex mystery–drama. A reclusive and conniving art dealer's efforts at amassing an outstanding collection might be compromised by his sudden, fierce desire for a beautiful young woman whom he catches in an unguarded moment. Rush is Virgil Oldman, the dealer; and Sylvia Hoeks is Claire, that obscure object of his desire. I'll stop with that much, for two reasons: 1) *The Best Offer* contains possibly the most convoluted – and enigmatic – plot of any title on my lists, so further explanation would be pointless and become tedious, and 2) It's really best to screen the movie repeatedly – and on consecutive days – because I guarantee you won't be able to absorb all of the nuances and misdirections in one sitting. [Caution: explicit sexuality] **[W]**

Camille Claudel (and) Camille Claudel 1915
1988 and 2013 – France – Bruno Nuytten (also co-writer) and Bruno Drumont (also writer)

The model who worked for 19th-century sculptor Auguste Rodin turned out to be a pretty fair sculptress herself. The problem was that Camille Claudel's relationship with Rodin grew less professional and more personal, to the point where her rising despair over their affair drove her to madness – including the destruction of many of her works. Here we have two films, a quarter-century apart, dealing with the same subject; each produced in France and directed by a man named Bruno, and each starring an actress of exceeding beauty and exceptional talent: Isabelle Adjani in the earlier version and Juliette Binoche in the latter. How to choose? It's difficult because both biographies are well-made – though both are shattering dramas. So, instead of ranking one over the other – as I do with other pairs in a later chapter – I'll just boil them down for your consideration. In nutshells, *Camille Claudel* focuses on the stormy relationship between the title character and Rodin, played by the great Gérard

Depardieu, while *Camille Claudel 1915* deals only with the artist's life after Rodin – and after her family has confined her in an asylum. My recommendation? If the artist's life interests you, see them both, and/or by all means seek out exhibitions of Claudel's works. [Caution: sexuality and adult themes in both] **[W]**

Cézanne et Moi
2016 – France – written and directed by Danièle Thompson
Two of the most renowned artistic figures in 19th-century France were painter Paul Cézanne and writer Emile Zola – Cézanne for his vivid human studies and landscapes, and Zola for his literary passion. The two men also shared a lifelong relationship, albeit tempestuously, and ended up alienated. The story follows that relationship. Cézanne (Guillaume Gallienne) is mercurial, while Zola (Guillaume Canet) is reserved and judgmental. Emotionally and physically exhausted, Cézanne eventually begins his most famous series of paintings, landscapes of Montagne Sainte-Victoire, above the town of Bouches-du-Rhône. [Caution: explicit sexuality and rough language] **[W]**

Frida
2002 – Julie Taymor
Talk about stormy relationships! Salma Hayek stars in an Oscar-nominated performance as Frida Kahlo, a Mexican artist of the 1920s who loved and married her mentor, artist Diego Rivera (Alfred Molina in a sly performance), despite his infidelities and fits of temper. Kahlo began her craft via a fluke of fate. As a teenager riding on a city bus, she was impaled and badly injured in a collision. To help her endure a lengthy and painful recovery, Frida's father gave her brushes, paints and a framed canvas, from which her innate talent quickly emerged. It's a lively, mature depiction of Kahlo's life, featuring an exceptional supporting cast that includes Geoffrey Rush as Bolshevik *capo* Leon Trotsky and Edward Norton as Nelson Rockefeller, plus Ashley Judd, Valeria Golino and Antonio Banderas. Like *Camille Claudel*, however, most of the movie focuses on Kahlo's love–hate encounters with Rivera, whose radical politics made him both notorious and world-famous for works such as "Man at the Crossroads,"

54

commissioned for, and partly completed at, Rockefeller Center in New York City. [Viewing note: Some of the movie's sequences begin with images of Kahlo's paintings that dissolve into matching live action] [Trivia note: The quality of the finished film notwithstanding, *Frida* was an extremely troubled production, largely because of the – let's call it what it was – unprofessional and inappropriate behavior of notorious studio head Harvey Weinstein. The specifics have been well reported, but suffice it to say the movie contains certain scenes inserted at Weinstein's insistence over the objections of both Hayek and director Taymor] [Caution: explicit sexuality] **[W]**

Incognito

1997 – John Badham

The versatile Badham, best known for *WarGames* (PF5) and *Saturday Night Fever* (P25), plus *Stakeout* and *Dracula*, here helms a high-stakes art-forgery caper wrapped within a murder mystery, a chase thriller, a love story and a courtroom drama. Notice that somewhere in the midst of those genres I included the term "art." It's the story of Harry Donovan (Jason Patric), a skilled painter who's been eking out a living by forging minor classical works for shady art dealers, who then sell them to private collectors on the black market. Meanwhile, Harry struggles unsuccessfully to earn a showing of his originals. Then, the opportunity of a lifetime knocks, sort of. One of Harry's clients offers him half-a-million dollars to forge a Rembrandt. Over the objections of his father (Rod Steiger in a minor role), also a painter, Harry accepts. In doing so, he sparks the myriad other elements of the story, including an improbable and convoluted affair with Marieke van den Broeck (French–Swiss actress Irène Jacob), a Rembrandt scholar and the only person who can expose the forgery. I confess, this one's a marginal entry – except that it includes a truly fascinating sequence midway where Harry researches, prepares and executes the faux Rembrandt (painted by veteran artist and scenic designer James Gemmill). It reveals some of the painstaking processes used by the old masters, and some of the techniques modern-day experts use to confirm the originals and expose the fakes. [Caution: sexuality, language and violence] **[W]**

Local Color
2006 – written and directed by George Gallo
Gallo, who wrote the screenplay for *Midnight Run* (PF5), one of my favorite caper comedies, here presents an autobiographical tale about an aspiring artist (Trevor Morgan) who seeks as a mentor an aggressively reclusive painter from the former Soviet Union (Armin Mueller-Stahl). It's loosely based on what happened to Gallo when he was a young man and became the protégé of Lithuanian impressionist George Cherepov. The lessons he learned from Cherepov must have stuck, because Gallo himself created all of the paintings displayed in the movie, and they're pretty good. [Caution: rough language and mild sexuality] **[W]**

Lust for Life
1956 – Vincente Minnelli
One of the supreme object lessons of history and culture is, as screenwriter William Goldman once so pithily declared about Hollywood, "Nobody knows anything." Unforgettably applied here, Goldman's aphorism paints … forgive the pun, enduring disdain on the many shortsighted individuals who not only viewed the works of Dutch painter Vincent van Gogh during his lifetime but also failed to purchase any of them. Available for pittances back then, today it would be difficult to obtain any van Gogh for less than eight figures. What does such rejection do to a man with van Gogh's talent and passion? As portrayed by Kirk Douglas in an Oscar-nominated performance, the conflict between his overwhelming desire to paint and his perpetual penury drove him into severe depression bordering on madness and led to his eventual tragic end. It's hard-going to watch, even though much of the movie was filmed in scenic locations frequented by the artist. The drama also features Anthony Quinn, winning his only Oscar as van Gogh's friend and fellow painter Paul Gaugin. [Technical note: Director Minnelli made, in retrospect, a terrible decision about the look of the movie. He shot

it using a film stock called Ansco Color, giving it a grainy quality with subdued colors; the idea was to suggest van Gogh's increasingly dark frame of mind. The problem is that Ansco Color deteriorates more rapidly than other stocks, something that rendered the eventual restoration more difficult than usual] **[W]**

Off the Map
2003 – Campbell Scott
I could easily have stuck this one in the Different Drummers category (below), though truth be told many if not most of these artistic profiles would fit there as well. Let's just say that of all artists I've profiled in this section, the fictional William Grubbs (Jim True-Frost) begins his avocation in the most unusual way. He's an Internal Revenue Service agent who travels to rural New Mexico to investigate a household that apparently has not filed income-tax returns for quite some time. When he arrives, he's startled by the sight of the wife, Arlene Groden (Joan Allen), standing naked in her vegetable garden. From there, one thing leads to another, and Grubbs ends up living with the family and beginning a series of striking landscape paintings, which he bequeaths to them after his death. [Caution: nonsexual nudity] **[W]**

Pollock
2000 – Ed Harris
Shades of Vincent van Gogh, Jackson Pollock (Harris, who stars as well as directs) was a painter of unique talent but a fiery, self-destructive personality; something that kept him in turmoil essentially all of his adult life. The movie, a pet project of Harris's for many years, follows Pollock's contrasting rising fortunes and reputation, and his descent into fatal alcoholism. Along the way, he romances and marries fellow artist Lee Krasner (Marcia Gay Harden in an Oscar-winning performance), while he continues dalliances with other women -- including, essentially, raping his potential matron Peggy Guggenheim (Amy Madigan, Harris's real-life wife), she of the family that would eventually build New York City's famed Guggenheim Museum. As with *Lust for Life*, it's difficult going most of the time, but Harris creates an unflinching

57

look at the character of an artistic genius. [Caution: sexuality, rough language and violence] **[W]**

The Red Violin
1998 – England and Italy and Canada – co-written and directed by François Girard

"A prophesy told of a masterpiece that would be born of tragedy," intones the narrator of the movie's trailer, a declaration that turns out to be literally true. The only title in the bunch not directly about painters – though the source of the instrument's mysterious hue is somewhat related. Similar in structure to *The Yellow Rolls Royce* three decades earlier (not on my lists), the story tracks three centuries of history and the sequence of ownership of *Le Violon Rouge*, as it's also known overseas, except the distinct chapters are linked to that prophesy, as denoted by particular tarot cards. Samuel L. Jackson stars as an art appraiser attempting to determine whether the legendary instrument is genuine. As we follow his investigation, we gradually learn the real story. [Caution: sexuality and violence] **[W]**

Renoir
2012 – France – co-written and directed by Gilles Bourdos

Famed impressionist painter Pierre-Auguste Renoir spent much of World War I at his country retreat at Cagnes-sur-Mere in the south of France. During that time, the aging Renoir (Michel Bouquet, a stunning lookalike) employed Andrée Heuschling (Christa Théret), a beautiful, lithe young model who whiled away many an afternoon posing in the altogether for him. Among Renoir's visitors was his eldest son (Vincent Rottiers). Wounded in the war, he went on to rival his father's reputation and fame as the celebrated filmmaker Jean Renoir (see *The Rules of the Game*). He becomes Heuschling's friend and suitor. It's a languid, pastoral tale, gorgeously shot by Taiwanese cinematographer Mark Lee Ping Bin, and paying some attention to the human subjects captured by the artist's brush. [Personal note: If ever in your lifetime you have an opportunity to see, in person, Renoir's "Luncheon of the Boating Party," on permanent display at The

Phillips Collection in Washington, D.C., don't deny yourself. I consider the painting one of the most stunning artistic creations I have ever seen and – trust me on this as well – no photograph can remotely approach the impact of the real thing] [Viewing note: I doubt anyone will complain about watching Théret's uninhibited posing for the artist's nude studies. But most of the real subjects of Renoir's nudes tended toward, shall we say, Rubenesque body types] [Historical note: Heuschling's relationship with Renoir the younger grew closer as the years passed. As the actress known as Catherine Hessling, she appeared in more than a dozen of the director's films, and the two eventually married] [Caution: sexuality and prolonged nudity] **[W]**

Séraphine
2008 – France and Belgium – co-written and directed by Martin Provost
Arguably one of the two most unusual titles of this section, and one of the saddest stories, it's based on a real character. But unlike Camille Claudel, Vincent van Gogh and Jackson Pollock, Séraphine Louis was not driven into insanity by poverty, lack of recognition or an ill-conceived love affair. Instead, prosperity apparently did it – or, at least, pushed her along a path for which she already had been destined. The life and works of Séraphine (Yolande Moreau) might have remained in permanent obscurity if not for her chance meeting with Wilhelm Unde (German actor Ulrich Tukur), an art critic who eventually became her patron. Alas, her good fortune was short-lived. Working for years as a housekeeper, when her paintings begin selling and she can afford to devote all of her time to them, she begins exhibiting bizarre behavior, to the point where she is eventually institutionalized. From there, her life proceeds in an irrevocable downward spiral. An award-winning actress, screenwriter and director, Moreau takes on a difficult role with skill and spirit. She makes you ache for Séraphine and her ill-fated life. [Viewing note: You can see most of Séraphine Louis's works at the Musée d'Art et d'Archéologie in Senlis, France. Interest in her paintings greatly

increased after the movie's release] [Caution: nonsexual nudity] **[W]**

Sirens
1994 – Australia – written and directed by John Duigan
In 1930s Australia, still nestled comfortably in Victorian mores, painter, sculptor and novelist Norman Lindsay (Sam Neill) was considered notorious, not only for his less-than-demure depictions of nudes but also for his bohemian lifestyle. Troubled and outraged at Lindsay's potentially demoralizing influence on the public, the Anglican Church in England dispatches Tony Campion (Hugh Grant), a young and proper priest, and Estella (Tara Fitzgerald), his shy wife, to meet with Lindsay and persuade him to moderate his views and paintings. There, on Lindsay's estate (the production used his actual New South Wales property for the movie), the couple quickly falls under the intoxicating spell of the place, including the artist, his wife Rose (Pamela Rabe); Pru and Sheela, two of Lindsay's models (Kate Fisher and world-famous fashion model Elle Macpherson); and Giddy, their young housekeeper (Portia di Rossi), who also occasionally poses. The story, ostensibly about the philosophical conflict between Norman and Tony, unexpectedly focuses more on Estella's sexual awakening, including several rather dramatic examples. The most explicit feature of the bunch, I suspect you'll either consider it a guilty pleasure or abandon it quickly. [Trivia notes: 1) Grant and Fitzgerald linked romantically onscreen again the following year, but as freer and more appealing characters, in *The Englishman Who Went Up a Hill But Came Down a Mountain* (PF5). 2) Neill's performance portrays Lindsay as a rather appealing character, but in real life the man was a bigot, a racist and an anti-Semite. 3) Many of Lindsay's paintings were lost just before World War II – in America, of all places. Shipped there to protect them from possible seizure by the Japanese, they were burned as pornography by U.S. Customs officials] [Caution: plentiful nudity and explicit sexuality] **[W]**

A Sunday in the Country
1984 – France – co-written and directed by Bertrand Tavernier

There's not much action or drama in *Un Dimanche à la Campagne*. But to say that nothing happens, or to describe its quiet nature as negative, would be like denying there is pleasure in sitting quietly outside on a lazy afternoon, or skipping stones across a pond, or listening to a gentle breeze. It also doesn't mean the movie lacks drama. Not at all. It's just that the drama is confined to the most ordinary – and therefore universal – family matters. Monsieur Ladmiral (Louis Ducreaux), an elderly and increasingly reclusive painter, hosts his son Gonzague (Michel Aumont) and his family nearly every Sunday. The family visits, the adults converse, the children play on the lovely grounds and along the verdant banks of the nearby river, and they all enjoy a meal before the day ends. On this particular Sunday, however, Ladmiral's independent-minded daughter Irène (the radiant Sabine Azéma) arrives and inserts a welcome jolt of energy into the routine. She creates some conflict, though it's mild. In the end, beyond a few hurt feelings, life for all returns to normal – except that Ladmiral makes a small shift in his artistic focus, a most satisfying gesture of hopefulness. **[W]**

Tim's Vermeer
2013 – co-written and directed by Teller

Last and most unusual. I assume you're familiar with the second name in the title, Johannes Vermeer, the 17th-century Dutch painter whose striking works depict still-life moments mostly in the town of Delft – and almost all within the same room of the same house. I also assume you're familiar with the director, who goes professionally by only one name and is the magician partner of Penn Jillette. What might not be familiar to you is the term camera obscura. It's a centuries-old device that allows certain images or views to be projected in a scale useful to artists. In this documentary, Teller portrays the five-year effort of Tim Jenison, a computer graphics specialist, to reproduce one of Vermeer's works using replicated subject material and a camera obscura. It's a fascinating process with a weird twist: "The Music Lesson," the

Vermeer painting Jenison is attempting to re-create, is the property of Queen Elizabeth II of England and is part of her collection at London's Buckingham Palace – where it cannot be seen by the public. Hence, all he had to go on were photographs and printed reproductions, so no direct comparison of the finished product is possible. But, as mentioned, it's fascinating to watch the attempt. **[W]**

Five Before the Code

Hollywood 1931-1934. Relevant titles from back then on my lists have included *42nd Street*, *Dr. Jekyll and Mr. Hyde*, *Dracula*, *Flying Down to Rio*, *Frankenstein*, *Gold Diggers of 1933*, *Grand Hotel*, *King Kong*, *Love Me Tonight*, *The Public Enemy*, the first two *Tarzan* movies and even *It Happened One Night*. What was so distinctive about the period? For one thing, it was early in the movie industry's sound era, which had begun just three years prior with *The Jazz Singer* (not on my lists), a musical starring Al Jolson that became a sensation. As a result, the movie industry rapidly retooled to give the public what it was now clamoring for; "talkies," as pictures with accompanying sound were called. For another – and relevant to this section – many movies back then continued a trend begun in the 1920s, depicting themes such as sexuality and mob violence in an increasingly frank manner, a manner more advanced than much of society comfortably tolerated. Some movies likewise became sensational for their relatively explicit nature. By 1930, objections to such themes (or, at least, the way Hollywood was treating them) arose from the guardians of public morality – churches, newspapers and politicians – forcing the industry to self-impose certain standards of content. Will Hays, president of the Motion Picture Producers and Distributors of America, drafted the Motion Picture Production Code, specifying what could be, and could not be, shown on the screen. The code was meant to head off laws and lawsuits alike aimed at the studios. Except that the studios, essentially, took their time falling into line. Finally, Hays intervened. In 1934, he began strictly enforcing the code, which defined acceptable movie content for the next three decades, and some of the actions were applied retroactively. For example, in *King Kong* (<u>PF5</u>), code censors removed three scenes from the original movie: one where Kong touches the heroine's (Fay Wray's) body and then sniffs his fingers; another where Wray, after a desperate dive into the ocean, resurfaces but momentarily topless; and a third where Kong snatches a fleeing native and devours him. It eventually took half a century to restore the suppressed footage. The same with *Tarzan and His Mate* (also in PF5), which contained a nude underwater scene. The battle between artistic freedom and public morality continues to this day Here are five titles from that period; four of them by well-known directors – three of whom went on to direct Best Pictures. With one exception, they illustrate how Hollywood was pushing the bounds of acceptable content until the Hays Code, as it became known, clipped its wings.

Bombshell
1933 – Victor Fleming
Twenty-two-year-old, "platinum blonde" Jean Harlow presaged Marilyn Monroe by two decades in this tale of corruption and deceit in Hollywood – though it's a comedy, and a screwball comedy at that. Harlow plays Lola Burns, a "bombshell" movie star (a sexy, scantily dressed and promiscuous woman) who longs for a quiet life but whose family and studio can't abide losing her as a source of substantial box-office revenues. So, they plot and scheme to keep her working. Fleming, who went on to direct, among other titles, *Captains Courageous*, *Test Pilot*, *Gone With the Wind* and *The Wizard of Oz* , (all in PF5), keeps things moving briskly, with inside jokes and sly references to other stars and movies galore. But notice the casual asides, the innuendoes and even the direct references to, shall we say, naughty behavior such as blatant infidelity, not to mention the direct references – and the loose clothing. [Trivia notes: 1) Harlow's designation as a platinum blonde had originated three years earlier with Howard Hughes, who used the term when he publicized his sound version of *Hell's Angels* (PF5) and continued when she starred in a 1931 movie of the same name (not here). 2) The real Harlow indeed longed for a quieter life and possibly less sexy roles, but her type-casting as a bombshell prevailed throughout the rest of her career, until her death in 1937 of kidney failure after a series of illnesses. 3) Speaking of Harlow's career, she appeared in more than 30 movies – but she holds the rare distinction of receiving no screen

credit for over half of them, all early on] [Caution: mild sexuality and adult themes] **[B&W]**

Call Her Savage
1932 – John Francis Dillon
This one might be, relatively speaking, the most *outré* of the five. Its themes include out-of-wedlock pregnancy, prostitution, homosexuality and interracial romance – all affecting Nasa Springer (Clara Bow), a free-spirited ("wild," as she is termed by family and outsiders alike) young woman whose unconventional life and background eventually lead her to true love with a kindred spirit; a "half-breed," as the pejorative was known at the time, named Moonglow (Gilbert Roland at his most dashing). Yes, such topics appear routinely and non-controversially in today's dramas and comedies. But in the early 1930s? Shocking! [Caution: mild sexuality and adult themes] **[B&W]**

Design for Living
1933 – Ernst Lubitsch
What a pedigree! Directed by Lubitsch with a screenplay by Ben Hecht and based on a play by Noël Coward, it stars Gary Cooper, Miriam Hopkins and Fredric March in an implied *ménage à trois* seven years before Bing Crosby, Bob Hope and Dorothy Lamour even began that particular storyline for laughs. Cooper's an artist; so's Hopkins, and March is a playwright, all living in Paris. Both men pursue – and eventually win – their mutual love interest, despite her marriage to wealthy executive Edward Everett Horton. It's all oh-so-discreet, however. Even though the movie was made pre-code, there were limits. The most explicit reference to the *ménage* is when Hopkins, shortly after her wedding, tells Horton, "It feels good to be a law-abiding citizen again." **[B&W]**

Dinner at Eight
1933 – George Cukor
Here's the exception. It's mature material but not really shocking, even for its day. Still, it was part of that period and well worth mentioning. Based on the hit play by George S. Kaufman and

Edna Ferber, and with a screenplay co-written by Herman Mankiewicz (forever remembered as the writer of *Citizen Kane* – see <u>PF5</u>) and Donald Ogden Stewart, it's a sparkling, sophisticated ensemble comedy, featuring the biggest stars of the time: John and Lionel Barrymore, Wallace Beery, Billie Burke, Marie Dressler and Jean Harlow. The plot involves a society couple (Burke and Lionel Barrymore) with failing fortunes who attempt to bolster their standing by hosting a lavish dinner party, one that will greatly strain their finances. As it turns out, the hosts aren't the only ones projecting a façade. John Barrymore, as a fading movie star and alcoholic, gives one of his greatest performances as a character who's fortunes are mirroring Barrymore's own. Unbeknownst to the host, the 47-year-old, thrice-divorced star has been having an affair with their 19-year-old daughter (Madge Evans), something inevitably revealed along with other secrets and scandals as the evening proceeds – or recedes. Everyone's in fine form, and the verbal sparring between Harlow and Dressler is priceless. [<u>Trivia notes</u>: 1) Beery and Harlow, who play an unhappily married couple, couldn't stand each other offscreen, either. Their mutual disdain had begun two years earlier in *The Secret 6* (not here) and didn't improve with this rematch. 2) No doubt Beery's and Harlow's stormy relationship influenced Cukor when he directed battling (unmarried) couple Broderick Crawford and Judy Holliday in *Born Yesterday* (<u>PF5</u>) 18 years later. 3) The two cast members who sparred onscreen but developed a mutual friendship were Dressler and Harlow. Dressler, in her memoir years later, wrote that Harlow's performance "all but ran off with the show!"] **[B&W]**

Little Caesar
1931 – Mervyn Leroy
"Mother of mercy, is this the end of Rico?" That's the lament, at movie's end, of Caesar Enrico "Rico" Bandello (Edward G. Robinson), an Italian immigrant who rose, temporarily, to the top of Chicago's rackets during Prohibition, the period from 1920 to 1933 when the sale of alcohol was banned in the United States by

the Nineteenth Amendment to the Constitution. During his rise and brief reign, "Little Caesar" Bandello waged a murderous campaign against his rivals and enemies, in scenes if not as explicit then for certain as intense as anything seen in the genre since. The unrelentingly ferocious look in Robinson's eyes frightened moviegoers but also made him a star. Even now, nearly nine decades later, his commanding presence is unforgettable. [Trivia note: "Eddie G.," as he was known, in real life in no way resembled the vicious Rico Bandello. A devout Jew, he often spoke out publicly during the 1930s against the fascists in Italy and the Nazis, and he generously supported relief organizations assisting the victims of tyranny. He also spent a great deal of his personal time collecting art and painting. His film career lasted an astounding seven decades] [Caution: violence] **[B&W]**

6. Biblical Proportions

During the 1950s and early '60s, Hollywood produced a lengthy series of spectacles based on biblical lore or prominent historical figures. Their common characteristics included the recruitment of popular stars – particularly Yul Brynner, Charlton Heston, Victor Mature, Susan Hayward and Jean Simmons – plus scripts by Philip Dunne or Jesse Lasky Jr., casts of hundreds or thousands of extras, exotic locations, the expenditure of (at the time) unheard-of sums and the frequent use of CinemaScope or other widescreen photographic processes. Sometimes, the epics worked spectacularly, such as *Ben-Hur* (a Best Picture winner) and *Spartacus* (both in <u>PF5</u>), as well as the first half of *Cleopatra* (<u>P25</u>) and in a wonderfully clunky way *The Ten Commandments* (<u>PF5</u>). But mostly, they turned out to be tedious extravaganzas. My second baker's dozen doesn't rise nearly to the heights of the above-named favorites – one colossal bomb in particular – but they're still entertaining even in their frequent preposterousness.

David and Bathsheba
1951 – Henry King

Gregory Peck and Susan Hayward play the title characters in this portrayal of one of Israel's most famous kings, and the concubine he desires and wins by sending her husband into battle and certain death. Even seven decades later, it's a surprisingly affecting story, elevated by Peck's strong performance. As I mentioned in my chapter about him in <u>P25</u>, Peck displayed remarkable versatility and enjoyed enduring appeal. He had worked with director King two years earlier in *Twelve O'Clock High* (<u>PF5</u>), the superb World War II drama about the early days of the U.S. Eighth Air Force in England. Here, he gives an earnest interpretation of the Old Testament saga, while Hayward, though beautiful, alluring and spirited, is as one reviewer wrote at the time more Hollywood than Bible. The script? The first of four in this section by Philip Dunne. [Caution: nudity – though seen at a discreet distance]

The Egyptian (and) Land of the Pharaohs
1954 and 1955 – Michael Curtiz and Howard Hawks

Two epics depicting the days of ancient Egypt from the perspective of 1950s Hollywood, under the direction of two heavyweights: Curtiz, who gave us the immortal *Casablanca* (PF5), and Hawks, associated with several of the best comedies ever made plus the classic western *Red River* (also in PF5). Here, unfortunately, both failed miserably at the box office, but their films still merit a look.

* * *

In *The Egyptian*, Victor Mature co-stars with Jean Simmons and with British stage actor Edmund Purdum in the title role. Featuring another script by Dunne, this one chronicles the character of Sinuhe (SIN-oo-way), a physician to Pharaoh whose fortunes rise and fall over many years as they parallel the intrigues and rivalries of the royal court. It's a strangely interesting look at an ancient culture, with some scenes shot on location in Egypt. [Trivia notes: 1) Sharp-eyed viewers might recognize some of the props appearing in Pharaoh's court, because they turned up again two years later, also decorating the royal palace in *The Ten Commandments*. 2) The movie, distributed by 20th Century-Fox under studio head Darryl F. Zanuck, for the first of two times featured a cast member who also was Zanuck's … um, romantic interest. Here, it's Bella Darvi as, perhaps fittingly, a courtesan from Babylon. Seven years later, it was Irina Demick in *The Longest Day* (PF5) as a *Résistance* fighter] **[W]**

* * *

Then there's Hawks's *Land of the Pharaohs*, starring Joan Collins and Jack Hawkins and boasting a script supposedly co-written by none other than William Faulkner. Like *The Egyptian*, Hawks shot the movie on location, using thousands of workers or soldiers supplied by the Egyptian government as extras. Unlike *The Egyptian*, which focuses on intrigues within the royal court, *Land of the Pharaohs* depicts the construction of one of the country's gigantic, familiar landmarks: a pyramid. The drama centers on an obsession of Pharaoh Khufu (Hawkins) to secure his eventual entombment from future grave robbers. He does this by 1) commissioning Vashtar (James Robertson Justice), the kingdom's best pyramid architect, 2) ordering Vashtar to develop a foolproof mechanism to seal the pyramid after Khufu's entombment, and 3) condemning to death anyone familiar with the structure's interior. Will Khufu's wishes prevail? Well, yes, but not without plot twists and surprises, giving the story a good measure of suspense. [Trivia notes: 1) Speaking of Faulkner, though his name appears in the credits, by all accounts he wrote very little of the script and often showed up on set in a drunken state. 2) Speaking of Egypt, that country never allowed the movie to be shown. The reason? The religious authorities considered Justice to be too … let's say, un-Egyptian in appearance. 3) In the previous chapter, I outlined how the Hays Code placed content restrictions on movies, and it was still in full force in the 1950s. Here, the censors decreed that Joan Collins's bare midriff could not display (I'm not kidding) her navel. So, for each day's shooting she wore a large jewel there, attached via a messy adhesive] **[W]**

El Cid
1961 – Anthony Mann
Charlton Heston, two years after winning his only Oscar for *Ben-Hur*, this time plays a (literally) legendary figure in the history of Spain who was credited with (temporarily) driving the Moors (Muslims) from that country. Born in Castille in the 11th century as Rodrigo Díaz de Vivar, he won the title El Cid (the Lord) from his battles with both Christian and Moorish armies at the time. The movie depicts his rise, not so much to power but to great influence because of his skill in battle, his fervent religious devotion and his magnificent white Andalusian stallion named Babieca. Sophia Loren co-stars as Jimina, Rodrigo's wife and eventual successor as ruler of the Spanish province of Valencia. Featuring the biggest cast of the bunch, with at least 7,000 extras, it's a marvelously overblown epic, leading to a miraculous – and

that aforementioned legendary – climax. [Historical note: You can visit the tomb housing the remains of El Cid, also known as the Prince of Castille, in the Spanish city of Burgos; located along the country's famous Camino de Santiago] [Viewing note: As with *The Ten Commandments*, in which Heston's character Moses ages over many years, Rodrigo's story spans decades and requires the actor to display the effects of time. Apparently, Loren's Jimina suffers no such diminishment; she looks the same throughout] [Trivia notes: 1) Another legend surrounding the real Rodrigo was how his horse was named. His godfather, Pedro El Grande, gave him a selection of steeds as a gift, but when seeing his choice, he reportedly yelled, *"babieca!"* ("stupid!"). 2) They might have been lovers onscreen, but otherwise Heston and Loren did not get along at all during the production. Three reasons: Heston resented the fact that Loren was paid more than he was, Loren resented that Heston's name appeared above hers in the credits and on the publicity posters, and Heston objected to his character's aging while Loren retained her beauty. 3) As with *The Leopard* and *The Red Shoes* (both above), Martin Scorsese greatly admired *El Cid* and helped fund the film's restoration] **[W]**

Genghis Khan
1965 – Henry Levin
It was a toss-up whether to include this one here or in the What Went Wrong? category, later on. I placed it here because I don't think anything could have fixed it. Egyptian-born Omar Sharif, who had made his stunning debut in the West in David Lean's *Lawrence of Arabia* three years earlier, and this same year starred in the title role in Lean's sublime romantic epic *Doctor Zhivago* (both in PF5), nearly squanders his appeal and credibility in a laughable biography of the 13th-century rampaging Mongolian warlord. Also starring Stephen Boyd (who upstages Sharif in every one of their scenes) as Jamukha, the Khan's lifelong rival; blonde French actress Françoise Dorléac as his childhood love and eventual wife; James Mason as a lisping Chinese – yes, Chinese! – envoy; British actor Robert Morley as the Chinese emperor, and Eli Wallach as a Persian noble and enemy, the movie contains not

a single Asian principal. It's Hollywood at its loopiest and most artificial. Shot mostly in Yugoslavia, which at the time was a Soviet satellite country, *Genghis Khan* has its entertaining moments. But if you want a superior treatment of Temüjin (his birth name, which means "blacksmith"), try *Mongol: The Rise of Genghis Khan* (P25). [Historical note: Sharif plays Temüjin as a heroic figure and uniter of tribes. The real Genghis Khan, however, in forming the largest geographic empire in history, slew millions – perhaps tens of millions – during his conquests, and his literally rapacious nature resulted in many thousands of offspring] [Trivia note: Dorléac, older sister of Catherine Deneuve, was tragically killed in an automobile accident two years later, at age 25] [Caution: violence and sexuality, both mild by today's standards] **[W]**

Hawaii
1966 – George Roy Hill

Not a Biblical epic, obviously, but not unrelated, either, because the theme of this big-screen version of James Michener's 1959 best-seller is the conflict between Abner Hale (Max von Sydow), a stern 19th-century Christian missionary from New England, and the native Polynesian culture as personified by Malama Kanakoa (Tahitian-born Jocelyn LaGarde), the Ali`i Nui, or ruler, of the Hawaiians. At greatest issue is the longstanding tradition of incest among the royal family, something obviously abhorrent to Hale and his young wife Jerusha (Julie Andrews). Malama and her husband Kelola (Ted Nobriga) are also brother and sister. Likewise, Malama's son Keoki (Fijian-born Manu Tupou, who narrates the movie's breathtaking prologue) and Noelani (Elizabeth Logue), his betrothed. Also repugnant is the practice of drowning babies born with birthmarks or other defects. And there's the natives' *laissez-faire* attitude about sex, including sex with outsiders. The principals clash frequently over these and other profound differences. Nominated for eight Academy Awards but shut out in all categories, it's an often-tragic but fascinating tale of the evolution of Hawaiian society. Elmer Bernstein composed the soaring score, which recalls his work for

The Magnificent Seven as well as *The Ten Commandments* (both in PF5). [Trivia notes: 1) LaGarde is the only Oscar-nominated actress to appear in one film. She never acted again. 2) Strange to consider; many of the materials appearing in the movie had to be imported because they were no longer available in Hawaii. These included roofing thatch from Japan, cloaks from Hong Kong, Tapa cloth from Ireland, straw from Mexico, silk from Taiwan and, incredibly, carved statues of Hawaiian gods from Hollywood! 3) *Hawaii* marks the screen debut of Bette Midler, who can be glimpsed, ever-so-briefly, as a seasick passenger on the voyage to the islands] [Caution: plentiful nubile nudity and, as described, adult themes] **[W]**

King of Kings
1961 – Nicholas Ray

Know that this was the first major production of the story of Jesus Christ to present his face – something that inevitably led to controversy, and rightly so, which I'll get to shortly. Adapted from the four books of the Bible's New Testament, the movie follows Christ's life from his birth to his three-year ministry in the Holy Land, including his gathering of the Apostles, his preaching to the multitudes, his performing miracles and his eventual betrayal, trial and condemnation to death on the cross – and his resurrection. To play the title role, director Ray chose 35-year-old, New Orleans-born Jeffrey Hunter, and therein lay the controversy. Hunter, of Scottish ancestry, was fitted with a prosthetic nose to make him appear more Semitic. After preview audiences winced at his extensive body hair, Hunter had it all shaved off and re-filmed the scourging and Crucifixion scenes. But the physical aspect that brought the most criticism was, ironically, his striking blue eyes – something Ray admitted later was the main reason he had cast the actor. No question, Hunter's gaze is arresting. But his whole physical appearance remains incongruent with the character. That wasn't the entire problem, however. The movie, despite its large cast, its dramatic locations (in Spain), its lush score by Miklós Rózsa (similar to his Oscar-winning work two years earlier for *Ben-Hur*), the whole thing often seemed stiff and strained. It ended up a borderline-silly portrayal of the life of Christ. [Trivia note: Though Hunter played 50 movie roles, and 20 more on television, before his untimely death eight years later from an on-set accident at age 43, he'll always be remembered most as Christopher Pike, original captain of the Starship Enterprise on the Star Trek TV series] **[W]**

King Solomon's Mines
1950 – Compton Bennett and Andrew Marton

Less visually imposing than the six widescreen epics above, this one nevertheless offers plenty of distinctions. Shot in four African countries (with some scenes in California and New Mexico), it was one of the few productions to cast Kikuyu, Maasai and Tutsi tribe members for the story and use their real villages. That authenticity remains dramatic and impressive. Also, the movie features footage of a real elephant shooting; still heartbreaking to view. Deborah Kerr stars as Elizabeth Curtis, wife of an explorer who apparently has become lost in Africa while seeking the legendary king's diamond mines. Distraught and determined to find him, Elizabeth secures the services of veteran guide Allan Quatermain (Stewart Granger) to lead the search. The quest leads them through deserts, snow-covered mountains and steamy rainforests (hence the multiple locations) as well as, inevitably, into a love affair. Movie audiences reacted enthusiastically enough to make it the second-highest-grossing attraction of the year. [Trivia notes: 1) Kerr had initially lobbied to play the character of Rose Sayer in *The African Queen* (PF5), a role that went to Katharine Hepburn. 2) As with *The African Queen*, parts of which also were shot on location, cast and crew were constantly beset with similar miseries, including dysentery and malaria, and insect and snake bites. 3) The crew filmed the elephant-killing sequence as part of an authorized culling by the Kenyan government. But the resulting reaction by the herd – a vivid and affecting group mourning – was spontaneous and unexpected] [Caution: several scary animal scenes]

The Robe (and) Demetrius and the Gladiators
1953 and 1954 – Henry Koster and Delmer Daves

The Robe's main distinction was its release in the CinemaScope format, making it the first of the widescreen epics. Co-written by Philip Dunne, it's based on Lloyd C. Douglas's bestselling, fictional chronicle of … the robe worn by Christ. Therein follows a plot as convoluted as the saga of *The Red Violin* (above). It involves Marcellus (Richard Burton), a Roman tribune who wins the robe in a game of chance during the Crucifixion; Demetrius (Victor Mature), a former slave turned Christian; Peter the Apostle (Michael Rennie – Klaatu in *The Day the Earth Stood Still* – see PF5); and the evil, ascendant Caligula (Jay Robinson, in a deliciously slimy performance), who seeks the robe because he believes it possesses supernatural powers. There's also Diana (Jean Simmons), beloved of Marcellus but betrothed to Caligula. And so forth. But better that you should watch it all unfold to your satisfaction, your inspiration or your amusement. Despite its melodramatic shortcomings (and Burton's half-stiff/half-over-the-top performance), the CinemaScope presentation seemed to thrill audiences, who made *The Robe* the biggest hit of the year. [Trivia note: Among the huge cast is Harry Shearer, former Saturday Night Live regular and a voice on the long-running series The Simpsons, here as a child actor; and, believe it or not, Marilyn Monroe, doing a voice-over in a pinch for an actress taken sick during production] **[W]**

*　　*　　*

In the sequel, continuing the fate of the robe, Susan Hayward plays Messalina, the beautiful, unfaithful wife of Claudius (Barry Jones), uncle of the notorious Caligula (Jay Robinson again). Demetrius (Victor Mature) becomes a … gladiator and, in this story, an off-again, on-again Christian. He also becomes, temporarily, Messalina's lover – naturally during his un-Christian phase – while retaining his real devotion to a young slave girl (the fetching Debra Paget). Another script by Dunne (also *The Robe*'s co-writer), it's more 1950s potboiler than biblical lore. And though the cast tries gamely to lend depth of the story, the silliness factor becomes overwhelming. Yet audiences loved this one as well, making *Demetrius*... the year's top box-office attraction. Future star Anne Bancroft appears in a minor role, and Ernest Borgnine, fresh from his villainous turn in *From Here to Eternity* (PF5), here plays a nasty Roman centurion. [Trivia question: How is this movie connected with Star Trek? Answer: Jay Robinson, along with William Marshall (one of the gladiators – a former Nubian king) and Julie Newmar (a dancing slave girl) all guest-starred in episodes of the original TV series] [Trivia note: Among the vast cast in a bit part was a young woman named Anna Maria Italiano – now better known as the late, Oscar-, Tony- and Emmy-winning Anne Bancroft] **[W]**

Samson and Delilah
1949 – Cecil B. DeMille

I'm fudging the category a little bit here with a release from the 1940s, well before the days of widescreen – though it did feature glorious technicolor. But I've included it because, in some respects, it's the best of the bunch. Victor Mature and Hedy Lamarr co-star in the title roles, and both give among their best performances. The excellent supporting cast includes George Sanders and Angela Lansbury. And Jesse Lasky Jr., who seven years later would write *The Ten Commandments* for DeMille, did the literate script. It's the Old Testament's story of a man with colossal strength whose Achilles Heel, so to speak, was that his power emanated from his hair. When it's shorn, Samson becomes a weakling and is captured by his enemies, who blind him. That sets up the climax, which places Samson between the pillars of the king's temple, and which results in a spectacular demolition, DeMille style. Like some of the other titles, the movie veers into stiffness and silliness at times. Despite the shortcomings, audiences loved *Samson and Delilah,* making it by far the biggest hit at the box office that year, and the third-highest-grossing movie ever up to then, behind *Gone With the Wind* and *The Best Years of Our Lives* (both in PF5). [Trivia notes: 1) The movie's acknowledged and glaring low point is Samson's battle with a lion. Even at the time, audiences could tell that Mature had been replaced by a lookalike stuntman fighting a tame lion in the

76

longshots, with the star basically wrestling a lion skin for the close-ups. 2) Groucho Marx once quipped about the movie, "There's just one glaring fault. No picture can hold my interest where the leading man's bust is larger than the leading lady's." 3) Throughout his career, Mature kept a refreshingly realistic view of himself. Once he was denied membership in a country club because of their policy not to admit actors. He shot back that he wasn't an actor and had the movies to prove it]

Solomon and Sheba
1959 – King Vidor

"The days of battle; the nights of desire." That's how the movie's trailer describes the whirlwind affair between Solomon (Yul Brynner), the biblical king, and the legendary Queen of Sheba (Gina Lollobrigida) – though perhaps taking more liberties with the story than any of the other titles. The famous King David (Finlay Currie) has ruled Israel for many years but is approaching the end of his reign. When he chooses Solomon as his successor, instead of his firstborn Adonijah (George Sanders), the elder brother begins plotting against him. Adonijah conspires with the Pharaoh of Egypt (David Farrar) to depose Solomon, and Pharaoh enlists Sheba to seduce him. And, boy, does she! But Sheba doesn't count on falling in love with the young king, and in doing so helps him redeem himself before God and his people, while Solomon devises a plan to defeat the invading Egyptians. Beautifully shot by the great Freddie Young, who did *Lawrence of Arabia* and *Doctor Zhivago* (both in PF5), it's a passable epic though frequently implausible. [Trivia notes: 1) The production contains a tragic element. The original actor playing Solomon was Tyrone Power. In fact, he had completed most of the filming when he suffered a sudden and fatal heart attack. After a great deal of debate and discussion, the producers decided to cast Brynner, who was a friend of Power's. He completed all of the love scenes with Lollobrigida as well as other scenes requiring him in close-up. But Power remains in many of the battle scenes and longshots. 2) There has been much debate about whether the legendary Queen of Sheba even existed, much less charmed Solomon. The

77

best evidence available suggests she ruled an area in the southern part of the Arabian Peninsula, in present-day Yemen] **[W]**

Troy
2004 – Wolfgang Petersen

Going back a millennium or so before Biblical times, to the legendary battle depicted in Homer's Iliad, the gorgeous Diane Kruger stars as the "face that launched a thousand ships." She's Helen, a Greek princess abducted by Paris (Orlando Bloom), a Trojan prince, and setting off what has become known as the Trojan War. Brad Pitt and Erik Bana play, respectively, the seemingly invincible Greek warrior Achilles and his Trojan rival Hector, with Brian Cox looking imposing as Agamemnon, king of Greece. The guest appearances include Julie Christie as Thetis, the mother of Achilles; Peter O'Toole as Priam, king of Troy; Saffron Burrows as Andromache, wife of Hector, and Brendan Gleeson as Menelaus, king of Sparta. Fine actors, all, they nevertheless often strain to remain serious, in or out of costume. Filmed on Malta and in Mexico, it's a sprawling, mostly CGI-created epic with a few thrilling scenes and a lot of overblown hokum. [Viewing note: If you'd like to watch a scholarly but captivating take on the legend, I highly recommend In Search of the Trojan War, British historian Michael Wood's six-part documentary series on the topic done for the BBC in 1985. Not a CGI moment in sight, it's nevertheless enthralling] [Caution: sexuality and computer-generated violence] **[W]**

7. Coming of Age

Ah youth, in all of its callowness, and bringing to mind Maurice Chevalier's delightful song in *Gigi* (PF5), "I'm Glad I'm Not Young Anymore." Here's yet another baker's dozen, this time a bunch of studies of the angst afflicting either impetuous youth or unrealized manhood.

The Apprenticeship of Duddy Kravitz
1974 – Canada – Ted Kotcheff

Richard Dreyfuss, following his bit role in *The Graduate* and his appealing debut in *American Graffiti* and before his breakthrough co-starring in the blockbuster *Jaws* (all in PF5), here portrays a callow, selfish young Jewish Canadian man taking his first fitful steps into the adult world. That's about as apt a description as necessary. Duddy plods his way through a job at a lakeside summer camp while harboring ambitions to get rich as a property developer. He competes with the college students also working at the camp, loses his virginity, and endures several harsh life lessons. He also receives advice and counsel from his ailing grandfather (Joseph Wiseman in a terrifically appealing performance). Randy Quaid is excellent as an ill-fated friend. A small, often touching movie, sensitively directed by Kotcheff, it was a smash hit in Canada. [Trivia notes: 1) Dreyfuss hated his performance here, and by his own admission still does. He had earlier turned down playing ichthyologist Matt Hooper in *Jaws*, but after seeing himself as Duddy Kravitz, he immediately begged director Steven Spielberg to give him the role. 2) Wiseman's performance is a delightful surprise if you've seen him in his previously notable roles; as the wild-eyed Civil War veteran in John Huston's western *The Unforgiven* (P25) and, of course, the evil Dr. No in the James Bond installment of the same name (PF5).

Here, he's all grandpaternal affection and wisdom] [Caution: language and mild sexuality] **[W]**

Big
1988 – Penny Marshall

You might not be familiar with the Hollywood term, high concept. It describes movie ideas that can be quickly summarized, usually prefaced by, "What if…?" Sometimes, even the movie's title fits the bill. And *Big* is a perfect example: What if a kid suddenly becomes an adult? In this comedy, which reflects the loopy fantasies of many youngsters, Tom Hanks plays the adult version of Josh Baskin, a 12-year-old boy granted his fondest wish by a carnival vending machine: to be … big. As the old saying goes, be careful what you wish for. Josh wakes up to discover that he's suddenly grown into an adult (in … um, the complete sense of the term). Of course, when his mother (Mercedes Ruehl) discovers the new Josh, she's terrified he's an intruder and has kidnapped her son. Therein begins a series of adventures, and misadventures, for Josh. This being a comedy, however, all must end happily. Thirteen-year-old David Moscow plays the young Josh, Elizabeth Perkins plays his adult love interest and object of sexual discovery, and veteran actor Robert Loggia does a charming, dancing-and-playing duet with Hanks on an electronic floor keyboard at New York City's famed FAO Schwarz toy store. [Trivia note: To achieve the best approach for his adult scenes, acting as though he were still a boy, director Marshall had Moscow perform the scenes first, with Hanks watching them and then mimicking the boy's behavior and reactions] [Caution: language and mild sexuality] **[W]**

Gregory's Girl
1981 – Scotland – written and directed by Bill Forsyth

A gentle tale about Dorothy (Dee Hepburn), a pretty girl wanting to play on a boys' high school "football" (soccer in the U.K.) team, while the Gregory of the title (John Gordon Sinclair), one of the team members, tries to court her. The catch is that Dorothy is not Gregory's girl. That distinction goes to Susan (Clare Grogan), who meets Gregory after he has been handed off on a date sequentially by two more of Dorothy and Susan's friends. Confusing? Not really. It's a breezy little story where not much happens, but you're attracted to the young cast, nevertheless. [Viewing note: Depending on your source for watching the movie, you might encounter its original U.K. release, which features heavy Scottish accents. In the version released for U.S. audiences, the voices have been redubbed with less of the brogue] [Trivia note: You might notice that in Clare Grogan's scenes she is photographed favoring her right side. That's because she had been injured as a bystander to a bar fight. Her left cheek was badly scarred by a piece of broken glass and had not yet healed] [Caution: mild sexuality – including a bit o' breathless voyeurism by the boys] **[W]**

The Karate Kid
1984 – John G. Avildsen
The director of the original *Rocky*, eight years earlier, presents another underdog hero, but of a younger age, in this simplistic but crowd-pleasing story. Danny LaRusso (youthful-looking but 22-year-old Ralph Macchio) is a bullied high-schooler. At first, Danny is constantly harassed by Johnny Lawrence (William Zabka), a martial-arts student under the tutelage of John Kreese (Martin Kove), his stern and borderline sadistic instructor. Danny and Johnny are also rivals for the attention of Ali Mills (Elisabeth Shue), a pretty classmate. But then Danny meets Mr. Miyagi (Pat Morita, in an Oscar-nominated role), a Japanese karate master. Gradually, under Miyagi's patient guidance, he gains skill and self-confidence, enough to compete in a local tournament where, no surprise, the two young men eventually face off for the championship. Formulaic to be sure, but the friendship that builds between Danny and Miyagi is touching to watch, and if *Rocky*'s improbable ending evoked cheers from you, this one probably will, too – maybe helped by the fact that Bill Conti, who composed the soundtrack for *Rocky*, did the rousing score here as well. [Trivia notes: 1) Bitter rivals throughout the movie, Macchio, Zabka and Kove ended up as lifelong friends. 2) About that bitter rivalry, the movie became so popular that, for years, Zabka and

Kove often had to persuade fans they weren't really the bad guys they portrayed] [Caution: language] **[W]**

The Last Picture Show
1971 – co-written and directed by Peter Bogdanovich
Teen angst and sexual awakenings in a tiny early 1950s Texas town, based on Larry McMurtry's novel. Timothy Bottoms and Jeff Bridges star as high school buddies and sometime romantic rivals for Cybill Shepherd, who debuted here as a spoiled rich girl seeking to lose her virginity. The solid supporting cast includes Ellen Burstyn, Eileen Brennan, Randy Quaid, Sam Bottoms (Timothy's brother) and Ben Johnson, along with TV's Cloris Leachman, who won an Oscar for her role as the frustrated wife of the school's athletic coach. Johnson likewise won as the owner of the theater that runs … the last picture show: the immortal western *Red River* (PF5). [Trivia note: The movie's music presages a similar treatment two years later in George Lucas's *American Graffiti* (PF5), in which it's only heard from juke boxes, car radios and the like appearing within the scenes, but except for the closing credits never directly] [Caution: plenty of sexuality and frontal nudity] **[B&W] [W]**

Mother
1996 – written and directed by Albert Brooks
In a change of pace, here's an offbeat, subtly biting comedy about a grown man's unresolved relationship with his … mother, played out when circumstances force him to move back in with her. Brooks, who co-wrote the script and directed, also plays the protagonist, John Henderson, a struggling novelist and recent divorcee, while Debbie Reynolds plays the somewhat thankless title role. If you're a fan of Brooks and his movies, you know that beneath much of the laugh-getting situations and lines of dialogue there's a mind at work probing the human condition. [Caution: language and mild sexuality] **[W]**

Pelle the Conqueror
1987 – Denmark and Sweden – co-written and directed by Bille August
In this adaptation of the popular 1910 novel by Martin Andersen Nexø, the winner of both the Foreign Language Oscar and the *Palme d'Or* at Cannes, Max Von Sydow stars as Lasse Karlsson, aging father of young Pelle Karlsson (Pelle Hvenegaard). Father and son have traveled from Sweden to a small island off the coast of Denmark. They are seeking a new life after Lasse's wife, and Pelle's mother, has died. That new life turns out to be much more difficult than expected for father and son, who are, respectively, too old and too young for most jobs. So, they end up doing farm work for a nasty, sexually predatory boss (veteran Danish actor Axel Strøbye). From there, the fortunes of the pair diverge, with Lasse's sinking and Pelle' slowly but surely improving. In the end, Pelle just might be maturing to the point where he can ... conquer the world at large. [Trivia notes: 1) *Pelle Erövraren* was the second consecutive Danish film to win the Oscar, following *Babette's Feast* (PF5). 2) Pelle Hvenegaard was actually named after the novel's titular character] [Caution: sexuality] **[W]**

Say Anything...
1989 – written and directed by Cameron Crowe
A rarity: a teen romantic comedy–drama intelligently written and sensitively performed. John Cusack, in his best role, plays Lloyd Dobler, a newly graduating high-schooler who's smitten with class valedictorian Diane Court (Ione Skye – pronounced eye-OH-nee – real-life daughter of folksinger Donovan Leitch). Their mutual romantic attraction becomes thwarted by opposition from Diane's father, Jim (John Mahoney), who soon must deal with more serious problems of his own. Better not to give away any more of the plot, because it's an enjoyable process to watch. Again, well-written by Crowe and well-acted by Cusack, Skye and the supporting cast. [Trivia notes: 1) Cusack and Mahoney had appeared together the previous year in the baseball drama Eight Men Out (P25); Cusack as Chicago White Sox player "Buck" Weaver, and Mahoney as his manager, William "Kid" Gleason. 2)

Three little connections between the movie and Frasier, the long-running TV series: Mahoney played radio psychiatrist Frasier Crane's father; Bebe Newirth, here making her movie debut in a minor part, played Frasier's ex-wife Lilith, and both the movie and the series were set in Seattle] [Caution: mild sexuality] **[W]**

Stand By Me
1986 – Rob Reiner
Make it a John Cusack double-bill, though he plays a minor role here. Four boyhood friends (Wil Wheaton, Corey Feldman, River Phoenix and Jerry O'Connell) hike a long way to see a dead body, encountering several harrowing adventures along the way. Based on a Stephen King short story, it's told in flashback by a narrator (Richard Dreyfuss), who's one of the boys all grown up. [Trivia note: The setting for the movie, a town called Castle Rock, Oregon, became the name of Reiner's production company] [Caution: language and depictions of some gross juvenile behavior] **[W]**

Summer of '42
1971 – Robert Mulligan
Maybe *the* youthful wish-fulfillment story – and based on an encounter the original author claims to be true – about a teenager's summer vacation at Nantucket in … 1942. There, amid his exploits with two friends in pursuit of the opposite sex – in the form of teen girls also vacationing on the island – he meets a gorgeous newlywed (gorgeous model Jennifer O'Neill), therein beginning an unforgettable episode in his life. The movie became a huge hit that year, enhanced by Michele Legrand's lush romantic score. [Caution: sexuality, both teen and adult] **[W]**

Tea and Sympathy
1956 – Vincente Minnelli
Deborah Kerr and John Kerr (unrelated) in a mildly suggestive version of Robert Anderson's more explicit stage play, in which they also appeared, about a sensitive young man's introduction to sexuality by an older woman. The plot involves the difficulties the young man has in reconciling traditional manliness with his interests in pursuits such as theater and literature. Those interests

frequently place him in conflict with the other young men at his school and with his athletic coach (Leif Ericson, also reprising his stage role). Eventually driven to despair and unsuccessful suicide, he seeks solace – echoed in *The Last Picture Show* – with the coach's wife, who deflowers him. Her most notable line, quoted many times since: "Years from now, when you talk about this, and you will, be kind." [Viewing note: Here's another case where the industry's Production Code, still in full force during the 1950s, required a significant toning down of aspects of the play such as homosexuality, adultery and prostitution] [Caution: adult themes] **[W]**

Vision Quest
1985 – Harold Becker
An intelligent and appealing character study about a high school wrestler spending his senior year focusing on his sport, contemplating his future and experiencing love for the first time. Louden Swain (Matthew Modine), occupying a decent spot on his team, decides to up the ante by dropping two weight classes, a common but difficult challenge in the sport, so he can challenge the region's reigning champion Brian Shute (Frank Jasper). Complicating his … vision quest, as he calls it, is the arrival of Carla (Linda Fiorentino, in her debut), a young woman temporarily staying with Louden and his father (Ronnie Cox). That's about it. Modine, who the previous year turned in fine performances as the lead in Alan Parker's extremely offbeat *Birdy* (P25), and Gillian Armstrong's fine historical drama *Mrs. Soffel* (PF5), here plays perhaps his most ordinary character. That said, it's an engaging movie. Veteran character actor Roberts Blossom shows up briefly but vividly as Louden's grandfather, and pop-singer Madonna contributes the popular song, "Crazy for You." [Caution: sexuality] **[W]**

The World of Henry Orient
1964 – George Roy Hill
This weird little comedy, co-written by Nunnally Johnson and his daughter Nora – who wrote the source novel – is based on a real-life incident. Val and Gil (Tippy Walker and Merrie Spaeth), two

85

young teen girls, become obsessed with the eponymous Henry, a concert pianist (Peter Sellers). In modern parlance, they stalk him. They show up at his performances, hang out near his apartment building and collect souvenirs of him, all of which Val compiles in an artful scrapbook. It's an initially harmless fantasy, until they discover that among Henry's conquests as a serial philanderer is Val's mother (Angela Lansbury). A bitter pill to swallow, but one that helps the girl's standoffish father (Tom Bosley) bind with her in a life lesson that, seemingly, helps her to begin transitioning into young adulthood. To tell the truth, the adult part of the story is ordinary and uninteresting; it's the interplay between Val and Gil – who are onscreen together much of the time – that remains touching and appealing, now some six decades later. [Trivia note: The real incident involved two girls who developed a similar fixation on pianist Oscar Levant] [Caution: mild sexuality] **[W]**

8. Cops 'n' Robbers

Plenty of movies deal with law enforcement and its eternal battle with those who commit crimes. The interesting thing about these 11 movies is they can occasionally focus on – and sympathize with – both sides and, in some of the cases, even add a bit of humor.

Angel Eyes
2001 – Luis Mandoki

Jennifer Lopez and Jim Caviezel co-star in a romantic mystery–drama about a policewoman (Lopez) whose life is saved by a mysterious stranger with a tragic and traumatic past. Lots of implausibilities and misdirections along the way, but Lopez is surprisingly effective as a lady cop – she even did most of her own stunts – as is Caviezel as the mystery man, a most troubled soul. If you can forgive those implausibilities and misdirections, you might be captivated and even moved by the story and the performances, with strong support from Sônia Braga as her mother and Shirley Knight as his mother-in-law.[Caution: street violence and sexuality] **[W]**

The Bank Job
2008 – Roger Donaldson

In 1970, somewhere in the Caribbean, an often-scandalous member of the British royal family is engaged in … um, scandalous behavior. Only this time it's photographed by operatives intending blackmail. The event figures prominently in a sensational bank robbery the following year. Based on a true story – though fictionalized – Jason Statham and Saffron Burrows star in the depiction of the robbery, which takes place in the underground safety-deposit vault of a London Bank. It's fascinating, engaging and, before it's over, it envelops not only the royal family but also some prominent politicians and at least one world-famous entertainer. Well-directed by New Zealander Donaldson, it will, as often promised but not always delivered by other movie publicity, keep you on the edge of your seat. [Trivia note: Speaking of world-famous entertainers (not the one depicted in the movie), Rolling Stones lead singer Mick Jagger appears in a cameo – though you'll have to watch closely for him] [Caution: language, violence and explicit sexuality] **[W]**

Bonnie and Clyde (and) The Highwaymen
1967 and 2019 – Arthur Penn and John Lee Hancock

Here's an interesting pair of features separated by over half a century, one focusing on the most notorious male–female bank-robbery team in U.S. history, Bonnie Parker and Clyde Barrow; and the other portraying Frank Hamer and Maney Gault, the former Texas Rangers who brought Parker and Barrow to justice after they had rampaged across the Midwest for two years in the early 1930s, leaving a trail of dead lawmen in their wake.

*　　*　　*

In Penn's glamorous portrayal of the murderous couple, Warren Beatty and Faye Dunaway star in the title roles. The movie, which Beatty also produced, is an almost-lighthearted look at the story, with some sequences underscored by lively bluegrass music performed by Lester Flatt and Earl Scruggs that make it resemble screwball comedy. But Penn being Penn, the laughs will cease, partly as he portrays some of the violent robberies and assaults by lawmen, and then completely as Barrow and Parker meet their fate. Gene Hackman plays Barrow's brother Buck, and Estelle Parsons, in an Oscar-winning turn, plays his hysterical wife Blanche. [Trivia notes: 1) Beatty once told of working with Frank Stahl, the movie's sound supervisor, to make the gunshots so loud they would startle the audience. Sometime later, while traveling in England, Beatty attended a showing at a local theater. There, he heard the movie playing at a low volume. Furious, he confronted the projectionist, who told him he turned down the audio because so many customers had complained about the noise. 2) In contrast with the real Bonnie Parker, who would be no one's idea of a glamorous woman, audiences loved Faye Dunaway's look so much they copied her fashion for years, particularly her signature beret. 3) The movie served as a career springboard for several prominent names in the business. Along with Hackman, who became a star four years later with *The French Connection* (PF5), Gene Wilder, who debuted here in a minor role, likewise rose to stardom the next year in *The Producers* (also in PF5), and first-time screenwriter Robert Benton went on to become a successful director, whose films included the Oscar-winning *Kramer vs. Kramer*] [Caution: sexuality and intense violence] **[W]**

*   *   *

As mentioned, Arthur Penn directed, essentially, a Hollywood version of the story of Bonnie and Clyde. Here, in great contrast, Hancock and screenwriter John Fusco go for historical accuracy while focusing on Hamer (Kevin Costner) and Gault (Woody Harrelson in a surprisingly strong performance), with relative unknowns Emily Brobst as Parker and Edward Bossert as Barrow. This movie presents important details that enabled the Barrow Gang, as they were known, essentially to carry out their crime wave with impunity. For example, Barrow purchased or stole only high-powered vehicles, particularly V-8 (8-cylinder) Fords that could easily outrun their opposition. He used high-speed escapes to cross state lines and frustrate local police pursuers. Also, Barrow became an expert at choosing, and firing, powerful weapons, an ability that made many lawmen leery of confronting him directly. On the other hand, where *Bonnie and Clyde* portrayed Hamer and other pursuers as clumsy fools, *The Highwaymen* leaves no doubt about his skills and his lethality – likewise Gault. It's a gritty and gripping account of the real events, with the famous climactic shootout filmed at the spot on the Louisiana road where the rendezvous with destiny took place for the pair. [Trivia note: Among the actors who considered playing Hamer and Gault in this story were Paul Newman and Robert Redford. But when Newman died in 2008, the project languished for another decade] [Caution: graphic violence] **[W]**

Dear Inspector
1977 – France – Philippe de Broca

A rarity in the U.S. market, it's nevertheless worth watching for because it's a clever and amusing police comedy–drama. Originally titled "Dear Detective," (in France, *Tendre Poulet*, or "Tender Chicken" for some reason), it stars Annie Girardot as Lise, a police … inspector. Middle-aged and a bit plump but considerably appealing, she accidentally runs into Antoine (the venerable Philippe Noiret, star of *Cinema Paradiso* – see PF5), with whom she shared a short romantic encounter many years earlier. The plot involves Lise's attempts to rekindle the flames with Antoine while being continually interrupted by her professional duty: investigating murders, including a political assassination. In Gary Arnold's Washington Post review, he called it "a delightful entertainment" and "overwhelmingly winning." I'd add it's breezy and consistently funny (yes, even among the crimes and crime scenes), and as mentioned worth keeping an eye out for. [Caution: violence and mild sexuality] **[W]**

Dick Tracy
1990 – Warren Beatty

A decent-sized hit when released, it's still a mystery to me why it wasn't a blockbuster, because it's so much fun from beginning to end. Beatty also plays the title role, but he's mostly a straight man to the large and delightful array of crime denizens – nearly two dozen of them – come to life from Chester Gould's longstanding comic-strip, particularly Dustin Hoffman as "Mumbles" and Al Pacino as mob boss "Big Boy" Caprice, all sporting hilariously distorted makeup and prosthetics. Madonna also puts in an appearance as "Breathless" Mahoney, Big Boy's moll who's smitten with Tracy but who might not be who she seems. It's big. It's brash. It's colorful. It's a blast – and boy, does Big Boy get his comeuppance! [Trivia note: As a Hollywood inside joke, Hoffman based his character's vocal mannerisms on producer Robert Evans (see *The Kid Stays in the Picture* in P25), with whom he had worked on several productions] [Caution: cartoon violence – though some of it is scary – and mild sexuality] **[W]**

90

The Flim-Flam Man
1967 – Irvin Kershner

George C. Scott, three years before he gained acting immortality as the famous general in *Patton* (PF5), here plays Mordecai C. Jones, an inveterate trickster who travels through the rural South defrauding gullible souls. Along the way, he picks up a protégé, the aptly named Curley Treadaway (Michael Sarrazin), an Army deserter. Together, the two execute several successful cons before running afoul of The Law. Filmed entirely in and around Lexington, Kentucky, it's a diverting caper comedy, with Sue Lyon as Curley's love interest, a small band of veteran character actors playing the pigeons and the pursuers, and many of the residents hired as extras. Jerry Goldsmith did the folksy score. **[W]**

Guarding Tess
1994 – Hugh Wilson

I wish I had a proverbial nickel for every movie I've seen where the two principal characters start out as antagonists and end up lovers, partners or, in this case, friends. Shirley MacLaine and Nicolas Cage star, respectively, as a widowed first lady and the Secret Service agent detailed to … guard her. Their relationship starts out prickly – he considers it a demotion to receive this detail, and she regards her protectors as nuisances at best. That changes, however, when the former first lady suddenly disappears, and her ostensible security people realize she's been kidnapped. At that point the search is on, growing desperate when they receive a ransom demand containing a threat and driving Cage's character to drastic measures. [Trivia note: Though antagonists for much of the movie, Cage and MacLaine ended up good friends in real life] [Caution: violence] **[W]**

King of Thieves
2018 – England – James Marsh

The previous year in *Going in Style* (P25), Michael Caine had teamed with fellow seniors Alan Arkin and Morgan Freeman in a pretty good bank-heist vehicle done mostly for laughs. Here, based on a true story, Caine teams with fellow seniors Tom

Courtenay, Michael Gambon and Jim Broadbent in an attempted robbery worth millions in cash, gems and other valuables – and though it's funny in places it's definitely not a comedy. Also, this time Caine's character, Brian Reader, isn't an ordinary guy caught up in desperate circumstances. He's a career criminal and an occasionally nasty fellow. Likewise, Broadbent's Terry Perkins is as ferocious a character as the actor has ever portrayed. As in *The Bank Job*, Reader and Perkins, with Courtenay's deceptively mild John Collins and two other accomplices attempt to rob the safety-deposit vault of a London bank. Also like *The Bank Job*, several severely unexpected circumstances develop to challenge the team's fortitude. True story or not, it's a compelling narrative, and Caine and Broadbent are particularly good, as is Francesca Annis as Reader's appealing wife Lynne. [Trivia note: Not to give away the robbery's outcome, but the gang here did overlook an inconvenient flaw in their plan, something similar to the goof committed by Chicago would-be hate-crime victim Jussie Smollett] [Caution: violence] **[W]**

Public Enemies
2009 – co-written and directed by Michael Mann
Mann, who previously had directed *Heat* (P25), an exceptional film dealing with criminal minds and based on real incidents and characters, here creates a portrait of one of American's most notorious outlaws of the 1930s, John Dillinger (Johnny Depp). Dillinger, a flamboyant personality who despite his ruthless nature was sometimes portrayed heroically by the press – because he was a bank robber, and banks were held in even lower esteem than many of the crooks at the time – eventually ran afoul of J. Edgar Hoover (Billy Crudup), director of the newly constituted Federal Bureau of Investigations. Hoover dispatched Melvin Purvis (Christian Bale), one of his top agents, to catch and/or kill Dillinger, a task that became more challenging and dangerous than Purvis initially imagined. Like *The Highwaymen*, this was filmed in many of the locations where the actual events unfolded. It's a well-crafted, well-acted, superior crime drama – though some of the action scenes are so complex you tend to lose track of

who's who. The always-excellent Marion Cotillard plays Billy Frechette, the nightclub singer who became Dillinger's lover. [Trivia note: As he did with the characters played by Robert De Niro and Al Pacino in *Heat*, Mann staged some scenes using the real dialogue by the individuals involved, based on transcripts or accounts at the time] [Caution: sexuality, torture and graphic violence] **[W]**

Stakeout
1987 – John Badham
I admit this is the weakest of the bunch, but director Badham keeps it moving along, the cast does uniformly good work, and though the ending is never in doubt the whole thing is entertaining. Richard Dreyfuss and Emilio Estevez are Chris and Bill, cops assigned to surveil mob mistress Maria (Madeleine Stowe), because her former Beau (Aidan Quinn), a vicious criminal, has escaped from prison and is on the run. As they say, complications ensue, particularly when Chris gets too close for comfort to Maria and falls in love with her. This leads to ostensible mortal danger for the two cops, but because this is more caper than crime drama, you shouldn't mind when I say it ends fittingly for the bad guy and the good cops. [Trivia note: Speaking of happy endings, two romances and weddings resulted from this production. Aidan Quinn met Elizabeth Bracco (sister of Lorraine Bracco, in a minor role here) during the shoot, and they married that same year. Bruce Willis met Demi Moore at a screening of *Stakeout*. They likewise married that year, but their union lasted only until 2000] [Caution: violence and sexuality] **[W]**

9. Cruisein'

Some actors, such as Russell Crowe and Daniel Day-Lewis, can inhabit their characters so thoroughly you forget they're just performing. Others, such as John Wayne and William Holden, would essentially insert themselves into roles without sublimating their identities – Wayne was always "The Duke," as he was affectionately known, and Holden was always that same handsome, appealing guy. Even James Stewart, who occasionally played tough *hombres*, never really altered his essential persona. The man born Thomas Cruise Mapother IV is part of that category. In good movies and bad, he's basically the man with the same piercing eyes and the same killer smile. Along with his fine performances in *A Few Good Men*, *The Firm*, *Valkyrie* and *War of the Worlds* (all in PF5), in *The Color of Money* and *Days of Thunder* (both in P25), and in this compilation in both *Top Gun* movies, a secondary role in *Interview with the Vampire* and the lead in the first *Jack Reacher*, here are seven more examples of his enduring star power, now in its fifth decade. In chronological order…

Risky Business
1983 – as Joel Goodson

A big hit in the year of its release, this was Cruise's breakthrough role, at age 20. Written and directed by Paul Brickman, it's a slick but deeply cynical comedy about a high school underachiever who manages to earn – and immediately lose – eight thousand dollars in one night by selling the services of prostitutes to his classmates. Joel Goodson (Get it?) lives a comfortable if boring life in the Chicago suburbs and is trying to figure out a post-graduation plan. All that changes when 1) his parents go out of town, and 2) one of Joel's buddies persuades him to hire, via a local tabloid's personals ad, a hooker for the night. The attempt at first backfires but soon brings the presence of Lana (Rebecca De

Mornay in a smashing debut), a glamorous hooker who seduces and gradually corrupts Joel, and then deprives him of his ill-gotten gains. Trust me when I say the movie is deeply cynical, about both adults and relations between the sexes. But along with Cruise's personal appeal (his rendition, in his underwear, of Bob Seger's "Old Time Rock and Roll" became legendary among females), the movie contains ultra-hip soundtrack instrumentals by Tangerine Dream, and veteran actor Joe Pantoliano contributes a smashing debut of his own as Lana's pimp, Guido. Paul Brickman wrote and directed. [Caution: explicit sexuality and rough language] **[W]**

All the Right Moves
1983 – as Stefen Djordjevic

Cruise quickly abandoned his Joel Goodson routine in *Risky Business* and adopted a more ambitious, wise-ass personality that he used repeatedly during his career, and here's the first example. "Stef" is a promising high school football player from a working-class family in a Pennsylvania mill town. When his quick temper and youthful indiscretion prompts his coach (Craig T. Nelson) to kick him off the team, thereby jeopardizing his chances of winning a college athletic scholarship, Stef must scramble to salvage his future. He's also on shaky ground with his girlfriend Lisa (Lea Thompson, in an appealing debut), who's furious at him for blowing his best chance at a better life. Directed by Michael Chapman, who previously had established himself as a first-rate camera operator (among his credits were *The Godfather* and *Jaws* – both in PF5) and cinematographer (*Taxi Driver* and *Raging Bull*), it's an earnest though imperfect effort. [Trivia notes: 1) Thompson initially balked at doing a nude scene in the story, so Cruise volunteered to shed his clothes as well. Thompson later expressed her eternal gratitude to him for the gesture. 2) Like *Slapshot* (PF5) six years earlier, this one was filmed in Johnstown, Pennsylvania] [Caution: sexuality] **[W]**

Rain Man
1988 – as Charlie Babbitt
Barry Levinson directs Cruise and Dustin Hoffman in this Best Picture winner. Hoffman also won an Oscar for his portrayal of an autistic savant named Raymond (the "Rain Man" of the title). But I'd argue this was Cruise's most challenging performance, and he did a better job than Hoffman, whose character remains unchanged through the story. Charlie, on the other hand, must evolve from a self-centered, opportunistic young man into a person who truly cares for his long-lost brother. And Cruise accomplishes just that. It's a subtle, nuanced role, and he handles it as well as anything he's done, before or since. Valeria Golino does fine in a brief appearance as Charlie's love interest. [Critic's note: It might appear that I'm denigrating Hoffman's performance here. I'm not. Hoffman spent months studying the habits and mannerisms of autistic savants, particularly Kim Peek, whom Hoffman befriended for the rest of Peek's life. It's just that I consider Cruise's performance here to be underrated] [Caution: language and sexuality] **[W]**

Born on the Fourth of July
1989 – as Ron Kovic
Co-writer and director Oliver Stone's second Vietnam War epic, based on Kovic's scathing memoir, became Cruise's most dramatic role. The story traces Kovic's youth and young adulthood to his enlistment in the Marines then portrays his second tour of duty in Vietnam in the late 1960s. During that tour, Kovic accidentally kills a fellow soldier and is severely wounded in a firefight, leaving him not only paralyzed from the waist down but also wracked with guilt. Both become worse as Kovic suffers both mistreatment and unsuccessful attempts at rehabilitation. He falls into deep depression and alcoholism, and, when things look their worst, he meets and is befriended by a small group of paralyzed veterans, including Charlie (Willem Dafoe), who helps him come to terms with his condition. It's a heartbreaking story of one man's tragedy in the midst of that unpopular war. John Williams composed the mournful but stirring score. [Trivia note:

Along with Dafoe, Tom Berenger also appears briefly as a Marine recruiting sergeant. Both had co-starred in Stone's *Platoon* three years earlier, Dafoe as the platoon's courageous leader, and Berenger as a murderous soldier and rival. Nine other actors from *Platoon* also appear here in minor roles] [Caution: sexuality, adult themes and wartime violence] **[W]**

Jerry Maguire
1996 – in the title role

The topic of sports has been given screen treatments galore, but few movies have featured characters such as Jerry, an agent who represents top-drawer athletes and their multi-million-dollar deals with the pro teams. Jerry has been phenomenally successful but emotionally detached – until he experiences an epiphany when trying to comfort the young son of a client who has become permanently disabled due to an injury. So, he begins questioning not only his behavior but also that of his colleagues. In a fit of manic zeal, he writes what he considers a new manifesto for the profession. His action costs him his job and all but one of his clients, a mercurial pro football running back (Cuba Gooding Jr., who won a Best Supporting Actor Oscar). Down and nearly out, Jerry must claw his way back to viability. In that process, three women figure prominently: Avery (Kelly Preston in a ferociously sexy performance), his soon-to-be former lover; Dorothy (Renée Zellweger in her breakthrough role), the office secretary and single mother who eventually wins his heart; and Laurel (the always appealing Bonnie Hunt), Dorothy's sister and protector, who tells Jerry at one point, "If you hurt her, I'll kill you." Sharply written and directed by Cameron Crowe, and superbly edited by Joe Hutshing, it's a nearly nonstop talkfest that's never tiring. [Caution: language and sexuality] **[W]**

Mission: Impossible
1996 – as Ethan Hunt

One of the most popular TV series of the 1960s here recast and reimagined for the big screen, with Cruise in the central role. He's bolstered by arguably the most prestigious team of screenwriters ever assembled for a single movie: Robert Towne, David Koepp and Steve Zaillian assisted by Sydney Pollack and Brian De Palma, who directed. Despite all the big names, the whole thing quickly disassembles into implausibility, beginning with the opening sequence, which finds the entire Mission: Impossible team murdered, except for Ethan, who suddenly finds himself the prime suspect. The rest of the story involves Ethan trying to discover who framed him, a trail leading him to, among other places, the Central Intelligence Agency's headquarters at Langley, Virginia; downtown Prague, in the Czech Republic; and aboard the TGV train rolling from England to France via the Chunnel under the English Channel. I'm not a great fan of this one. For one thing, it ditches the solid premise underlying the TV series that the Mission: Impossible team merely outsmarted their adversaries, to the point where no one even suspected they had been fooled. Still, I give this iteration two nods: It's better than its five sequels, which grow progressively more outrageous; and Cruise worked hard at it, both producing and doing most of his own stunts. [Trivia notes: 1) Veteran actor Martin Landau, who played master of disguises Rollin Hand in the original series, disclosed in an interview that the producers wanted the entire TV team to appear at the beginning of the story – only to be killed off, as the movie portrays. Landau refused, and the idea died. 2) One of Cruise's co-stars in *The Firm* (PF5) was Stephen Hill, playing an FBI official. Hill had played Jim Phelps in the first season of TV's Mission: Impossible before being replaced by Peter Graves] [Caution: violence and intense suspense] **[W]**

Jack Reacher: Never Go Back
2016 – in the title role
I regard it as the more interesting title of the two Reacher movies starring Cruise (see *Jack Reacher*, elsewhere). Some years ago, my Jessie became hooked on Lee Child's novels about former Army military policeman Jack Reacher, an extreme loner of a man and eccentric drifter who maintains no permanent residence or even a personal vehicle. This installment follows parallel plotlines, one involving a criminal conspiracy and the other a personal mystery.

In the first, Reacher must spring a wrongly imprisoned female military officer (Cobie Smulders) and track down whoever is trying to kill her – and now him. In the second, he must determine whether a teenager (Danika Yarosh) is his illegitimate daughter. Like John Rambo in *First Blood* (P25), Reacher is an invincible fighter. But unlike Stallone's character, Cruise portrays Reacher as a supercool, calculating expert at hand-to-hand combat who resists the urge unless absolutely necessary – but when lethal force becomes necessary, he dispatches his adversaries quickly and with brutal efficiency. I prefer this second movie because Cruise gets to play off Smulders and Yarosh instead of working alone, and their interplay is appealing and often funny. Some fans have complained about Cruise in this role. The Reacher of the novels is a bit of a beast, standing well over six feet and weighing well over 200, while Cruise is not-quite-average height and of slender build – even with his pre-production physical training. Such comments remind me of something director William Wyler once told Terence Stamp during the filming of *The Collector* (not here). When Stamp complained about the differences between how Wyler wanted Freddie Clegg, his character, to behave and how author John Fowles had described him in his novel, Wyler leaned in to Stamp and whispered, "I'm not making the book." The director is Edward Zwick, known for weightier dramas such as *Glory* and *Defiance* (both in PF5), but he does good work here as well. [Viewing note: If you would prefer Reacher portrayed more closely to the character in Child's novels, maybe sample the Reacher series released in 2022 on Amazon Prime] [Caution: sexuality and violence] **[W]**

10. Darth Vader's Other Life

That deep voice with the raspy breath became a legendary presence in the first three Star Wars movies (now the middle trilogy of the nine-part saga with the endless spinoffs). Vader's towering physique belonged to British bodybuilder David Prowse, but the voice was none other than James Earl Jones, one of America's greatest actors, who characteristically resisted receiving a screen credit for his work. Gradually gaining experience and reputation as a young man as a superior Shakespearian stage actor, Jones got his start on film in his thirties in, of all things, *Dr. Strangelove* (P25), playing a B-52 nuclear bomber crewmember. Now 91, Jones has appeared in 85 movies. Along with *The Hunt for Red October* and *Sneakers* in PF5, as well as *Field of Dreams* and *Clear and Present Danger* in P25, here are three more favorites, including his first two leading roles. [Trivia note: His world-famous voice and gift of articulation notwithstanding, Jones as a child suffered from a severe speech impediment to the point where he almost never spoke. He credited his high school English teacher, who encouraged him to write and recite poetry, with helping him overcome his handicap – to the great benefit of his millions of fans]

The Great White Hope
1970 – as Jack Jefferson

Starring in the screen version of Howard Sackler's Pulitzer Prize-winning play, Jones is at his most versatile here. He plays mercurial heavyweight boxer Jefferson (based on the real, early 20th century champion Jack Johnson) in a drama directed by Martin Ritt and co-starring Jane Alexander as his lover, Eleanor Bachman. Jones and Alexander reprised their stage roles, for which they had both won Tony Awards, and both received Oscar nominations for the movie. Jones suffered the misfortune of competing against George C. Scott in *Patton* (PF5), which I consider the greatest screen performance of all time. Unbelievable as it seems, this was his only nomination. The story concerns a boxer, but it isn't really a boxing movie, though there is an eight-minute fight sequence at the end – and Ritt expanded the theatrical version by staging three large outdoor set pieces. Yes, because of the timeframe and situation, racial disparities and racism appear throughout, but they aren't the main themes. Instead, as Sackler once described, it's a study of an individual in the social crosshairs, in this case a black man targeted for having the audacity to defeat his presumed white superiors in the ring but gaining little admiration from his own community because of his, let's say, nonstandard behavior. The striking thing about Jones here is how well he balances it all. Not only does he seem so different from just about everything else he has done, he also projects an emotionally fearsome character; not a physically intimidating one. The tool, as usual, is his voice. The depth and timbre are there, but he's speaking not as a classically trained actor; rather as an uneducated black man and talented athlete who has clawed his way up the professional boxing ladder. He's completely believable. Alexander, as Eleanor, gives her greatest performance in her debut role. Hard going a lot of the time, it's an affecting drama, and the two leads are terrific together, their chemistry no doubt honed by hundreds of repeats on stage. [Trivia notes: 1) The title refers to the white boxer whom the press and the public expected would finally put Jefferson down. In the real history, it was former champion James Jeffries, who was persuaded out of retirement to face Jack Johnson. Johnson defeated him badly, and Jeffries admitted he couldn't have beaten Johnson even back in his prime. 2) Jones wasn't the only classically trained actor playing against type here. Moses Gunn, whom you can see as an elegant but corrupt African diplomat two years later in the caper comedy *The Hot Rock* (PF5), likewise was arresting in a brief role as Scipio, sort of a singleton Greek chorus who challenges Jefferson's behavior] [Caution: sexuality and adult themes] **[W]**

The Man
1972 – as President Douglass Dilman

Probably his least-known role but one of his best performances, Jones plays a distinguished and learned senator whom fate suddenly thrusts into the Oval Office and the presidency. The premise is highly contrived. Attending an event in Europe, the sitting president and speaker of the House are killed in a building collapse. The vice president, normally the immediate successor, declines the succession because of failing health. That allows the awesome burden of the presidency to fall on Dilman, who's President Pro Tempore of the Senate. From there, it's an organizational scramble by the former president's cabinet to educate and indoctrinate the unexpected, and racially inconvenient, new … man in the White House. Directed by TV veteran Joseph Sargent and originally intended for that medium, *The Man* was considered topical entertainment – released as it was during the lingering turmoil of the civil rights movement. And despite its strong supporting cast – including Martin Balsam, Burgess Meredith, Lew Ayers and William Windom – and a script by the legendary Rod Serling based on Irving Wallace's novel, it's otherwise run-of-the-mill. But Jones elevates it into a solid character study. He commands attention, and he conveys, unambiguously, the overwhelming emotions any of us would feel in facing such a radical upheaval in our lives. Not a perfect production by any means, but a fine performance by an actor ascending. [Trivia note: The movie opens at a fictionalized version of the annual White House Correspondents Association dinner, with Jack Benny providing the traditional humorous remarks. It was the beloved comedian's last screen appearance] [Caution: adult themes] **[W]**

The Bingo Long Traveling All-Stars & Motor Kings
1976 – as Leon Carter

Just about the time he was recording that growly voice for George Lucas in the original *Star Wars* (PF5), Jones was co-starring in this tale about a traveling Negro baseball team in the 1930s. Back then, the country's two professional baseball leagues, National and

American, would not permit African Americans to play regardless of their ability. Likewise, the minor leagues would not accept black players. Such exclusions forced the most talented athletes into what were called the Negro leagues, featuring teams spread out across America. *Bingo Long...* depicts players who, though not necessarily less talented, tended toward a less-organized approach to the game. Their team functioned a bit like the Harlem Globetrotters of basketball. They traveled around the American heartland, challenging local teams to games and entertaining the crowds with their antics. Led by the eponymous Bingo Long (Billy Dee Williams), the team features Leon Carter (Jones), a catcher and heavy hitter; and Charlie Snow (Richard Pryor), who's trying to break into the majors by pretending he's a Cuban named Carlos Nevada. Not nearly as good as the other two titles here, it's nevertheless diverting. Directed by John Badham, whose Alabama roots included days in the stands as a boy watching some of the great Negro players. [Trivia notes: 1) Pryor's character reflected the reality in the early days of baseball, where some African Americans adopted Caribbean accents and pseudonyms to pass, as it was called, as Cubans or Puerto Ricans. A few exceptional players made it into the majors that way. 2) Jones and Williams would again appear onscreen together, sort of, four years later in *The Empire Strikes Back* (PF5), the fifth chapter in the Star Wars saga, with Williams as Lando Calrissian and Jones as ... well, you know] [Caution: adult themes] **[W]**

11. Different Drummers

Twenty-seven individuals in 20 films who, as the ballad by Fleetwood Mac describes, go their own way – most of them real people.

The African Doctor

2016 – France – co-written and directed by Julien Rambaldi

How's this for rubbing against the grain? Also known as *Bienvenu à Marly-Gomont*, it's based on the true story of Dr. Seyolo Zantoko, a Congolese man who has taken his medical training in France in the 1970s and decides to begin practicing there instead of his war-torn home country. So, he summons his wife and family to Marly-Gomont, a small town in the northern Provence of Picardy (today, Hauts-de-France). There, Dr. Zantoko (Marc Zinga) by his very presence creates a host of unintended consequences, many stemming from the fact that most of the town's residents have never seen a black man, much less a black doctor. But this isn't a drama. It's a comedy–drama, and one with a happy though bittersweet ending. The movie's co-writer is Congolese–French comedian and singer Kamini Zantoko, the doctor's real-life son. It's a minor treasure. [Caution: adult themes] **[W]**

The Aviator

2004 – Martin Scorsese

These days, America's best-known eccentric billionaire is Elon Musk, creator of the Tesla electric car and SpaceX, one of the world's most successful private rocket-launch companies. But for half a century, beginning in the 1920s, the same distinction went to Howard Hughes, who for much of that period divided his time between moviemaking and trailblazing achievements in … aviation. Scorsese's sprawling, three-hour epic casts Leonardo

DiCaprio as the brilliant but obsessive Hughes, whose understated but powerful personality and force of will brought him both fame and notoriety most of his life. Unlike Hughes, DiCaprio portrays him as relentlessly manic and a bit over-the-top, particularly when depicting the man's severe obsessive-compulsive disorder. Cate Blanchette plays Katharine Hepburn, whose friendship and affair with Hughes ended when she began a lifelong relationship with Spencer Tracy (played here by Kevin O'Rourke); and Kate Beckinsale is Ava Gardner, the second love of his life. Scorsese spared no expense in re-creating the period of the story, even to the point of digitally adjusting the film stock's tinting to match what color movies looked like back then. For the aviation sequences, he largely abandoned CGI animation and used detailed miniatures, with impressive results – the best since *The Right Stuff* (PF5). The extensive supporting cast includes Alan Alda, Alec Baldwin, Willem Dafoe, Edward Herrmann, Ian Holm, Jude Law, John C. Reilly and Brent Spiner, better known as the android Lt. Commander Data in the Star Trek: The Next Generation television series. *The Aviator* is big, flashy and, like its subject, audacious in the extreme, but take it more as entertainment than true-to-life portrait. [Critic's note: No offense to Blanchette, but her Oscar-winning portrayal of Hepburn was, in my humble opinion, more impersonation veering into caricature than personification] [Caution: language, sexuality and adult themes] **[W]**

The Big Year
2011 – David Frankel

From a big, sprawling epic to a simple story on a small scale – though it depicts individuals at least somewhat obsessed. *The Big Year* is about a birdwatching competition. Specifically, it's about three individuals, played by Jack Black, Steve Martin and Owen Wilson, who spend an entire year competing to accumulate the most sightings of different species. Based on Mark Obmascik's nonfiction book of the same name, it depicts the lengths to which serious birders will go to spot the rarest and remotest avian critters – though California, Alaska and British Columbia stand in

105

for some of the more widespread locations. The excellent supporting cast includes Dianne Wiest, Anjelica Huston, Rosamund Pike, JoBeth Williams and John Cleese. A genial little movie, it features 18 songs, including one written and performed by Martin. [Trivia note: I used the word "spend," above, literally. Attempting a big birding year tends to cost as much as climbing Mount Everest] [Caution: sexuality] **[W]**

The Distinguished Citizen
2016 – Argentina and Spain – Gastón Duprat & Mariano Cohn
Consider Daniel Montovani (Oscar Martinez), a Nobel Prize-winning author and longtime resident of France who's suddenly inundated with invitations from organizations worldwide, asking him to speak and make presentations about his work. But he accepts only one of them: from his old hometown in Argentina, a place that knew him long ago and where he lost the love of his life. They want him to come and judge a local art contest. Shunning the international limelight, Montovani thinks he'll achieve a temporary respite and enjoy visiting with old friends and acquaintances. Little does he know what challenges – and dangers – await him. Lots of surprises and fascinating details in a most unusual story. [Caution: language, sexuality and some violence] **[W]**

The Endless Summer
1966 – produced, directed, photographed and narrated by Bruce Brown
Who on this planet moves to the "beat of a different drum" (a lyric from a nice oldie by Linda Ronstadt, back when she sang with the Stone Poneys) more than those seeking to hang ten and find the perfect wave? Surfers and surfing are the topics of this classic documentary, produced and directed by Brown, whose son Dana made the superb *Step Into Liquid* (PF5) nearly four decades later. The title is literal. Brown and his crew followed surfers Mike Hynson and Robert August as they visited surfing haunts during their respective peak summer days. Aside from being … endlessly enjoyable, *The Endless Summer* is possibly the most laid-back movie ever made, with footage from eight of the best surfing

beaches on Earth. It's credited with spurring worldwide enthusiasm for the sport, and its theme song, by The Sandals, became a hit. [Trivia note: The movie itself sports an odyssey as unusual as its topic was at the time. Lacking a conventional distributor, Brown and Hynson at first hauled their reels from town to town and played the movie to school and community audiences. Also lacking a soundtrack (Brown shot it on 16-millimeter, silent film), Brown supplied the narration in person]

A Fine Madness
1966 – Irvin Kershner
Probably Sean Connery's least-known role is also his most unusual and uninhibited. He plays Samson Shillitoe, a frustrated poet and serial philanderer with anger-management issues whose temperament lands him in one scrape after another. When he ends up in a mental institution and runs afoul of one of the psychiatrists (Clive Revill) by having an affair with his wife (Jean Seberg), Shillitoe must undergo a lobotomy – which remarkably doesn't affect him. Sound manic? It is, he is and the movie is, unceasingly so. Connery radiates an energy here that he never displayed in any of his other roles, at least not to this degree. He isn't exactly likeable, but Sean being Sean, you can't help but watch him in action. The cast also includes Joanne Woodward as Shillitoe's steadfast lover, plus a bunch of character actors whose names you might not know but whose faces you'll likely recognize – including Richard Castellano, better known as Clemenza in *The Godfather* (PF5). [Trivia note: If you've never heard of New Zealand actor Revill before, chances are you've heard his voice, albeit briefly. He supplied it for the holographically projected Emperor in the Star Wars episode *The Empire Strikes Back* (PF5)] [Caution: sexuality and adult themes] **[W]**

Florence Foster Jenkins
2014 – Stephen Frears
Chances are, at some point in your life you've met an individual who 1) yearns to perform before a large audience, 2) is convinced of their exceptional appeal or talent and 3) is, unfortunately, clueless about the lack thereof – a variation of Hans Christian

Andersen's fairy tale "The Emperor's New Clothes." Meryl Streep in the title role is such a person, a bubbly New York socialite and patron of the arts in the 1940s who fancies herself a songstress, but who can barely sing a note. Based on a true story, the movie chronicles Jenkins in her quest to become an opera star. In a way, her wish comes true, because she ends up performing at New York's celebrated Carnegie Hall to a packed house of well-wishers and soldiers. You can guess the outcome. It might sound comedic, and some parts are, but overall, it's a surprisingly touching story, made so by Streep's fine performance (she did all of her own singing), and well-supported by Hugh Grant as St. Clair Bayfield, Jenkins' manager and life partner. [Caution: adult themes and sexuality] **[W]**

Good Morning, Vietnam
1987 – Barry Levinson
Robin Williams is Adrian Cronauer, a disc jockey on an Armed Forces Radio station in Saigon during the Vietnam War who, shall we say, breaks with standard protocol in an effort to boost troop morale. It's a showcase for Williams's brilliant, nonstop improvisations, particularly his sensational first broadcast, but it's in no way a true biography of Cronauer, who praised Williams's performance but cautioned that his real experience was completely different – including finishing his entire year of duty in Vietnam and being honorably discharged. As Cronauer himself said of the movie, it's a Robin Williams standup performance disguised as a tale about Vietnam and the war. Along those lines, Cronauer is the only real person portrayed; everyone else is fictional. [Trivia note: One of the DJs who replaced Cronauer after he returned to the States was Pat Sajak, much better known over here as host of the long-running TV game show, Wheel of Fortune] [Caution: language, sexuality and violence] **[W]**

Hampstead
2017 – Joel Hopkins
Diane Keaton and Brendan Gleeson co-star in a slight but endearing romance based on a true story. Gleeson is Donald Horner, a bit of a hermit living off the land – but within the city

limits of London. Keaton is Emily Walters, an American widow also residing in London, still settling matters in the aftermath of her husband's death. One day, she spots Horner in the park across the street and becomes fascinated by his odd behavior. Eventually, she discovers his hand-crafted hovel in the woods and pays him a visit. Things go awkwardly at first, but a friendship builds between Emily and Donald, leading to an unlikely but touching love affair. All isn't well, however, because a developer wants to build condominiums on the land Horner occupies, and a legal battle ensues to determine whether he can claim property rights. It's all pleasant and nicely done. The cast also features Jason Watkins, who played Prime Minister Harold Wilson in the British miniseries The Crown, as a potential suitor. [Caution: sexuality] **[W]**

Heart Like a Wheel
1983 – Jonathan Kaplan

Imagine a young girl growing up in the 1950s who's fascinated with speed, automotive speed. This girl, who possesses natural abilities, would love to become a racecar driver, but she lives in an era when the thought of a woman competitor in that sport is unthinkable. Miraculously, because of her courage, persistence and talent, she does end up racing professionally – on the dragstrip circuit. And she becomes a champion. Bonnie Bedelia plays legendary dragster Shirley Muldowney in this well-made biography about her uphill climb to the top of a male-dominated, extremely dangerous milieu. Country singer Hoyt Axton plays her father, who encourages Shirley to pursue her dream. Leo Rossi is Jack Muldowney, her automobile-mechanic husband who builds her first competition vehicle. And Beau Bridges is Connie Kalitta, her professional rival and sometime lover. [Trivia note: Regarding the dangers of pro drag-racing, Muldowney was nearly killed in 1973 in an accident on the strip that destroyed her car, shattered her leg and burned her severely] [Caution: adult themes]

Housekeeping
1987 – written and directed by Bill Forsyth

Forsyth, who specialized in quirky comedies featuring unusual characters, such as the beguiling *Local Hero* (<u>PF5</u>) and the simple but charming *Gregory's Girl* (elsewhere), here moves into the world of drama. You can tell from the opening scene, where a single mother in the 1950s drives out into the countryside, lovingly drops off her two young girls by the roadside, gets back in the car and promptly rolls off a cliff. The shocking act leaves the sisters in the care of their grandmother, who dies several years later of natural causes. Then the girls, now teenagers, fall into the custody of their only remaining relative, an extremely eccentric aunt (Christine Lahti) living in a small Idaho town. Let's just say the move intensifies their strange life's odyssey. If you're intrigued enough by the premise, discover the rest of the movie for yourself. I admit, this one's a stretch but not without its appeal. Forsyth, a Scotsman, possesses an unusual story sense, to say the least. [<u>Caution</u>: adult themes] **[W]**

King of Hearts
1966 – Philippe de Broca

During the 1970s, repertory movie houses often double-billed this one with *A Thousand Clowns* (<u>PF5</u>), both to appreciative audiences, because each portrayed what I call in this section a different drummer, one who hates living within the bounds of established society, and one who's drawn away from conventionality. The time is 1918, near the end of World War I. In a small town in France, the German Army is in retreat. To slow down the pursuit of the Allies, the Germans have planted boobytraps – landmines awaiting the advancing enemy troops – all over the town. Witnessing what the Germans have done, the residents flee to the countryside. Remaining and ignored, however, are two small populations: the caged animals in the town's tiny zoo and the inmates at the local asylum. Meanwhile, the British learn about the boobytraps, so the commanding officer sends an enlisted man, Charles Plumpick (Alan Bates, in one of his best roles). His duty had been to care for the unit's messenger pigeons. But now his commander orders him to locate and disarm the German mines. When Plumpick arrives, he encounters the remaining Germans, who try to capture him. They pursue him inside the asylum, where he hides among the inmates. What happens next is too precious to give away. Just know that Plumpick and the movie's title are inextricably connected, and you might find yourself thoroughly charmed. The supporting cast features a young Geneviève Bujold at her most appealing. [Trivia note: Early on, a young soldier appears who strongly resembles Der Führer of Germany's later years. It's director de Broca's cameo] [Caution: sexuality and violence] **[W]**

Leave No Trace
2018 – co-written and directed by Debra Granik
Probably the most different drummer in the category, it's another one based on a true story. Granik, whose brooding and dark *Winter's Bone* (P25) won her critical acclaim, presents a fascinating but wrenching tale of a troubled Iraq War veteran and his daughter attempting to live way, way off the grid in the Oregon wilderness. Ben Foster plays Will, whose wartime experiences have left him with a severe case of post-traumatic stress. Tom (Thomasin McKenzie), his teenage daughter, stays with Will and tries to keep him grounded in reality. It's a difficult task, to say the least. For one thing, some of the people they encounter suspect Will of having abducted Tom and using her for sex trafficking. For another, the father and daughter are frequently subject to attempted intervention by welfare agencies. Spare of dialogue, with long periods of silence, it's a captivating, touching story of two souls, one perhaps irretrievably lost, and the other torn between love for and devotion to her father, and her basic desire to live a normal life. [Caution: adult themes] **[W]**

Memento
2000 – written and directed by Christopher Nolan
Yet another different drummer for you: a man who cannot retain short-term memories, a condition known as anterograde amnesia. To help himself retain things, he takes Polaroid photos, writes himself notes and even tattoos his body with important

information. Much more complex than *Slaughterhouse-Five* (P25), where the protagonist experiences his life out of sequence, the movie does a skillful job of balancing two storylines, one shown in black & white in which Leonard Shelby (Guy Pearce), the protagonist, continually finds himself in situations, some of them dangerous, where he can't remember where he is or how he got there. In the other, in color, the movie presents sequences in reverse chronological order, leading back to the traumatic event that most likely caused Shelby's amnesia. This one isn't for the casual viewer. The two storylines jump back and forth more than 100 times, so it's easy to lose yourself in the plot if you don't pay close attention. I'm not a big fan of Nolan, but here, in only his second directorial effort, he holds things together fairly well. [Viewing note: For a strictly comedic take on a similar plotline, see "The Betrayal," episode 8 in the ninth and final season of Seinfeld] [Caution: adult themes] **[B&W in selected sequences] [W]**

Morgan!
1966 – Karel Reisz

David Warner over the years has played many villainous characters, on TV as well as the movies. This is his one comedy, his one sympathetic protagonist, his first starring role and my favorite of the bunch. Full title *Morgan! – A Suitable Case for Treatment*, Warner is Morgan Delt, an eccentric but appealing London artist who's obsessively devoted to his wife Leonie (Vanessa Redgrave). Eventually, Morgan's eccentricities – in addition to everything else, he's a committed communist – become intolerable for her, and she files for divorce. The action triggers even more bizarre behavior in him. How bizarre? Imagine Morgan, escaping from Leonie's wedding to her new husband (classical stage actor Rober Stephens) on a motorcycle in a gorilla suit that's on fire. Strange you want? This one's got it. [Trivia note: Redgrave received an Oscar nomination as Leonie, the same year her sister Lynn also received one for the title role in *Georgy Girl* (P25). Both lost to Elizabeth Taylor in the detestable *Who's Afraid of Virginia Wolf?* (not on my lists)] [Caution: sexuality] **[B&W]**

My Dinner with Andre
1981 – Louis Malle

How about a movie whose sole content is a 110-minute conversation in a restaurant? Boring? No, actually, it's fascinating – though I readily admit it isn't for everyone. You might not have heard of the eponymous character; actor and playwright Andre Gregory, but you'll probably recognize his dinner companion; Wallace Shawn, forever known as the scheming Vizzini in *The Princess Bride* (PF5). Gregory and Shawn meet for ... dinner in Manhattan, where Shawn begins by asking Gregory what he's been up to. That begins a one-hour monologue where Gregory answers the question, followed by 50 more minutes of back-and-forth between the two men where they touch on a wide range of topics such as their respective worldviews and the meaning of life. The conversation isn't, strictly speaking, scripted – though both men wrote their basic monologues. A lot of it was improvised. As mentioned, not for everyone but unusually fascinating. [Trivia note: Shawn's dinner with Andre is supposed to be taking place in Manhattan, but due to budgetary restrictions the movie was shot at an abandoned – and unheated – hotel in Richmond, Virginia, in winter. Cast and crew reportedly compensated for the lack of heat by wearing long underwear and, where possible, ski clothes] **[W]**

The Peanut Butter Falcon
2019 – written and directed by Tyler Nilson and Michael Schwartz

This might be the most unusual title of all. It's the story of Zak (Zack Gottzagen), a young man with Down Syndrome (played by Gottzagen, who likewise has Down Syndrome), an inmate at an assisted-living facility. One day, Zak escapes and, with the help of Tyler (Shia LeBoeuf), another young man on the run, attempts to become a pro wrestler. Via several twists of fate, that's what happens. Under the tutelage of the Salt Water Redneck (Thomas Haden Church in a witty performance), a supposedly legendary figure in the sport along the southern East Coast, Zak earns his first match. Meanwhile, the pair attempts to keep avoiding their

113

pursuers, including Eleanor (Dakota Johnson), the social worker back at the facility who's responsible for Zak. From there, well, a few surprises emerge on the way to a happy ending. A little gem. [Trivia note: The movie had a most unusual genesis. Nilson and Schwartz happened to meet Gottzagen at a camp for the disabled, where Gottzagen expressed a desire to become a movie star. So, they created the storyline to fulfill his dream] [Caution: adult themes] **[W]**

Rose Island
2020 – Italy – co-written and directed by Sydney Sibilia
Also known as *L'incredibile storia dell'Isola delle Rose*, it's based on the improbable but true story of Giorgio Rosa (Elio Germano), an engineer who craves independence so much that he builds an artificial island of his own just off the Italian coastal town of Rimini, on the Adriatic Sea. Rosa is the quintessential different drummer. He hates conventionality, to the point where he builds his own automobile from scratch and yearns to live somewhere that permits total freedom. So, he goes the car project one better. Along with Maurizio (Leonardo Lidi), a friend and fellow engineer, Rosa builds a structure resembling an offshore oil rig just outside the limits of Italian coastal waters. Soon, the Republic of Rose Island begins attracting like-minded characters from all over Europe. Unfortunately, the tiny new nation also attracts the disdain, and enmity, of the Italian government, which takes a series of increasingly harsh measures to force Rosa and his fellow islanders to abandon the place, even to the point of threatening a naval bombardment. Like the legendary Camelot in the days of King Arthur, Rose Island was a fleeting wisp of glory. And it was a beguiling prospect while it lasted. [Caution: sexuality] **[W]**

Swimming to Cambodia
1987 – Jonathan Demme
A natural double-bill with *My Dinner with Andre*, here is Spalding Gray's 85-minute monologue on his experiences as a cast member of *The Killing Fields*. Gray, a sometime actor but more consistently a standup performer, stages his first filmed monologue in front of a small group of onlookers on a cabaret-like set. There, he

expounds at length on his small role in Roland Joffé's epic about the Khmer Rouge's genocide in Cambodia, presenting some astute takes on the quirks about both the movie business in general and Joffé in particular. He also engages in frequent asides, including if not swimming *to* Cambodia, then swimming offshore from a Cambodian beach. Like *My Dinner with Andre*, not for everyone. But worth sampling for a glimpse of Gray's unique perspectives and personality. [Caution: language] **[W]**

Unstrung Heroes
1995 – Diane Keaton

A gentle, touching drama about a pair of dysfunctional brothers (Maury Chaykin and Michael Richards – playing far, far against his famous, manic comedic role as Kramer on the Seinfeld TV series). The brothers, Arthur (Chaykin) who obsessively collects everything in sight, and Danny (Richards) whose paranoia frequently veers into delusion, become the temporary caretakers of Steven (Nathan Watt), their young nephew whose mother (Andie MacDowell) has become ill, potentially fatally so, with ovarian cancer. Despite the traumatic situation, and through the patient intervention of the brothers, Steven discovers aspects of life he had never considered before. Based on the real-life memoir by Franz Lidz (his uncles decided to change his name from Steven to Franz), it's a fine job by the principals – including John Turturro as Steven's father – and by Keaton, directing her only fictional story for the big screen. [Caution: adult themes] **[W]**

115

12. Disorder in the Court

Five outstanding dramas, helmed by four distinguished directors, dealing with or involving the judicial system.

12 Angry Men
1957 – Sidney Lumet

Lumet's landmark behind-the-courtroom drama, in which Henry Fonda and 11 superlative character actors play a jury attempting to determine the guilt or innocence of a young man accused of murder, has long been considered a classic. Indeed, the dozen jurors do get angry a lot of the time, trying to sort out the evidence. Eventually, all decide that the prosecution's case was sufficient to produce a guilty verdict, which would mean execution via the electric chair. All, that is, except one. Fonda, as juror number 8, cannot shed the nagging suspicion that the evidence contains sufficient gaps to trigger the legal concept of reasonable doubt, and therefore a not-guilty verdict. So, he must argue against the collective opinion of his peers, creating an obviously tense situation, made even more so by Lumet's subtle but brilliant filming scheme. For one thing, almost the entire movie takes place in the cramped jury room. For another, Lumet begins the scenes by shooting from a high angle, above the heads of the jurors. Then, gradually but inexorably, he brings the cameras lower and closer, until the last discussions are filmed within inches of the actors' faces. Based on Reginald Rose's 1954 teleplay, it's an ordeal but worthwhile, and the cast is terrific. The other jurors include Oscar-winners (along with Fonda) Martin Balsam and Ed Begley; Oscar nominees Jack Warden and Lee J. Cobb; Emmy winner Jack Klugman and TV, stage and screen veterans E.G. Marshall and Edward Binns. The other four, not as well known, are no less skillful. [Trivia note: Speaking of ordeals, along with the unusual photographic technique, Lumet forced the actors to rehearse and re-read their dialogue for hours in that jury room, producing discomfort that seeped deeply into their performances] [Caution: adult themes] **[B&W] [W]**

Anatomy of a Murder
1959 – Otto Preminger

A far less powerful drama but still an entertaining one, and not without its connections to a real courtroom. James Stewart is Paul Biegler, an Upper Peninsula Michigan lawyer who loves to fish but takes time out occasionally to accept a worthwhile defendant, in this case a soldier (Ben Gazzara) accused of killing a man he suspects raped his wife (Lee Remick). It's a tough case and a sharp battle of legal minds, pitting Biegler against out-of-town prosecutor Claude Dancer (George C. Scott in a strong early role). Lots of complications and surprises, and both Stewart and Scott received Oscar nominations. It is, as mentioned, entertaining. [Cultural note: The movie proved controversial in many areas where it screened – even in Chicago, where Mayor Richard J. Daley attempted to have it banned. One of the reasons? One item of evidence introduced and shown in the trial included Remick's character's panties. Shocking back then, they're amusingly modest, demure even, by today's standards] [Trivia notes: 1) As to that real courtroom connection, the story was based on a U.P. murder case in 1952, in which counsel for the accused employed a similar defense. 2) *Anatomy of a Murder* received seven Oscar nominations but zero wins. Where it did score well was at the Grammy Awards, winning in all three nominated categories for an excellent jazz score by none other than Duke Ellington] [Caution: adult themes] **[B&W] [W]**

Inherit the Wind
1960 – Stanley Kramer

Also inspired by a real case but veering quite a bit into theater – it was, after all, based on the play five years earlier by Jerome Lawrence and Robert Edwin Lee – the story nevertheless involves issues relevant to this day. Spencer Tracy and Fredric March star as old friends but dueling lawyers in a fictionalized version of the famous and so-called "Scopes Monkey Trial" in 1925 Tennessee. The ostensible issue was the teaching of Darwin's Theory of Evolution in the classroom, in a state where such instruction was, literally, unlawful. The defendant, a young teacher named Betram Cates (Dick York, best-known later as Darren Stevens in the TV series Bewitched), whose character was based on the real defendant John Scopes, was accused of introducing the illegal subject to his biology class. In perhaps a sane world, the debate would have been waged between the students' parents and the local school board. In this instance – as tends to happen today – the case drew three nationally known figures to the small town to carry on the legal battle before the whole country. For the prosecution, there was Matthew Harrison Brady (March), based on Illinois Democratic senator and three-time presidential candidate William Jennings Bryan. For the defense, there was Henry Drummond (Tracy), patterned after famous attorney Clarence Darrow. And chronicling the event was journalist and commentator E.K. Hornbeck (Gene Kelly) of the fictional Baltimore Herald (a version of renowned Baltimore Sun columnist H.L. Mencken). Given the personalities involved, the arguments could not be waged in a low-key manner. The encounters advance from quiet monologues to fiery dialogue, from congenial honesty to theatrical bombast. And the drama centers on those largely unresolved exchanges, not on any particular conclusion. In the end, the central contentious issue remains: How can we reconcile a local community's need to control its schools with issues that will ultimately transcend places and times? Here's Hollywood's attempt at an answer, eloquently performed by the three principals, with a quietly powerful ending scene between Kelly and Tracy. [Trivia notes: 1) One of the movie's scriptwriters was Nedrick Young, who had been blacklisted in the 1950s and forced to use the name Nathan E. Douglas. 2) The story has been remade three times for television over the years; in 1965 with Melvyn Douglas and Ed Begley, in 1988 with Jason Robards and Kirk Douglas, and in 1999 with Jack Lemmon and George C. Scott, all, respectively, as Drummond and Brady. 3) Here's a weird coincidence for you. March and Tracy

118

both starred in the dual title roles in the two classic versions of *Dr. Jekyll and Mr. Hyde*; March in 1931 and Tracy a decade later] [B&W]

Judgment at Nuremburg
1961 – Stanley Kramer

Among all of the movies listed in my three volumes, this one is arguably the most thoughtful, the most thought-provoking and the most conscience-wrenching – not because of what it portrays directly but because of the implications it conjures. Here's Spencer Tracy again, one year later, returned to the courtroom under Kramer's direction, but this time behind the bench as a jurist trying accused Nazi war criminals – in particular, four members of the German judicial system who participated, indirectly, in the unspeakable atrocities of Adolph Hitler's Third Reich. This isn't a re-creation of the real Nuremberg Trials, which took place beginning in the fall of 1945. Instead, it's a condensed dramatization featuring a group of fine actors, most of them playing against type. Burt Lancaster, for example, is Ernst Janning (YANN-ing), a stoic, apparently learned man who nevertheless sentenced thousands of Jews and others to death. Judy Garland, in one of her last roles, plays Frau Hoffman-Wallner, an ordinary German whose friendship with an older Jewish man led to his arrest. Marlene Dietrich plays Frau Berthold, widow of a Nazi general executed by the Allies. Montgomery Clift, bloated and disheveled in a disturbing performance, bears personal witness to one of the non-lethal monstrosities of the Nazis. And Maximillian Schell delivers a towering, Oscar-winning performance as the defense attorney for the Germans. Tracy again gets the last word, with a shattering, six-minute monologue that was filmed in a single take from multiple angles. Nominated for 12 Academy Awards, including Abby Mann's superb, Oscar-winning screenplay, it's an uncomfortable 3 hours, listening to the testimonies and the mounting evidence. Part of that discomfort derives from the realization that some of the warnings and lessons contained within the plot remain valid to this day. We ignore or forget them at our peril. [Viewing note: The moviemakers faced an awkward problem involving the need for many of the characters to wear headphones, ostensibly to hear simultaneous translations into English or German. The solution remains slightly awkward, but after a while it becomes only a minor distraction] [Trivia notes: 1) About Tracy's closing monologue: extras and onlookers poured onto the set that day just to hear the great actor perform. 2) Kramer helped Clift play his part more effectively by allowing him to treat the script, which had been giving him trouble anyway, loosely and speak extemporaneously. That, plus Kramer's tolerance for the actor's drinking on the set, and Clift's generally unkempt appearance, contributed to the intensity of his performance. 3) *Judgment at Nuremberg* proved the last major role for both Clift and for Garland, who hadn't done a movie since *A Star Is Born* (PF5) in 1954. Both plagued by ill health and addictive behavior, Clift died five years later at age 46, and Garland passed away at 47, four years after that. 4) The movie marked three consecutive titles – and years – in which Kramer cast top MGM *musical* stars in dramatic roles: Fred Astaire in *On the Beach* (PF5) in 1959, Gene Kelly in *Inherit the Wind* in 1960 and Judy Garland here. 5) The cast includes two future TV stars: William Shatner, aka Captain James T. Kirk of the Starship Enterprise in the original Star Trek; and Werner Klemperer, an expatriate German and U.S. Army veteran who played the incompetent Colonel Klink in the POW comedy series Hogan's Heroes] [Caution: adult themes] [B&W] [W]

Reversal of Fortune
1990 – Barbet Schroeder

A story narrated by a corpse? Well, yes, in this case by Sunny von Bülow (Glenn Close), whose husband Claus (Jeremy Irons, in an Oscar-winning turn) was accused and then convicted of attempting to murder her, with the vast court of public opinion considering him guilty. In desperation, he turned to one of America's most skilled and celebrated attorneys, Alan Dershowitz (Ron Silver, in his best role) – even though at first Dershowitz likewise suspected von Bülow's guilt. This is the story of the case's appeal, with Dershowitz marshaling a crack team of his Harvard law students to identify the holes in the prosecution's case. It's a fascinating, amusing look at both American upper-class society and the painstaking process required to fight a legal battle. The outcome? It's a matter of record, as are the eventual fates of both Sunny and Claus (pronounced KLOUSE). What remains unanswered to this day is why Sunny lapsed into a diabetic coma on December 27, 1979, and into a second one a year later. Even Sunny, the deceased narrator, doesn't explain why. [Trivia note: This was the second of three pairings of Irons and Close. They had played lovers onstage six years earlier in "The Real Thing," directed by Mike Nichols, and three years later they would be siblings in *The House of the Spirits*] [Caution: adult themes] **[W]**

13. The Electrician's Son

He played a bicycle racer in *American Flyers* and a witty, edgy gunslinger in *Silverado*, both in the same year. He later portrayed aging ballplayers in *Bull Durham* and *For Love of the Game*, and a pro football GM in *Draft Day*. He was crusading federal lawman Elliot Ness in *The Untouchables*. Of course, he did a superlative directorial/starring turn in *Dances with Wolves* (all seven in PF5). Changing pace, he played a criminal on the run in *A Perfect World*, an estranged but supportive father/psychologist in *Molly's Game* and a borderline demented dream-chaser in *Field of Dreams* (all in P25). Elsewhere, he also plays a relentless Texas Ranger on the trail of Bonnie Parker and Clyde Barrow in *The Highwaymen*. And as of this writing, Costner stars as John Dutton, patriarch of the Dutton ranching clan in the monumental TV series Yellowstone, about to run its fifth season. If there is a unifying characteristic in these disparate roles, other than his appealing good looks and his winning smile, it's probably his working-class background. Here are five more appearances by the son of a small-California-city tradesman who rose to become a bona fide American star, creating a career now in its fifth decade. In chronological order…

Fandango
1985 – as Gardner Barnes

Costner's breakthrough was supposed to be in *The Big Chill* (PF5) two years earlier, but writer–director Lawrence Kasdan removed his part as Alex, a suicide victim, compensating Costner with his aforementioned role of Jake in *Silverado*. But chronologically speaking, *Fandango* was his first star vehicle, a coming-of-age tale of four Texas college graduates about to begin their separate lives in the early 1970s, with one of them departing for the Army during the Vietnam War. Facing the great unknown, the young men decide to undertake one last adventure together; heading to a location along the Rio Grande River to unearth what they keep calling "Dom," something that eventually becomes self-evident. Along the way, they of course encounter several adventures, including attempting to jump-start their car by hitching it to a moving freight train, initiating one of the four (Judd Nelson) to the sport of skydiving, and reuniting another to his lost love (Suzy Amis). There's also a nifty chase scene involving a small plane and a police helicopter. Definitely dated and no doubt a bit juvenile in quite a few places, it also has its loopy, appealing, sentimental moments. Kevin Reynolds directed. [Caution: language and sexuality]

Tin Cup
1996 – as Roy McAvoy
Working with director Ron Shelton for the second time, Costner stars in this fanciful golf story. He's "Tin Cup" McAvoy, a formerly competitive pro golfer who's somehow lost his way and spends endless idle hours at his Texas driving range with best friend Romeo (Cheech Marin). The aimlessness suddenly changes, naturally, when 1) Molly Griswold (Rene Russo), a beautiful psychologist, arrives seeking a lesson; and 2) McAvoy discovers she is involved with David Simms (Don Johnson), a long-time rival. That rivalry sparks two competitions between the men, one professionally as McAvoy decides to re-qualify himself for the approaching U.S. Open tournament, and one (no surprise) romantically. From there, you can basically guess what happens – but you'd be partly wrong. [Trivia note: Almost all of the shots taken by McAvoy were done by Costner, who's an avid and skillful golfer – something evident in the beauty of his swing] [Caution: language] **[W]**

Rumor Has It...
2005 – as Beau Burroughs
Start with the premise that 1) *The Graduate* (PF5) was based on a true story, and 2) a young woman has grown up not knowing that her own mother and grandmother had been the story's inspiration. Add to it 3) that she likewise ends up falling under

the spell of the man who had … um, relations with the other two women, and start from there. Costner and Shirley MacLaine play the "Benjamin" and "Mrs. Robinson" roles, now three decades later. This most fanciful story also includes the convenient device that the "Elaine" character (Katherine Ross in the original), died when her daughter (Jennifer Aniston) was young. And when I use the term "start," I mean that from there the plot proceeds with so many more twists and turns it's likely to give you a case of whiplash. Through it all, however, Costner remains Costner: charming, appealing and, despite all the improbabilities, dignified. Rob Reiner directed. [Trivia note: The movie originally was conceived as a literal sequel to *The Graduate,* starring Dustin Hoffman and Anne Bancroft. But Bancroft died before production could begin] [Caution: language and sexuality] **[W]**

The Guardian
2006 – as Ben Randall
Here, Costner takes on arguably his most physically demanding role since *American Flyers,* portraying a former Coast Guard rescuer of those in peril on the sea, now an instructor of young cadets attempting to follow in his footsteps. Among the most talented of those new recruits is Jake Fischer (Ashton Kutcher, in a strong performance), a champion swimmer who shares an affliction with Ben: survivor's guilt. Randall lost his entire crew in a rescue-helicopter accident in heavy seas, while Fischer survived a highway crash that killed several of his high school teammates. Eventually, the two form a strong bond, leading to a climactic scene where only one of them can survive, and subsequently fulfillment of the legend represented by the title. Excellent training and rescue sequences, a rock-solid performance by Costner, and well-crafted moviemaking by Andrew Davis, best known for *The Fugitive* (PF5), 13 years earlier. All-in-all, a fine tribute to the amazingly courageous men and women of the U.S. Coast Guard, whose motto is, "So Others May Live." [Trivia note: Some of the shots of training or rescues at sea were taken from real sessions or incidents] [Caution: intense rescue sequences] **[W]**

Hidden Figures
2016 – as Al Harrison

Plenty of movies and documentaries – most notably *The Right Stuff* and *Apollo 13* (both in PF5) – have portrayed the early days of the NASA and the U.S. space program. This one, written and directed by Theodore Melfi, covers an important but little-known aspect of that period – though it does take certain liberties to hype the drama involved. Here, Costner plays one of his few supporting roles, a mission controller charged with safely bringing back astronaut John Glenn in February 1962 when instruments warned that his Friendship 7 spacecraft could have damaged or lost its heat shield. The real stars are Katherine Johnson, Mary Jackson and Dorothy Vaughn (Taraji P. Henson, Octavia Spencer and Janelle Monáe), three black mathematicians, all women, who must race against time – and the disdain of their white supervisors – to determine the proper … figures in the complex formula for the spacecraft's re-entry angle and placement. It's their remarkable story and their show, and rightly so. But Costner blends in well and plays his role persuasively. [Trivia notes: 1) Katherine Johnson's reputation became so solid at NASA that John Glenn insisted she personally review the calculations for his orbital flight before it launched. 2) Johnson died in 2020 at age 101] [Caution: adult themes] **[W]**

14. Father Figures

Nine strong male presences – including three real-life fathers – influencing the lives of the younger generation.

Blue Miracle

2021 – Raymond Cruz as Hector

Directed by Julio Quintana and based on a true story, Hector is a former street kid now running Casa Hogar, an orphanage in Cabo San Luca, Mexico, with his wife Becca (Chilean actress Fernanda Urrejola). Facing foreclosure of the property, Hector attempts to raise funds by entering the city's world-famous marlin-fishing tournament. It's a simple tale affectingly told, about a man whose strength of character can steer wayward youth away from lives among gangs and crime toward a wholesome adulthood. Produced for Netflix, the movie features co-starring turns by Dennis Quaid as a crusty fisherman who conveys Hector and the boys – one of whom attempts to wrestle a prize-winning fish with rod and reel – to the marlin grounds, and Bruce McGill as a competitor. [Caution: language] **[W]**

Boys Town

1938 – Spencer Tracy as Father Flanagan

Directed by Norman Taurog, another one based on a true story. Tracy, winning his second consecutive Oscar, plays the famous Catholic priest and founder of the eastern Nebraska home for wayward boys. As portrayed in the story, Flanagan actually began his charitable career caring for homeless men. But when he heard a condemned murderer describing how he grew up homeless and friendless, Flanagan resolved to create a unique institution to help indigent youth. He begins raising funds and recruiting candidates, including one seemingly incorrigible delinquent (Mickey Rooney in an electrifying early performance). Predictable and a bit overly dramatic by today's standards, it's nevertheless a compelling dramatization of the venerable institution's early days, produced by Hollywood's crown jewel, Metro-Goldwyn-Mayer, at the peak of its collective skills. [Trivia notes: 1) Rooney's behavior during filming presaged what happened between Steve McQueen and Yul Brynner when shooting *The Magnificent Seven* (PF5). Rooney, like McQueen, would continually try to attract attention to himself on camera via nervous habits such as pulling on his face – to the point where the antics so infuriated Tracy that he threatened to have Rooney fired unless he cut it out. 2) Among the boys is a character named Tony Ponessa. He's played by a young Gene Reynolds, who would grow up to become co-creator of the long-running and beloved M*A*S*H television series] **[B&W]**

Cheaper by the Dozen
1950 – Clifton Webb as Frank Bunker Gilbreth

Three in a row based on real characters, featuring the versatile Webb in one of his best performances as an efficiency expert, with Myrna Loy plays his psychologist wife Lillian, with whom he had a … dozen children. Directed by Walter Lang, it's an earnest if slightly stilted portrayal of the real-life Gilbreth family's story, based on the biography written by their son Frank Jr. and daughter Ernestine. (Jeanne Crain, who plays daughter Ann, narrates the movie). The elder Gilbreth indeed serves as a family patriarch, both by example and by insisting on (soft) discipline for and achievement by all of the children. Frank's parental approach proves invaluable to the brood when tragedy strikes suddenly, and all must share the burden and make what proves to be a fateful decision. It's a captivating if dated tale. Two years later, the sequel *Belles on Their Toes* (not on my lists) continued the Gilbreth saga, likewise based on a second book by the Gilbreth siblings and featuring most of the same cast. In 2003, an updated version of *Cheaper by the Dozen* (also not here) starred Steve Martin and Bonnie Hunt, but he was a football coach and the couple's name was Baker. [Trivia note: If the Gilbreth home's exterior seems familiar, you might have seen it before. It's the same house used in *Meet Me in St. Louis* (PF5) six years earlier] **[W]**

Conrack
1974 – Jon Voight as Pat Conroy
In the late 1960s, Donald Patrick Conroy, a novice teacher, took a job at a one-room schoolhouse on Daufuskie Island in South Carolina, whose small student body spoke an isolated dialect called Gullah. The closest the children could come to pronouncing his name was "Conrack;" hence, Voight's character. Based on Conroy's 1972 novel The Water Is Wide and directed by Martin Ritt, the story concerns his interactions with the students on fictional Yamacraw Island and his conflict with the school district's superintendent, Mr. Skeffington (Hume Cronyn). It seems that Skeffington, and a good portion of the local community, do not want Conroy to introduce the children to the possibilities of the outside world. They seem satisfied to push the kids quickly through school and confine them to life on the island. But Conroy aspires more for them. He plays Beethoven's 5th Symphony on a gramophone. He shows them *The Black Swan* (not here), a pirate movie starring Tyrone Power and Maureen O'Hara. He even helps them go trick-or-treating on the mainland. Eventually, opposition to his methods ends his tenure, and he must leave the island. Filmed using some of Conroy's real students, it's a poignant portrayal of one man's attempt to do something seen less and less frequently in our public schools today: inspire. [Trivia note: Conroy's efforts did seem to affect at least some his charges – three of them went on to become teachers themselves] **[W]**

Cry Macho!
2021 – Clint Eastwood as Mike Milo
Clint does it again, at age 90, directing and starring as a (temporary) father figure to a young Mexican–American boy trapped in Mexico in 1980. Milo is a retired Texas rodeo rider whose former employer (Dwight Yoakam) entreats him to travel to Mexico City to find and retrieve Rafo (newcomer Eduardo Minett), his teenage son currently in the custody of his mother

(Fernanda Urrejola, who also appears in *Blue Miracle*). Mike indeed finds Rafo and heads back to Texas with him, therein beginning a life-changing odyssey for both man and boy. It's a poignant tale, full of surprises – and even romance – with strong performances by Clint and the young Minett. The title? It's about a rooster – you'll see. [Trivia note: The odyssey of this story is almost as fascinating as the movie itself. It began as a 1975 novel by Richard N. Nash (who died before *Cry Macho* was released), and over the years attracted interest of ... *macho* stars such as Robert Mitchum and Arnold Schwarzenegger before Clint was finally cast] [Caution: adult themes] **[W]**

The Freshman
1990 – Marlon Brando as Carmine Sabatini
The most lighthearted of the bunch, and not without its charms, Matthew Broderick co-stars with Brando in this comedic takeoff of *The Godfather*. Broderick is Clark Kellogg, a Vermonter come to Manhattan to attend college but who is quickly scammed by Victor Ray (Bruno Kirby), nephew of Carmine, a prominent resident of the city's Little Italy whom Victor claims served as the basis for Vito Corleone (played, of course, by Brando). Victor introduces Clark to Carmine, and little by little the elder man draws the youngster into an increasingly complex and mysterious series of tasks, including transporting a Komodo dragon to an associate of Carmine's who specializes in preparing exotic dishes (the great Maximillian Schell, in a wry performance). Clark also becomes romantically involved with Carmine's daughter, Tina (Penelope Ann Miller), while apparently participating in criminal trafficking in endangered species – or is he? Written and directed by Andrew Bergman, it's harmless fun finding out, and the movie indeed provides elements of *The Godfather*, as well as *The Godfather Part II* and even a bit of *The Sting* (all in PF5) thrown in. [Trivia notes: 1) Because Komodo dragons are dangerous and potentially lethal creatures, the moviemakers used less-aggressive monitor lizards as stand-ins – and a tame one for the scenes in close contact with the actors. 2) Speaking of *The Godfather*, the other cast member to appear here is Gianni Russo, who played the Don's ill-

fated son-in-law Carlo. Russo was the only individual in either movie with real Mafia connections. 3) Brando was 66 when filming *The Freshman*, Vito Corleone's age at death – not 48, as Brando was when he played him. 4) Broderick and Miller had played a romantic couple many times, beginning in 1985 in Neil Simon's "Biloxi Blues" on Broadway, and three years later in the film version (P25)] [Caution: sexuality] **[W]**

The Great Santini
1979 – Robert Duvall as Lieutenant Colonel Wilbur "Bull" Meechum

A few years after Pat Conroy wrote about his experiences teaching children on that South Carolina island, he stepped back in time a bit and moved onshore to probe his relationship with his own father. Written and directed by Lewis John Carlino, and based on Conroy's novel of the same name, the movie wrenchingly depicts that relationship and elicits so many of the strains and tensions that can emerge between father and son – though usually not to this extreme. Robert Duvall's Bull Meechum, the self-described "Great Santini" of the title, a disciplinarian Marine pilot living with his family in Beaufort, South Carolina, in the early 1960s. This time, Michael O'Keefe stands in for Conroy as the fictional Ben Meechum, a high school basketball star who nevertheless remains under the critical gaze and physical domination of his high-achieving parent bordering on the sadistic. Though Duvall and O'Keefe are excellent in difficult roles (both were nominated for Oscars) – as is Blythe Danner as Bull's wife and Ben's mother – I've got a quibble with the movie's convenient (fictional) resolution. Namely, it relieves father and son of painfully, painstakingly hammering out a reconciliation as adult males. Speaking from personal experience, the process can be extremely rewarding if successful. And Conroy has admitted as much when describing how his relationship with his father eventually evolved. [Trivia note: Another movie location you might recognize (see *Cheaper by the Dozen*, above), the Meechum home in Beaufort appeared four years later as the vacation residence of

Harold and Sarah Cooper in *The Big Chill* (<u>PF5</u>)] [<u>Caution</u>: adult themes]

King Richard
2021 – Will Smith as Richard Williams

A notorious incident at the 2022 Academy Awards – which I'll cover shortly – rendered problematic Smith's superb, Oscar-winning performance in a fine movie based on a true story. Williams is a small-businessman running a private security company in Compton, California, while attempting to teach tennis to his two daughters, Venus and Serena (Saniyya Sidney and Demi Singleton in solid debuts as the nascent superstars). Richard and his wife Brandy Price (Aunjaneu Ellis, in an equally solid performance) run an admirably tight family ship. They impose behavioral and achievement expectations on their collective five children with firm but loving hands, and they make personal sacrifices to help them rise out of their working-class background. Some of those sacrifices involve refusing early sponsorship and endorsement offers for the girls, offers which would have quickly eased their financial strains. But the Williams family's collective wisdom prevailed and, as history has shown, Venus and Serena became two of the finest players in history – with Serena rising to the very top. It's a fascinating odyssey to watch unfold, skillfully directed by newcomer Reinaldo Marcus Green. Central to the whole story, regardless of the sensational outcome, is Richard's fierce, exemplary devotion to his daughters. It's truly inspiring. [<u>Cultural note</u>: The outcome of that incident involving Smith, in which he physically struck comedian and host Chris Rock at the Oscar ceremony, seems to have been resolved at this writing. Shortly after the encounter, Smith resigned from the motion picture academy. Then the academy banned him from attending the ceremony for 10 years. It's unknown whether further action against him by Rock will take place. Regardless, it reflects badly on the actor. I try hard to separate the art from the artist, but it seems to grow more difficult by the year. Too bad so many celebrities can't behave themselves] [<u>Trivia notes</u>: 1) Saniyya Sidney's fine performance as Venus Williams was made even more impressive because a) before making the movie the young actress had never played tennis before, and b) she's actually a southpaw and had to spend weeks and weeks practicing and training to play righthanded. 2) As of this writing, Serena and Venus Williams, playing one last time in the U.S. Open at Forest Hills, New York, in 2022 at ages 41 and 42. Lost their doubles match in straight sets] [Caution: language and violence] **[W]**

A River Runs Through It
1992 – Tom Skerritt as Reverend John Maclean

Robert Redford directed this beguiling tale of two sons, Norman and Paul Maclean (Craig Sheffer and Brad Pitt in his debut), one of them who develops into a respectable writer and honest citizen, and the other whose destiny is ill-fated, both under the tutelage and loving guidance of their Presbyterian minister father. Skerritt, in his gentlest and most appealing role, offers his boys a solid role model to follow, and though he sometimes expresses displeasure at their actions, he prefers setting behavioral examples rather than making demands or using intimidation. And among the life skills John imparts to the boys is a passion for fly fishing, frequently undertaken in the Blackfoot River near their home in Missoula, Montana in the 1920s. The activity, sublimely portrayed and photographed, eventually inspires Norman to write the autobiographical novel that became the basis for the movie, which Redford narrates. Mark Isham composed the melancholy bucolic score. [Caution: adult themes] **[W]**

15. Grade B Bond

For those of my age and generation, British Secret Service Agent 007, who has been portrayed 27 times to date on the screen, will always be personified by that lanky, sexy Scotsman with a distinctive brogue lisp named Sean Connery. He introduced the character in *Dr. No* (PF5) 60 years ago, and to my mind the six other actors* who attempted the role never matched his perfect combination of winning charm, sex appeal and potentially lethal menace. Still, once in a while the others approached Connery's prowess, particularly Daniel Craig in *Casino Royale* (also in PF5), who landed a terrific performance. Here are four also-rans (and I've included another one in the Epilogue) in chronological order…

Live and Let Die
1973 – Roger Moore as 007

Except for George Lazenby's brief appearance in the series, Moore inherited the role of 007 after Connery's disastrous previous effort in *Diamonds Are Forever* (not here) in this lively and witty romp that features voodoo, black organized crime, a spectacular chase (on the ground) involving aircraft, an even more spectacular boat chase through the Louisiana Bayou and a clever hairbreadth escape from hungry 'gators (done for real by stuntman Ross Kananga). Among the movie's other distinctions are Jane Seymour's debut and a catchy theme song by Paul McCartney and his post-Beatles group, Wings. Guy Hamilton, who had helmed *Goldfinger* (PF5), directed. [Trivia note: Though *Live and Let Die* was the eighth movie of the official Bond series, it was the second novel author Ian Fleming completed after Casino Royale, his first] [Caution: violence and sexuality] **[W]**

A View to a Kill
1985 – Roger Moore as 007

Moore's seventh and last outing as Bond (tying him with Connery for the most times in the role and making him, at 57, the oldest playing Bond) pits him against Christopher Walken as Zorin, a crazed and murderous tycoon, with a climax high above San Francisco's Golden Gate Bridge. Tanya Roberts steps in as Bond's momentary love interest, and the tall, lanky Grace Jones does a witty turn as Zorin's bedmate and partner in crime. There's also a neat appearance by Patrick Macnee, late of The Avengers TV series, and the throbbing theme song is by the group Duran Duran. [Trivia note: Moore might have been aging at the time, but he wasn't without certain skills from his earlier years. He ended up driving the firetruck through the city's streets when a suitable stuntman couldn't be found for the scene] [Caution: violence and sexuality] [W]

The Living Daylights
1987 – Timothy Dalton as 007

Dalton's brief turn as Bond presented a return to a more youthful character, though he never seemed to devote much energy or his full attention to the role – he even looked halfhearted when firing his gun at the camera in the traditional opening bit. That said, the movie excels at two stunt sequences, one involving a drive down the hairpin turns on the slopes of Gibraltar (directed by master driver Remy Julienne), and the other a fight on a thick net trailing from a large cargo aircraft. The delicately beautiful Maryam d'Abo plays Bond's eventual love interest, while Art Malik and John Rhys-Davies drop in as unexpected allies, and Joe Don Baker and Jeroen Krabbé supply the necessary villainy – the whole lot of them either lackluster or downright silly. [Trivia note: Dalton's stint as Bond, short as it was, took a long time to materialize. He previously had been approached to play the role five times, beginning in 1969 with *On Her Majesty's Secret Service* (not here). He might have been shut out entirely had Pierce Brosnan, next in the series of actors, been available instead of committing to continue his TV series Remington Steele] [<u>Caution</u>: violence and sexuality] **[W]**

Licence to Kill
1989 – Timothy Dalton as 007

Dalton's second Bond movie, and the better or the two, pits him against a Central American drug lord (character actor and singer Robert Davi) and requires him to give up his "00" status to avenge the murder of the wife (Priscilla Barnes) of his friend and colleague, CIA operative Felix Leiter (David Hedison), himself badly mauled by a shark. Once again, the stunts are superb, including a mid-air capture by a helicopter of a light plane and heavy-truck chase along a cliffside road. The plot involves maybe a bit too many double-crosses and implausible escapes, but it moves along at a good clip. Carey Lowell and Talisa Soto play the Bond girls, and Gladys Knight belts out the theme song. [<u>Trivia note</u>: *Licence to Kill* represents a reunion of sorts. The previous year, Davi and fellow cast member Grand Lee Bush played a pair of FBI agents, both named Johnson, in *Die Hard* (<u>PF5</u>) while composer Michael Kamen did that movie's score as well] [<u>Caution</u>: violence and sexuality] **[W]**

<u>**A Bond series viewing note:**</u> Of the franchise movies featuring Agent 007, almost all begin with a now-standard formula: a clever, often over-the-top action showpiece followed by the theme song and an equally clever title sequence. I've mentioned five here as well as five in my chapter on Sean Connery in <u>PF5</u> – the latter bunch my true favorites. As for the remaining (at this writing) 15, here's a suggestion how best to sample them: Watch the opening and theme song/credit sequence to gain the flavor of that particular episode. From there, you usually can decide quickly whether to continue or resume browsing. Don't have access to Netflix or Amazon Prime or other streaming services? No problem. You can find all of the Bond movie openings on YouTube. Best one? My choice would be *The Spy Who Loved Me*, featuring a death-defying ski jump over a precipice followed by one of the best theme songs, "Nobody Does It Better," sung by

Carly Simon. [<u>Bond trivia note</u>: Speaking of those opening title/theme song sequences, beginning with *Thunderball*, the fifth in the series, and running all the way through *Casino Royale* (both in <u>PF5</u>), every title sequence featured a bevy of shapely and unclothed females, usually cleverly photographed to obscure their bodies. My guess is the producers stopped the practice because the video releases of the movies made the nudity much more obvious]

---

*The seven actors who have played James Bond, along with Connery, include David Niven in the dreadful 1967 comedy version of *Casino Royale* (not here), George Lazenby in 1969's *On Her Majesty's Secret Service* (also not here), Roger Moore in seven of the movies (five not here), Timothy Dalton in the two above, Pierce Brosnan in four (none here) and Craig as mentioned in the 2006 *Casino Royale*, *No Time to Die* above, and three others not on my lists.

16. Hearts of Darkness

At the beginning of "The Shadow," a popular radio program airing in the 1930s, the narrator (actor Frank Readick Jr.) would voice the ominous question, "Who knows what evil lurks in the hearts of men?" Indeed, ever since Cain murdered Abel and then denied it (consult the Old Testament), humans have been wrestling with evil instincts, often hiding behind an emotional façade or an insistent rationalization, but sometimes erupting unrestrained. With apologies to novelist Joseph Conrad, these 26 titles depict individuals who must deal with some of the darkest places of the human psyche – involving others or themselves.

The 39 Steps
1935 – England – Alfred Hitchcock

Who better to kick off this category than the director known as the Master of Suspense. Here, he presents a groundbreaking story about one man's efforts to stop a network of spies stealing secrets in the years leading up to World War II. Also somewhat groundbreaking, the movie begins with an unsuspecting but gullible male charmed by a beautiful and mysterious woman. The real distinction of this spy thriller, however, is its resemblance to the most popular of Hitchcock's 46 films in the sound era, *North by Northwest* (PF5), made over two decades later. The similarities are striking. There's an early stabbing of a preliminary character. There's the aforementioned gullible male (Robert Donat, in his best role), wrongly accused of murder and pursued across the landscape by the police. There's a sequence aboard a train where our man makes his getaway – including meeting up with another beautiful woman (Madeleine Carroll at her most appealing), plus a shot from the exterior of the train as it rolls along a lakeshore. There's a desperate foot chase across a perilous landscape. There's a dashing but duplicitous adversary looking to sneak out of the country. There's our hero trying to hide in plain sight. There's the indispensable but improbable device of salvation (no, it isn't a starter's pistol). And, of course, there's the trademark "MacGuffin," which Hitchcock used so often, here for the first time. Not to mention the director's signature cameo appearance, likewise approximately repeated in *NxNW*. Sound familiar? Crudely made by today's technical standards, and a little rocky for a while, it eventually hits its stride and proves enduringly witty and entertaining. Watch for a young Peggy Ashcroft in a small role as a rural Scotsman's comely but frustrated wife. **[B&W]**

Changeling
2008 – Clint Eastwood
This creepy tale, based on a true story, is bound to disturb any parent of a young child – as well as anyone who has run afoul of the law unjustly. Angelina Jolie stars as Christine Collins, a 1920s Los Angeles single mother whose son was kidnapped but whom the LAPD finds and returns to her several months later. She quickly realizes, however, that the boy is not her offspring. That's bad enough. What's worse is that her claim generates negative reactions from the newspapers and law enforcement to the point where authorities take her "son" from her, and she is institutionalized as delusional. Only through the dogged investigation of Detective Lester Ybarra (Michael Kelly), who believes her, and a publicity campaign by an evangelical radio host, Reverend Gustav Briegleb (John Malkovich), does the real story begin to materialize. What they discover represents, indeed, the one of dark aspects of the human condition. But that isn't all, either. It turned out both the LAPD's leadership and the city's public health department were severely corrupt, and the Collins case helped to expose that corruption. As for Collins and her son … well, as mentioned, this is based on a true story, a story that didn't end happily. Another solid piece of moviemaking by Eastwood. [Trivia note: The movie's title is literal. It's taken from European folklore, in which demons or evil spirits would steal an

infant or young child and then replace it with a "changeling," a sick or evil being. Apparently, the legend grew as an explanation for children who died young or who exhibited the condition we now call autism] [Caution: violence, adult themes and nonsexual nudity] **[W]**

The Conformist
1970 – Italy – written and directed by Bernardo Bertolucci
Bertolucci's first international hit is a taut, anti-fascist political thriller starring Jean-Louis Trintignant as Marcello Clerici, a willing government operative caught up in a time of extreme political corruption and betrayal. He's willing because he will do anything to maintain his position, even assassinate one of his former college professors deemed by authorities to be dangerous to the regime. That's essentially the plot. But Bertolucci and his editor, Franco Arcalli, rearranged and mixed up the timeline so much that the story begins to resemble Kurt Vonnegut's *Slaughterhouse Five* (P25), in which the protagonist Billy Pilgrim experiences his life totally out of order. Few moviemakers had ever attempted such a blatant temporal unhinging before, so it was a risky device. But audiences and critics alike raved about the technique, coupled with Vittorio Storaro's dark but striking cinematography. It's a brooding masterpiece. [Trivia note: One of Clerici's superiors is played by Gastone Moschin. Four years later, he portrayed local mob boss Don Fanucci, who was assassinated by the young Vito Corleone in *The Godfather Part II* (PF5)] [Caution: violence and sexuality] **[B&W] [W]**

The Contender
2000 – written and directed by Rod Lurie
This one's a marginal choice, primarily because it's blatantly biased politically, though it retains entertainment value, and the two co-stars do a nice job. Jeff Bridges is Jackson Evans, a second-term U.S. president approaching the end of his time in office and contemplating who might succeed him in the White House. That privilege would usually go to the vice president, but the man has just died. So, Evans lines up two ... contenders to be nominated

and approved by both houses of Congress. One, Arkansas governor Jack Hathaway (William Petersen), a moderate who has been proclaimed a national hero after he risked his own life unsuccessfully attempting to rescue a young woman trapped in a car that drove off a bridge. (Yes, I know; it's a mashing of parallels to Bill Clinton, former governor of Arkansas, and to Teddy Kennedy at Chappaquiddick) The other, Laine Hanson (Joan Allen), is an Ohio senator known for her unapologetically liberal views. Standing between them is Sheldon Runyon (Gary Oldman), a powerful and scheming Republican congressman from Illinois who favors Hathaway and has uncovered potentially damaging background information about Hanson. So, the games begin, and what follows exposes the dark underbelly of Hathaway's candidacy and an explanation for Hanson's behavior. Too neat? Maybe. For sure, the way Oldman's character is portrayed, he might as well have sported a twirlable mustache. But Bridges is congenial and appealing as president – though he seems to spend a bit too much time ordering up unusual items for his meals – and Allen does fine work in her first starring role. [Caution: language, adult themes and sexuality] **[W]**

The Courier
2021 – Dominic Cooke

Among dark hearts, you can't get much darker than the old Soviet Union, particularly in the days of Stalin and then Khrushchev, in which everything emanating from the state was a lie, and the entire Russian population was under surveillance and kept in constant fear. That's when this increasingly gripping, and ultimately tragic true-life story takes place. The year is 1960, and Benedict Cumberbatch stars as Greville Wynne, an English businessman who's persuaded by operatives of MI6, the British intelligence service, and the CIA to contact a high-ranking Soviet official willing to help the West avoid a nuclear confrontation. Wynne accepts, meets and eventually befriends the official (Merad Ninidze, who played the Jewish émigré husband in Caroline Glick's haunting *Nowhere in Africa* nearly 20 years earlier – see P25). The movie begins deceptively, with the intrigued

Wynne traveling to and from Moscow, ostensibly to promote trade but enjoying himself in the process. Then, as tensions increase between the U.S.S.R. and the West – the story updates to 1962 and the Cuban missile crisis – so do the stakes and the dangers for Wynne and his contact. Where things lead is likely to leave you shocked and sickened. It's a stark lesson in both the evil lurking within all authoritarian governments, and in the lack of resolve and cowardice often displayed by those professing to protect our lives and our freedoms. Never forget either one. [Viewing note: Don't confuse this title with two inferior but similarly named thrillers released around the same time, one starring Olga Kurylenko and Gary Oldman, and the other with Jason Statham and, of all people, Joan Allen] **[W]**

Dangerous Liaisons
1988 – Stephen Frears

John Malkovich, Glenn Close and Michele Pfeiffer co-star in Frears's absorbing tale about sexual and political intrigue in 18th-century France. Based on Christopher Hampton's play, in turn based on the epistolary novel by Pierre Choderlos de Laclos, the story depicts how clever, scheming individuals can exploit a tightly structured society's strict social rules for their own purposes. In a vicious act of romantic revenge, the Marquise de Merteuil (Close), who has been dumped by a lover for a younger, virginal love object (Uma Thurman), plots to deflower the young woman – thereby rendering her undesirable – via Merteuil's sometime lover, the Vicomte de Valmont (Malkovich). Unfortunate, but Valmont is uncooperative. He's on the amorous trail of Madame de Tourvel (Pfeiffer), the wife of a political rival. Therein begins a trail of deception and betrayal that will require your full attention just to keep track. An elegantly mounted and costumed production – you can almost smell all the perfume – and beautifully photographed by Philippe Rousselot, it's a pretty picture of a pair of amusing but ugly souls. [Trivia notes: 1) Hampton's play inspired two screen versions at the time. The other, *Valmont* (not here), directed by Miloš Forman and released the following year, starred Colin Firth in the title role with

141

Annette Bening as Merteuil and Meg Tilly as de Tourvel. It bombed at the box office. 2) Also regarding Hampton's stage version, the production exemplifies how casting decisions, including rejections, can often determine the course of an actor's career. Alan Rickman, not Malkovich or Firth, had played Valmont on the stage. Unknown to screen audiences, he was passed over for the part in favor of Malkovich – so he was free to accept his sensational breakthrough role as chief villain Hans Gruber in *Die Hard* (PF5)] [Caution: sexuality and violence] **[W]**

Experiment in Terror
1962 – Blake Edwards
What sort of person would kidnap an innocent teenager and then use her to blackmail her older sister into committing theft? Given the annals of crime, there's no shortage of such characters, and this tense drama presents one of them. Lee Remick stars as Kelly Sherwood, a San Francisco bank teller whose younger sister (Stephanie Powers) is taken by sadistic killer "Red" Lynch (Ross Martin). He tells Kelly he will torture and murder her sister unless she extracts a hundred thousand dollars from her bank, and he warns her to say nothing to the police. Terrified but courageous, she nevertheless confides in local FBI agent John Ripley (Glenn Ford), who tries to track down Kelly's tormentor. It's gripping, among Edwards's best work, and supported by a rare dramatic score by Henry Mancini and a likewise rare villainous turn by the otherwise affable Martin. [Trivia note: You might not be familiar with Martin's best-known role. He played Artemus Gordon, a U.S. Secret Service agent who's a master of disguise and a fellow crime-fighter with James West (Robert Conrad) in the popular 1960s television series The Wild, Wild West] [Caution: violence and intense suspense] **[W]**

Gaslight
1944 – George Cukor
If you've ever heard the term "gaslighting," meaning severe emotional manipulation, it originated here. The great Ingrid Bergman stars as Paula Anton, fragile wife of Gregory Anton

(Charles Boyer), an obsessive, controlling personality who might have been responsible for Paula's aunt's death – and might not even be who he claims to be. Slowly and methodically, Gregory persuades Paula that she is experiencing hallucinations, that she suffers from kleptomania and, perhaps, she needs to be institutionalized. He does so by creating situations within their house that Paula perceives to be real but are denied by Gregory. He's assisted by their young and complicit maid Nancy (18-year-old Angela Lansbury in her film debut). Adapted from Patrick Hamilton's play, it's an engrossing drama, with Boyer playing heavily against his traditional benign roles and employing the simple premise once expressed by Groucho Marx: "Who are you going to believe – me or your own eyes?" [Trivia notes: 1) A year older than England's Queen Elizabeth II (who granted her the feminine equivalent of knighthood), Dame Lansbury's incredible career has included notable roles on stage and television as well as movies. On screen, she appeared in such classics as *National Velvet* (PF5), *The Manchurian Candidate* and *The Court Jester* (both in P25), and *Samson and Delilah, The World of Henry Orient* and the Disney feature *Mary Poppins Returns* (all elsewhere). She's most famous, however, as writer–sleuth Jessica Fletcher in her long-running, popular TV series Murder, She Wrote. 2) Lansbury's lengthy career – which continues at this writing and is approaching 80 years – is made even more remarkable by the fact that before she auditioned for the role of Nancy in *Gaslight*, she had never studied acting] **[B&W]**

The Informer
1935 – John Ford

Ford won the first of his still-unmatched four Best Director Oscars for this gritty tale of a desperate man's descent into guilt and despair in Dublin, Ireland, in the early 1920s. The inimitable Victor McLaglen is Gypo Nolan, a former Irish Republican Army member who … informs on his best friend Frankie McPhillip (Wallace Ford) to collect a reward. He wants the money so he and his ladyfriend Katie Madden (Margot Grahame) can sail to America to escape the country's civil war and begin a new life.

After Nolan fingers McPhillip, however, he is killed in a gunfight with the local British constabulary, known as the Black and Tans. From there, Nolan's soul is in constant torment. He's bereft about McPhillip's death, suspected by his other former comrades as well as Katie and unsure where to turn. It's a stark drama, leading to a tragic but redemptive conclusion. [Trivia note: Long before Ford's well-known belittling and verbal abuse of John Wayne during filming, the legendary director applied the same tactics, and worse, to McLaglen. Much of his Oscar-winning portrayal of Nolan resulted from Ford's constant prodding and deceiving him. For instance, Ford, knowing McLaglen's fondness for the bottle, would often force him to film his scenes when suffering from severe hangovers] [B&W]

The Mission
1986 – England – Roland Joffé

Stepping back in time a bit, to the mid-18th century and the northern rain forests of Argentina near Iguazú Falls on the country's border with Brazil and Paraguay, we witness two other aspects of the dark side of humanity: colonialism and the slave trade. Loosely based on a true historical incident, the story involves Father Gabriel (Jeremy Irons in an excellent and appealing role), a Jesuit priest attempting to bring Christianity to the Guarani, an indigenous tribe whose members at first violently resist him. Eventually, Gabriel's gentle manner wins favor with the tribal leaders, but those efforts also place him in the middle of a political conflict involving his home country of Spain as well as Portugal and the Roman church hierarchy. More directly, Gabriel faces opposition from Rodrigo Mendoza (Robert De Niro, playing way against type), a slave-trader whose interest in the Guarani is purely financial. Yet Gabriel's deep faith eventually forces Mendoza to repent and seek forgiveness. Now allied, the two men must face Cardinal Altamirano (Irish actor Ray MacAnally), sent by the Vatican to determine whether the Guarani may remain protected and free, or placed under the jurisdiction of the Portuguese, who ruthlessly ply the slave trade. Given the economic and political pressures involved, you can guess the outcome of this tragic tale. Written by Robert Bolt and winner of the *Palme d'Or* at Cannes and nominated for seven Oscars, it's a handsomely mounted production, with a cast that includes future stars Liam Neeson and Aiden Quinn, and with Argentinian and Colombian indigenous people playing the Guarani. [Caution: violence and nonsexual nudity] **[W]**

Mystic River
2003 – Clint Eastwood

Call this the dark side of *Stand By Me*, in which four boys experience a traumatic event but grow up into fairly normal adulthood. Here, it's a trio of Boston boys, one of whom suffers a kidnapping and sexual abuse and never entirely recovers. Based on Dennis Lahane's novel, with a solid script by Brian Helgeland, the movie stars Sean Penn and Tim Robbins in Oscar-winning roles (respectively, Best Actor and Best Supporting Actor), along with Kevin Bacon as the adult versions of the boys. Robbins is Dave, the former abuse victim, while Penn is Jimmy, a liquor-store owner and Bacon is Sean, a police detective. They've grown apart over the years, with Jimmy and Sean also enduring personal demons of their own. Their destinies converge once more when Jimmy's daughter Katie (Emmy Rossum) is found murdered. Sean begins investigating the case, which leads him eventually to the killer. But Jimmy, whose rage already has been unleashed by the loss of Katie, goes over the top when Dave's wife Celeste (Marcia Gay Harden) confesses that Dave could be Katie's murderer. Unhinged and unaware of Sean's discovery, Jimmy exacts his vengeance. It's a raw and brutal tale of the deepest and darkest emotions that can lurk within us. Clint as usual directs sharply, using the Boston locations skillfully – including the ... Mystic River. Laura Linney appears, in a rather weird role, as Jimmy's long-suffering wife, and watch for Eli Wallach in a brief and uncredited cameo. [Trivia note: You might recall that Wallach appeared 37 years earlier with Eastwood as one of the three title characters in *The Good, The Bad and The Ugly* (not here)] [Caution: violence, sexuality and plentiful rough language] **[W]**

145

No Way to Treat a Lady
1968 – Jack Smight
Another marginal entrée, but it's worth a look because of the trio of stars: George Segal and Lee Remick playing, respectively, a police detective investigating a series of murders and a key witness to one of the crimes; plus Rod Steiger as the prime suspect, a theater director and actor who can change his speech and appearance at will. Based on an early novel by the great William Goldman, there isn't much mystery because we learn, early on, who the killer is. But it's fun to watch these actors work, and Remick was at the peak of her allure. [Trivia note: Steiger was originally set to play the detective, but when he read the script he decided it would be more fun, and more of a challenge, to play the chameleon-like murderer. Also, he had won an Oscar for *In the Heat of the Night* (PF5) the previous year as a southern small-town sheriff] [Caution: sexuality and violence] [W]

Notorious
1946 – Alfred Hitchcock
If you've read the capsule above on *The 39 Steps*, you should know what a MacGuffin is, and this movie contains maybe the most dangerous MacGuffin of all, disguised in an otherwise innocuous bottle of wine. It's Ingrid Bergman again, this time working with Hitchcock in a mystery–romance co-starring Cary Grant and set in Rio de Janeiro, with Claude Rains as a villainous ex-Nazi. Also again, she's caught in the middle of a conspiratorial whirlwind. Bergman plays Alicia Huberman, the American-born daughter of a Nazi spy. At the end of World War II and pleading her loyalty to the United States, she agrees to help the government break a vestigial spy ring in Rio de Janeiro. She's placed under the supervision of Special Agent T. R. Devlin (Grant), who quickly and predictably falls in love with her. Of course, complications ensue, particularly when Huberman is ordered to marry Alex Sebastian (Rains), leader of the ring. And those complications create potentially lethal consequences for all three corners of the love triangle. It's nail-bitingly tense at times, with a knockout climax. But should we worry about Grant and Bergman? Well,

maybe a little, given the stakes and players involved. [Trivia notes: 1) Speaking of Grant and Bergman, that kissing-and-talking scene between them was a contractual necessity and a technical challenge. They needed to express their characters' passion for each other, but the Hays Code, strictly enforced at the time, forbade any kiss lasting more than three seconds. Hence, kiss, release, talk; kiss, release, talk, and so on. The challenge resulted from the fact that they needed to repeat their moves and lines several times, exactly, to accommodate the different camera angles edited into the scene. 2) And speaking of Rains, you might remember him as Louis Renault, the corrupt chief of police in *Casablanca* (PF5) – co-starring with Bergman] [Caution: adult themes] **[B&W]**

One Flew Over the Cuckoo's Nest
1975 – Miloš Forman

Winner of the Best Picture and three other top Oscars, the story involves Randle P. McMurphy (Jack Nicholson), a misguided individual sentenced to an Oregon prison farm in the early 1960s. Averse to hard labor, he decides he could cruise through his sentence by having his incarceration transferred to a mental institution. He succeeds but quickly discovers the facility presents challenges of its own, particularly in the form of Mildred Ratched (Louise Fletcher), the stone-cold head nurse. She imposes quietly tyrannical, sometimes sadistic rule over the other inmates, played by a host of skilled character actors including Danny DeVito and Christopher Lloyd, Will Sampson as an evidently mute but towering Native American, and a number of real patients. The battle of wills – and occasionally fists – begins soon after McMurphy's arrival, leading to an inevitable climactic confrontation. Based on Ken Kesey's counterculture best-seller, this wrenching story is elevated by the Oscar-winning performances of both Nicholson and Fletcher, and by the supporting cast, most of whom remained in character long after the cameras stopped rolling. [Trivia notes: 1) Forman and Nicholson both ended up with Oscars, but they never saw eye-to-eye during the production, to the point where they barely spoke directly to each other and never agreed about how certain scenes should be staged. 2) A decade before the movie, Kesey's novel was produced on Broadway and starred Kirk Douglas as McMurphy with Joan Tetzel as Ratched. Douglas had wanted to reprise his role on film, but by the mid-1970s he was deemed too old. 3) Lily Tomlin was originally cast to play Nurse Ratched, while Fletcher was planning to appear in Robert Altman's *Nashville* (PF5). Eventually, the two actresses switched roles, and while Fletcher won Best Actress that year, Tomlin was only nominated for Best Supporting] [Caution: sexuality, violence and shocking medical procedures] **[W]**

The Pawnbroker
1964 – Sidney Lumet
Rod Steiger again, here in a powerful, Oscar-nominated earlier role in a landmark film. Steiger plays Sol Nazerman, a tortured, emotionally numbed Holocaust survivor trying to live a quiet life in 1960s Harlem, in New York City, while still dealing with the memories of what the Nazis did to his wife and children two decades earlier. Skillfully directed by Lumet, with Steiger portraying a man who will not show feelings but whose inner life boils like a cauldron, the film presents the aftermath of one of the world's most horrible episodes. You're not likely ever to forget it. [Trivia note: *The Pawnbroker* marked the debut of composer Quincy Jones as well as a great American actor, Morgan Freeman, who appears as an extra in one of the last scenes] [Caution: adult themes and sexuality – the first American film to feature frontal nudity above the waist] **[B&W]**

Primary Colors
1998 – Mike Nichols
Whatever your position on Bill Clinton's presidency, two undeniable facts remain: 1) He stood up, wagged his finger and lied to all of us about his Oval Office affair with a young intern, and 2) he attempted to persuade aides and other members of his administration to make excuses for his reprehensible behavior. What kind of man looks you in the eye and (forgive the mixed

148

metaphors) lies through his teeth? In this profile of presidential candidate Jack Stanton (John Travolta), based on the eponymous novel, itself a thinly veiled chronicle of the Clintons by political reporter Joe Klein, you get a glimpse of what drives him – or, at least, how he can be devilishly seductive to everyone around him. Travolta's character conjures something reporter Aaron Altman (Albert Brooks) uttered in *Broadcast News* (PF5), the fine feature about a TV network newsroom. Describing Tom Grunick (William Hurt), an attractive but shallow news anchor, Altman calls him "The Devil" who (I'm paraphrasing) never does anything wrong; he just lowers our standards a little at a time. How does that apply here? When caught in an inescapable scandal, Stanton and his team don't contemplate for an instant that they should come clean, ask forgiveness and atone for their bad behavior – let alone resign in disgrace. Instead, they figuratively circle the wagons and begin scheming how to spin – as that now-common political term goes – the disclosure to place Stanton (Clinton) in the best favorable (or least unfavorable) light. Right or wrong has no bearing. Amusing in places, you can't mistake the movie's attempt at a cautionary tale. With strong supporting performances by Emma Thompson as Stanton's wife, Billy Bob Thornton as his closest adviser, and Kathy Bates as his scandal-suppressor. With a wry script by Elaine May (director Nichols's former standup-comedy partner), it's an unnerving look at the dark underbelly of politics. [Caution: language and adult themes] **[W]**

The Russia House
1990 – Fred Schepisi
Watching this romantic but somber adaptation of the John Le Carré novel of the same name, you might think 1) the sun never shines in the Soviet Union and 2) all intelligence agencies, East or West, are hopelessly cynical and corrupt – though the latter point is probably true. Cinematographer Ian Baker must have laid on extra filters to portray every scene – actually filmed in the U.S.S.R., only the second Hollywood movie to do so – as though the place was the most depressing on Earth. On the other hand, the

production traveled to Moscow in the newly established atmosphere of *glasnost*, or openness, promoted by Mikhail Gorbachev, the Russian premier at the time. The cast and crew received plenty of cooperation during their stay, in stark contrast to the often-deadly rivalry between the West and the Soviets in previous years. In this story, Sean Connery plays Barley Blair, a British publisher in Moscow initially seeking business opportunities in the form of promising new writers to present to western audiences. What he discovers instead, from a mysterious source, is an ostensible manuscript that's actually a secret document revealing Soviet nuclear capabilities. The encounter launches desperate attempts by both sides – with the CIA also joining the fray – to secure both the document and its author. And it leads Blair to a romantic liaison with Katya (Michelle Pfeiffer), a beautiful Russian woman somehow linked to the whole affair. Backed by a stellar supporting cast – including Klaus Maria Brandauer, Roy Scheider, James Fox, John Mahoney and even notorious director Ken Russell – and with an unusually moody jazz score by Jerry Goldsmith and a script by playwright Tom Stoppard, it's a class act. [Trivia note: *The Russia House* marks the third time Connery and Brandauer collaborated, sort of. In *Never Say Never Again* (P25), they played enemies and romantic rivals. Then, Brandauer was picked to star in *The Hunt for Red October* (PF5), but when he became unavailable, he recommended Connery for the role. And here, the two play honorable but uneasy allies] [Caution: adult themes] **[W]**

Salvador
1986 – co-written and directed by Oliver Stone
The same year he wrote and directed the Oscar-winning *Platoon* (P25), Stone did likewise for this deeply disturbing tale of a country in unrelenting turmoil. James Woods in an Oscar-nominated performance is Richard Boyle, a veteran but struggling photojournalist who attempts to revive his fortunes by covering the ongoing civil war in El Salvador. He's accompanied by his friend Doctor Rock (Jim Belushi), who's likewise struggling and looking for opportunity in what was then one of the world's most

dangerous places. The men do find opportunity, but they also encounter raw evil – among those fighting on both sides of the war – than they could have possibly imagined. Based on the true story of both lead characters (Boyle was a friend of the director), the movie heavily reflects Stone's leftwing politics. But it also reflects a perspective borne of his own combat experiences, making Stone (except for Samuel Fuller) unique among directors. He has seen the type of brutality that affected El Salvador in the 1980s. Not for the fainthearted. [Caution: extreme violence, including execution and rape] **[W]**

Shattered Glass
2003 – written and directed by Billy Ray

Irish poet William Butler Yeats ended the epitaph to be inscribed on his gravestone with the words, "Cast a cold eye on life, on death." It sounds cryptic, I know, but Yeats meant that he was most concerned with the legacy he would leave to succeeding generations – how he would be remembered. This fact-based drama presents a cautionary tale about a journalist whose quest for fame and prestige outweighed his professional integrity. And when his fraud was revealed, he lost his credibility for all time. Such was the story of Stephen Glass (Hayden Christiansen), who wrote for The New Republic magazine in the late 1990s and became a sensation via his vivid chronicles of young technology pioneers and entrepreneurs. The problem was, much if not most of his writing was fabrication – he made things up. This is the story not about Glass but about the honest and determined journalists who exposed him. It also represents a serious, almost catastrophic comedown for The New Republic, a weekly political journal whose editors once prided themselves in their thorough vetting of all copy submitted by their writers. Yet in this case they took what Glass was writing at face value because he boosted their readership. It's a shameful situation that continues in various news and commentary outlets to this day. Good performances by Steve Zahn, in a rare dramatic role as Adam Penenberg, the skeptical Forbes reporter who first unearthed Glass's fraud; and Peter Sarsgaard as Charles Lane, the New

Republic editor charged with cleaning up the mess. [Caution: adult themes] [W]

The Silence of the Lambs
1991 – Jonathan Demme

Here's a Faustian bargain for you: accept the Devil's cooperation in the hope of catching another, possibly worse devil. That's what happens to Special Agent Clarice Starling (Jodie Foster), newly recruited to the FBI. Charged with tracking down a serial killer who calls himself Buffalo Bill, because he removes the skins of his victims, Starling must pay a visit to the permanently imprisoned Hannibal Lecter (Anthony Hopkins), another serial killer who has been given the nickname Hannibal the Cannibal. You can guess how he earned that one. Easily the darkest of the bunch, yet a Best Picture winner, this rendition of the Thomas Harris novel remains one of the most disturbing movies ever made. Watching it, you almost feel as though a thin greasy film is enveloping you. Yet it's skillfully plotted and superbly acted by Hopkins and Foster, both of whom won Oscars. [Trivia note: Hopkins in an interview described his concept of Lecter as a human version of the all-seeing and all-knowing but murderous HAL 9000 computer in *2001: A Space Odyssey* (PF5). He added that for Lecter's voice he conjured a mix of author Truman Capote and actress Katharine Hepburn. You can discern the Hepburn element clearly, but Capote? That might be a stretch] [Extreme caution: disturbing themes and violence] [W]

A Simple Plan
1998 – Sam Raimi

Sometimes, the prospect of fast fortune results only in ruin. It depends on how carefully you can resist the temptation to take unfair advantage of the situation. So it is with Hank and Jacob Mitchell (Bill Paxton and Billy Bob Thornton), brothers out hunting in a snowy rural Minnesota landscape who run across a crashed small plane carrying several million dollars in cash. Faced with the prospect of sudden and ill-gotten wealth, the Mitchells, along with their friend Lou Chambers (Brent Briscoe), conspire to hide the money until they're sure the haul – a ransom collected by kidnappers – is no longer sought by law enforcement. Simple. Hide the money. Wait. Get rich. But given human nature, and the powerful lure of so much cash, sticking to the plan becomes a futile strategy – leading to a shocking cascade of disastrous results. [Trivia note: Though the movie might be called *A Simple Plan*, its evolution was anything but. At least four other directors considered doing the project before Raimi took it on, with three other actors vying for the role of Hank, and four actresses contending to play Hank's wife Sarah, a role that went to Bridget Fonda] [Caution: violence] **[W]**

The Social Network
2010 – David Fincher
Facebook, at this writing at least, is the world's most popular location for online human expression and interactions. Founded in 2004 on a tiny scale, the site eventually exploded onto public consciousness and has maintained its dominance ever since. Ironic, but this marketplace of interactions began as a means for Mark Zuckerberg (Jesse Eisenberg), a Harvard University student with abundant intelligence but an enormous chip on his shoulder, to demean and humiliate female students. Subsequently, on the way to fame and titanic fortune, Zuckerberg managed to outsmart, alienate and betray just about everyone else associated with the nascent ... social network, including Harvard president at the time Lawrence Summers, who needed to resolve one of the many disputes involving Zuckerberg and his classmates. Sharply directed by Fincher, with a fine script by Aaron Sorkin, it's an unsparing portrait of the man who became the world's youngest billionaire. [Trivia notes: 1) In the opening scene, where a college-age Zuckerberg tries to woo a co-ed but can't help insulting her, that attractive, fresh-faced, appealing young woman is played by Rooney Mara, who made her spectacular starring debut the following year as *The Girl With the Dragon Tattoo* – also directed by Fincher. 2) The Zuckerberg saga involved a dispute with twin brothers at Harvard who were champion rowers. Failing to find a suitable pair of twins, Fincher cast Armie Hammer as one of them;

153

Josh Pence, an actor with a similar build as the other, and then digitally applied Hammer's face onto Pence's when necessary] [Caution: language, sexuality and adult themes] **[W]**

Sunset Boulevard
1950 – co-written and directed by Billy Wilder

"All right, Mr. DeMille, I'm ready for my closeup." Gloria Swanson's line as faded silent-film idol Norma Desmond, spoken while descending the staircase at the movie's finale, has become immortal in one of the loopiest scenes in cinema history. Once again, here's a plot involving an ordinary man whose circumstances and poor judgment lead him into a devilish arrangement. William Holden plays Joe Gillis, an aspiring writer down on his luck and getting nowhere in Hollywood. His fortunes seem to improve when he meets Norma and contrives, for a handsome fee, to help her polish a screenplay she intends as a comeback vehicle. Instead, good fortune quickly deteriorates into folly when Norma, far from treating Joe as her protégé, begins … well, let's say the term gigolo applies to the arrangement. No surprises where things head from there – Joe narrates the story beginning with him floating, dead, in the pool outside Norma's mansion. But Swanson's performance as a woman descending into madness is breathtaking and personally courageous. Likewise, German director Erich von Stroheim as Norma's obsessively loyal manservant Max. Nominated for 11 Oscars, it won three, including Best Screenplay for Wilder and Charles Brackett. In PF5, I described Wilder's *Some Like It Hot* as everybody's favorite comedy, and his *Witness for the Prosecution* as the best courtroom drama. Now, I need to include *Sunset Boulevard* as *the* classic Hollywood saga. [Technical note: That shot of Joe floating face-down in the pool, with police and onlookers standing at the edge, presented a tough logistical challenge: You can't capture surface objects sharply if you film from underwater. The crew solved the problem by placing a mirror at the bottom and shooting the reflected image from above] [Viewing note: As impressive as Swanson's performance was, it almost pales compared to Carol Burnett's brilliant parodies of the character on

154

her weekly television show, which featured Harvey Korman's hilarious portrayals of Max] [Trivia note: When Norma visits Cecile B. DeMille at the studio, the set where he's working is real. It's for *Samson and Delilah*, directed by DeMille and released the year before *Sunset Boulevard* premiered] [Caution: violence and adult themes] **[B&W]**

The Talented Mr. Ripley
1999 – written and directed by Anthony Minghella
The poet Sir Walter Scott got it right when he wrote:
> *Oh, what a tangled web we weave*
> *when first we practice to deceive.*

Tom Ripley (Matt Damon) is a young man of limited means who attempts to capitalize on a case of mistaken identity. The deception leads him into deeper and deeper problems that eventually require him to commit murder to prevent his exposure. Scandalous and immoral, no question, but among the complications is the fact that other characters in the story are nearly as corrupt as Tom. Dickie (the always arresting Jude Law), for example, seems to behave entirely without a moral compass. Freddie (Philip Seymour Hoffman) isn't particularly immoral, but he is obnoxious and snobby, to the point of engendering indifference when Tom … um, dispatches him. That's the rub here. Tom acts in increasingly ruthless ways, but he never seems to lose your sympathies. In effect, he lures the audience into accepting his solutions as well – into entering his personal heart of darkness. [Caution: violence and sexuality] **[W]**

Three Days of the Condor
1975 – Sydney Pollack
Robert Redford worked with Pollack seven times over a 20-year period. They made this spy thriller together in the middle of that time span and at the height of Redford's popularity. Here, he plays Joe Turner, an analyst at a low-level CIA operation in New York City. His code name is "Condor," for reasons that remain unclear. Also, for reasons seemingly unexplained, Turner steps out to grab some takeout food for lunch one day, only to return to

the office and find out that everyone else has been murdered. From that point on he finds himself 1) in dire peril from villains unknown and 2) obsessed with finding out who was responsible for the terrible deed. Along the way, he abducts an innocent bystander (Faye Dunaway), who turns out to be an angel of mercy in more ways than one. Eventually, Turner discovers the reason for his being targeted, and he meets the assassin (Max von Sydow) directed to kill him. Because this is a rather contrived thriller, those and other loose ends get resolved maybe a bit too neatly. [Trivia note: *Three Days of the Condor* holds the sad distinction of being the only film to feature scenes shot inside the World Trade Center, though the exteriors of the ill-fated twin towers appear in many other movies] [Caution: language, violence and sexuality] **[W]**

The Ugly American
1963 – George Englund
A predicament that has faced Western governments for as long as they have attempted diplomacy: trying to deal honestly with resentful populations and corrupt or ideologically opposed regimes in the Third World. Marlon Brando stars as Harrison Carter MacWhite, an American diplomat dispatched to the fictional land of Sarkhan, and whose arrival generates fierce and dangerous protests. Despite his longtime friendship with Sarkhanian politician Deong (Japanese actor Eiji Okana), a communist, MacWhite becomes increasingly alienated from both his friend and the people he has been charged to serve, to the point where he eventually admits defeat and returns to America, convinced permanent diplomacy cannot work in that benighted country. Produced in the early 1960s and shot in Thailand, the movie foreshadows America's tragic experience in Southeast Asia. [Trivia notes: 1) Kukrit Pramoj, a former journalist and scholar, and a member of the Thai royal family, here plays Kwen Sai, Sarkhan's prime minister, in a couple of brief but important scenes. About a decade later, Pramoj became the *real* prime minister of his country for a short time. 2) Brando, a notorious practical joker, nearly got himself in trouble at the movie's

156

premiere in Bangkok when he called Pramoj a liar and a thief. Before the stunned crowd could react, Brando explained that though Pramoj had told him he couldn't act, he had acted well enough to steal the movie] [<u>Caution</u>: adult themes and violence] **[W]**

17. Hillwilla Heaven

I write about the movies in my off-hours, but I publish books as my day job. One of my authors, Melanie Forde, created the <u>Hillwilla</u> trilogy, the captivating saga of a Boston woman who ends up owning a llama farm in southern West Virginia, in the heart of Appalachia (pronounced Appa-LATCH-ah by the locals). Her love interest gives her that nickname as the feminine counterpart of "hillbilly," a derisive term some would apply to the real-life characters portrayed in this quintet of titles. Never forget, though, that some of the finest individuals this country ever produced emerged from the deepest hollows of Appalachia, including Alvin York, the extraordinary hero of World War I portrayed by Gary Cooper in *Sergeant York*; and Chuck Yeager, America's greatest test pilot and one of the subjects of *The Right Stuff* (both movies in <u>PF5</u>). Not that these characters qualify as so noble. They are, however, uniformly fascinating.

Blaze
1989 – written and directed by Ron Shelton
This loosely constructed profile of Louisiana politician Earl Long and his affair with stripper "Blaze" Starr pairs Paul Newman with sexy Lolita Davidovich in her first significant role. Earl Long was a member of the dynastic Louisiana political family from the 1930s through the '60s that included his brother Huey, the state's governor – who was assassinated – and his nephew Russell, who became a U.S. senator. Earl was elected governor as well, for three terms. But this movie has relatively little to do with the Long family's political fortunes. Instead, Shelton's script concentrates on – and takes great artistic liberties with – Starr's rise from poverty in West Virginia to successful striptease artist and her affair with Earl. Born Fannie Belle Fleming in a hamlet called Twelvepole Creek, in the western part of the state, she eventually

moved to Baltimore, became a waitress, and was lured onto the stage by her longtime manager Red Snyder (comedian and actor Robert Wuhl), who persuaded her to include a striptease with her act. The combination of her backwoods simplicity, her demure politeness and her stunning figure quickly made her a ... star. Long's attraction to her was instantaneous, and Shelton plays their affair for laughs. As for Newman, at 64 –20 years after *Butch Cassidy* (PF5) – he portrays Long with more of an elder's twinkle in his eye than overt masculinity or sexual charm. Probably a wise move, given that he was 36 years older than Davidovich. [Caution: sexuality, and quite a bit of it, given Ms. Starr's occupation and Mr. Long's proclivities] **[W]**

The Coal Miner's Daughter
1980 – Michael Apted

An earnest, straightforward biography of Loretta Lynn, the singer known as the "First Lady of Country Music." She's portrayed by Sissy Spacek in an Oscar-winning role. The title, based on Lynn's autobiography, is literal. Her father Ted Webb (here played by actor and singer Levon Helm) worked in the coal mines of Kentucky to support his wife and eight children. Loretta marries "Doo" Lynn (Tommy Lee Jones) at age 15 (he's 22) and bears four children of her own in four years. Unending poverty would seem to be their lot, but fate intervenes, in a complicated way, when Loretta's singing talent emerges, and she eventually becomes a Country & Western sensation as well as a close friend of established star Patsy Cline (Beverly D'Angelo). In some ways, it's a standard backstage saga elevated by the fine cast and their arresting performances, particularly Spacek and D'Angelo, who performed all of their songs. [Trivia notes: 1) Spacek's singing Lynn's songs in the movie started out as a bluff the actress used to attempt to escape the role. Preferred by Lynn to portray her life, Spacek and her husband, production designer Jack Fisk, decided to demand that she perform the numbers instead of lip-syncing to Lynn's voice. To their surprise, both Lynn and the studio accepted. Spacek studied Lynn's speaking and singing voice, and she ended up delivering an excellent impersonation. 2) C&W fans also showered their approval of Spacek's singing performance, as well as D'Angelo's, by pushing the soundtrack album into the Top 40 on Billboard magazine's list in that category. 3) Loretta Lynn died in 2022 at age 90] [Caution: language, domestic violence and mild sexuality] **[W]**

Cold Mountain
2003 – written and directed by Anthony Minghella

There's a scene in Stanley Kubrick's *The Shining* (not on my lists), in which one of the characters attempts a desperate journey to save one of the other characters, only to … well, let's say the word "futile" immediately comes to mind. The connection here? A wounded Confederate soldier abandons his post to return home to his lover, undertaking a long and dangerous journey, only to … um, this one's better left undisclosed. Setting aside the denouement, the title refers to a region of western North Carolina, amid Appalachia's Blue Ridge Mountains, that has sent many of its young men to fight for the South in the Civil War. One is W.P. Inman (Jude Law), a craftsman in civilian life who loves Ada Monroe (Nicole Kidman), a preacher's daughter. Ada loves him back and promises to remain faithful until he returns from the fighting. Inman resolves to do just that after he nearly dies in battle. He undertakes the perilous trek home, knowing he would be executed for desertion if discovered. Along the way, Inman meets an array of odd but vivid backwoods characters. Ada, who meanwhile is struggling to keep body and soul together awaiting Inman's return, encounters an assortment of her own. Most of both groups are played by well-known actors, including Eileen Atkins, Kathy Baker, James Gammon, Brendan Gleeson, Philip Seymour Hoffman, Natalie Portman and Donald Sutherland, as well as Renée Zellweger, who won a Best Supporting Actress Oscar. It's a big, sprawling epic, lavishly produced and beautifully shot (mostly in Romania) by John Seale, with a memorable, twangy score by Gabriel Yared. There's just that issue about the outcome, which owes its origin to the source novel, Charles Frazier's best-seller. [Viewing note: Yes, *Cold Mountain* was shot in Romania, standing in for North Carolina. That's a common practice in movies, such as *Doctor Zhivago* (PF5) shot in Spain and Finland instead of Russia, and *Moonstruck* (PF5, too) shot mostly in Toronto and not Brooklyn] [Caution: periodic gruesome violence and explicit sexuality] **[W]**

Hillbilly Elegy
2020 – Ron Howard

What an American success story! J.D. Vance, who at this writing is seeking to win a seat in the United States Senate for the state of Ohio, began as a member of a dirt-poor family in rural Kentucky. His path could have ended up in a number of pathetic ways. Yet through the stern but patient guidance of "Mamaw," his maternal grandmother (an almost-unrecognizable Glenn Close in a sensational performance), Vance managed to enter the U.S. Marines, gain entrance to Yale Law School and eventually write the best-selling autobiography on which the movie is based. Yes, it's a success story, but it's a brutal, punishing ordeal for Vance, both as a child and a young man (played, respectively, by Owen Asztalos and Gabriel Basso). One reason is his mother, Bev (Amy Adams, in a tough role but a fine performance of her own). She's a drug addict, an alcoholic and is mentally unstable. Difficult going for practically the whole length of the story, it's nevertheless a worthy attraction because of its emphases on the ability of the human spirit to overcome the toughest challenges and, as Close's character demonstrates, on the precious fact that wisdom and inspiration can be found in the most unlikely individuals. [Trivia note: Close's performance garnered her an eighth Oscar nomination without a win, tying her with the late Peter O'Toole for the most in that dubious distinction – in his case, an utter travesty given his monumental performance as T.E. Lawrence in *Lawrence of Arabia* (PF5) in his debut] [Caution: adult themes and constantly rough language] **[W]**

Minari
2020 – written and directed by Lee Isaac Chung

A surprisingly poignant, skillfully directed and solidly acted story about a family of Korean immigrants trying to carve out a living on a farm in rural Arkansas in the 1980s – "this hillbilly place," as one of the principal characters complains. The movie chronicles the ordeal of Jacob and Monica Yi (Steven Yeun and Han Ye-ri), along with their pre-teen daughter Anne (Noel Kate Cho), their young son David (seven-year-old Adam Kim) and Monica's mother Soon-ja (veteran actress Youn Yuh-jung, a major star of South Korean cinema). The Yi's have arrived in Arkansas from California, where Jacob and Monica were earning a modest living, but not prospering, separating baby chicks by gender for a food-processing company. So, Jacob buys a plot of Arkansas farmland, hoping to raise vegetables to sell to Korean grocers in the Midwest. It turns out to be much more challenging than he imagined, both in managing the farm – where water turns out to be scarce – and in his marriage. Placid at times, punctuated by a few emotionally explosive moments, it's thoroughly compelling. Filmed in and around Tulsa, Oklahoma, in less than a month, *Minari* was nominated for six Oscars, including Best Picture and acting nods for Yeun and Yuh-jung. The versatile Will Patton appears as Jacob's somewhat unglued but well-meaning farmhand. And Yeun is worlds away from his former membership in Chicago's Second City comedy troupe and his TV roles in popular series such as The Walking Dead and The Big Bang Theory. Oh, and the title? Minari is a type of celery that's widely grown in Korea. [Trivia notes: 1) The movie represents one of those miraculous Hollywood turnarounds, à la Sylvester Stallone and *Rocky*, for writer–director Chung. An unsuccessful screenwriter, Chung had returned to Korea to accept a teaching job when he decided to attempt one more script. Modeling his situation after Willa Cather, who kept trying and failing to sell manuscripts about urban topics before becoming famous writing about her life in rural Nebraska, Chung decided to create a fictionalized memoir of his own childhood in Arkansas. It worked, and this lovely movie is the result. 2) In *Hillbilly Elegy*, I mentioned it was Glenn Close's eighth Oscar nomination without a win. Who did win? Youn Yuh-jung as the Yi family's feisty grandmother] [Caution: language and adult themes] **[W]**

162

18. Loves Won, Lost or Regained

As song lyricist Johnny Burke once wrote, "Love is funny or it's sad, or it's quiet or it's mad; it's a good thing or it's bad – but beautiful." Love certainly can encompass all of those aspects, including the beauty, as I hope I've shown in some of my previous picks. Here, however, I've chosen to highlight something else; the "bumpy road to love," a phrase written by the immortal Ira Gershwin in "They Can't Take That Away from Me," sung by Fred to Ginger – twice, in *Shall We Dance* and *The Barkleys of Broadway* (both in P25). I offer these 20 romances not because they're particularly beautiful but because they're difficult. Each in its own way – even the comedies – portrays the process of human coupling, which almost always involves the other, inevitably bumpy aspects of love.

About Last Night...
1986 – Edward Zwick

Let's begin with a story that covers several of those adjectives above. It's ostensibly about the freewheeling singles scene in the 1980s but at its core delves into the natural yearnings of the human heart. That's because it's based on David Mamet's sharp-edged play of a decade earlier, "Sexual Perversity in Chicago." It concerns the meeting and one-night stand between Danny Martin (Rob Lowe) and Debbie Sullivan (Demi Moore), two attractive Windy City residents who weren't initially looking for commitment. Yet they quickly form a live-in attachment despite the disapproval of Bernie and Joan (Jim Belushi and Elizabeth Perkins), their respective best friends. It isn't smooth sailing between them, either. Their basic differences and unfamiliarity with relationships soon breaks them apart, a development that Danny eventually regrets. In his efforts to regain Debbie's affections, they both begin to learn the real meaning of love. A pretty good ensemble piece, a pretty fair directorial debut by Zwick and one of Moore's best roles. [Trivia note: Zwick once confessed that he was drawn to the story because it reflected his own experiences as a young single man] [Caution: language and sexuality] [**W**]

Bridget Jones's Diary
2001 – England – Sharon Maguire

Based on Helen Fielding's best-seller, it's a semi-comedic love triangle featuring Renée Zellweger in the title role opposite two of the most appealing British male stars of the period, Colin Firth and Hugh Grant. Bridget is a plump, rather foul-mouthed, 32-year-old single living in London (Zellweger was 32 at the time, gained weight for the role and adopted a British accent). Working at a publishing company, she lusts after her boss, Daniel Cleaver (Grant). Then, at a holiday party, she meets Mark Darcy (Firth), whom she instantly – and justifiably – dislikes. From there, Bridget alternately pursues Daniel but keeps encountering Mark, all the while keeping a … diary to record her attempts at improving her appearance. Whom will she end up with? As the trailer puts it, Bridget must decide "between a man who seems too good to be true, and a man so wrong he could be right." No disclosure here, but it's passable fun finding out. [Trivia notes: 1) The movie brims with subtle references to Jane Austen's Pride and Prejudice, but the most interesting is the casting of Firth. In her source novel, Helen Fielding based Mark Darcy not only on the immortal Mr. Darcy but also on Firth's portrayal of the character in the glorious 1995 miniseries rendition of the novel. 2) Here's another connection with the miniseries: The movie was co-written by Andrew Davies, who did the adaptation for British TV] [Caution: language and sexuality] [**W**]

Collateral Beauty
2016 – Dave Frankel

This one's likely to make you shake your head, trying to figure out what you've just seen. That's exactly how it affected me. Yet it isn't without its charms. Will Smith stars as Howard Inlet, an advertising executive deeply grieving for his lost child, to the point where he writes letters to the abstractions of love, time and death, complaining about their treatment of him. His worried colleagues (Edward Norton, Keira Knightly and Michael Peña) decide to hire three actors (Kate Winslet, Jacob Latimore and Helen Mirren) to personify Love, Time and Death, and visit Howard one by one. But rather than hoping the "spirits" will shake him out of his depression, their motive is mercenary. They need to prove he has become mentally incompetent so they can sell the company out from under him. It's wrenching, compelling and hugely sentimental, but is it effective? I've struggled with it for a while, granting lots of leeway because of the quality of the talent involved. But I haven't been able to get beyond the huge misdirection that lies at the center of the plot – and the utterly puzzling epilogue. Maybe you'll have better luck. [Caution: adult themes] **[W]**

Comfort and Joy
1984 – Scotland – written and directed by Bill Forsyth
In the "Loves Lost" category, Bill Paterson plays Allan "Dicky" Bird, a radio DJ in Glasgow whose girlfriend Maddy (Eleanor David) leaves him just before Christmas and turns his life upside down. This being another in director Forsyth's line of quirky but endearing narratives, the split eventually leads the now-despondent Dicky into bizarre territory – he gets caught up in a turf war between, of all things, two rival Mafia-owned ice cream trucks. It's best not to reveal much more; it probably wouldn't make much sense, anyway. I'll just mention that Dicky becomes more than a bystander in the ice cream war, he slowly regains his bearings after losing Maddy, and fate even presents the prospect of a new romance. [Trivia note: Though the movie plays it for laughs, Glasgow did experience a turf war involving ice cream trucks – a lethal one – and just before the movie's release. It turned out the trucks were being used as fronts for organized crime activities] [Caution: language, mild violence and sexuality] [Second caution: Ever hear of an earworm? Well, this movie contains a doozy – and I'm speaking from experience] **[W]**

Creator
1985 – Ivan Passer
Talk about carrying a torch! Dr. Harry Wolper (Peter O'Toole) is a medical researcher, a Nobel Laureate and a widower still grieving for his wife after 30 years, to the point where he has been trying to clone her cells into a new person by seeking a willing egg donor. He finds the donor in Meli (Mariel Hemingway), a free spirited young woman who agrees to carry the fertilized egg – not so much because Wolper is paying her but because she is falling in love with him. It's a wildly implausible story, yet O'Toole, as always, is so appealing – and believable – that you might find yourself rooting for his success. Hemingway is appealing as well, but she's playing a contrived character. Considerably more interesting are Boris and Barbara (Vincent Spano and Virginia Madsen), Harry's lab assistant and a local college student. Their courtship is delightful, and Boris turns out to be Barbara's literal lifesaver. The basic plot implausible? Well, yes. No doubt O'Toole is one of the most attractive men who ever lived. But an eventual March–December romance with Meli? Mm … maybe asking for too much. [Caution: adult themes and plentiful sexuality] **[W]**

The Decoy Bride
2011 – England – Sheree Folkson
Alice Eve and Kelly Macdonald as, respectively, a real prospective bride and her … decoy in a romantic comedy of errors. Eve plays Lara Tyler, a Hollywood star and international celebrity constantly hounded by the *paparazzi*, particularly in her efforts to marry James Arber (veteran Scottish TV actor David Tennant), a best-selling British author. With me so far? Good, because from here the plot takes more twists and turns than a narrow mountain road. Much of it involves a pert young woman named Katie (Macdonald), who steps in to impersonate Lara and help her avoid Marco, a pesky Italian photographer. But Katie quickly falls for James, and he quickly begins falling for her. As for Lara and Marco, well, he stays tenaciously on the hunt for celebrity photos, but there's much more, and it's better to discover firsthand than to read it in summary. Besides, it's a fun bit o' romcom, shot on

the scenic and charming Scottish Isle of Hegg. [Trivia note: If Marco, that pesky Italian photographer, looks familiar, it's because he's Federico Castelluccio, who played Furio, the fearsome bodyguard and enforcer in the TV series The Sopranos] [Caution: mild sexuality] **[W]**

Defending Your Life
1991 – written and directed by Albert Brooks

In the "Loves Won" column, there's good news and bad news about the afterlife. The good news is there doesn't seem to be a Hell for the worst of us. The bad news is that Hinduism seems to be correct – if you can't make it into Heaven, you must return to Earth in a different guise for as many repeat performances as required. The routine is revealed to Daniel Miller (Brooks), who dies in a highway crash and is sent to a place called Judgment City, where he must … defend his life in front of a pair of stern-looking judges. It isn't a single trial, however. It's a series of sessions, in which Miller's personal history is replayed and reviewed. In between, he's allowed the run of the place, which includes such amenities as unlimited buffets – which can be consumed without consequences – and various recreational opportunities. That's where Daniel meets and falls in love with Julia (Meryl Streep), who apparently has led an exemplary life and is cruising through her judgment, while Daniel seems to be heading toward an earthly restart. The dichotomy sets up a climax aboard twin celestial shuttles, one carrying Julia to her heavenly reward, the other conveying Daniel back to terra firma. Is this the couple's end? Well, it's an Albert Brooks comedy, so don't lose hope that love will conquer all. Also because it's an Albert Brooks comedy, the humor is consistently biting and clever. **[W]**

Enchanted
2007 – Kevin Lima

It's fitting in a chapter featuring love stories to include at least one fairy tale. Here it is, in a clever "What if?" scenario, and produced by the Disney organization to boot, at a time when they were capable of such things. Amy Adams plays Giselle, a Snow White-like character in a romantic musical. Except that Giselle is exiled by the evil queen Narissa (Susan Sarandon) from her animated world to modern-day Manhattan. There, she can still commute with her friends from the animal world, especially pigeons and rats (in both cases, trained live animals), and she sings either to them or to other humans (and it's Adams's real voice). So, the romance? That's initially in the form of Edward (James Marsden), a handsome but dim prince with whom Giselle falls in love. But when Narissa intervenes and exiles Giselle, she's befriended by Robert (Patrick Dempsey), a lawyer and single dad. From there, it's misdirection, chaos and suspense galore on the way to … well, it's a classic Disney plot, updated to 21st-century sensibilities. [Trivia notes: 1) Inside jokes abound in the movie, harkening back to Disney's better days. An example: Robert's law firm, Churchill, Harline and Smith, is based on the three of the songwriters for the original *Snow White and the Seven Dwarfs* (P25): Frank Churchill, Leigh Harline and Paul Smith. Another: Judy Kuhn and Jodi Benson, two voice/singing actresses from the studio's animated features, appear in bit parts here. Keep a close eye out for more because they're plentiful. 2) The only principal cast member who doesn't sing is Tony Award-winning *singer* Idina Menzel, playing Robert's fiancée Nancy] [Caution: mild sexuality] **[W]**

Infinity
1996 – Matthew Broderick
One of my chapters in P25 dealt with pet projects; movies produced and directed by stars who pushed heavily for them. *Infinity* fits that category. Broderick and his mother Patricia co-wrote this gentle story about Richard Feynman and his marriage to Arline (Arr-LEEN) Greenbaum, and Broderick plays the world-renowned physicist. In interviews, he described how he had studied the man's two memoirs, Surely You're Joking, Mr. Feynman and What Do You Care What Other People Think? for years, trying to figure out how to bring his story to the screen. Broderick settled for portraying a distinct period in Feynman's life, well before he won the Nobel Prize in physics. The story takes place from the 1920s to the early '40s, when his father (played by

Peter Riegert) introduces him to the wonders of the universe, he meets and marries Arline (appealingly played by Patricia Arquette), participates in developing the atomic bomb and loses his wife to cancer. It's a well-balanced effort and an appealing love story, and Broderick carries off both the role and directing with skill. [Caution: adult themes] **[W]**

Love is a Many-Splendored Thing (and) The World of Suzie Wong
1955 and 1960 – Henry King and Richard Quine
A pair of love stories, both set in Hong Kong in the mid-20th century and both starring William Holden.

* * *

In *Love Is a Many-Splendored Thing*, Holden co-stars with Jennifer Jones in a big-budget, CinemaScope romance set in the late 1940s. Jones plays Han Suyin, a Eurasian doctor who has been widowed with a young daughter. He plays Mark Elliott, a (married) journalist covering the civil war in China. Based on the real Suyin's memoir of the same title, the story follows the pair's introduction, rapid friendship and eventual affair that elicits racial bigotry – from both the European and Asian societies – and leads to a bittersweet conclusion. A modest box-office success in its day, the movie's theme song, popularized by The Four Aces, became a top-hit song at the time and a romantic standard. [Trivia note: This might have been a love story, but no love was lost, both between the two stars and between Jones and the movie crew. She continually complained about Holden and treated the offscreen workers with indifference or outright disdain] [Caution: adult themes] **[W]**

* * *

Five years later, in *The World of Suzie Wong*, Holden paired with stunning Eurasian dancer-turned-actress Nancy Kwan in her debut. This time, Holden is Robert Lomax, an architect spending a year in Hong Kong to try his hand as a painter. Almost immediately, he meets Kwan's titular Suzie Wong, a young Asian woman who captivates but deceives him. Eventually, he learns she's a prostitute. Her livelihood notwithstanding, Robert offers

169

to pay Suzie to pose for him, an action that leads, eventually, to genuine friendship, a love affair and a lasting relationship. Improbable? In concept, maybe. But the story, based on Paul Osborn's play – in turn based on Richard Mason's novel – is as compelling as it is convincing. [Trivia note: Re: the Broadway play: Instead of Holden and Kwan the stage production had starred France Nuyen and, of all people, William Shatner – both of whom reprised their roles as lovers in an episode of the original Star Trek television series some years later] [Caution: adult themes and mild sexuality] [W]

Marnie
1964 – Alfred Hitchcock
In the same year he starred as British secret agent 007 James Bond in *Goldfinger* (PF5) – which I still regard as the best movie in the series – Sean Connery took on this difficult assignment. He's Mark Rutland, a Philadelphia publisher who meets the title character (Tippi Hedren at her most alluring) and engages in what's best called a tortured romantic relationship. Marnie is constantly disingenuous. Nevertheless, Mark marries her and then, over time, steadfastly pursues and eventually exposes the central reason for her deceitful personality – through great effort, he saves both her and their marriage. It's uncomfortable to watch sometimes, but it's a fascinating character study, and Connery is first-rate in a strictly dramatic role. He gives much of the credit to Hitchcock, about whom he said, "[His] preparation for moviemaking is second to none. In terms of what he wanted in the script, he visualized everything. I honestly enjoyed working with him." Not to neglect Hedren, whose performance ranks among the best and most nuanced in this genre. Reports at the time quoted her as saying that disputes during filming killed her relationship with Hitchcock and ended her movie career, though she regarded *Marnie* as her favorite. [Caution: violence and adult themes] [W]

A Place in the Sun
1951 – George Stevens

Boy does this one define the "Loves Lost" part of the chapter. Based on Theodore Dreiser's 1925 novel <u>An American Tragedy</u>, itself based on a real incident two decades earlier, it's the story of a lonely young man whose momentary indiscretion literally destroys three lives. Montgomery Clift plays George Eastman, a working stiff who travels to his uncle's factory seeking a new job and a possible better life. Early in the process, George meets and romances Alice (Shelley Winters, in an early role), a dowdy co-worker. Later, as he begins to advance his position in the company, he meets and falls in love with Angela (Elizabeth Taylor, only 17 years old at the time), a refined, upper-class young woman. Thereafter, George's affections and sense of duty are severely torn between the two women. And, as the title suggests, therein lies the tragedy – a terrible one. No, dear readers, this one doesn't end happily, but it's riveting. [<u>Trivia notes</u>: 1) Though they played onscreen lovers, *A Place in the Sun* marked the beginning of a close and lifelong but platonic friendship between Clift and Taylor. 2) About Taylor's age; the movie was actually filmed in 1949, but its release was held up for two years. This fact makes the famous kissing scene between her and Clift all the more remarkable. 3) The movie marked the last for one of the great movie craftsmen of all time, art director Hans Dreier, who had worked on more than 500 productions during his 30-year career] [<u>Caution</u>: adult themes] **[B&W]**

River of No Return
1954 – Otto Preminger

No one personified sex appeal more in the 1950s than Marilyn Monroe, particularly in screen comedies. Here, however, she's pretty impressive in a CinemaScope romantic drama, co-starring with Robert Mitchum in what you could call a northwestern. In 1875, somewhere in that part of the country, widower Matt Calder (Mitchum) arrives in a town looking for his son Mark (Tommy Rettig), whom he had to abandon when imprisoned for killing a man. Mark has been temporarily raised by Kay Weston (Monroe), a dance hall singer married to Harry (Rory Calhoun), a prospector and gambler. Soon, the two men clash, and Harry strands Matt, Mark and Kay in the back country. As they try to make their way back to town via a log raft floating down the river, and they face a series of dangers, the couple forms a romantic attachment. The attachment partly sparks the climactic conflict between Matt and Harry. It's a testament to the two leads that despite the movie's flaws their onscreen bond always seems genuine. [Trivia notes: 1) When Mitchum and Monroe made this film they were already old friends. A decade earlier, when Monroe went by the name Norma Jean Dougherty, Mitchum worked with her first husband, Jim Dougherty, at a Lockheed aircraft plant in Los Angeles. 2) Those who knew Monroe often mentioned her sensitivity to suffering. Mitchum once said that during the studio filming of the rapids sequence, she suddenly refused to continue a scene because she noticed one of the technicians was apparently shivering from handling the coldwater stream] **[W]**

Shadowlands
1993 – Richard Attenborough

Another romantic drama, and like *A Place in the Sun* based on a true story but based only on personal loss. Anthony Hopkins is British author C.S. Lewis, living comfortably within 1950s academia at Oxford University. Lewis's comfort is suddenly disrupted by the appearance of Joy Davidman Gresham (Debra Winger). Gresham is a poet touring England with her young son, Douglas (Joseph Mazzello, the same year he co-starred with Attenborough in Steven Spielberg's *Jurassic Park* – see PF5). Lewis is quiet and reserved, while Gresham is direct and outgoing. Yet they quickly fall in love and marry. But their happiness is soon disrupted when she is diagnosed with terminal cancer, a development that severely challenges Lewis's deep religious faith. A most unconventional love story, it's also thoughtful and engaging, and elevated by its talented stars. [Trivia note (and spoiler alert): Ten years earlier, Winger portrayed another doomed soul, in Best Picture-winner *Terms of Endearment* (P25)] [Caution: adult themes] **[W]**

Sideways
2004 – written and directed by Alexander Payne

Another comedy amid the dramas. Paul Giamatti is Miles Raymond, a San Diego teacher and wine enthusiast. A recent divorcé, he's also depressed about his lack of romance. To distract himself, he agrees to take a road trip with his old friend Jack Cole (Thomas Hayden Church in an Oscar-nominated role), an actor living in Los Angeles and soon to be married. The two men start by visiting Miles's mother (film and TV actress Marylouise Burke), where Miles steals a thousand dollars from her before the two men sneak away. He wants to use to money to play golf and drink the very best wines during their trip, but Jack has something else in mind: one last, wild affair before his marriage. At one of their first stops, Miles meets Maya (Virginia Madsen, also Oscar-nominated), an old acquaintance, and Jack meets Stephanie (Sandra Oh), another friend of Maya's. Jack wants the foursome to double-date, and that's where the many, many complications begin. Central to the story is whether Miles and Maya will get together despite Jack's extreme ability to … um, mess things up. It's to the two actors' credit that you tend to root for them to bond despite how incredibly stupid Miles also can be at times. [Trivia note: Hard to believe, but the script for this movie, in 2004, was the first ever to win writing awards from *all* of the major associations: the National Board of Review; the New York, Los Angeles and Broadcast Film Critics; the National Society of Film Critics, the Golden Globes, the British Academy of Film and Television Arts (BAFTA), the Writer's Guild and, of course, the Oscar] [Caution: explicit sexuality and rough language] **[W]**

Somewhere in Time
1980 – Jeannot Szwarc

Perhaps the strangest of the bunch, this one will require your patience and some slack. It's a romantic time-travel fantasy based on a novel by sci-fi writer Richard Matheson, who also wrote the screenplay. It concerns Richard Collier (Christopher Reeve), a playwright who attempts to shake off a bout of writer's block by spending some time away at a resort, in this case the magnificent

Grand Hotel on Michigan's Mackinac Island. There, Collier becomes obsessively fascinated by a photograph of a beautiful woman named Elise McKenna (Jane Seymour) who had visited the hotel six decades earlier. He also discovers that Elise apparently was the woman who had once visited him and gave him a pocket watch before dying that same day. From there, the story moves inexorably toward its central fantasy, uniting Collier and McKenna, sparking a romance between them, threatening to separate them and resolving their severe temporal difficulties – in an ending reminiscent of *The Ghost and Mrs. Muir* (P25). The great John Barry supplied the richly romantic score. [Technical note: There's a scene where Richard appears in the foreground and Elise is in the deep background that employed a rarely used technique, called a split diopter, a special lens that allowed both subjects to stay in focus without the need for visual effects] [Trivia note: Bill Erwin, the hotel doorman in the contemporary scenes, compiled more than 250 roles over his 65-year career] [Caution: mild sexuality] **[W]**

Splendor in the Grass
1961 – Elia Kazan

One of the most famous screen romances, featuring a grown-up and vivid Natalie Wood, and Warren Beatty in his debut. It's a bittersweet story of young love written by William Inge, who won the screenplay Oscar. In smalltown Kansas in the late 1920s, Deanie Loomis (Wood) struggles to maintain her virginity despite her powerful attraction to Bud Stamper (Beatty), who's struggling with more than his share of young male urges. But the normal teen angst takes a back seat to the powerful dramas surrounding both families – at least temporarily. Soon, however, the family problems interfere with Bud and Deanie's romance, and they break up. The event traumatizes Deanie to the point where she attempts suicide and is institutionalized. Meanwhile, Bud is sent off to college – Yale, to be exact – where his fortunes quickly fall. In a lesser drama, maybe the two estranged lovebirds would find their way back to each other. But here, in Inge's scenario, Bud and Deanie eventually find happiness separately. And in the aforementioned bittersweet aspect of the story, they reunite briefly but only to exchange polite greetings and move on. It's here, near the fadeout, that Deanie's voice recites the William Wordsworth verse from which the movie's title is derived.

> *Though nothing can bring back the hour*
> *Of splendor in the grass, glory in the flower*
> *We will grieve not; rather find*
> *Strength in what remains behind.*

[Trivia note: Deanie's attempted suicide required Natalie Wood to jump into a pond. She did, despite a lifelong fear of drowning – which, ironically, was how she did die, 20 years later at age 43] [Caution: sexuality and adult themes] **[W]**

The Station Agent
2003 – written and directed by Tom McCarthy

An unusual romance that's more about a friendship and potential romance that grows between Emily (Michelle Williams), an unmarried but pregnant librarian; and Fin (Peter Dinklage), a train enthusiast who inherits an abandoned station along a commuter railway in New Jersey. Fin, who is occasionally taunted because of his dwarfism, just wishes to be left alone. Wishes aside, three individuals enter his life, seemingly to stay. Along with Emily, there's Joe (Bobby Cannavale), who's running a food truck for his father while the man recuperates from surgery. There's also Olivia (Patricia Clarkson), who is attempting to deal with the death of her son, an event that ended her marriage. One way or another, the four lives keep intertwining, the main issue being whether Emily and Fin, who do spend the night once, will end up together. It's a pleasant and engaging little movie, a nice debut effort by McCarthy, who went on to write and direct the Oscar-winning *Spotlight* (P25) 12 years later. [Caution: language and sexuality] **[W]**

Young Cassidy
1965 – Jack Cardiff (and John Ford)

I admit this one's a stretch, because it's more about the history of Ireland in the early 20th century than a romance. Nevertheless, I included it because the relationship between the protagonist John Cassidy (Rod Taylor, adopting a bit o' brogue but giving a fine performance) and Nora (Maggie Smith, in her prime), though brief, is vivid and memorable. Cassidy (based on Irish playwright Sean O'Casey) is an aspiring writer in the midst of a growing Irish revolution. His plays are so provocative they tend to cause riots among emotional theatergoers. But he maintains the support and confidence of the legendary poet William Butler Yeats (Michael Redgrave, father of Vanessa and Lynn), which eventually enables Cassidy to travel to America to continue his work. That opportunity means a separation, possibly a permanent one, with Nora, setting up a painful conflict between his love for her and love of his craft. Both actors are excellent, while Julie Christie – the same year she blazed as "Lara" in *Doctor Zhivago* (PF5) – appears in a small role as a prostitute. [Trivia note: The movie carries two directing credits – Ford and Cardiff – because Ford took ill almost at the beginning of the production and had to be replaced] [Caution: sexuality and adult themes]

19. Marty, We Hardly Knew Ye

In 1977, Martin Brest, a graduate of New York University's film school and a fellow at the American Film Institute's Center for Advanced Film Study in Los Angeles, produced the most sensational student film I've ever seen, *Hot Tomorrows* (<u>PF5</u>). I wasn't alone in my assessment. Critics all over the country raved about the 26-year-old's talent. As Gary Arnold wrote in The Washington Post, "movie freaks should recognize Brest as the next young American filmmaker with a potentially great future." He added, "Brest demonstrates a literary flair almost as distinctive as his visual flair, and ... one relishes the thought of the comedies, dramas, musicals and horror melodramas that could be simmering in his imagination." His special talent in evidence, Brest broke into the movie biz with great anticipation. What happened over the next quarter-century, however, became one of the strangest and perhaps saddest installments in Hollywood lore. After a modest success with his first feature, *Going in Style*, followed by an early misstep when he was fired as director of *WarGames* (<u>PF5</u>), Brest rebounded with two rousing smash hits in *Beverly Hills Cop* and *Midnight Run* (both also in <u>PF5</u>). He helmed *Scent of a Woman*, which won Al Pacino his only Oscar. Then he directed only two more features, the somber *Meet Joe Black* and finally *Gigli* (not on my lists) in 2003, a star vehicle for Ben Affleck and Jennifer Lopez that critics savaged unmercifully. Ever since, Brest has been inactive – reclusive, even. A shame, but a cautionary tale echoing the last line of *Patton* (<u>PF5</u>), that "all glory is fleeting." [<u>Historical note</u>: The great director David Lean, after receiving a critical thrashing in 1970 for his Irish epic *Ryan's Daughter* (<u>P25</u>), refrained from making another film for 15 years. He returned with a magnificent rendering of E.M. Forster's *A Passage to India* (<u>PF5</u>), regrettably, his last. Whether

177

Brest will attempt a comeback after what is now 19 years remains unknown]

Going in Style
1979

Expanding on the theme of inevitable death that he explored in *Hot Tomorrows* (PF5), writer–director Brest here enlists George Burns, Art Carney and the legendary Lee Strasberg in a tale about three oldsters who, feeling they have nothing left to lose, decide to rob a bank. The actors play, respectively, Joe, Al and Willie. Long retired, they while away their days in increasing fits of boredom, until Joe gets the bright idea that they should rob a bank. The other two are skeptical, with Willie even asking, "What if we get shot?" To which, Joe answers, "So what?" End of discussion. With a little bit of planning, simple disguises and three borrowed handguns, the robbery takes place and is surprisingly successful – until the emotional strain eventually proves too much for Willie, who dies of a heart attack. There's another death, as well as a bit of justice in the form of the long arm of the law. But those developments are better left discovered. Know, however, there's a scene that's emotionally overwhelming, a sober reminder of the destiny we all face, and what can happen when we're unprepared. Watching the movie's trailer you might think it's a gentle comedy about oldsters. *Going in Style* isn't without humor, but unlike the 2017 remake (P25), it packs a strong emotional punch, largely due to Burns in his best role. [Trivia note: Carney's role suggests he's a contemporary of Burns and Strasberg, but he was considerably younger than his co-stars] [Caution: language and adult themes] **[W]**

Scent of a Woman
1992

An extremely loose remake of an Italian movie of 1974 starring Vittorio Gassman, and an unusual movie in its own right, here Brest crafts a fine human drama in a two-character study that, as mentioned and incredible as it sounds, won Pacino his one and only Oscar. It also garnered Brest his one and only Best Director nomination. Pacino plays Lieutenant Colonel Frank Slade, a retired military officer whose accident-induced blindness has confined him to a permanent state of depression. His condition changes when Charlie Simms (Chris O'Donnell), a prep-school student, takes on the paid task of babysitting Slade over a Thanksgiving holiday weekend. Simms is nursing a demon of his own, resulting from his witnessing a prank carried out by some of his classmates against the headmaster of his school (James Rebhorn, master of playing weaselly characters), and from the headmaster offering him a prize recommendation letter if he fingers the pranksters. But there's a lot of drama – and some humor – before Simms encounters his inevitable showdown at school, with some excellent byplay between the two leads, plus an iconic tango performed by Pacino and a lovely restaurant patroness (Gabrielle Anwar). And that showdown? Pacino owns the scene. Hoo-ah! [Trivia notes: 1) Anwar, playing a sighted woman who tangos with Pacino, just the year before played the lead in *Wild Hearts Can't Be Broken* (not here), the biography of Sonora Webster, a woman blinded in a horse-riding accident. 2) In the original film, *Profumo di donna*, Gassman's character claims that despite his blindness he can spot beautiful women purely by their scent. Here, Frank Slade merely identifies one woman's perfume] [Caution: sexuality and adult themes] **[W]**

Meet Joe Black
1998

Brest's expansive (3 hour) reworking of the 1934 fantasy *Death Takes a Holiday* (not on this list) features Anthony Hopkins as Bill Parrish, a tycoon facing his 65th birthday and, suddenly, the prospect of confronting his mortality. That prospect arrives in the foggy persona of a spirit who identifies himself as the dark angel. Meanwhile, Bill's daughter meets a young man (Brad Pitt), who is killed in a pedestrian accident soon thereafter. And when Bill encounters the spirit again, it's now in the form of Pitt, whom Bill eventually introduces to family and friends as … Joe Black – but not before Bill and the spirit make a deal. Essentially, if Bill will instruct him in the ways of mortals, "Joe" will not summon him

179

to the afterlife. As in *Collateral Beauty*, 18 years later, some of Bill's family and associates attempt to capitalize on his suddenly strange behavior. But Joe intervenes and saves Bill's fortune – but not his life. Written by Bo Goldman, who also adapted the screenplay for *Scent of a Woman*, it's a strange and in some ways confusing plot. Among Brest's five financially successful titles, artistically this one's a near-miss. [Trivia notes: 1) About the movie's financial success: Given its lukewarm critical reception, the box office revenues were mostly incidental. *Meet Joe Black* turned out to be the first movie to feature the trailer for the new Star Wars *Episode One: The Phantom Menace* (not here). Theater owners across the country reported that many of the patrons who bought tickets watched the trailer and then left soon thereafter. 2) Hopkins and Pitt had played father and son four years earlier in *Legends of the Fall* (also not here)] [Caution: adult themes] **[W]**

20. Master Class: Kurosawa

I admit it; the man's films with one or two exceptions require extreme patience. But there's no denying his extraordinary craftsmanship and artistry. Japan's legendary director was the equivalent of America's John Ford – and both men admired each other's work. His array of period pieces is staggering. His *Seven Samurai* (PF5) is widely regarded as one of the greatest films ever made. *The Hidden Fortress* (not on my lists) became the rough model for the Star Wars saga. His *Yojimbo* (also in PF5) essentially created the template for Clint Eastwood's most iconic characters. And moviemakers all over the world have acknowledged Akira Kurosawa's influence. Here are three more of his most notable.

Rashômon
1950 – and co-written by Kurosawa

I don't often use the term "landmark" to describe a movie, but here's a case where it's entirely appropriate. The acclaimed director's pessimistic but strangely compelling drama is based on a deceptively simple premise, which has since been imitated countless times. During a deluge of a rainstorm, a woodcutter and a priest take shelter under a massive city gate. They're soon joined by a third man, who notices they both looked troubled. He asks them what's wrong, and they begin telling a story about the murder of a Samurai warrior and the rape of his wife in the forest. What they're really telling, however, is the story of a trial that had taken place three days earlier, in which the priest, the woodcutter and two other individuals, plus the Samurai's wife, shared their accounts of the events – and they all conflict with one another. The witnesses, including the notorious bandit Tajomaru (the great Toshiro Mifune, in the first of his 16 collaborations with Kurosawa), who's accused of the murder, all address the camera.

181

The trial judge and other officials remain unseen. It's as though they're making their individual pleas directly to you, the viewer. In the end, however, you're not sure who is telling the truth, who is lying and who is simply wrong. It's what has become known as the "Rashômon effect" – conflicting accounts beyond resolution. As the priest asserts in the first line of dialogue, "I can't understand it. I can't understand it at all!" He's right. But that's the point. How do you deal with not receiving a convenient answer? It can be maddening. A genuine landmark film, but again, like so many of Kurosawa's, it demands patience. The movie's title? It means "city gate," in this case in feudal Kyoto, where the story begins. [Trivia notes: 1) *Rashômon* didn't win the Best Foreign Film Oscar for the simple reason that the award didn't yet exist. So, the motion picture academy gave it a special Oscar and instituted the category the following year. 2) If the movie's music, by Fumio Hayasaka, sounds familiar, it's because the composer loosely adapted Ravel's "Bolero" for his score. 3) The Samurai's wife (played by Machiko Kyō) sports the strangest eyebrows I think I've ever seen. In real life, however, the actress's brows were reassuringly normal. She died in 2019 at age 95] [Caution: adult themes] **[B&W]**

Kagemusha
1980 – and co-written by Kurosawa

The title translates as "Shadow Warrior," and it refers to a common thief employed to impersonate a warlord who has taken ill at a critical time and dare not appear weakened to his enemies. Then, à la the delightful Kevin Kline comedy *Dave* (PF5), when the warlord dies from battle wounds, his operatives hire the thief to impersonate him permanently. Which he begins to do, and convincingly. Also as in *Dave*, veteran actor Tatsuya Nakadai plays both roles. When his deception is eventually exposed, it sets off a chain of events that culminates in a massive and decisive battle – which Kurosawa introduces with exquisite suspense – and elicits some deeply buried courage within the impersonator. That's enough of the plot because, for one thing, it's extremely complex and convoluted, and for another, given the historical and cultural aspects, it's difficult to follow under any circumstances. Nevertheless, the movie is gripping, once again because of Kurosawa's extraordinary craftsmanship. In contrast with *Rashômon's* crude black & white photography, *Kagemusha* is sharp and vividly colorful. Nominated for the Best Foreign Film Oscar, the movie won the *Palme d'Or* at Cannes. Based on a real 16th-century battle, this could be regarded as Kurosawa's masterpiece. Some scenes approach the sweep and scale of David Lean's *Lawrence of Arabia* (PF5), which I consider the greatest film ever made. The production involved thousands of costumed extras and took months and months to shoot. Obviously, an expensive proposition. That's what Toho, Kurosawa's studio, concluded when he presented *Kagemusha's* formidable (at the time) budget. Their executives balked, so none other than George Lucas and Francis Ford Coppola stepped in to cover the costs. And when the movie premiered in Tokyo, the two were joined by William Wyler and a host of other prominent directors and stars, arriving to pay homage to their formidable peer. [Trivia note: The big battle required so many skilled riders that several hundred needed to be imported from America – including equestriennes playing male warriors] [Caution: graphic violence] **[W]**

Ran
1985 – and co-written by Kurosawa

Meaning "Chaos" in Japanese, this is Kurosawa's loose adaptation of "King Lear," the story of Hidetora Ichimonji (Tatsuya Nakadai, again), a powerful feudal warlord with three sons who eventually turn against him. The intrigue begins when the elder Ichimonji divides his territory among the sons but unsatisfactorily to the two younger siblings. There's also a scheming wife, somewhat like a Lady MacBeth in that other Shakespearean tragedy, except this one is the spouse of the eldest son, and she's bitter about her family's past battles with the father. As with *Kagemusha*, the plot complexities and intrigues of *Ran* quickly multiply, with betrayals, subterfuges and lethal attacks galore. Also like *Kagemusha*, big battles develop. Though visually arresting, they're not quite on the scale of the predecessor. What's surprisingly vivid is the emotional punch carried by the interfamilial rivalries and interactions. Because of the language barrier, the words are difficult to follow, even with subtitles. But because of the actors, the powerful emotions are unmistakably conveyed. Once again, a master storyteller at work. [Trivia note: *Ran*'s production was smaller in scale than *Kagemusha*'s but not its preparation and detail. Kurosawa spent a decade planning it and had every scene storyboarded via paintings – done by his own hand – before he shot a single foot of film. Even the costumes took two years to craft] [Caution: graphic violence, including one particularly shocking scene] **[W]**

21. Master Class: Truffaut

French director François Truffaut was known not only as one of the founders of the French New Wave in the 1950s and '60s but also as arguably the moviemaker most devoted to the medium – and his encyclopedic knowledge of cinema was renowned. Truffaut spent quite a few years writing about and reviewing films – largely for the venerable French magazine *Cahiers du Cinéma* – before he began directing them. That's partly why his filmography totals a mere 21 features over a career that lasted only 24 years. Also, he died young, at age 52. Lesser known about the man was his extremely difficult childhood and rebellious youth. He fell afoul, as they say, of the law several times as a teenager, and he dropped out of school at 14. Ironic, but that background formed the basis for two of Truffaut's outstanding qualities: his vast knowledge of film and literature, and his affinity for working with children. When he ended his formal education and for the rest of his life, Truffaut read voraciously and attended movies almost every day – his encyclopedic knowledge was hard-won. His personal background also formed the character of Antoine Doinel in his acclaimed first film, *The 400 Blows* (PF5). And his love of the medium eventually drew him to make the Oscar-winning *Day for Night* (likewise in PF5), a creation that inspired one commenter to call him, "the man who loved film." Along with *Jules et Jim* (P25), plus his acting role in *Close Encounters of the Third Kind* (PF5 again), here are seven more of Truffaut's notable titles, in chronological order…

Fahrenheit 451
1966 – England
Based on the Ray Bradbury science-fiction novel of the same name, this was Truffaut directing his only English-language title (and his most difficult production). As far as the story goes, it's a

warning for the ages. In the world of Bradbury's tale, men work as firemen. But they don't put out fires – they *start* fires with the purpose of incinerating forbidden books, the titles of many of which you'll easily recognize. Guy Montag (Oskar Werner) is one such man, dutifully responding to calls to destroy unacceptable literary and intellectual properties. That is, until two things happen. First, he witnesses a woman (little-known Irish actress Bee Duffell) who loves books so much she allows herself to be burned to death with her collection rather than submit to authority. Then, he meets Clarisse (Julie Christie), a teacher who begins to open Guy's eyes about a far better world than the one in which he lives – a world in which ideas are freely promulgated via books. Both events begin to affect his thinking, eventually turning him away from his job and his service to the state and leading him to a development too good and precious to give away. About the production, it was difficult for two reasons. First, Truffaut clashed almost daily with Oskar Werner (who four years earlier had co-starred in his *Jules et Jim*), to the extent that the two ended up hating each other. And second, because Truffaut spoke almost no English, he tended to avoid contact with cast and crew in his off hours, secluding himself in his hotel room during the entire shoot. I admit this one's a marginal choice, but it's an interesting movie; as mentioned, the story presents a cautionary tale, and Bernard Herrmann contributes a chilling but beautiful score. [Viewing notes: 1) If you have the option, choose the French version with subtitles. Truffaut's unfamiliarity with English rendered the dialogue in that version stilted, awkward and occasionally grammatically incorrect. The version *en Français* is superior in that respect. 2) You'll notice there are no opening titles or written end credits. A deliberate choice, keeping with the movie's theme of the attempted destruction of written words. 3) Julie Christie's role here was her most unusual performance, for reasons that quickly will become evident] [Trivia note: Terence Stamp was originally cast as Guy. If he had played the role, he would have co-starred romantically with Christie twice in the same year; here, and in *Far from the Madding Crowd* – see P25)] [Caution: adult themes] **[W]**

186

The Wild Child
1970 – and co-written by Truffaut

Not only Truffaut's most unusual story, *L'Enfant sauvage* is one of the most unusual stories ever filmed – and it's based on a true incident. As the title suggests, the movie chronicles the discovery of Victor of Aveyron (12-year-old Jean-Pierre Cargol, in an astounding performance), a feral boy in the late 18th century in southern France. His case attracts the interest of Dr. Jean Itard (played by Truffaut), a physician specializing in deaf–mutes who first diagnoses the boy's condition and attempts to break through to him. In a sense, Truffaut designed his character to mimic the "deaf–mute" theme. The movie contains very little dialogue – which would have been difficult anyway, given the situation. Instead, he imposed a voice-over narration based on a fictional diary of Dr. Itard, who documented his work with the boy only via clinical reports. And to emphasize the theme of Victor's primitive state, Truffaut had cinematographer Néstor Almendros shoot the movie in black & white and in the pre-widescreen standard format, giving *L'Enfant sauvage* a retro look à la Kurosawa's *Rashômon*. [Trivia note: One other unusual aspect; a personal one for the director: Truffaut said later in an interview that playing Dr. Itard had created for him the sensation he was directing from in front of the camera instead of behind it] [Caution: adult themes] **[B&W]**

The Story of Adèle H.
1975 – and co-written by Truffaut

One of the giants of French literature, Victor Hugo, had two daughters, one of whom fell obsessively in love with a soldier. Adapting the story from the diary of the younger daughter, Adèle (Isabelle Adjani in her breakthrough role at age 20), Truffaut begins the story in midstream, with a young woman arriving in Halifax, Nova Scotia, in 1863 under an assumed name. She is seeking a Lieutenant Pinson (Bruce Robinson) of the British Army who is stationed there and who is her fiancé. We quickly discover, however, that the engagement is illusory, that Pinson has no interest in her and that Adèle is, essentially, stalking him. We also learn she is haunted by the drowning death of her older sister Léopoldine. The twin obsessions eventually drive Adèle to madness. Not a particularly appealing premise. But Truffaut's direction and Adjani's riveting, Oscar-nominated performance (Pauline Kael once called her acting talent "prodigious") make a powerful drama. This time, the great cinematographer Nestor Almendros has free reign, and the movie looks just grand. [Trivia notes: 1) It took Truffaut seven years to bring *L'Histoire d'Adèle H.* to the screen – the longest delay of any of his films – with difficulties ranging from obtaining the rights to Adèle's diary, financing and casting. 2) Watch for Truffaut, looking dashing, in a cameo] [Caution: adult themes] **[W]**

Small Change
1976 – and co-written by Truffaut

A deceptively simple story, marking the third and fourth time Truffaut featured a child – along with Antoine in *The 400 Blows* and Victor in *The Wild Child* – as a primary character. In some ways, it's his most sympathetic exploration of the theme. Known in France and elsewhere as *L'Argent de poche* ("Pocket Money"), it involves the youngest residents of the town of Thiers in central France. Patrick (Georges Desmouceaux), whose mother has died, is just beginning to notice the opposite sex. His pal Julien (Philippe Goldmann) must deal with physical abuse at home. Both boys, along with their schoolmates, live an otherwise ordinary smalltown life, alternating between humor and pathos – the latter involving Julien and his predicament. It's relatively low-key but captivating. Low-key? One of the highlights is an innocent first kiss. The ending includes an admonishment by one of the kids' teachers for parents and adults to love and protect children. Truffaut, given his background, must have believed it passionately. And I can't think of another director – except for perhaps Steven Spielberg – who has shown more skill working with the youngest actors. **[W]**

The Man Who Loved Women
1977 – and co-written by Truffaut

No two ways about it, Bertrand Morane (Charles Denner) adores women. Young, old, tall, short and otherwise, they captivate him and dominate his thoughts. He can wax endlessly about the shape of their legs and the flow of their skirts. And he attracts and beds them by the dozens. Then, in his prime, he dies in a pedestrian accident. At his funeral appear many of his former conquests, each reacting in her own way to his loss. One of them, Geneviève (Brigitte Fossey), observes the procession of feminine pulchritude and reminisces about her own relationship with Bertrand. In the process, she opens a lengthy flashback sequence that reveals the story: Before his untimely death, Bertrand had been lovingly chronicling his relationships in book form, thereby leaving an unfinished manuscript. I have no proof of this, but I suspect Truffaut wrote *L'homme Qui Aimait les Femmes* as a counterpoint to Bertrand Blier's *Calmos* (P25), released the previous year. In that film, Blier presented the idea that men actually hate women because they are incapable of understanding them. Here, Truffaut posits a somewhat opposite view; that some men not only understand women but can easily seduce them with compliments and enthusiasm. Yet, just like the two protagonists in *Calmos*, women ultimately become Bertrand's undoing. Comedic, yes, but as with all of Truffaut's films, underpinned by drama. As Geneviève comments at Bertrand's funeral, "I have no doubt that he loved them all, in his way. And he was right to. Each one has something the other doesn't. Each one is unique. Bertrand loved them all as they were." [Trivia notes: 1) Speaking of Spielberg (see above), Truffaut drafted his script during idle moments while working for the director on *Close Encounters*. 2) One of Bertrand's most prominent conquests is a character named Vera, played by Leslie Caron in a small but vivid role. 3) Six years later, director Blake Edwards attempted a remake co-starring Burt Reynolds and Julie Andrews. It bombed] [Caution: sexuality] **[W]**

The Green Room
1978 – and co-written by Truffaut

Here's a particular favorite of mine among Truffaut's films. I feel compelled to state as much because I'm the only person I know who liked it. Everyone else seemed either indifferent or outright repelled. Gary Arnold particularly despised it, writing in The Washington Post, "Although obviously conceived in utterly sincere homage to [Henry] James, the resulting hybrid is so stilted and literal minded – and so trivialized by Truffaut's own autobiographical marginalia – that it would surely have James himself fit to be tied." Yet, I admire it. Arguably his most personal film, it's based on a James short story, "The Altar of the Dead," with references to two others. *La Chambre Verte* follows Julien Davenne (played by Truffaut), a newspaperman in a French town in the late 1920s who is responsible for writing obituaries. That's his job, but death is his obsession, particularly the death of his wife Julie. Struggling to keep her memory alive, Julien uses a … green room in his home as a shrine to her. Then, when fire destroys the room, he transfers the shrine to an abandoned chapel in the town and further expands it to include memorials to those buried in the chapel's cemetery. The process builds to a stunning scene in which the extent of Julien's memorial – and his obsession – is revealed. As with *The Wild Child*, Truffaut spent seven years developing the story. Not anybody's idea of casual viewing, it's nevertheless an engrossing character study. In an interview, Truffaut said he wanted "to show on screen a man who refuses to forget the dead." He does so, and in the process contributes a solid and sympathetic performance. [Caution: adult themes] **[W]**

Love on the Run
1979 – and co-written by Truffaut

Truffaut's first film, *The 400 Blows* (PF5), introduced the character of Antoine Doinel (Jean-Pierre Léaud), a wayward young boy. Here, exactly 20 years later, Truffaut portrays Doinel (Léaud again) as a grown man and still thoroughly perplexed by the ways of the opposite sex. In between, Truffaut had featured the character in two other films, *Stolen Kisses* and *Bed and Board*, both also starring Léaud, with the quartet eventually comprising what's now known as the Antoine Doinel Cycle. *L'amour en fuite* picks up where *Domicile conjugal* had left off, with Antoine and his wife Christine (Claude Jade – yes, this "Claude" is a woman) reunited. Except that Antoine cannot seem to keep his (ahem) to himself, and the couple divorces. The split leaves Antoine to seek new relationships, which he does seemingly with abandon – at least, for a while. Then, further complications arise, casting doubt on whether Antoine will ever find lasting love again. Will Truffaut leave us hanging? No. He closes out the saga with a glimmer of hope in a clever fade-out. And as one of the participants in that fade-out (French singer Dorothée – aka Frédérique Hoschedé) declares, "I'm totally under your spell, you bastard!" [Trivia note: The character of Liliane, one of Antoine's lovers, is played by French actress Dani. Coincidentally, she and Léaud also played lovers six years earlier in *Day for Night*. So, when Truffaut needed a flashback of the couple, he lifted one of their scenes from the previous movie] [Caution: sexuality] **[W]**

Trivia postscript to Truffaut

I noted his nifty cameo in *The Story of Adèle H*, but that wasn't his only brief appearance where he hadn't officially joined the cast. Truffaut, who wrote a fine 1967 biography, Hitchcock, paid periodic homage to the legendary director, who was the king of cameos. Beginning with *The 400 Blows*, Truffaut inserted himself into seven more of his films.

22. Master Class: Rohmer

I mentioned that François Truffaut was one of the founders of the French New Wave of filmmakers. Éric Rohmer was the last of the New Wavers, getting his start as a writer–director well after his colleagues had already become established. Like Truffaut, he wrote for a time for *Cahiers du Cinéma*. Despite the late start, Rohmer managed to carve a creative niche for himself, persisting as an *auteur* long after most of the others had passed on. You could call him the cinematic version of a short-story writer. Not that Rohmer's titles are unusually short – though a few of them are, very. They just seem to pass by quickly, offering vignettes of ordinary life and concentrating on that eternal topic, interactions and misunderstandings between men and women. On the other hand, his repertoire consists mostly of groups of movies, thematically linked and released under collective titles such as "Tales of the Four Seasons," "Six Moral Tales," and so on – hence, the short-story analogy. Regarding his creative niche, Rohmer frequently used unusual techniques. For example, he rarely employed experienced actors, preferring to work with novices and non-professionals. He also avoided complex camerawork – he even used close-ups sparingly – an approach that gave his films a sense of what's called neorealism: as though you're observing real life, not a movie. Most of all, Rohmer's films present literate dialogue – you want to *hear* what all of the characters are saying (or, not miss the subtitles) because what they're saying is interesting and often meaningful. That's a timeless quality. How about instead of CGI-based epics with bloated budgets and standard plots, sometime try one of these six gossamer tales by Rohmer, plus one of his rare dramas. In chronological order…

Claire's Knee
1970 – and written by Rohmer

Starting with the fifth of his "Six Moral Tales," it's the simplest of this bunch. But it is also Rohmer's most popular, a story about a grown man's fixation on a beautiful teenager's knee. Nothing more to add, except that Vincent Canby of The New York Times called *Le Genou de Claire* "close to a perfect film," and I have personally witnessed audiences erupting into gleeful applause the moment the man's hand (chastely) touches said knee. With Jean-Claude Brialy as the man and 16-year-old Laurence de Monaghan as the girl. [Caution: mild sexuality] **[W]**

Chloé in the Afternoon
1972 – and written by Rohmer

Now titled *L'Amour l'Après-midi* ("Love in the Afternoon," not to be confused with the Billy Wilder comedy of the same name – see P25), it concerns Frédéric (Bernard Verley), a successful and happily married businessman who begins what he thinks will be a platonic affair with an old flame, the eponymous Chloé (actress, model and singer Zouzou). Frédéric is married to Hélène (Françoise Verley, Barnard's real-life wife), who has already given him a son and is pregnant again. Frédéric by all appearances *should* be happy. Yet he misses the single life when he could pursue any romantic attraction he wished. Then Chloé suddenly re-emerges, destitute. Frédéric immediately springs to her aid, first by giving her a secretarial job and then by spending an increasing number of … afternoons with her. Eventually, they both are confronted with the opportunity to cast off the sexless nature of their affair, and Frédéric must choose between the wife he loves and the woman he again desires. The last of Rohmer's "Six Moral Tales," nothing tests personal morality more than the opportunity for sexual adventure. [Caution: sexuality] **[W]**

The Marquise of O
1976 – Germany – and written by Rohmer

Rohmer received a *Grand Prix Spécial du Jury* for this one at the Cannes Film Festival, the event's second-highest honor and the only such award he ever won. It's an early 19th-century mystery about rape and redemption. A mystery because, in the beginning, no one is sure that a rape actually took place. The Marquise of the title (Edith Clever) places an announcement in the local paper of an Italian town (yes, a French director making a film in Germany, in German, with a German cast but set in Italy). A widow, the Marquise [Mar-KEE-sah] claims she is nevertheless pregnant, the father is unknown, and she demands that he immediately present himself to her. Even after repeated tries, no one owns up to the deed. We then flash back some weeks to see the Marquise's estate being overrun by Russian soldiers, some of whom gather together to rape her. The men are stopped, however, by their commander, the Count (the great Bruno Ganz in an early role), who orders them away and urges the Marquise's servants to give her a sedative to help her rest and recover from the trauma. You might guess where the plot develops from there – or not. I'll only say that in either case it becomes an engrossing if stagey drama involving the couple. [Caution: adult themes] **[W]**

Pauline at the Beach
1983 – and written by Rohmer
One of Rohmer's "Comedies and Proverbs," it concerns a teenager's sexual awakening, which begins on a vacation … at the beach with her older cousin. Pauline (Amanda Langlet), a bit of an awkward and gangly girl, is new and unknown to the ways of *amour*. Meanwhile, Cousin Marion (Anelle Dombasle), a gorgeous young woman, has had several such experiences, including a failed marriage. As the story develops, Marion interacts with various men, while Pauline essentially sits back and observes the sexual dynamics. Things change, and rapidly, when she meets Sylvain (Simon de la Brosse), a local teenager on whom she quickly develops a crush. But Sylvain, being a teenage boy, and not a particularly bright one, inadvertently hurts Pauline, and she ends her vacation a bit saddened but more experienced, and made a little wiser by her brief ordeal. I'd call it standard Rohmer, but that would seem demeaning. Better to describe it as typical of his keen observational skills. [Viewing note: If you happen to see the

movie's poster, it features a lovely blonde looking toward a boy and girl sitting among beachgoers. The blonde isn't Pauline; it's Marion, while Pauline is sitting in the background with Sylvain] [Caution: plentiful sexuality] **[W]**

Boyfriends and Girlfriends
1987 – and written by Rohmer

The last of the "Comedies and Proverbs," *L'Ami de mon amie* concerns angst and mutual discovery among young adults in suburban Paris. As the title suggests (the French version is "My Girlfriend's Boyfriend"), it involves coupling – specifically, five young adults with four them romantically linked as pairs. There's Lea (Sophie Renoir), who's been going with Fabien (Éric Viellard). There's Adrienne (Anne-Laure Meury), paired with Alexandre (François-Éric Gendron). And there's Blanche (Emmanuelle Chaulet), currently unattached. Don't worry about the alignments. Just know that at the end of the movie they'll be somewhat different from the beginning. An interesting aspect: The story's setting is Cergy-Pontoise, a brand new (at the time) complex on the northwest outskirts of Paris. Far from the iconic and unique landmarks of the City of Lights, Cergy-Pontoise resembles hundreds or even thousands of similar commercial–residential developments that have sprung up outside urban areas across the globe. The location gives the story a bit of universality. [Trivia note: Among the actors and actresses I've mentioned in this entire volume, Ms. Renoir holds arguably the most impressive pedigree. She's the great-granddaughter of the painter, Pierre-Auguste Renoir; grand-niece of director Jean Renoir and the daughter of cinematographer Claude Renoir] [Caution: mild sexuality] **[W]**

A Tale of Winter
1992 – and written by Rohmer

If the title brings to mind Shakespeare's "The Winter's Tale," you can be forgiven, because the two works bear striking similarities. For example, both involve a woman torn between the loves of two men. For another, both involve a child of uncertain parentage –

though leave it to Rohmer to cast his own spin and subtle variations on the theme. Despite the title, the movie begins in summer. Félicie (Charlotte Véry), a young woman on holiday, meets and falls in love with Charles (Frédéric van den Driessche), a cook. The two enjoy a brief summer fling, which Félicie wants to extend even after she returns home. She gives Charles her address and urges him to stay in contact. The problem is, it's the wrong address. Flash forward five years, and Félicie has a five-year-old daughter, Élise, assumedly Charles's, with whom she lost touch. Complicated enough, but Félicie has since been having two concurrent affairs; one with Maxence (Michel Voletti), her employer; and another with Loïc (Hervé Furic), a librarian. Stuck in indecision, she attends a performance of "The Winter's Tale," is struck by the identical predicament of the character Queen Hermione (who also has given birth to a fatherless daughter) and decides to leave them both. Then, Charles suddenly reappears! As with Rohmer's other films, the plot points in *Conte d-Hiver*, the second of his "Tales of the Four Seasons," seem less important than the fascinating characters and how they interact. I liked what critic Roger Ebert said about this movie; "There is sadness in [Rohmer's] work, but not gloom." [Caution: sexuality] **[W]**

23. A Masterful Septet

Here's a variation on the theme of the last three segments. Instead of one exceptional filmmaker, I'm covering seven acknowledged international masters of cinema, craftsmen whose work is either imitated repeatedly or is so unique it's inimitable. Not that their movies are perfect or universally acclaimed. Every one of them has been panned, occasionally, either by the critics or the public at large. Nevertheless, they've all created movies that have thrilled, amused or simply entertained legions of sophisticated fans, and here I offer one such example from each, in directorial alphabetical order.

After the Rehearsal
1984 – Sweden – written and directed by Ingmar Bergman

If you're seeking imitators of the venerable Swedish director you need look no further than Woody Allen. Like Bergman, the Wood Man has written or co-written almost all of his movies, and he has made several attempts at "scaling Mount Bergman," as Gary Arnold once described Allen's folly. They include the somber *Interiors* and the awkward and unfunny *Midsummer Night's Sex Comedy* (neither among my favorites). But Allen never even approached the sheer raw honesty of Bergman's work. I think you can trace that quality to the man's background; a strict religious, Scandinavian upbringing by a disciplinarian minister of a father. Instead of suppressing the young Ernst Ingmar, however, the restrictions merely encouraged him to look elsewhere for fulfillment – to "the smell of eternity, the coloured sunlight quivering above the strangest vegetation of medieval paintings … there was everything that one's imagination could desire" – as he wrote in his memoir Laterna Magica ("The Magic Lantern"). Somehow, Bergman's childhood and upbringing helped create one of the world's finest filmmakers, and *After the Rehearsal*, one of his television features, reinforces his reputation. It's all the more impressive because of its brevity. At just over 70 minutes, it's the cinematic equivalent of a one-act play. Theater director Henrik Vogler (longtime Bergman regular Erland Josephson) is preparing a production of August Strindberg's early 20th-century "A Dream Play." He's backstage after a ... rehearsal, as his character says, "to reflect on the day's work in solitude" (actually, he's been dozing). Then cast-member Anna (Lena Olin in an early but sensational performance) bursts in, and her appearance sets off a flashback to Vogler's earlier affair with Anna's mother, Rakel (Ingrid Thulin). But that's just a pretext for the real themes of the story: the difficulty of creating collaborative art and the minefield of combining personal and professional relationships. As always, Bergman explores the themes through his strength: dialogue. What passes between Henrik and Anna, and Henrik and Rakel, is plain but penetrating, subtle but with emotional clarity and altogether satisfying. If I hadn't created this category, I would have placed *Efter repetitionen* right at the beginning of the book, because it's "Adult, in the Best Sense." As Gary wrote in his review for The Washington Post, the movie is "the most artful and eloquent valedictory address a great stage and screen director ever composed." [Caution: adult themes] **[W]**

That Obscure Object of Desire (and) *Un Chien Andalou*
1977 and 1929 – France and Spain – both co-written and directed by Luis Buñuel

What you need to know about Buñuel is that he was notorious for creating bizarre, surrealistic storylines. In the previous volume, I devoted a short chapter to France's Bertrand Blier, arguably Buñuel's closest filmmaking cousin in that respect. The difference between the two, however, is that Blier stuck almost exclusively to comedy, while Buñuel often veered well into drama and violence – often grotesquely. That isn't the case here, in his last film. It's a comedy, and a romantic comedy at that – though the old master can't resist inserting a bit of violence, both domestic and political. Come to think of it, this is as close as Buñuel has ever come to the theme Blier continually explored: the comic inability of men to understand or avoid becoming addled by women. Told in flashback, it's the story of an aging aristocrat (Fernando Rey, who played the cunning drug-smuggler in *The French Connection* – PF5) who falls for a beautiful young woman, which is where his troubles begin. The movie's gimmick is that the woman – the object of desire – is actually played by *two* actresses, Carole Bouquet and Angela Molina. Moreover, Buñuel doesn't even pretend to have the pair behave or even look alike. He simply switches them into and out of the story at will. It's a uniquely funny bit, and though the movie meanders somewhat it's an entertaining, sophisticated, occasionally outrageous comedy about the eternal conflict between the sexes. But be forewarned: Even in a comedy, Buñuel can't resist spoiling what appears to be a happy ending. [Caution: violence and plentiful sexuality] **[W]**

* * *

I'm not counting *Un Chien Andalou* ("An Andalusian Dog") in my 500 here, nor do I consider it a favorite. But I've included it because 1) at 20 minutes it's a quick screening, and 2) it was Buñuel's first effort, done with surrealist painter Salvador Dali, and therefore it bookends with *Cet obscur objet du désir*. Briefly described, not only is there no plot but the two collaborators deliberately attempted to avoid making any sense whatsoever. Instead, they present a long, long string of unrelated images. Conventional entertainment it isn't, but worth a look for its glimpse at a budding international talent. [Trivia note: The man you see at the beginning is Buñuel] [Caution: disturbing images and sexuality] **[B&W] [Silent]**

Postscript to Buñuel

His sense of dark humor extended even to his own demise. He once joked that at the reading of his will, where his family would be gathered presumably in anticipation, he would direct his attorney to invite billionaire and politician Nelson Rockefeller. Then the attorney would announce that Buñuel had bequeathed his entire estate to Rockefeller! Laughing, he mused at how his relations would no doubt storm away in anger and curse his memory forever.

Beauty and the Beast
1946 – France – written and directed by Jean Cocteau
You might be familiar with the 2017 box-office blockbuster or the 1991 Disney animated feature (neither on my lists), or maybe the hit television series of the late 1980s. Also, there was a 1976 made-for-TV movie starring, of all people, George C. Scott, looking like a humanoid wild boar as the Beast, not to mention several other iterations in cinema and on the small screen. This, however, was the first and in some ways still the best interpretation of Jeanne-Marie Leprince de Beaumont's 18th-century tale of a beautiful young woman who falls in love with a ... beast. Known as *La Belle et la Bête* in France – and, for some strange reason, in England – it's Cocteau's haunting, surreal romance. The Beast, tyrannical ruler of the land, threatens to kill a man for trespassing unless he is willing to offer his daughter as a concubine. The man is the father of Belle (Josette Day), who accepts her fate to spare his life. Belle arrives at the Beast's haunted and magical castle, preparing for the worst. But instead of facing an evil creature, she finds him surprisingly disarming, to the point where he eventually wins her heart. Crudely made by today's standards, *Beauty and the Beast* remains a cult classic. [Language note: As anyone with even a year of French in school should know, articles accompanying nouns in the language are either the masculine "*le*" or the feminine "*la*." So, it's curious why the obviously male *Bête* of the movie's title is given the feminine modifier] [Trivia notes: 1) One aspect of the movie that, essentially, created the mold for all subsequent versions was the Beast's noble nature. It was by Cocteau's design. He wanted the audience to fall for the Beast as well. He succeeded to the point where (spoiler alert) when the Beast is transformed into a handsome but dull prince, certain moviegoers rejected the change, complaining about the denouement. Greta Garbo, for instance, reportedly declared, "Give me back my Beast!" and Marlene Dietrich uttered something similar. 2) Around the time of the movie's release, Walt Disney was considering an animated

version. But when he saw Cocteau's film he declined, thinking his people could not match such artistry] **[B&W]**

8-1/2

1963 – Italy – co-written and directed by Federico Fellini

Otto e mezzo, so named because Fellini had previously directed seven films plus two shorts, might be called indescribable. It's the director's imagination realized on a grand, big-budget scale. Where *Day for Night* (PF5) was François Truffaut's love letter to the process of moviemaking, you could say this was Fellini's therapy session on the same subject. I won't even try to describe the plot. Instead, think of *8-1/2* as an exercise in stream-of-consciousness filmmaking. Consider also that 1) Fellini basically made up the story as he went along, and 2) he didn't record any of the dialogue while the actors were speaking because he wanted to be free to yell instructions to them during filming. Instead, they had to loop – as the task is called in the trade – their dialogue later on in the studio, something that allowed Fellini to alter their lines even after filming had completed. What emerged here is an admittedly confusing but undeniably mesmerizing concoction. It stars Marcello Mastroianni as Fellini's alter ego, a director suffering creative block while trying to complete, of all things, an epic sci-fi picture; and French star Anouk Aimée as his wife. Winner of Oscars for Best Foreign Film and Best Costume Design, *8-1/2* remains a perennial favorite among critics and fans the world over, and many other filmmakers have liberally stolen from its scenes and concepts. For example, Woody Allen's dreadful *Stardust Memories* (not on my lists) is a pale imitation. [Viewing note: I mentioned Fellini not recording any of the dialogue live and requiring his actors to loop their lines later in a recording studio. You'll probably be focusing on the subtitles (and I always recommend avoiding whenever possible versions of foreign-language movies that have been dubbed into English), but you'll notice that in certain scenes what you're hearing from the actors does not match the movement of their lips. That's because of the altered dialogue in the looping process] [Trivia note: You might recognize Madeleine Lebeau among the cast. She played Yvonne, the nightclub performer smitten with Rick Blaine (Humphrey Bogart) in the immortal *Casablanca* (PF5) 20 years earlier] [Caution: sexuality] **[B&W]**

Boudu Saved from Drowning
1932 – France – written and directed by Jean Renoir

Director Renoir was renowned for his political and social satires such as *La Grande Illusion* (PF5) and *Rules of the Game* (not on my lists), and *Boudu Sauvé des Eaux* provides one of his earlier examples. Boudu (Michel Simon) is a wretch … saved from attempted suicide in the Seine by Edouard Lestingois (Charles Granval), a kindly local merchant who immediately brings him home. From there, well, it's better and more enjoyable to discover on your own. François Truffaut once wrote about Renoir, "I think Renoir is the only filmmaker who's practically infallible, who has never made a mistake on film. And I think if he never made mistakes, it's because he always found solutions based on simplicity – human solutions." Fifty-four years later, writer–director Paul Mazursky attempted a remake, *Down and Out in Beverly Hills* (not here), a cringeworthy attempt with Nick Nolte assuming the "Boudu" role, and Richard Dreyfuss and Bette Midler as the wealthy couple that takes him in. [Trivia note: If Boudu looks familiar, you might remember him as the gruff and stubborn but heroic "Papa Bull" in 1963's *The Train* (PF5)] **[B&W]**

The Leopard
1963 – Italy – co-written and directed by Luchino Visconti

In some ways, the odyssey of *The Leopard* (*Il Gattopardo* in Italy and *Le Guépard* in France – it was an Italian–French co-production) parallels the fate of Abel Gance's *Napoleon* (PF5) nearly four decades earlier. Distributors kept trimming its original 195-minute running time (the length for its premiere at Cannes, where it won the *Palme d'Or*) until the version shown in America ran 161 minutes. Thirty-four minutes might not seem like a lot in a feature running nearly 4 hours, but the missing footage severely disrupted the plot and resulted in a strong negative critical reaction. It eventually took 20 years for the original version to be restored, at which time the film received the praise it rightfully deserved. Burt Lancaster stars as Don Fabrizio Corbera, a 19th-century Sicilian nobleman during the long and tempestuous period of Italy's *Risorgimento*, or unification, slowly transforming it from a fractious collection of city–states into a single nation. Yes, much of the film involves political intrigue. But what elevates it to international-classic status is its exquisite portrayal of the upper-class life of that era; in particular, the extraordinary, 45-minute ballroom scene, with its hundreds of elegantly dressed nobility lit by thousands of candles. Few interior sequences before or since have been so breathtaking. Gorgeously shot by Giuseppe Rotunno, the supporting cast features Alain Delon and Claudia Cardinale in early roles. [Trivia notes: 1) At first, Visconti and Lancaster (the only American in the cast) clashed frequently on the set. But finally Lancaster lashed back so furiously that he convinced the director he could display enough passion to carry the role. The two eventually became friends, with Lancaster calling him, "the finest director I've ever worked with." He also appeared in Visconti's *Conversation Piece* (not on my lists) a decade later. 2) Lancaster again played an Italian nobleman in 1976, as the *Padrone* in Bernardo Bertolucci's *1900* (P25). 3) Martin Scorsese once declared *The Leopard* his favorite film, something that no doubt influenced his nearly manic pursuit of period authenticity, down to the smallest detail, 30 years later in his own portrayal of upper-class life, *The Age of Innocence* (also in P25)] **[W]**

The Magnificent Ambersons
1942 – written and directed by Orson Welles

Few moviemakers will fail to acknowledge the enormous influence Welles had on their creative evolution, particularly from 1941's *Citizen Kane* (PF5). If nothing else, the very idea of a 25-year-old writer–director–star behind one of the all-time classics is astounding. His follow-up, a lushly produced rendition of Booth Tarkington's Pulitzer Prize-winning novel, stood as the most anticipated release of the following year. That said, in the annals of Hollywood, *The Magnificent Ambersons* remains one of its most troubled and controversial productions. An exaggeration?

Consider that audience cards at preview screenings were routinely and equally divided between those calling Welles's new work a masterpiece and those who hated it so much they thought he should never be allowed to direct again. Consider also that although accounts differ, the RKO studio's supervising editor (and future Oscar-winning director) Robert Wise was ordered to remove between 25 minutes and a full hour of the finished film. Worse, that excised footage was destroyed and is permanently lost. Where was Welles during the process? He had been ordered by RKO to go to Brazil to produce a goodwill documentary during the early days of World War II – a project he never finished. When he returned and saw what had been done to his film, he was furious. He was particularly angry at Wise, whom he said must have done his editing "with a lawnmower." They didn't speak again for decades. Bernard Herrmann, the film's composer, became so angry at the music editing he demanded that his name be removed from the credits. To this day, 80 years later, *The Magnificent Ambersons* remains incomplete, with its ending radically changed by RKO. [Historical note: Those screenings, in which preview audiences panned the movie's somber ending, were held soon after Pearl Harbor, when most of America remained in shock at the Japanese attack on the American Navy. Understandably, many moviegoers weren't in the mood for unhappy endings]

*   *   *

Why recommend the movie? Because it is brilliant in parts. Because it remains a lavish and fascinating glimpse at Midwest American society in the late 19th and early 20th centuries. And because, after all, it's Orson Welles, still in his 20s, showing flashes of genius and promise like few in Hollywood ever have. One example: Welles insisted on building a set representing the entire interior of the Ambersons' three-story mansion, something never tried before, not even in *Gone With the Wind* (PF5). The edifice allowed Welles's cameras to follow the characters from room to room and floor to floor. Give it a look, and see what you think. [One small bit of trivia: The main poster for the movie was created by another American icon, Norman Rockwell] **[B&W]**

204

24. Master of Masters: Wyler

I couldn't present a group of acknowledged masters of cinema without paying tribute to the other American (along with Orson Welles) in their midst, William "Willi" Wyler, who directed 87 films in a career that spanned half a century. He worked in both the silent and sound eras, in black & white and in color, in standard formats and in epic widescreen. Master of Masters? Yes. What else would you call someone who won more Best Picture Oscars (3) than anyone else, including a Best Director Oscar with each? Only the legendary John Ford, with four, won more director's accolades. Wyler's third Best Picture, *Ben-Hur* (PF5), is tied for the most Oscar wins: 11. He holds the record for Best Director nominations: 12. And here's the topper. His combined cast of actors and actresses earned 36 Academy Award nominations and won 14, by far the most for any director. I covered four favorites – *The Best Years of Our Lives*, *Roman Holiday*, *Ben-Hur* and *Funny Girl* – in PF5. I added four more – *The Westerner*, *The Desperate Hours*, *The Big Country* and *The Children's Hour* – in P25, plus two of his World War II documentaries, both shot in the midst of combat, *The Memphis Belle* and *Thunderbolt*. Add the following five, and Willi Wyler becomes, arguably, the unsurpassed master of the medium. In chronological order…

Dodsworth
1936

Wyler directs the great Walter Huston playing Sam Dodsworth, a retired businessman caught in a marital crisis. The drama earned Wyler his first of those unsurpassed 12 Best Director nominations. The crisis involves Sam's wife, Fran (Ruth Chatterton), who had been supremely bored with her life during his working years but suddenly finds herself liberated and uninhibited during a transatlantic cruise to Europe. She's liberated to the point of engaging in a series of flings, first with the young and dashing Captain Lockert (David Niven), then with playboy Arnold Iselin (Paul Lucas) and last with sophisticated nobleman Baron Von Obersdorf (Gregory Gaye). Those aren't the only challenges to the marriage, however. During Fran's liberation, Sam meets Edith (Mary Astor), an attractive divorcée whom he finds *sympatico*. Fran's dalliances and Sam's love affair drive a wide wedge between them, and their differences seem irreconcilable despite their becoming grandparents. Resolving those differences is the stuff of excellent drama. [Trivia note: Astor faced challenges of her own during the production as she was experiencing a scandalous divorce] **[B&W]**

Wuthering Heights
1939

Made during what many cinephiles – myself included – regard as Hollywood's best year, and garnering Wyler his second Best Director nomination, *Wuthering Heights* is considered one of the greatest romantic tragedies ever filmed. A partial adaptation of the 19th-century Emily Brontë novel, the story of doomed lovers Heathcliff (Laurence Olivier in his first significant screen role) and Cathy (the hypnotic Merle Oberon) experiencing passion, withdrawal, estrangement and reconciliation has reduced generations of fans to tears. I regard Wyler's Oscar nomination more deserved than for *Dodsworth* because he managed to create this classic despite the constant conflicts he encountered with the cast. That assessment applied particularly to a young, flamboyant and self-centered Olivier. The conflict arose from Olivier's extensive stage experience but his limited familiarity with performing for the screen. As I've mentioned occasionally in my books, the stage requires projection while film demands subtlety. At the beginning, Olivier had none, and he and Wyler battled almost daily over the director's insistence on doing many, many retakes. At one point, an exhausted Olivier complained that he had done a scene every possible way and asked the director what else he wanted. Wyler responded, "I want you to do it better." He did, and his portrayal of the self-tortured Heathcliff remains among his best. Credit also goes to Greg Toland's gorgeous, Oscar-winning cinematography and the literate script by Ben Hecht and Charles MacArthur, with a few choice insertions by a young John Huston. It's a chick flick, but a great one. [Trivia note: Speaking of Hecht, whose screenwriting reputation grew with each passing year, he was invited to Hollywood in the late 1920s by Herman Mankiewicz, the writer of *Citizen Kane* (PF5), via what some have called the most legendary telegram in movie history:

WILL YOU ACCEPT THREE HUNDRED PER WEEK TO WORK FOR PARAMOUNT PICTURES. ALL EXPENSES PAID. THE THREE HUNDRED IS PEANUTS. MILLIONS ARE TO BE GRABBED OUT HERE AND YOUR ONLY COMPETITION IS IDIOTS. DON'T LET THIS GET AROUND.

Hecht, broke at the time and living in New York, hurried to L.A. and proceeded to turn out superior screenplays for the next quarter century – including his Oscar-nominated work for *Wuthering Heights*] **[B&W]**

Mrs. Miniver
1942

In Wyler's first Best Picture and Best Director winner, Greer Garson stars in the title role (although the title has a double meaning). She plays Kay Miniver, a British housewife and remarried widow living outside London with her second husband, Clem (Walter Pidgeon), and their family as the specter of war with Hitler's Germany looms. When war breaks out, their son Vin (Richard Ney) joins the Royal Air Force, becomes a fighter pilot and joins the action. By arrangement with his parents, Vin buzzes the family home each time he returns from a mission. Clem takes the family boat to Dunkirk, France, to help with the evacuation of stranded British and French troops. While he's away, Kay encounters a downed Nazi pilot (Helmut Dantine), who temporarily takes her hostage. Eventually, the war affects them even more when their home is partially destroyed. Nevertheless, the Minivers, and their fellow citizens, soldier on, even participating in the local town's annual garden show. The winning rose is named the "Mrs. Miniver." But the war continues, bringing unexpected casualties both to the family and the community. The twin tragedies lead to the movie's centerpiece, a rousing, heartrending sermon by the local minister (Henry Wilcoxon) delivered in the town's partially destroyed church. The sermon so moved President Franklin Delano Roosevelt that he ordered a recording of it to be broadcast by radio stations across America. And the movie, and its patriotic climax, energized audiences in England and America alike. Winner of four other Oscars, including for Garson as Best Actress, for Theresa Wright in a supporting role, and for its screenplay and cinematography; next to *Casablanca* (PF5), *Mrs. Miniver* remains the most iconic movie about civilians in World War II ever made. [Trivia notes: 1) They might have played mother and son here, but Garson and Ney – who was 11 years younger – married the following year. 2) Dantine, an Austrian by birth, often played Nazis during the '40s. He also played the young refugee husband in *Casablanca*, the next Best Picture winner. 3) No doubt part of Wilcoxon's motivation for his sermon scene was personal. His brother Robert had been killed while assisting in the Dunkirk evacuation] **[B&W]**

Friendly Persuasion
1956
Here's another story directed by Wyler about a family trying to hold together and persist despite gathering war clouds. But unlike *Mrs. Miniver*, it doesn't serve as a rallying cry for resistance against tyranny; it's a paean to pacifism. It begins innocently enough, with a sampler image that dissolves into a real setting à la *Meet Me in St. Louis* (PF5), followed by a delightful sequence involving a crafty goose tormenting a young boy. One by one, we then meet the Birdwells, including Gary Cooper and Dorothy McGuire as Jess and Eliza, devout Quakers and parents of three children. They seem to be living a pleasant life in 1862 in southern Indiana amid a peaceful farming community and among their "friends," as members of the faith call one another. This being Wyler, however, intense human drama must inevitably appear,

which it does as the war between the states reaches the Birdwells and their neighbors directly. The story deals with their moral conflict when they encounter Union and Confederate troops in combat, and when their older son (Anthony Perkins in his second film role) joins the fight. Cooper adopted a variation of his Oscar-winning performance in *Sergeant York* (<u>PF5</u>), but it seems awkward and less authentic here. Indeed, Cooper and Wyler argued frequently about the character. McGuire is more natural and appealing as Eliza, who becomes a force of nature when defending that goose, her beloved pet Samantha, from hungry soldiers. The battle scenes notwithstanding, *Friendly Persuasion* is a captivating, humane portrayal of a family and a community caught up in forces beyond their control, and it's a powerful drama about the deepest convictions of the heart and soul. The international community must have agreed, because the movie won the coveted *Palme d'Or* at Cannes. Dmitri Tiomkin composed the lovely score, and Pat Boone sang the popular title song. [<u>Critic's note</u>: A quibble, actually. To save money, Allied Artists required Wyler to shoot the movie in the San Fernando Valley, and despite the production crew's best efforts to disguise the location, it's definitely California] **[W]**

How to Steal a Million
1966

The venerable Wyler, late in his career, tried his hand at a romantic caper comedy set in Paris and carried it off divertingly. Peter O'Toole and Audrey Hepburn co-star as a most unusual pair of art thieves in the service of Hugh Griffith, who plays Audrey's father. They conspire to steal a supposedly priceless work of Italian sculptor Cellini: his "Venus." It's currently on display at the fictitious Kléber-Lafayette Museum, and Audrey, for reasons necessary to the plot, must steal it. So, she enlists O'Toole's character because she believes him to be an art thief. But in this story very little of anything is what it seems, and truth be told most of the plot, by veteran screenwriter Harry Kurnitz, is an excuse for the gorgeous couple to make eyes at each other while Audrey sports a series of dazzling gowns by Givenchy. John

Williams (then, "Johnny") composed the score, his first notable work. Also notable was the appearance of Eli Wallach in a straight role as an art-loving tycoon. **[W]**

25. Men at Work

Hollywood sometimes veers from its staples of thrillers, romantic comedies and special-effects extravaganzas to make movies about people pursuing their crafts and livelihoods, often when those activities involve extreme danger, but sometimes simply pursuing the objects of their passion, such as the individuals in these 18 tales of life on the job.

Backdraft
1991 – Ron Howard

I've been a fan of Howard's for six decades, ever since his appearance as a young boy in *The Music Man* (PF5). When he moved into directing, he helmed several terrific movies, particularly *Apollo 13*, *Cinderella Man* and *A Beautiful Mind* (all in PF5), the latter of which won Best Picture. If I have a criticism of him, it's that he sometimes takes a solid basic story and overloads it – needlessly, I think – with melodrama. In *Cinderella Man* he inflamed the professional rivalry between boxers Jim Braddock and Max Baer. In *Rush*, he did the same with James Hunt and Niki Lauda. And much earlier, he did it here, in this story about Chicago firemen. He also takes some liberties with the laws of physics, but I'll get to that shortly. *Backdraft* concerns two second-generation firefighting brothers, "Bull" and Brian McCaffrey (Kurt Russell and William Baldwin). Their job is hazardous enough, but apparently there's an arsonist afoot, and the men are attempting to find him, aided by "Shadow" Rimgale (Robert De Niro), a veteran former firefighter himself. The McCaffreys are also trying to keep their women (Rebecca DeMornay and Jennifer Jason Leigh) happy – not necessarily an easy task. And they're trying to expose some political intrigue. But paramount in their lives is fighting the fires that erupt periodically in their district, and Howard and his crew and cast produce some truly frightening blazes and harrowing situations. To their credit, much of what you see on the screen is real, albeit carefully controlled and sometimes the product of camera tricks. <u>About the physics</u>: Fires in big buildings are scary enough. But here the flames take on an artificially organic quality, as though they've become demons. It's a bit much. Quibbles aside, it's a well-executed story. And it's a tribute to the cast that they spent time both with real Chicago engine companies and at the bootcamp the city runs to train its brave firefighters. [<u>Caution</u>: language, sexuality and intense firefighting scenes] **[W]**

Beneath the 12-Mile Reef
1953 – Robert D. Webb

Here's an unusual occupation that can be as dangerous as firefighting: sponge-diving. Gilbert Roland and Robert Wagner (in his first starring role) play Mike and Tony Petrakis, father-and-son Greek–American divers working in the only location in America where the "most dangerous of all occupations," as described by the narrator, is pursued. That would be Tarpon Springs, Florida, near Tampa. And the danger emanates from the necessity of harvesting sponges using old-fashioned diving suits, with heavy weights attached to the feet and a rigid, globe-like helmet receiving oxygen via hose from the surface. Much can go wrong – and does – with such a system. As with the other sponge fishermen in the town, the Petrakises struggle – both to earn a living and stay safe from harm. That struggle eventually draws them to go … beneath the 12-mile reef, a location in the Gulf of Mexico that's fraught with danger. As Mike tells Tony,

> "First time you go down in deep water, you get scared. You don't know how scared you can be. After a while, you forget. But the reef … never forgets. It waits … all the time. Then one day when you are not looking, it grabs you."

That danger, and more, confront the Petrakises before the drama – and the melodrama – fully unfolds, including a Romeo-and-Juliet romance between Tony and Gwyneth (Terry Moore),

212

daughter of a rival sponge-diving clan, and a confrontation with an unusually large (but obviously artificial) sea creature. An early CinemaScope production, the movie features the first underwater widescreen photography, and those sequences are thrilling. Bernard Herrmann composed the suitably nautical score, and future TV stalwart Peter Graves supplied the romantic rivalry and villainy. [Trivia notes: 1) Tarpon Springs is still the largest concentration of Americans of Greek ancestry, and the occupation of sponge-diving was invented by the Greeks on the island of Kalymnos, two millennia ago. 2) Wagner almost drowned in an early scene when accidentally kicked by another swimmer. Nearly thirty years later, his wife Natalie Wood did drown off California's Santa Catalina Island after falling into the water from their yacht. 3) The venerable, Mexican-born Roland, who's riveting here, enjoyed one of the longest careers in Hollywood, lasting nearly 70 years] **[W]**

Breaking In
1989 – Bill Forsyth

Much less dangerous than the previous two titles but not without its own brand of hazards. Burt Reynolds is Ernie Mullins, who's what's known in the trade as a safecracker – he figures out ways to break into vaults, whether in banks or residences. Not so much a caper or crime story, in terms of the protagonists aiming for that big score. It's more of a tricks-of-the-trade tale. Ernie meets Mike (Casey Siemaszko), a bit of a schnook who's squatting in a home that Ernie robs. Soon they become, forgive the pun, thick as thieves, as Ernie instructs Mike in his skills and provides nuggets of life's wisdom. As with most of Forsyth's films (see *Gregory's Girl* and *Comfort and Joy*), it's a low-key but absorbing story peppered with colorful characters, such as Ernie's poker buddies Johnny and "Shoes" (TV veteran Albert Salmi and John Ford regular Harry Carey Jr.), plus a pair of bickering lawyers (Maury Chaykin and Stephen Tobolowsky), one defending and one prosecuting. Ernie tries to teach Mike everything he knows, but he can't seem to convey the need to be careful with newfound loot. Mike doesn't listen, and soon his excesses lead to an encounter with the law – and a choice of whether to squeal on his mentor or face justice alone. An engaging little movie, written by John Sayles. [Caution: language and mild sexuality] **[W]**

Captain Phillips
2013 – Paul Greengrass

Back to the lethal-hazards column. Tom Hanks in the title role commands the Maersk Alabama, en route off the coast of East Africa. Based on a true incident, the giant container ship is overtaken by Somali pirates in a small, speedy launch, from which they board and capture Phillips and his crewmembers. Therein begins a long and harrowing ordeal for the men of the cargo ship, including several escape attempts, retaliatory beatings and negotiating sessions. How the incident ended is a matter of record. Just as Greengrass did with *United 93* (PF5), his landmark depiction of the hijacking and subsequent retaking of the ill-fated fourth airliner in the Islamic terror attacks of September 11, 2001, he and screenwriter Billy Ray re-create the episode, taking minimum dramatic license. Instead of the Indian Ocean off Somalia, which remains under constant threat of piracy, cast and crew gathered in Malta and shot the sea-surface scenes in the Mediterranean – using a real ship on loan from the Maersk merchant fleet. For the pirates, Greengrass recruited a group of Somali-Americans from Minnesota, four young non-actors who were trained in both seafaring and weaponry. They're quite convincing, especially Barkhad Abdi as the leader. A dramatization, yes, but under Greengrass and crew – who spent 12 weeks shooting on the water, à la Steven Spielberg and *Jaws* (PF5) – it's a nail-biter of a thriller with a powerful, cathartic ending. [Trivia note: Greengrass had originally agreed to direct *Rush* (below), while Ron Howard was set to direct *Captain Phillips*. But as projects often develop in Hollywood, the two men eventually swapped directing duties, and Greengrass, the son of a merchant mariner, took on this one] [Caution: violence] **[W]**

Captains of the Clouds
1942 – Michael Curtiz

Actually, two hazardous occupations unveil themselves here. In the first, James Cagney is Brian MacLean, a hotshot bush pilot delivering supplies and mail to residents living on lakes in remote parts of northern Ontario. The hazards are aplenty, such as the possibility of crashing in a vast wilderness, or even being struck by a rotating propeller, something that happens to MacLean early in the story. Recovered, he continues flying the supply runs, partly in partnership and sometimes in competition with Johnny Dutton (Dennis Morgan), and definitely the latter when both men seek the charms of dark-eyed Brenda Marshall. The rivalry eventually turns bitter, but other events suddenly intrude, in the form of Canada's entry into World War II. Eventually, both MacLean and Dutton enter the Royal Canadian Air Force and continue their animosity. But both end up flying a desperate mission to deliver badly needed bombers to England, which is where one of the men must sacrifice himself to save the other aircraft. Filmed entirely in Canada, it's somewhat formulaic. But the aerial scenes – both civilian and military – are exciting; Cagney, as usual, commands the screen, and it's an opportunity to see Marshall in one of her few roles. She retired from movies a few years later to become the full-time wife of William Holden. Two Warner Bros. stalwarts, George Tobias and Alan Hale Sr., play fellow pilots.

Diamond Men
2000 – written, produced and directed by Dan Cohen

As Burt Reynolds taught the ropes of safecracking and getting the goods to Casey Siemaszko in *Breaking In*, here Robert Forster as traveling jewelry salesman Eddie teaches the ways of protecting the goods. Miller, a 30-year veteran of the trade, and proud that in all that time he's "never lost a line," as they say in the trade, is nevertheless assigned a young associate, Bobby Walker (Donnie Wahlberg, younger brother of Mark). Walker is company management's indelicate way of forcing Miller into retirement. Initially wary of each other, during their visitations to Miller's customers – small jewelry stores across Pennsylvania – they develop a budding friendship and mutual respect. There's also the sudden prospect of romance, though in an unusual form, as Miller meets a proverbial hooker with a heart of gold (Bess Armstrong). And there might even be an opportunity for Miller to exact a little larcenous revenge on his employers. A taut, diverting, solid little movie. [Caution: explicit sexuality] [W]

Fisherman's Friends
2019 – England – Chris Foggin
Okay, this one isn't about men on the job; it's about their recreational activity – in which they sometimes indulge during working hours. In the tradition of *Local Hero* (PF5), it's a charming tale about Danny (Daniel Mays), a London music promoter who encounters a group of fishermen in a Cornish village who sing traditional ballads called sea shanties. Goaded by his corporate superior, Danny persuades the group to sign a contract on a bet that he can make them famous. Which he does, eventually, but not before he and the fishermen must overcome a convoluted set of obstacles, and he can win the heart of Alwyn, a lovely local girl (Tuppence Middleton, charming in a break from her nasty, nasty role as Princess Hélène Kuragina in the BBC television series War & Peace). Based on a true story, it's an affectionate profile of a group of working men dedicated to each other, their community and their music. [Caution: language (though the accents are thick) and mild sexuality] [W]

The Frogmen
1951 – Lloyd Bacon
Not all wartime dramas involve direct combat. Some, like this one, require brave men to fight the battles indirectly and underwater, operations that were – and remain – among the most hazardous in warfare. So it is with the members of Underwater Demolition Team 4, serving in the Pacific in World War II. While Marines prepare to storm the beaches, the Frogmen – so named because most of the time they operate with only fins and swim masks – approach the landing zones ahead of time and search

underwater for obstacles and boobytraps. The melodramatic plot and contrived ending are secondary to the movie's positively nerve-wracking action scenes mid-way (filmed in Caribbean locations), giving a good look at the team's dangerous work, particularly deploying and recovering the men, done from speedboats and under enemy fire. Richard Widmark, Dana Andrews and Gary Merrill star. [Trivia notes: 1) *The Frogmen* marked the beginning or early work of four actors who went on to prominent screen and television roles: Jeffrey Hunter, Warren Stevens, Robert Wagner and Jack Warden. You'll see them all featured elsewhere in my trilogy. 2) You might never have heard of Lloyd Bacon, who also directed *Kill the Umpire* (below). He didn't achieve the prominence of some of his contemporaries, but he maintained a solid reputation in Hollywood and directed more than a hundred films over his four-decade career, including some pretty good musicals such as *42nd Street* (P25)] **[B&W]**

Hooper
1978 – Hal Needham
If you know anything about moviemaking, you know about stunt performers, the men – and occasionally women – who put themselves in real danger to complete scenes supposedly featuring the principal actors in harm's way. Burt Reynolds, a former stunt man himself, stars in the title role, and that's what his character has been doing for most of his adult life. Now he's on the verge of retirement but is resisting the inevitable while Delmore "Ski" Shidski (Jan-Michael Vincent), a young and brash rival, is goading Hooper to perform his valediction: driving through the biggest, the baddest, the most irrational scene of mass destruction in movie history – purely for thrills and laughs. But forget the plot – it's all ridiculous, anyway. The movie's real attraction is its tribute to stunts, and there are a ton of them, performed by the 72 professionals in the cast, plus another that Needham – another former stunter – performed himself. Sally Field (linked romantically with Reynolds through the '70s) plays his girlfriend, and immortal Pittsburgh Steelers quarterback Terry Bradshaw appears in a witty brief role. It's an affectionate sendup

217

of the craft. As Reynolds commented later, receiving a life-achievement award by fellow stunters, particularly for his work here, "I never wanted to be John Wayne. I wanted to be Hal Needham." [Cautions: 1) language and sexuality, and 2) lest it need be said, do not try any of this at home] **[W]**

Kill the Umpire
1950 – Lloyd Bacon
Most movies about baseball concentrate on the players and, occasionally, the coaches. Here's one about umpires; baseball people who don't play, they work – and usually under glaring criticism from the players, the coaches and, especially, the fans. Bill Johnson (William Bendix), a former ballplayer – and perennial umpire-hater – learns this firsthand and gets a taste of his own medicine when he's forced to call balls and strikes after failing at several other jobs and facing an ultimatum from his wife. Graduating from an umpire academy run by Jimmy O'Brien (William Frawley), he wins a pro contract after displaying an unusual style – the result of a mishap with eyedrops – that earns him the nickname "Two-Call" Johnson. After a few other hitches along the way, he settles into his new career, finally believing, as he admits, "without an umpire, you can't have a clean and honest game of baseball." It's silly in places and a bit uneven, with even some slapstick thrown in, but Bendix is delightful. [Trivia notes: 1) Bendix's character resembles the persona he developed for Chester Riley, his lead role in the TV series The Life of Riley, which started in 1953. 2) Meanwhile, the gruff character Frawley played resembled his immortally gruff Fred Mertz of I Love Lucy, beginning the following year. 3) *Kill the Umpire* marked the first of two baseball-themed movies directed by Bacon in succeeding years. In 1951 he did the delightful fantasy *Angels in the Outfield* (PF5)] **[B&W]**

Man of a Thousand Faces
1957 – Joseph Pevney
James Cagney again, this time playing legendary silent-screen actor Lon Chaney Sr., who went to great lengths to meet the

physical-appearance requirements of his roles, including distorting his own face. This one's tough to watch, however. It's a morose drama about Chaney's early years, extremely troubled marriage to his first wife Cleva (Dorothy Malone) and the persistent difficulties of his career and personal life. All that said, Cagney is still Cagney, and in this role he's mesmerizing as Chaney, particularly in portraying the man's specialty, his exceptional ability to contort his face and body to personify his characters. [Trivia note: Like *The Frogmen*, above, *Man of a Thousand Faces* features a quartet of secondary cast members who later rose to distinguished careers: Jim Backus (in the TV series Gilligan's Island and as the voice of the animated character Mr. Magoo), legendary producer Robert Evans (*The Godfather* and *Chinatown* – see PF5), Roger Smith (TV regular and longtime spouse of Ann-Margret) and Oscar-winner Jack Albertson] [B&W]

Medicine Man
1992 – John McTiernan

Making an exception here for a woman working alongside a man – albeit with some standard romantic tension, a bit of political melodrama and, unfortunately, not the best work from the actress. Sean Connery, whom McTiernan had directed three years earlier in *The Hunt for Red October* (PF5) co-stars with Lorraine Bracco (she the saucy mafia wife in *Goodfellas* (also in PF5) and psychiatrist to Tony Soprano, everybody's favorite mafioso, in TV's The Sopranos). They're Robert Campbell and Rae Crane, research botanists stationed deep in the Mexican rainforest to seek cures for what ails the people of our planet. That they do, often at odds with each other while dealing with the hackneyed plot elements. Getting the idea I didn't like this one? No. I did like it, but *in spite of* its flaws, because Connery is so reliable and watchable. By the way, the title is literal; Campbell is deemed a … medicine man by a nearby indigenous tribe for curing one of their children of a stomachache – by giving him Alka Seltzer. Jerry Goldsmith contributed the lush soundtrack, ever-so-slightly reminiscent of John Barry's overpowering, unforgettable suite for *Out of Africa* [PF5]. [Caution: mild sexuality] **[W]**

North Dallas Forty
1979 – co-written and directed by Ted Kotcheff
No series about working men would be complete without at least one title featuring professional athletes – particularly like Kotcheff's uneven but probing look at football players. Based on former Dallas Cowboys wide receiver Peter Gent's novel of the same name, it's the story of Phil Elliott (a bulked-up Nick Nolte in his best performance), an aging receiver with the fictional ... North Dallas Bulls (the "Forty" in the title derives from the number of players on the team). We first meet Elliott as he wakes up one morning and, as he frequently must do, removes the blood clots that have formed in his nostrils overnight. That's a foreshadowing of the ordeals we'll be witnessing as Elliott and his teammates struggle against injuries and pain to remain gameworthy. Part of that struggle involves the constant use of painkillers and other drugs – legal, recommended and otherwise. There's also quite a bit of sexual mischief and recreational drug use by the players, including Elliott and his quarterback Seth Maxwell (country musician Mack Davis). Such behavior, if not sanctioned, is ignored by Bulls head coach B.A. Strother (J.D. Spradlin) – anything to keep winning. In the end, as the story shows, pro football is more of a business than a game (though both topics arise regularly in the dialogue), and the men it chews up in that process tend to lead lonelier and sadder lives when retirement or termination arrives. I agree with Gary Arnold's take on *North Dallas Forty*, which he called "[p]rofanely funny, wised-up and heroically antiheroic," adding that "there's never been a better fictional film about pro football." [Trivia note: As Elliott's character is based on author Gent himself, Davis's character emerged from Cowboys quarterback Don Meredith. When "Dandy Don" saw the movie, he reportedly quipped, "If I'd known Gent was as good as he says he was, I would have thrown to him more"] [Caution: language, on-the-field violence and crude sexuality] **[W]**

220

Rush

2013 – Ron Howard

In the mid-1970s, in the international sport of Formula One (aka F1) racing, a rivalry emerged between two drivers of decidedly different character; a haughty, dashing Brit named James Hunt (a slimmed-down Chris Hemsworth) and a sullen, mousy, straight-arrow Austrian named Niki Lauda (Brazilian–German actor Daniel Brühl, who's terrific in this role). Both had to overcome serious difficulties – Hunt's alcoholism, playboy lifestyle and propensity toward recklessness; and Lauda's severe injuries from a near-fatal crash – to continue to compete at the top of the Grand Prix circuit. Both did, leading to their unusual showdown at the end of the 1976 season. Honestly, I don't rate this movie nearly as highly as James Mangold's sensational *Ford v Ferrari* (P25), which covered two seasons of the 24 Hours of Le Mans circuit a decade earlier. But it's a game effort by director Howard and his cast and crew, and it does portray the sport and its extreme hazards well. [Critic's note: *Rush* marked the second time Ron Howard took the story of a mostly friendly professional rivalry and turned it into a borderline nasty feud. Hunt and Lauda definitely were rivals, but the two remained friends throughout their careers; they even shared a house at one point. Howard had done the same with the story of boxing champions Jim Braddock and Max Baer in the otherwise superb *Cinderella Man* (PF5), turning Baer into an outright villain when his strength of character matched Braddock's – and the two were friends outside the ring] [Trivia notes: 1) About the Hunt–Lauda rivalry: It might have seemed an equal match here, as well as in some of the media at the time. But reality told a different story. Hunt won the F1 championship once, while Lauda won it three times, and Lauda's achievements were far superior in all other categories. He is considered the greatest F1 driver of all time, and he was a brilliant automotive technician. 2) Hunt's private life made headlines in 1976 when his wife, model Suzy Miller (here played by Olivia Wilde), left him for actor Richard Burton – who himself had left Elizabeth Taylor the previous year. 3) In contrast, Lauda's wife Marlene (Romanian–German actress Alexandra Maria Lara) *ended* an affair with a married celebrity, German actor Curt Jurgens, to be with him, whom she eventually married. 4) I mentioned Hemsworth slimming down. To play Hunt, he needed to lose 25 pounds from his muscular persona as Thor in the Marvel Comics Avengers series, whom he has played eight times to date. 5) Irony of ironies, despite the extreme dangers of their sport, both Hunt and Lauda died in their sleep; Hunt in 1993 at age 45, and Lauda in 2019 at 70] [Caution: language, intense racing scenes and plentiful sexuality] [W]

Tin Men
1987 – written and directed by Barry Levinson
Now *here's* a nasty rivalry but with a hopeful ending. In the early 1960s, B.B. Babowsky and Ernest Tilley (Richard Dreyfuss and Danny DeVito) are literally hurled together one day when they crash Cadillacs on a Baltimore street. They're both aluminum-siding salesmen – "tin men" – from competing companies, and they quickly become bitter foes and locked in a love triangle with Nora (Barbara Hershey) Tilley's wife. After nearly coming to blows, they eventually reach a mutual understanding and the possibility of friendship. The unpleasantness aside, *Tin Men* is essentially a sequel to Baltimore-native Levinson's charming breakthrough movie, *Diner* (PF5), set in 1959. But instead of the quintet of young men gathering at the diner at night, here's a quartet of middle-age working men (Tilley and three cronies) convening at the same place in the mornings. The movie even features one of the original characters, a contractor nicknamed "Bagel" (Michael Tucker). While the younger group had concentrated on pursuing the opposite sex, this bunch has moved on to more mundane concerns. For example, Sam, (comedian Jackie Gayle) is fixated on the TV show Bonanza, which he characterizes as a non-western about a "fifty-year-old father with three forty-seven-year-old sons." Among the other titles in this category, the movie portrays less of men working and more of their pursuits after hours. Nevertheless, it's entertaining. [Caution: language and sexuality] [W]

Unzipped
1995 – Douglas Keeve
Briskly clipped documentary coverage of New York fashion designer Isaac Mizrahi preparing his new collection for the fall of 1994. It's probably the ultimate man-at-work title here, because the movie relentlessly presents Mizrahi as he conducts the entire process of his trade: conceiving and designing the clothing, producing the garments, auditioning runway models and, finally, presenting his creations at the climactic fashion show – all sprinkled liberally with brief appearances by the supermodels and celebrities of that time, nearly 30 years ago. Unfamiliar territory for most of us, but fascinating, largely because of Mizrahi, who looks like a cross between Bob Woodward of The Washington Post and Michael Richards as Kramer on Seinfeld. [Trivia notes: 1) Director Keeve was involved with Mizrahi before and during the filming, but disagreements arose and the two split shortly thereafter. 2) The ambient music playing before the fashion show begins is the theme from That Girl, a '70s TV series starring Marlo Thomas] [Caution: language and adult themes] **[B&W – with one color sequence]**

White Nights
1985 – Taylor Hackford
Dancers Gregory Hines and Mikhail Baryshnikov face off in this tale about an expatriate Russian ballet star inadvertently returned to his homeland and meeting an expat American living there. An airliner carrying "Kolya" Rodchenko (Baryshnikov) must make a rough emergency landing in Siberia, where he is injured, arrested and then pressured to resume performing in the world-famous Kirov Ballet. Among the measures employed to persuade him are goading from rival (non-ballet) star Raymond Greenwood (Hines) and appeals from ballerina and Kolya's former lover Galina Ivanova (the great Helen Mirren, whose father was Russian). There's also an extended sequence where Kolya, Raymond, Galina and Raymond's wife (Isabella Rossellini, Ingrid Bergman's daughter, in her first role) plot an escape to the West, but the real interest and pleasure derive from watching the

dancing interplay between these two masters of their respective styles. This goes particularly for the scene where Baryshnikov, on a bet, performs 11 pirouettes from a standing start in his street shoes. It's jaw-dropping. [Trivia notes: Obviously, the producers could not win permission to film in the old Soviet Union. So they shot the Siberian scenes in late summer on an island off the coast of Finland, where the proper light of the titular white nights could be portrayed. 2) Mirren's real romance here was with director Hackford, whom she soon married] [Caution: adult themes] **[W]**

X-15
1961 – Richard Donner (as "Richard D. Donner")
Presaging *The Right Stuff* (PF5) by over two decades, this handsomely mounted but melodramatic production stars Charles Bronson as a pilot testing the eponymous rocket plane, which could fly twice as fast as the legendary SR-71 Blackbird reconnaissance aircraft. Some thrilling actual footage of the test flights, as the X-15 is dropped from a B-52 bomber in the California desert above Edwards Air Force Base. That's along with a few of the frightening – and often lethal – accidents befalling the brave souls who boarded that "hurtlin' piece of machinery," as the test pilots called their ride. Donner, who went on to direct blockbusters such as the original *Superman* (PF5) and *Lethal Weapon* (P25), contributes a workmanlike effort here. The supporting cast features Mary Tyler Moore in her first film role, the same year she began co-starring in The Dick Van Dyke Show. There's also the Stanley Livingston, who became youngest of TV's My Three Sons, also that same year. Former World War II pilot, Air Force General and beloved actor James Stewart supplies the narration. **[W]**

26. Misfortunes of War

Many war dramas depict virtues such as personal bravery and the struggle for freedom over tyranny. Others attempt to portray the strategic forces in play during wartime and the personalities involved in the fateful decisions. These 10, however, concentrate on the personal costs exacted whenever nations take up arms against one another.

Air Force

1943 – Howard Hawks

On the 6th of December 1941, the crew of the Mary-Ann, a B-17 bomber, takes off from San Francisco with eight other B-17 crews bound for Hickam Field in Honolulu, Hawai`i, on a routine mission. One by one, we meet the nine men aboard the Mary-Ann; ordinary Joes and good guys all. By the following morning, as the squadron prepares to land, the Japanese attack has begun, and the bombers, restricted by the rules of America's pre-December 7th neutrality, are unarmed and must flee from the marauding enemy aircraft to neighboring islands. Next, the Mary-Ann must fly across the Pacific, first to the besieged Wake Island and then to Clark Field in the Philippines, where fighting aircraft are desperately needed. There, we learn how badly the American forces are faring during the first few days of their involvement in World War II. And we eventually watch Mary-Ann's crew and some incredibly brave Marines on the ground endure some of those brutal combat experiences – though not before getting their licks in. It's a sober, serious portrayal of the Pacific War, when the outcome was well in doubt, and the battle tolls were often severe. Former aviator Hawks managed some gripping and authentic-looking sequences, filmed in Texas and Florida. [Trivia notes: 1) Hawks filmed the aerial scenes far from the West Coast because the sight of aircraft displaying Japanese markings there could have triggered, literally, anti-aircraft fire as well as panic on the ground. 2) The movie's title is generic. At the time, all military aircraft flew under the authority of the United States Army Air Forces. Congress didn't establish the U.S. Air Force as a separate service until 1947. 3) Made early in the war, *Air Force* was meant to boost America's war-fighting resolve. That included portraying Japanese-Americans as saboteurs and assassins – though in real life no such acts were ever documented] **[B&W]**

The Battle of Britain
1969 – Guy Hamilton
Despite Adolph Hitler's fervent desire, the German Army never invaded England during World War II. The country remained protected by the relatively narrow waters of the English Channel, which der Führer's hordes couldn't manage to cross. What the Nazis did do, however, was for a time rain death and destruction from the skies via the Luftwaffe, the German Air Force. That effort, most of which was waged in 1940, would have continued through the duration of the war were it not for the heroic resistance of a small group of fighter pilots flying – and dying – for crown and country. Hamilton, best known for directing *Goldfinger* (PF5), at the top of many fans' favorite James Bond thrillers, here helms a meticulous, large-scale re-creation of that desperate fight – in the war rooms as well as in the air – by the Royal Air Force against the Luftwaffe. Then Hamilton builds to a most unusual climactic sequence, mirroring the real battle, waged on September 15, 1940, an all-or-nothing strike by the Germans. It's a vast aerial ballet, absent dialogue and sound effects, played out over a performance of a symphonic suite composed by Sir William Walton – it's breathtaking. A star-studded cast, including Michael Caine, Trevor Howard, Laurence Olivier, Christopher Plummer, Ralph Richardson and Robert Shaw help enact the incredibly clever, courageous and self-sacrificing effort that blunted the German offensive and eventually defeated it. An effort of such collective valor that it caused Winston Churchill to declare:

Never in the field of human conflict was so much owed by so many to so few.

[Trivia notes: 1) *Battle of Britain* (the original title) displayed the biggest collection of aircraft ever assembled for a motion picture – enough to rank, temporarily, among the world's largest air forces. 2) About the meticulous re-creation: The production crew reproduced the period paint colors and designs on the aircraft so well that – as originally designed – they couldn't be seen easily from the ground or from the air over land. The planes had to be photographed either with clouds in the background or above water to counteract their camouflage] [Caution: wartime violence] **[W]**

The Fighting 69th
1940 – William Keighley

Stepping back in time to World War I, this hard-edged, fact-based drama stars James Cagney as Jerry Plunkett, a member of the 69th New York Regiment of the 165th Division. Plunkett is a poor excuse for a soldier. He's undisciplined, arrogant and insubordinate. He's also a coward; something that threatens his continued status in the outfit. But the 69th's chaplain, Father Francis Duffy (a real person played by the venerable Pat O'Brien), pleads with Major William "Wild Bill" Donovan (another real person, played by George Brent) to give Plunkett another chance. Donovan agrees but sends him on a dangerous mission – which he corrupts via bad judgment, resulting in two of his comrades being killed. Court-martialed and condemned to death, Plunkett is spared when his jail is hit by an enemy shell. He finally finds his courage, leading him to sacrifice himself to save others in his unit. Cagney, as always, is riveting in the role, and his (fictional) character's transformation mirrors the actions of thousands of real soldiers – ordinary men who have laid down their lives in service to their units and their country. [Trivia notes: 1) Donovan went on to head the Army's Office of Strategic Services in World War II, precursor of the Central Intelligence Agency. 2) Another real-life character in the movie is poet Joyce Kilmer, most famous for "Trees." He was killed in France near the end of the war] **[B&W]**

Flags of Our Fathers (and) Letters from Iwo Jima
2006 – both by Clint Eastwood

In early 1945, in the closing months of World War II in the Pacific, one of the fiercest battles occurred on the heavily defended Japanese island of Iwo Jima. In fact, the struggle for the island marked the only time in the war since Pearl Harbor where American casualties exceeded those of the Imperial Japanese Army. Here, director Eastwood presents, in two separate movies, fact-based and unique portrayals of the brutal conflict from the American and Japanese sides.

*   *   *

Flags of Our Fathers, written by William Broyles and Paul Haggis, and based on the book of the same name by James Bradley and Ron Powers, portrays the experiences of the six U.S. Marines who raised the American flag on the island's Mount Suribachi in the iconic image duplicated at the Marine Corps memorial in Arlington, Virginia. The movie actually begins with the aftermath of that event, when the three surviving soldiers (the other three, plus two more associated with the flag-raising, had been killed in the battle) return home to a heroes' welcome. Then the story flashes back, first to preliminary training and then to the beginning of the terrifying assault on Iwo Jima's beaches. After two days of fighting, the Marines secure the mountain, and a small group raises the flag. It's then that Eastwood tells the real story of the flag-raising: The famous image, taken by Associated Press photographer Joe Rosenthal, was actually of the *second* flag hoisted above the island. The first flag, raised while still under enemy fire, attracted the interest of Navy Secretary James Forrestal, who had just arrived on the beach and cheered the men on from below. He ordered the first flag lowered and delivered to him, and a replacement flag raised – hence the mission of Bradley and his five comrades, and the image for the ages. There's more to the story, but better to experience it yourself and contemplate the morally complex nature of the event and its impact on the lives of those brave and good men. [Trivia notes: 1) Forrestal's motivation for ordering the second flag wasn't selfish. He wanted a larger one displayed on the mountaintop so it could be better

228

seen from the Navy's ships and inspire the incoming troops. 2) Eastwood filmed the battle scenes in Iceland, where the black-sand beaches and general terrain resemble the volcanic island. Shooting on Iwo Jima's beaches and mountainside would have been prohibited; it is preserved as a national war memorial by the Japanese government] [Caution: graphic wartime violence] **[W]**

*   *   *

In *Letters from Iwo Jima*, Eastwood takes the unusual approach of producing the movie in Japanese with subtitles. The story concerns two of the thousands of Japanese soldiers taking shelter from the relentless American artillery barrages in the network of caves dug into the sides of Mt. Suribachi, under orders from General Tadamichi Kuribayashi (Ken Watanabe, a highly regarded actor in Japan), who commanded the island forces. Kuribayashi's strategy was to have his troops stay hidden instead of directly confronting the U.S. Marines – a plan that allowed the Japanese to deny the Americans a victory for over a month instead of a few days. It's a dark, brooding, ultimately horrific tale of suicidal determination of the island's defenders. But it portrays the Japanese, irrespective of their motivation, as human beings just as dedicated to their cause as their enemy. [Trivia note: I mentioned Watanabe's reputation because when Eastwood cast him as Kurbayashi, a flood of young Japanese actors sought to be included in the production] [Caution: wartime violence] **[W]**

Mrs. Henderson Presents
2005 – Stephen Frears

Not technically a war movie, though it takes place in London at the beginning of World War II, it addresses a genuinely poignant issue related to young men of the armed forces facing the distinct possibility of dying in battle. Based on a real character and played by Judi Dench, widowed heiress Mrs. Laura Henderson discovers that among her late husband's properties is the Windmill, a dormant downtown theatre (British spelling). Intrigued at the idea of dabbling in show business, and despite her lack of experience, she attempts to reopen the Windmill and present stage productions. To help her, she hires a male manager named

229

Vivian van Damm (Bob Hoskins). Despite their best efforts, the enterprise fails. At that point the war begins, and young British men are heading overseas in droves to fight the Germans. That's when Mrs. Henderson experiences a eureka moment: She decides to produce musical revues at the Windmill featuring beautiful young nude women. Her inspiration, based partly on personal history, is that the Windmill's show might be the only chance many of the young men will ever have to see naked females in the flesh. Needless to say, Mrs. Henderson's plan proves sensational to the soldiers but controversial in the extreme to the guardians of public morals. Who will win? It's well worth watching to … um, see it all play out, and Dench and Hoskins are solid gold together. [Trivia note: The versatile Christopher Guest, playing a prissy British lord here, actually *is* a member of British nobility and a former member of the House of Lords in Parliament. He served nearly four years under the title 5th Baron Haden-Guest, until the seat was abolished by law] [Caution: language, sexuality and plentiful nudity, ever-so-tastefully displayed] **[W]**

Paths of Glory
1957 – co-written and directed by Stanley Kubrick
One of the greatest and most persistent *personal* conflicts in war is the battle between one's duty and one's conscience. Must all orders be followed even if unwise or, in the worst cases, immoral? Kirk Douglas, working with Kubrick for the first of two times, is a French colonel in World War I who faces just such a dilemma. His Colonel Dax is ordered to lead a regiment against a superbly defended German position, a move that Dax knows will result in heavy casualties but without achieving the objective. He protests the order but eventually obeys, and unsurprisingly all of his men are killed in the first assault. Despite Dax's efforts to motivate the rest of the regiment, they refuse to head into certain slaughter. The refusal leads to a court martial of three of the soldiers, and Dax, an attorney in civilian life, attempts to defend them. Three things about the movie: 1) The imagery, by cinematographer Georg (GAY-org) Krauss with scenes and compositions conceived by Kubrick, is overwhelming, even more so in black & white; 2) the

230

script, by Kubrick and Calder Willingham, is as literate and thought-provoking as anything ever written for the screen on the subject; and 3) except for *Spartacus* (PF5), which he also did with Kubrick, Douglas gives arguably the performance of his career. In this genre, *Paths of Glory* is a heartbreaking classic. [Trivia notes: 1) Wayne Morris, who plays the slimy and cowardly Lieutenant Roget, was a highly decorated fighter pilot during World War II who turned to acting when his military career ended. 2) The movie's title is taken from Thomas Gray's poem "Elegy in a Country Churchyard."

The paths of glory lead but to the grave.

[Caution: adult themes and wartime violence] **[B&W] [W]**

The Railway Man
2013 – Jonathan Teplitzky

The timeframe is 1980, and the location is Scotland. Colin Firth is Eric Lomax, a self-described railway enthusiast and an aging veteran of the British Army in Southeast Asia in World War II. On one of his frequent train journeys, Eric meets, falls in love with and quickly marries Patti Wallace (Nicole Kidman, in a brief but fine role). After a quick and appealing honeymoon, Patti discovers, to her horror, that Eric harbors deep and terrible memories of his war experiences, to the point where seemingly innocuous happenings can trigger those memories as well as hallucinations. The situation threatens his marriage and his first real chance at happiness. Then, through the intervention of Finlay (Stellan Skarsgård), Eric's comrade from the war and his enduring friend, he discovers that one of his wartime tormentors is still alive. That man, a Japanese soldier named Nagase (martial arts movie regular Hiroyuki Sanada), now leads museum tours at the site in Thailand where he had once held Eric captive. Enough of the plot. Know, however, that Eric's memories are portrayed in excruciating detail, that his frequent fits of mental torment force both Patti and Finlay to desperate measures, and that Eric finally confronts Nagase. Based (albeit loosely) on the true story of both men, with huge, expansive wartime sequences shot in Thailand, it's one of the most redemptive war sagas ever produced. [Trivia note: The movie marked a reunion and a prequel of sorts – and a step up in quality – for the principal cast. Five years earlier, Firth and Skarsgård co-starred in the mediocre musical *Mamma Mia!* Then, five years later, they co-starred again, as well as Jeremy Irvine, who plays the younger Eric during the war, in the even-more-mediocre sequel *Mamma Mia! Here We Go Again.* And 10 years earlier, Skarsgård co-starred with Kidman as a married couple in the stagey *Dogville* (none on my lists)] [Caution: mild sexuality but explicit wartime violence, including torture] **[W]**

Taking Chance
2009 – co-written and directed by Ross Katz
The ultimate misfortune of war, or course, is the loss of human life, particularly young men in combat. This short (78-minute) HBO production nevertheless packs a lot of emotion. The title derives from the first name of Private First Class (PFC) Chance Phelps, a real 19-year-old American soldier who was killed in Iraq in 2004. Kevin Bacon, in his finest performance, plays Lieutenant Colonel Mike Strobl, a Gulf War veteran who volunteers for one of the most difficult non-combat assignments in the military: escorting the body of a soldier back to his hometown for burial. This is not a political story; it passes no judgment one way or another on the decision to invade Iraq. What it does, and what makes it such an affecting drama, is that it depicts in great detail the precise task of processing and serving as an escort for a military casualty. You're with Strobl – on whose personal story the movie is based – at every stage of the journey, from Dover, Delaware, where the Iraq casualties were sent for preparation, back to the small town in Wyoming where Chance Phelps was born and raised. You also get to glimpse some of the painstaking work performed by the men and women at Dover. And you get to see both Strobl's odyssey and the many gestures of support he receives from ordinary people along the way. It's a unique piece of moviemaking. [Caution: language] **[W]**

The Water Diviner
2014 – Australia – Russell Crowe

The phrase "inspired by true events" appears at the beginning of the movie, which in this case fits the story perfectly. It's based on the flimsiest of sources, one sentence in a letter by an Australian officer detailed to recover the bodies of servicemen killed in the Gallipoli campaign in Turkey during World War I (see *Gallipoli*, elsewhere). The sentence reads, "One old chap managed to get here from Australia, looking for his son's grave."

From that tiny tidbit, Crowe and his screenwriters, Andrew Anastasios and Andrew Knight, crafted an expansive, captivating, sometimes electrifying story of a father's obsession with finding his three (presumably) dead sons at the site of the Gallipoli battleground and bringing them home. Along the way, his character, Joshua Connor, an Outback farmer and … water diviner, faces a series of encounters; one personally tragic, several extremely dangerous and one romantic. At times, the story edges well into implausibility but never enough to spoil its impact. And overall, Crowe's directing (his first time in that chair) and performance are masterful. Likewise his supporting cast, including Ukrainian–French actress Olga Kurylenko as the romantic interest, and Turkish actors – and comedians – Yilmaz Erdoğan and Cem Yilmaz as two sympathetic and helpful Turkish officers. As Erdoğan's character tells the Australian commander of the burial detail, who at first rejects Connor's request to search for his sons, "He is the only father who came looking." The film won Australia's equivalent of the Best Picture Oscar. [Trivia notes: 1) Crowe's team received, for the first time ever for an international production, permission to film inside Istanbul's fabled Blue Mosque. 2) As with *Gallipoli* and Clint Eastwood's twin movies about Iwo Jima (all above), the scenes of the battle and the battlefield were filmed in Australia because the real location is now protected and considered sacred ground. 3) A diviner, as Connor's character demonstrates, is a person who seems to possess an uncanny ability to determine where a water reservoir might be lurking underground, often via the use of what's called a divining rod] [Caution: wartime violence] **[W]**

27. (Mostly) British Capers

Of the many genres in the movie business, one of the most audience-pleasing involves when "the game is afoot," as Sherlock Holmes used to call the process. That's how Arthur Conan Doyle's legendary sleuth described attempts by clever, unscrupulous or desperate individuals to get away with something before the long arm of the law could reel them in. And among the world's audiences, none seem to enjoy such stories more than the Brits. For over a century, British readers, moviegoers and eventually television viewers have lavished attention on such tales, particularly when humor is involved. Mostly, however, fans of caper movies want endings that surprise, shock or delight them, particularly when the plotters succeed. Here are 11 such examples.

Agatha
1979 – England – Michael Apted
Swiping a page – though unsuccessfully – from writer–director Nicholas Meyer's sparkling *The Seven-Per-Cent Solution* (<u>PF5</u>) three years earlier, here's a story about another famous Brit in the mystery-genre, Agatha Christie. Like its predecessor, the plot takes an unsolved gap in the life of Christie (luminously played by Vanessa Redgrave) and speculates on what might have happened. Unlike Meyer, who took a similar disappearance by the legendary-but-fictional detective Sherlock Holmes and crafted a captivating scenario about treatment for drug addiction during his absence – by none other than Sigmund Freud – screenwriter Kathleen Tynan delivers a muddled mess of a plot about Christie's marital distress. Worse, she fictionalizes an otherwise documented episode in Christie's life. That said, the movie is saved by the performances of Redgrave and Dustin Hoffman; her in the title role and him playing Wally Stanton, a fictional

journalist figuratively on Christie's tail. The other star here is cinematographer Vittorio Storaro, whose work elevates the movie to a "pictorial knockout," as Gary Arnold wrote in his Washington Post review. He added, "What Storaro and his crew don't know about the creative possibilities of light sources may not be worth knowing." Gary also praised Hoffman for "one of the most winning portrayals of his career." Superior acting and beautiful-looking images outweigh the pedestrian plot. [Trivia note: *Agatha* enjoys a direct connection to *The Seven-Per-Cent Solution* in Redgrave. Though she appeared as two different characters, she graced both movies as an alluring woman in distress] [Caution: adult themes and non-sexual nudity] [W]

A Big Hand for the Little Lady
1966 – Fielder Cook
Back on the other side of the Pond, as the Brits sometimes call the Atlantic expanse between England and America, Joanne Woodward stars as a desperate widow whose only remaining asset is the poker hand held by her husband (Henry Fonda), who has collapsed during the game. Or is it? Based on a TV play by Sydney Carroll, it's a clever little swindle/revenge comedy also starring Jason Robards, Charles Bickford and Paul Ford. [W]

Deathtrap
1982 – Sidney Lumet
Here's a story idea likely to leave you shocked at its evil intentions but shocked again because the evil was worse than you thought – and then laughing at how it fooled you. Sidney Bruhl (Michael Caine) is a failing playwright who plots to murder Clifford Anderson (Christopher Reeve, smack in the middle of his four performances as Superman), a promising drama student who has written a brilliant play titled … "Deathtrap." Bruhl wants to kill the young man, steal his work and revive his own sagging fortunes. That he does, to the extreme distress of his wife Myra (the always-bewitching Dyan Cannon). But therein begins a series of feints and double-crosses involving the three characters plus one more, Helga Ten Dorp (venerable stage actress Irene – "eye-

REE-nee" – Worth), a psychic who constantly bedevils Bruhl. The mystery quickly becomes who exactly is aligned with whom and to what end. Based on Ira Levin's play, and adapted by Lumet's longtime collaborator Jay Presson Allen, *Deathtrap* is consistently "fun to watch," Gary Arnold wrote in The Washington Post, "Caine has never been funnier," and "this classy quartet appears to take so much humorous pleasure in the material." He also singles out Cannon's performance as "so full of surprising reflexes and expressions that you want more of this endearing, wobbly helpmate than circumstances allow." And he praises Reeve for "ingratiat[ing] himself in a fresh way by impersonating a charming menace, extending his range to the amoral, treacherous aspects of human nature." All-in-all, not British (except for Caine), but a jolly caper. [Trivia note: In case you haven't figured it out, "Ten Dorp" is an anagram of "portend"] [Caution: adult themes and violence] **[W]**

The Great Train Robbery
1978 – written and directed by Michael Crichton
A hybrid caper movie, featuring an American writer–director working with two British stars. Together, they've re-created one of the biggest heists in England's history, which took place in 1855 during the Crimean War. Sean Connery is Edward Pierce, a sophisticated thief. Pierce's quest is to remove millions in gold bullion from a safe contained within a secure car of a moving train. The term "moving" is critical, though that's an understatement. The train is careening down the track, and Pierce must traverse the tops of several other cars to reach the safe's location. A couple of chapters back, I included the Burt Reynolds comedy *Hooper*, about the work of movie stuntmen. Incredibly, in this obviously dangerous scene, it's really Connery atop the train, and he's continually ducking under low-hanging bridges traversing the railway. The sequence is heart-pounding. As for the heist, Connery's character is assisted by Agar (Donald Sutherland), a nimble-fingered pickpocket, and Miriam (the gorgeous Leslie-Ann Downe), his love interest and, when required, a compelling distraction. [Trivia notes: 1) The movie's

British title is *The First Great Train Robbery*, intended to distinguish it from a similar caper executed in 1963. 2) Again, about the train: During Connery's rooftop sequence it was clocked at 55 miles an hour for some stretches, leaving precious little time for him to duck under those bridges] [Caution: sexuality – including one gratuitously vulgar moment – and mild violence] **[W]**

The Lavender Hill Mob
1951 – England – Charles Crichton

From an American Crichton to a Brit – but no relation – also dealing with a gold robbery. It's the story of Henry Holland (Alec Guinness), a schnook of a London bank clerk who masterminds a plot to steal a large amount of bullion and, with the help of Alfred Pendlebury (Stanley Holloway), his metalworking neighbor, smuggle the loot out of the country and onto the black market by disguising it as cheap souvenirs. At least, that's the plan, also involving Lackery and Shorty (Sydney James and Alfie Bass), two other neighbors in London's … Lavender Hill neighborhood. But this being a caper comedy, and with the characters involved, unintended consequences surely must arise, which they do in increasingly abundant amounts, and with karma having the final say. That seems fitting, given the movie's plot was devised by a production committee. Still, it's an enjoyable ride while it lasts – the movie's trailer humorously compares Holland and Pendlebury to such real outlaws as Jesse James and John Dillinger. Watch for future stars Audrey Hepburn and Robert Shaw in small roles in their respective debuts. [Trivia note: Speaking of Hepburn, 13 years later she would star in the title role in *My Fair Lady*, with Holloway playing her father] **[B&W]**

Mr. Holmes
2015 – England – Bill Condon

We now turn to the most famous British sleuth, Arthur Conan Doyle's legendary crime-solver Sherlock Holmes (Ian McKellen in a terrific performance), now in his 90s and struggling with memory loss. The year is 1947 and … Mr. Holmes is trying to clear up one final case, one that has troubled him for years. He's helped in his efforts by an unexpected source: Roger Munro (11-year-old Milo Parker), the young son of Holmes's widowed housekeeper (Laura Linney in a nice supporting role). Through his youth and curiosity, Roger nudges Holmes back somewhat from the abyss of onset dementia. In the process, the two develop a touching friendship, and the great detective finally recalls the missing details of that lingering case, the source of his decades-long depression. There's also an interesting subplot involving Holmes visiting Hiroshima while the city recovers from atomic destruction and meeting a Mr. Umezaki (Hiroyuki Sanada, whom I mentioned in *The Railway Man*). Umezaki is the son of an old acquaintance, and he helps Holmes weather his inevitable decline a little more gracefully. A fine, well-acted drama. [Trivia notes: 1) Sanada and McKellen both appeared in the Marvel Comics fantasy *The Wolverine* (not here) in 2013, with Sanada in a major role and McKellen in a cameo. [Caution: violence] **[W]**

Murder on the Orient Express
1974 – Sidney Lumet
A handsomely mounted though – forgive me – somewhat overrated mystery based on an Agatha Christie novel with an eye-popping cast and featuring her most famous detective, the legendary Belgian, Hercule Poirot (Albert Finney, turning in a damned good performance in a difficult role). The year is 1935, and an illustrious slate of characters is boarding the equally legendary Orient Express in Istanbul, bound for London. They include an American widow (Lauren Bacall), Poirot's friend and owner of the rail line (Martin Balsam), a Swedish missionary (Ingrid Bergman in her last Oscar-winning role), a mysterious countess (Jacqueline Bisset), a British Army colonel (Sean Connery), an English governess (Vanessa Redgrave), a cynical American businessman (Richard Widmark) with two employees in tow (Anthony Perkins and John Gielgud), and a Hungarian count (Michael York). As the transcontinental journey begins, all seems ordinary, though early tensions emerge, until … well, this being Agatha Christie, there's bound to be a murder. This occurs in due time, complicated by the sudden immobilization of the

train by an avalanche blocking the rail line. It then falls upon Poirot to solve the murder, which he does after interviewing the passengers and later explaining it all to them in a marathon, eight-minute monologue. Given the lavish production values and stellar cast, it's passable entertainment, though the solution to the murder strains credibility. [Viewing note: Personally, I prefer the far simpler but slicker and more enjoyable plotline of *The Seven-Per-Cent Solution* (PF5), in which another famous detective, Sherlock Holmes, unravels a case with humor and aplomb – and in which Vanessa Redgrave also co-stars] [Trivia notes: 1) Poirot's extended monologue proved challenging to star and co-stars alike. The problem was the setting: a relatively cramped railroad car. Space limitations required Finney to perform his lines over and over again – a difficult task, even for stage performers. The rest of the cast, however, had to sit passively in exactly the same positions through all of the takes so the single camera could capture the necessary angles and reactions. 2) Agatha Christie, in her 80s at the time, attended the movie's premiere and approved of the rendering of her story. She died about a year later] [Caution: mild violence] **[W]**

Saving Grace
2000 – England – Nigel Cole

A contrived but engaging little comedy about a Cornish widow (Brenda Blethyn) suddenly confronted with the massive debts left by her late husband who struggles to stay afloat by surreptitiously growing marijuana in her greenhouse. If nothing else, the movie is worth watching for one side-splitting scene. It involves two otherwise prim spinster shopowners (Phyllida Law and Linda Kerr Scott) mistakenly steeping weed instead of tea and consuming the result. Liberating for them and hilarious for us; a little reminiscent of the two pixilated sisters (comediennes Margaret Seddon and Margaret McWade) in *Mr. Deeds Goes to Town* (PF5). **[W]**

239

Scandal
1989 – England – Michael Caton-Jones

In 1961, John Profumo, 46 years old, began serving as the British Secretary of State for War under Prime Minister Harold Macmillan. He also began an affair with a 19-year-old prostitute named Christine Keeler, who also happened to be servicing Yevgeny Ivanov, a Soviet naval officer. Thus commenced what came to be known in England as the Profumo Affair, a … scandal so sensational it eventually brought down the Macmillan government. Here's Ian McKellen again, playing Profumo, with Joanne Whalley as Keeler; Bridget Fonda as Mandy Rhys-Davis, an … um, associate of Keeler's, and John Hurt as Stephen Ward, the socialite doctor who brought Profumo and Keeler together. It's a solid, straightforward telling of the drama that rocked 10 Downing Street and Parliament and filled the British tabloids for years with gossip about the principals. [Trivia note: Though Profumo was never charged with or convicted of a crime, the scandal ruined his reputation. He resigned his position and spent the rest of his life as a private citizen working for charitable causes – making him one of only two politicians I can think of who ever attempted to atone for their sins. The other was Nixon White House counsel Charles Colson. Imprisoned for his part in the Watergate scandal, Colson spent the rest of his life helping fellow inmates to redeem themselves] [Caution: explicit sexuality] **[W]**

Topkapi
1964 – Jules Dassin

Elizabeth Lipp (Melina Mercouri), a Greek tourist, visits the titular museum in Istanbul and becomes smitten with one of its treasures: a jeweled dagger once belonging to Sultan Mahmud the First. Lipp begins plotting to steal it, first recruiting Walter Harper (Maximillian Schell at his most dashing), an exceptional thief and her former lover. Then, one by one, the couple adds to the team, including inept conman Arthur Simpson (Peter Ustinov in an Oscar-winning role), with old pros Robert Morley and Akim Tamiroff rounding out the cast. From there, the plot proceeds and thickens, with complications and double-crosses galore. Yes, the gang actually steals the prized dagger – in a thrilling sequence – but do they get away with it? I'm not telling. Instead, you'll have to wait and see if a little bird tells you. [Trivia notes: 1) Romance blossomed during the production between Mercouri and director Dassin. They became a married couple two years later and until her death in 1994. 2) *Topkapi* represents another in a series of unfortunate decisions by actor Peter Sellers. Two years earlier, he became so inured to the idea that *Only Two Can Play* (P25) would be a dud that he relinquished his financial interest in it. The movie became the third-biggest hit in England, behind *The Guns of Navarone* and *Dr. No* (both in PF5). Here, Sellers was originally cast as Simpson but dropped out, allowing Ustinov to play the role – and win Best Supporting Actor] **[W]**

Whiskey Galore!
1949 – England – Alexander Mackendrick
The year is 1943 and, aside from the woes of World War II, the most severe problem befalling the residents of the little Scottish island of Todday is a shortage of whiskey. Whether the Toddayans prayed for divine deliverance, appealed to lesser gods or just stumbled onto good luck, something intervenes to solve their problem. One night, in a dense fog, a freighter runs aground near the island. Its cargo: thousands of cases of fine whiskey, enough to last the residents perhaps for the rest of their lives. Normally, the authorities would order the cargo to be impounded – but there's a complication. One of the island's couples has become engaged. By ancient Scottish custom, a *rèiteach*, or betrothal ceremony, cannot become official without a ceremony at which ... whiskey is served. So, the islanders are out of legal whiskey; the freighter is full of it. The only thing standing in the way of a most convenient solution is Captain Waggett (Basil Radford), the stiff and stern local Home Guard commander. How he's hoodwinked from impounding the cargo becomes a delightful comedy – based on Compton MacKenzie's novel of the same name, in turn based a true story. [Trivia notes: 1) The real shipwreck cargo only mostly contained cases of whiskey. The rest was currency – worth millions of dollars in today's equivalent.

241

The money was never recovered, and its disposition remains a mystery. 2) For the movie's American release, Hollywood censors insisted on an epilogue declaring that the islanders suffered nothing but unhappiness from their ill-gotten gain; the opposite of the movie's ending – and of the real-life incident. Widespread joy reigned supreme. 3) Also in America, the distributors changed the title to *Tight Little Island*] **[B&W]**

28. My Home Town

You might not know this, but America's first theater devoted exclusively to movies originated in Pittsburgh in 1905. That's when Harry Davis and John P. Harris opened their Nickelodeon on Smithfield Street, and the phenomenon spread like wildfire. Something else about the place of my birth: Warner Bros., one of the major studios, got its start there, with the literal four brothers –Albert, Harry, Jack and Sam Warner – showing motion pictures around and in Pittsburgh in the early years of the 20th century before moving to Hollywood. Yes, I'm a Pittsburgh boy, born in the city and raised on a farm to the north. Though I spent 44 years in the Washington, D.C., area and have lived over a decade in the endless hills of western Maryland, my deepest roots still lie in William Pitt's namesake at the confluence of the Allegheny, Monongahela and Ohio Rivers – also known at various times as Steel City, City of Bridges and City of Champions. Along with its other residents, I wildly celebrated Bill Mazeroski's World Series-winning homerun for the Pirates in 1960, and Franco Harris's "immaculate reception," propelling the Steelers into the Super Bowl in 1972. Most members of my family are buried there. I visit their graves periodically, and I treasure the memories Pittsburgh has given me, including the movies that have been shot there. Along with *Angels in the Outfield* and *Mrs. Soffel* in PF5, these five features showcase the rugged, working-class charms of one of the country's bedrock metropolitan areas.

Jack Reacher
2012 – written and directed by Christopher McQuarrie

I admit I was reluctant to include this one, despite its generous use of the city's locations, because it's so fundamentally unsavory. Based on Lee Child's popular novels, the movie introduces the title character (played by Tom Cruise, a talented actor but of a much smaller stature than the literary Reacher). The story begins with an event that has become horrifically common these days: a mass shooting. Someone with a high-powered rifle and a telescopic sight murders, at a distance, five seemingly unrelated individuals. Law enforcement acts quickly and finds the suspect, a deeply troubled Iraq war veteran, and plenty of evidence. That's when Reacher, a retired military police officer, appears. Immediately, he's under constant surveillance by police and frequent attack from an unknown group. Each time, we learn more about this mysterious man's background and his exceptional prowess at self-defense as he confronts an organization apparently capable of unlimited evil. Cruise is ably supported by Rosamund Pike as the accused's defense attorney, Robert Duvall as a crusty rifle range owner, and director Werner Herzog in a particularly creepy role as Reacher's ultimate nemesis. Lots of hand-to-hand (Reacher's exceptional at it), an extended shootout and a thrilling car chase through the downtown streets. [Trivia note, and a bit o' Pittsburgh trivia to boot. Shooting on location required one fight scene to take place in an old tract house in the city – one with a traditionally small bathroom. The lack of space not only made both the staging and the filming difficult, it also resulted in the scene playing partly for laughs] [Caution: graphic violence] **[W]**

The Next Three Days
2010 – written, co-produced and directed by Paul Haggis
Haggis, who wrote and directed *Crash* (PF5), the Best Picture five years earlier, here does the same with a thriller starring Russell Crowe as John Brennan, an ordinary man required to accomplish several extraordinary deeds in order to save his wife Lara (Elizabeth Banks), who has served three years of a life sentence in prison for murder. The movie's gimmick is we're not sure whether Lara is guilty, and there are suggestions she did commit the crime. But John remains convinced of her innocence and resolves to spring her. He seeks the help of Damon Pennington (Liam Neeson), an expert on prison escapes. Pennington advises John but warns him of the obstacles and extreme dangers in

attempting such a radical act. Nevertheless, John begins a painstaking, months-long effort to plan the escape, after which he will leave the country with Lara and their young son. Then he learns that Lara will be moved from her current location in ... three days, thereby accelerating both the planning and John's sense of desperation. Based on the French thriller *Anything for Her* (not here), Haggis has crafted a solid and consistently nail-biting story that showcases many Pittsburgh locations, including one of the city's crown jewels, the beautiful Highland Park Zoo. Crowe, as usual, contributes a compelling performance as Lara's rescuer. [Caution: violence] **[W]**

One for the Money
2012 – Julie Ann Robinson

Stephanie Plum (Katherine Heigl) is a Jersey girl and an unemployed lingerie clerk. Joe Morelli (Jason O'Mara) is a Jersey boy and a cop accused of murder. He's on the lam and has jumped bail. They both share a not-completely unpleasant memory some years ago of a sexual encounter. With bill collectors and auto-repo people after her, Stephanie takes the first available job from her bail-bondsman cousin to bring in Morelli, her lack of any relevant experience notwithstanding. From there, the chase is on, with Stephanie learning quickly to think on her feet – a good quality, because her inexperience gets her into several potentially lethal situations. She also receives help, occasionally, from Morelli, and from an experienced bounty hunter known as Ranger (Daniel Sunjata), both of whom pull her fat from the fire, as they say, on more than a few occasions. Based on the Stephanie Plum series of novels by Janet Evanovich (One for the Money was the first of 27 at this count, with each succeeding novel containing its number in the series in its title), it's meant to capture the atmosphere of and the characters populating New Jersey's working-class neighborhoods. As directed by Robinson, it does to a reasonable extent. The movie's problem is its star. Heigl tries to seem hard-edged, but it's a tough sell. Still, eventually I warmed to her. Besides, in terms of not fitting the role, that distinction had to go to, of all people, Debbie Reynolds, playing Stephanie's grandmother. Sorry, no sale there. Despite its shortcomings, the movie clicks along fairly well, and whether or not Stephanie and Morelli end up together you do tend to keep a rooting interest in their survival. [Trivia note: For reasons known only to the producers, instead of the story's setting in Trenton, the entire movie was filmed in or near Pittsburgh – even the opening shot!] [Caution: violence and sexuality] **[W]**

Pittsburgh
1942 – Lewis Seller
Though the story is set partially in Steel City, the title refers to the nickname of Charles Markham (John Wayne), a self-centered coal miner who rises, Scrooge-like, through the ranks across two decades to become a ruthless, money-grubbing steel tycoon. Moving up along with him for a while are Cash Evans (Randolph Scott), a fellow miner and Pittsburgh's best friend; and Josie Winters (the improbably cast Marlene Dietrich), his love interest, whose lower-class roots mirror his own. But Pittsburgh's ambitions cause him to discard Josie and marry Shannon Prentiss (Louise Allbritton), daughter of steel-mill owner Morgan Prentiss (Samuel L. Hinds, who played George Bailey's father in *It's a Wonderful Life* – see PF5). Unlike old Ebenezer, whose change of heart occurred via supernatural intervention and whose fortunes remained whole, Pittsburgh's avarice eventually causes his complete downfall. Finally humbled, he begins rebuilding his life at a time when the entire country's fate falls into doubt because of World War II. Not one of the Duke's greats, and a bit obvious with its morale-building message, but a diverting period drama, nevertheless. Watch for Shemp Howard of the Three Stooges in a semi-straight role. [Cultural note: Dietrich's character has a nickname, too. It's "Hunky," a derisive term primarily for people of Hungarian descent. One of many slurs hurled by Pittsburgh's many ethnic groups at one another, it also could be used to define anyone from Central Europe or even Russia. Growing up there, I soon learned them all – including the ones aimed at me] **[B&W]**

The Valley of Decision
1945 – Tay Garnett

In the early '40s, it seemed that Greer Garson was the go-to star for adaptations of best-selling novels. Consider *Blossoms in the Dust, Random Harvest, Madam Curie, Mrs. Parkington* (none here) and, of course, her Oscar-winning role in *Mrs. Miniver*. Here's another one, based on Pittsburgh author Marcia Davenport's tale about a 19th-century steel company scion (Gregory Peck), his rise to take over the family business and his love affair with Mary Rafferty (Garson), the family's Irish maid. Metro-Goldwyn-Mayer infused many of its most popular character actors in the cast, including Lionel Barrymore, Donald Crisp, Gladys Cooper, Reginald Owen and even a young Jessica Tandy. And Peck is fine in one of his early roles. But Garson anchors the whole story with her grounded performance as a working-class young woman who sees all too clearly the difficulties of marrying a man not only high above her social station but who also represents the management opposition to her own family members' attempts to unionize the mills. The result is a sprawling epic supporting the central romance. Melodrama aside, the story probes the suspicious rivalry that existed in Pittsburgh's early steel industry between the mill owners and the emerging union movement, a rivalry that often broke out into violence. [Trivia note: I mentioned those other movies for a reason. When Garson was nominated for *The Valley of Decision*, it marked her fifth consecutive nomination, tying her with Bette Davis for that achievement. 2) Speaking of *Mrs. Miniver*, Garson's Best Actress acceptance speech changed Hollywood history. At five-and-a-half minutes, it was deemed much too long, and from then on the motion picture academy imposed time limits on the winners] **[B&W]**

PS to this section

You can see a lovely series of shots of downtown Pittsburgh, beginning with a beautiful panorama of the area known as the Golden Triangle, under the opening credits of *Groundhog Day* (PF5).

29. Another Pittsburgh Boy

I share my hometown with many individuals who succeeded in Hollywood, including a few who even became immortal, such as Eugene Curran Kelly, born nine years earlier than my father and growing up just a few blocks away. As a pure dancer, Fred Astaire will remain forever for me as the best. But Kelly's dancing exhibited a singular physical quality, an unsurpassed manly gracefulness shown by no one before or since. Plus, he had a pleasant singing voice and a flair for comedy – all of which he demonstrated superbly in *An American in Paris* and *Singin' in the Rain* (both in PF5). And he often attempted – and succeeded at – something Astaire never tried: Kelly became a superb choreographer. Here are five examples of him starring plus taking on that role, and a sixth demonstrating his unparalleled athleticism, in chronological order…

Cover Girl
1944 – as Danny McGuire
Starting with Kelly's fourth musical, where he meets his dancing match in a surprising and delightful performance by Rita Hayworth, here at the peak of her talent and flaming red-haired beauty. She's Rusty, a chorus girl in Danny McGuire's nightclub, and therefore Hayworth is given several opportunities to dance with Kelly, such as "Put Me to the Test" and the lovely "Long Ago and Far Away," with music and lyrics by Jerome Kern and Ira Gershwin. No need to … cover for Hayworth's dancing. It's all her, and she's terrific – though veteran voice actress Martha Mears provides her singing voice. Kelly's choreography is competent, though standard for the time – except for two snazzy numbers; "Make Way for Tomorrow," where Kelly and Hayworth and Phil Silvers dance out of a café and down a street; and the "Alter Ego" dance, where he performs opposite a ghostly image of himself. A

big hit in its day, largely due to Hayworth's skyrocketing popularity, the movie inspired red-headed girls across the country to begin calling themselves "Rusty." Charles Vidor directed, with Silvers and Eve Arden supplying comic relief. Watch for a very young Shelley Winters appearing in a tiny, uncredited role. [Trivia note: You might have noticed my occasionally mentioning the Production Code where certain movies and scenes are concerned. Cover Girl features a song titled "The Show Must Go On," which under normal circumstances would never have gotten past the censors in '44 because it features Hayworth and seven other chorus girls bumping and grinding in skimpy costumes. But it stayed in the movie because Columbia Pictures successfully argued the girls would boost morale for wartime audiences, particularly young men in uniform]

The Three Musketeers (and) The Pirate
1948 – as d'Artagnan and as Serafin

I'm combining these two, both made in the same year and both showcasing Kelly's extraordinary athletic abilities – though only *The Pirate* features his dancing and choreographing talents.

*　　*　　*

The biggest hit of that year, *The Three Musketeers* is nevertheless problematic in a modern context because it's so darned silly most of the time despite its impressive cast. You'd think the production team was making, in earnest, "The Dueling Cavalier," the preposterous movie-within-the-movie in *Singin' in the Rain*. Following the classic novel by Alexandre Dumas, Kelly plays the young French swordsman who joins forces with comrades Athos, Porthos and Aramis (Van Heflin, Gig Young and Robert Coote), and fights to protect the honor of the Queen (Angela Lansbury). Rounding out that stellar cast are Frank Morgan, Vincent Price, June Allyson and Lana Turner. But all that pales now except for Kelly's extraordinary physical performance, including some thrilling swordsmanship, acrobatics and even horseback riding. [Personal quibble: This movie, along with the many succeeding versions of the story, fails to answer a lingering but obvious question: Why didn't the Three Musketeers carry muskets?]

249

In *The Pirate*, Kelly performs many of the same stunts but in a more limited way and couched within a musical. Kelly's Serafin is an itinerant performer visiting a Caribbean village who meets and falls in love with Manuela (Judy Garland), a local girl. To win her heart, Serafin pretends to be the notorious pirate Mack "the Black" Macoco, whom Manuela desires. The requisite misunderstandings and reconciliations follow. Kelly as choreographer created two show-stopping numbers. One is "Be a Clown," composed by the immortal Cole Porter, in which he partners with the fabulous Nicholas Brothers, Fayard and Harold, arguably the greatest dance team ever to hit the floor. There's also the four-minute fantasy "Pirate Ballet," where Kelly expertly wields a sword and swings high above the stage. Garland, meanwhile, is almost shockingly unenergetic, the likely result of marital strife (with her husband, and director, Vincente Minnelli), a variety of illnesses and medications, and a multi-pack-per-day cigarette habit. Kelly mostly carries her in their scenes together. A box-office bomb, *The Pirate* nevertheless led Kelly to begin directing, which he did as well as choreograph in *On the Town* (P25) the following year; likewise with Minnelli three years later in *An American Paris* (PF5), the Best Picture-winner. [Trivia notes: 1) About those controversies, one involved Kelly's number with the Nicholas Brothers. Metro-Goldwyn-Mayer cut it from reels of the movie shown in the South, where "interracial" dances were considered immoral. The action so enraged the Nicholases that they left the country for Europe and didn't return for over a decade. 2) Along similar lines, the original script included a nice part, and at least one solo, for MGM star Lena Horne as Manuela's best friend. But her entire part was cut in subsequent rewrites. 3) Speaking of immoral, Kelly and Garland's "Voodoo" dance was considered so outrageous by MGM head Louis B. Mayer that he ordered all of its film footage destroyed. 4) Four years later, songwriters Nacio Herb Brown and Arthur Freed were accused of plagiarizing Cole Porter's music from "Be a Clown" for Donald O'Connor's immortal number "Make 'em Laugh" in *Singin' in the*

Rain (PF5). You gotta admit, the songs sound suspiciously identical]

Summer Stock
1950 – as Joe D. Ross

Kelly again teams with Judy Garland for the third and final time (the first was 1942's *For Me and My Gal* – not here) in this problem-plagued but sprightly musical about community theater. Once again, Kelly does a memorable number, a solo reprise of "You Wonderful You," in which he delightfully and brilliantly uses a sheet of newspaper and a squeaky floor board as props. Judy does two of her own; first the lovely solo "Friendly Star," followed by the show-stopping "Get Happy," one of her most memorable songs, at the finale. The pair also performs a terrific tap-dance faceoff in "The Portland Fancy." Problem plagued? Prior to filming, Judy had suffered a breakdown and as a result gained considerable weight, necessitating some skillfully designed costumes to hide her condition. She also depended on several medications to help her through the shoot, requiring strategically placed – and fastened-down – props to aid her balance. And persistent emotional problems caused her to miss shooting several key scenes, which needed resourceful cuts, substitutions and dissolves in the editing room. All that said, *Summer Stock* retains a delightful quality and some brief but sublime moments where Judy shines as only she can. [Trivia notes: 1) Ironic, but the "Get Happy" number was choreographed by director Charles Walters, not Kelly. They shot it a couple of months after the production had wrapped, and after Judy had gone on a radical diet – you might have noticed she appeared a little heavy during most of the movie. 2) You also might wonder why Kelly kept working with Judy Garland despite her difficulties. The two had become close friends doing *For Me and My Gal* together, and Kelly remained fiercely loyal to her – to the point of jumping at the chance to co-star with her again, and even faking an injury on the set one day so she could take a desperately needed rest]

Brigadoon

1954 – as Tommy Albright

Kelly, working once again as actor and choreographer with director Vincente Minnelli, is supported by Cyd Charisse and Van Johnson in a beguiling musical about a mythical Scottish village that appears once every hundred years. His Tommy Albright is caught, literally, between two worlds: the urban life of New York City and his fiancée Judy (Elaine Stewart) and the magical atmosphere of Brigadoon and Fiona Campbell (Charisse), the love of his life. Based on Alan Jay Lerner's Broadway musical, the movie features several wonderful songs, particularly Kelly's solo, "Almost Like Being in Love," and "The Heather on the Hill," a gorgeous courtship dance by the two leads. The strange aspect of the screen adaptation is its staginess. Though MGM built a huge set and backdrop for the Scottish sequences, you're always aware that the movie is essentially a filmed musical. That same year, the studio produced *Seven Brides for Seven Brothers* (P25) nearly the same way. Yet that movie seemed much more lively and became a smash hit, while *Brigadoon* languished. Still, I prefer it because it manages to produce moments of exquisite beauty and pathos, largely due to the onscreen chemistry between Kelly and Charisse. [Technical notes: 1) Movies in the early 1950s suffered from problems similar to those made in the late '20s, when studios were struggling to transition from silent features to the talkies. Here, widescreen epics had become the rage, and Hollywood scrambled to employ the new formats such as CinemaScope and VistaVision. The problem was that many theaters weren't yet equipped to handle the changes. So, every shot and every scene in *Brigadoon* had to be done twice; once in widescreen and once in the decades-old standard format – a nightmare for cast and crew alike. 2) For unfathomable reasons, MGM decided to shoot Brigadoon using Anscochrome film, instead of the excellent and durable Technicolor. The result is the colors look unpleasantly washed out instead of vivid] [Trivia note: Remember the scene in *Singin' in the Rain* (PF5) where Don Lockwood (Kelly) and Lina Lamont (Jean Hagen) squabbled between takes while filming a romantic scene? Reportedly, that's what happened often between

252

Kelly and Charisse – though she later said *Brigadoon* was her favorite among the films she made with him] **[W]**

It's Always Fair Weather
1955 – as Ted Riley

Kelly co-directs again with Stanley Donen (as they did in *Singin' in the Rain*), in this tale of three Army buddies reuniting 10 years after the end of World War II. Also as in *Singin'* he's joined by co-writers Betty Comden and Adolph Green, plus Cyd Charisse again as Kelly's love interest, and a young André Previn providing the music. Great ingredients, but for some reason this one never caught on with audiences. It lost money and began a long, slow slide in popularity at the box office for movie musicals made by Metro-Goldwyn-Mayer. But don't sell it short. Kelly does "I Like Myself," a wonderful tap number on roller-skates up and down a busy street. In "The Binge," he romps with co-stars Dan Dailey and Michael Kidd using, of all things, trash can lids as props. Then there's Charisse's show-stopper, "Baby, You Knock Me Out," in which she first recites the entire roster (up to then) of heavyweight champion boxers and then dances with an assortment of local gymnasium denizens. Wow! Once again Charisse shows why she's arguably the most glamorous dancer who ever lived. [Trivia note: Again, for unfathomable reasons (see *Brigadoon*, above), MGM decided to release this movie in a double-bill with *Bad Day at Black Rock* (PF5). A fine postwar drama and one of my original favorites, it isn't what you would call light entertainment; nor would it put audiences in a receptive mood for a musical] **[W]**

30. Nastyfellas*

*plus, some nasty dames and a couple of bad, bad cats

In 1990, Martin Scorsese directed the ironically titled gangster saga *Goodfellas* (PF5). In that same vein, but without the irony, these 14 titles feature fellas, gals and a pair of marauding lions that go about their business with little or no regard for the harshness of their actions. Or they've been driven to take such measures by the enormity of the evil confronting them. I know, I know, 14 chapters ago (coincidentally) I listed movies whose themes closely resemble some of the plots here. The difference is these stories focus more sharply on the nasty subjects themselves. They do what they do as Ian Holm's Ash, the rogue robot in *Alien* (PF5), described that rampaging creature. They are, applying his quote, "unclouded by conscience, remorse or delusions of morality." Despite their frightening characteristics, you might just love to hate a few of them and possibly even root for them – though please do so entirely in the company of adults. None should be viewed by youngsters or those easily disturbed by screen violence.

48 Hrs.

1981 – co-written and directed by Walter Hill

Eddie Murphy, who burst on the scene as a member of the second cast of NBC's Saturday Night Live, here eases effortlessly into big-screen stardom in Hill's raw and violent comedy–drama. Murphy is Reggie Hammond, a career crook serving out a sentence for armed robbery but temporarily sprung by Jack Cates (Nick Nolte), a hard-bitten San Francisco cop. Cates is after Albert Ganz (James Remar), the real nasty in the story, a prison escapee, murderer of two of his fellow cops and a former associate of Hammond's. Cates is warned by his superiors that he has only … 48 hours to find Ganz before he must return Hammond to the slammer. Of course, Cates and Hammond take an immediate dislike to each other, but Hammond must cooperate in the hunt because Ganz wants for himself a huge stash of ill-gotten cash Hammond has hidden away. It's an express train of a crime thriller, with plenty of rough-hewn, mostly improvised banter between Nolte and Murphy, while the hunt frequently turns lethal for everyone around Ganz and his two pursuers. Annette O'Toole makes an appealing but brief appearance as Elaine, Cates's girlfriend, and James Horner contributes a throbbing, visceral score in an early work – one of the best things in the movie. [Caution: sexuality, constant coarse language and extreme violence] **[W]**

Death Wish
1974 – Michael Winner
If you can accept Charles Bronson as a successful architect, instead of his usual assortment of western hombres and other tough guys, you'll probably go along with the rest of the plot. Bronson is much more plausible when he turns avenger, looking to fight crime personally after his wife is killed and his daughter raped by a trio of vicious thugs. In the nearly half-century since the movie's release, it has continually raised hackles among critics and politicians alike because of the visceral satisfaction it provides each time Paul Kersey (Bronson's character) dispenses vigilante justice to the lowlifes he encounters on the streets of New York. The thing is, in all those years, the issue of taking revenge against criminals because of law enforcement failures has never gone away. It remains depressingly relevant and uncomfortably satisfying. Watch for comedian and *auteur* Christopher Guest in his second early role as a young cop. [Trivia notes: 1) One of the three murderous thugs in that brutal early scene is played by Jeff Goldblum in his movie debut, and one of the subway muggers is now-veteran actor and playwright Saul Rubinek. 2) Another weird bit of casting – a coincidence, actually. Vincent Gardenia plays Lieutenant Frank Ochoa, the cop charged with tracking down the notorious vigilante, while Olympia Dukakis, in an early uncredited role, is also a police officer. Thirteen years later they

255

would play Cher's parents in the beguiling *Moonstruck* (PF5)] [Caution: particularly nasty violence, including rape] **[W]**

Fletch
1985 – Michael Ritchie
The publicity materials and poster art for this one pushed the idea that it's just another somewhat raunchy but light Chevy Chase comedy. And there are some funny – and raunchy – scenes, with Chase in the title role playing a Los Angeles Times investigative reporter. But much of the story contains darker elements, and its overall premise is indeed nasty. Consider this: Alan Stanwyck (Tim Matheson), a wealthy businessman, approaches Fletch, who's pursuing a story by pretending to be a beach druggie. Unaware of who he really is, Stanwyck attempts to hire him as an assassin in a forced-suicide scheme. But Fletch suspects something else is afoot and that Stanwyck isn't going to be the victim. He spends the rest of the movie trying to unravel the puzzle. As far as the funny scenes, most involve Fletch in silly aliases, disguises and situations, including an unexpected rectal exam. Meanwhile he meets, becomes smitten with and romances Gail (Dana Wheeler-Nicholson), Stanwyck's soon-to-be-widowed wife. When the climax arrives, however, the humor disappears and the really unsavory stuff emerges, in all directions, including a confrontation between the movie's two villains, Stanwyck and Jerry Karlin (Joe Don Baker), a crooked police chief. Richard Libertini and Geena Davis appear in likeable roles as, respectively, Fletch's editor and a newsroom assistant improbably named "Larry." And Harold Faltermeyer, who had done a superior score for *Beverly Hills Cop* (PF5) the previous year, here contributes a disappointing but still catchy clone. [Caution: sexuality and violence] **[W]**

The Ghost and the Darkness
1996 – Stephen Hopkins
A couple of rough scenarios here – both in the story and the production. In the story, based on a real incident, the nasties are two marauding lions willfully attacking workers building a

railroad bridge in the Tsavo region of Kenya at the end of the 19th century. Even more terrifying, the predatory pair seem to be working in tandem, something unheard of in males of the species. Perhaps they are attempting to drive away the humans invading their territory or satisfying their voracious appetites. Or maybe it's simply because they can take what they want. Whatever, the lions (maneless males in the real incident but conventionally portrayed here) frequently ambush the workers with relentless and horrific attacks. They seem unstoppable. When the crisis finally halts construction, the chief engineer and project commander, Lieutenant Colonel John Henry Patterson (Val Kilmer), hires safari hunter John Remington (Michael Douglas), to track down and kill the lions. The task proves much more difficult, and costly, than either man can imagine, particularly Remington. The story often seems to veer into improbability – except the events depicted really happened. Based on Patterson's memoir The Man-Eaters of Tsavo, with a screenplay by William Goldman, the movie vividly conveys how the attacks kept the tens of thousands of workers in sheer terror for nine months, and cost more than 30 lives.

*　　*　　*

About the production, a huge endeavor that took place in South Africa and involved thousands of cast and crew, director Hopkins in an interview described it this way:

> "We had snakebites, scorpion bites, tick-bite fever, people getting hit by lightning, floods, torrential rains ... hippos chasing people through the water, cars getting swept into the water and several deaths ... including two drownings."

In other words, a "nightmare," as Hopkins added in an interview. Plus, he and Douglas, who co-produced the movie, argued constantly. And the perpetually severe heat often fried the electronic equipment. Then there were the daily difficulties with Bongo and Caesar, the two trained, full-sized lions used for certain scenes (alternating with elaborate mechanical duplicates). The big cats disdained their confinement and their restraints, breaking free at every opportunity and scaring the bejeebers out

257

of those nearby. Given all that, *The Ghost and the Darkness* (the names given the real predators by the railroad workers) remains a remarkable achievement.

*   *   *

[Trivia notes: 1) Remington's character is fictional, invented by Goldman for the movie. In reality, Patterson killed both animals. 2) You can view the real lions, stuffed and preserved, in a diorama at the Field Museum in Chicago. The museum purchased their remains from Patterson in 1924. 3) What seems remarkable about the mounted beasts is their size – no bigger than large dogs. That's because their skins had shrunk over time, before the museum specialists could work on them. The living animals were considerably larger, possibly weighing 400 pounds or more each. 4) Researchers studying the cats' skulls have speculated on why the Lions of Tsavo preferred human flesh to their regular prey. Both were found to have injured teeth, something that could have led the cats to hunt the workers, who were slow and easy to catch and eat, versus the quick, tough-hided and large-boned animals roaming the savanna. 5) Though Patterson asserted – and the movie's background material repeats – that the lions claimed more than 130 victims, subsequent research lowered that total to about 35. 6) Ironic, but Tsavo, in the language of the Akamba people of Kenya, means "place of slaughter." 7) The railway car, scene of one of the attacks, had been used 11 years earlier as the one carrying Karen Blixen to her destination in *Out of Africa* (PF5)] [Caution: extremely violent animal attacks] **[W]**

High Plains Drifter
1973 – Clint Eastwood

As my dear Jessie often reminds me, there are only two essential story plots; a person goes on a journey, and a stranger rides into town. This one's the latter, with Clint at his most unapologetically brutal as the stranger. As soon as he, literally, rides into Lago, a mining town in an unspecified part of the 19th-century West, he's immediately challenged by three local hoods, whom he quickly dispatches. Then he's insulted by the local trollop (TV veteran Marianna Hill, miscast here), so he … um, takes her involuntarily.

258

Et cetera. It's the typical character and plot that propelled Clint's earlier Spaghetti Westerns, which he made in Europe in the 1960s with director Sergio Leone. Except here he steps up to directing himself. It turns out this nameless man has ridden into Lago on a mission of deadly revenge, something he deals out to various townsmen and outsiders alike with abandon while continuing to take advantage of the women (Hill and Verna Bloom, both in thankless roles). Naturally, they all plot to kill him and rid themselves of this nuisance – a bad, bad mistake. [Caution: violence and sexuality, including rape] **[W]**

Misery
1990 – Rob Reiner
Here's one of the nasty gals of the category, the mother of all deranged fans. Based on the Stephen King novel, and adapted by William Goldman, Kathy Bates stars in an Oscar-winning role as Annie Wilkes, a literary fan whose obsession with author Paul Sheldon (James Caan) rises nearly to the same league as Norman Bates with his mother in *Psycho*, except in reverse. That is, when Sheldon suddenly appears on Annie's doorstep – actually, he gets lost in a blizzard and she finds him and brings him home – well, she just can't let go of him. In particular, Annie is obsessed with Sheldon's … "Misery" novels (Misery is the first name of his heroine). She becomes positively psychotic when she learns how Sheldon's latest installment ends. Annie forces him – injured, bedridden and isolated – to burn his only manuscript and begin writing a new novel more suitable to her sensibilities. When he attempts to spike her wine with sleeping pills so he can escape, let's just say he suffers greatly for his attempt. It all eventually leads to a desperate, life-or-death battle between the two. In Goldman's second adapted screenplay in this category, *Misery* is full of his trademark dark humor. It's also Reiner's second successful adaptation of King, following *Stand by Me* four years earlier. [Trivia note: Reiner mercifully moderated what Annie does to Sheldon to keep him from escaping. In the novel, she actually takes an ax and … well, you can probably imagine] [Caution: adult themes and brutality] **[W]**

Payback
1999 – co-written and directed* by Brian Helgeland

Whoever invented the term "black comedy" could have been inspired by this one. Mel Gibson plays a character named, only, Porter, whom we see at the start being treated by a back-alley doctor for gunshot wounds. From there, he tells us via narration how he will plot his revenge on those who betrayed him out of a $70,000 illegal payday. Among the paybackees, in ascending order, are *caporegimes* William Devane and James Coburn, and their non-Italian don Kris Kristofferson, all part of a Chicago criminal cartel. Naturally, they dismiss Porter's demand, particularly for such a relatively small amount. So, one by one – though not without difficulty – Porter must work his way up the chain of command, using whatever means necessary to obtain his … payback. The story is constantly brutal, with several shocking scenes, but somehow you don't take it as seriously as you should. Does Porter exact his revenge and win back his due? Well, in a similar vein as *Misery*, he must first surrender, most painfully, a couple of body parts. Now, here's the kicker. Notice that asterisk (*) above, beside the word "directed"? That's because *Payback*, as Helgeland delivered it, was actually much more violent than it now appears. Studio executives were so shocked at some of the scenes that they fired Helgeland and ordered a toned-down rewrite – and this was after Gibson had handpicked him to direct. Makes you wonder what they deemed too shocking to show. [Caution: sexuality and extreme violence, including torture] **[W]**

The Professional
1994 – France – written and directed by Luc Besson

In the introduction I mentioned that some of these characters go about their business with little regard for its impact, or they are driven to take revenge on the evil that has confronted them. Léon (Jean Reno), the title character here, does so for a different reason: He's a paid assassin and troubleshooter – though personal reasons do eventually enter the picture. Those aspects involve 12-year-old Mathilda (12-year-old Natalie Portman in her debut), a girl living in an adjoining apartment to Léon's in New York City.

Mathilda's family, including her little brother, has just been wiped out by crooked federal drug officers headed by Norman Stansfield (Gary Oldman, in by far his creepiest role), and she persuades Léon to hide her from the assassins. Therein begins one of the most unusual screen relationships you're likely to see, and although nothing overt ever happens between the pair, some of the scenes do veer perilously close to the inappropriate. Nearly as troublesome, when Mathilda learns that Léon is a hitman, she becomes fascinated with his … profession and urges him to instruct her in the tools and tricks of the trade. Léon refuses. In fact, the longer they are together, the more paternal and protective he becomes, to the point where those protective emotions begin to take over his behavior, leading him to self-sacrifice (in a shockingly witty scene) to save her. Portman is so effective as Mathilda she will make you feel frequently uncomfortable. Reno, meanwhile, is sensationally understated as Léon, maybe the coolest and most methodical assassin ever. [Trivia note: It might seem strange to complain about a wrong note in a movie like this one, but I found the casting of Broadway actress and singer Ellen Greene as Mathilda's addled and ill-fated stepmother to be a step too far] [Caution: extreme violence] **[W]**

Sudden Impact
1983 — Clint Eastwood
A complicated plot involving revenge for a decade-old gang rape showcases the Bay Area's baddest cop, "Dirty Harry" Callahan, in this fourth installment of the series, the only one Clint directed. Sondra Locke, with whom he was romantically involved at the time, plays a woman avenging the assault on her and her sister by systematically and gruesomely assassinating the rapists and their associates. Callahan – in between several crowd-pleasing scenes in which he dispatches bad guys – is the San Francisco detective who tries to track her down. Formulaic? Yes, but with all of the blood-rush touches that made the Callahan movies so popular, including the now-classic Dirty Harry epithet, "Go ahead, make my day." [Trivia notes: 1) Albert Popwell, the wounded bank robber of whom Harry asks, "Do you feel lucky?" in the original

Dirty Harry, returns here as an associate of Harry's. Popwell appeared two other series installments as well. 2) When Clint ran for mayor of Carmel, California, in 1986 he used the slogan, "Go Ahead – Make Me Mayor." He won!] [Caution: graphic violence and brutality] **[W]**

Taken
2008 – France – Pierre Morel
In the vein of *Death Wish*, Liam Neeson joins the action genre as an avenging father with covert skills in this French thriller. He's Bryan Mills, a former Special Forces operative whose daughter Kim (Maggie Grace), visiting Paris with a friend, has been kidnapped by unknown perpetrators. When Kim tries to call Bryan to describe her attackers, and one of them takes the phone, Bryan, let's say advises the man to release her immediately or face lethal consequences. To which he replies, "good luck." Bryan then begins a desperate effort to find his daughter, whom he learns has been … taken by an international prostitution ring. Realizing he has only a limited time to find Kim before she's transported out of France, his actions become increasingly relentless – and ruthless. Given the brutality that Bryan dishes out, and the astoundingly rapid body count, you can only wonder what extreme measures he took during his professional career. As with Charles Bronson's Paul Kersey, however, you might find yourself enjoying the unofficial justice delivered to men who prey on innocent young women. [Caution: extreme violence] **[W]**

Taxi Driver
1976 – Martin Scorsese
"Are you talkin' to me?" Another line now firmly ensconced in popular culture. This seemingly innocuous question actually precedes a cascading torrent of violence undertaken by Travis Bickle (Robert De Niro), the titular character, as he faces the camera and prepares to confront a dangerous foe before drawing a handgun to do battle. The general theme of this section involves characters who must either confront manifestations of evil or their own descent into moral darkness or insanity. In Scorsese's morbid

and surrealistic tale, written by Paul Schrader, Bickle must do both. He's a Vietnam War veteran taking a job as a ... taxi driver in New York to pass the time and earn some money. He's quickly confronted by examples of the city's rot, such as a teenage prostitute (a plump and very young Jodie Foster in her debut) managed by a disgusting pimp (Harvey Keitel, who had played De Niro's friend in Scorsese's *Mean Streets* – see P25 – three years earlier). And that's a mild example. Scorsese intended the movie as a nightmare vision but not as a horror movie. What's presented might be impressionistic, but it's also shockingly real, as raw a portrait of big-city life as ever has been shown, intensified by Michael Chapman's deeply muted cinematography. Cybill Shepherd and Albert Brooks appear in small roles, and Bernard Herrmann, generally associated with Alfred Hitchcock's movies, composed the quietly unnerving score. [Trivia notes: 1) De Niro drove a cab in New York for weeks before shooting started to gain familiarity with the job and the milieu. Even though he had won an Oscar for *The Godfather Part II* (PF5) two years earlier, only one passenger recognized him – a fellow actor who nervously asked De Niro if he was having trouble finding work. 2) Foster was so young (age 12, the same as Natalie Portman in *The Professional*) when she did the movie that her 19-year-old sister had to double for her in some of the explicit scenes] [Extreme caution: language, sexuality and graphic violence] **[W]**

The Usual Suspects
1995—Bryan Singer

Actually, they're a group of *un*usual suspects, and what a motley crew – acted by Stephen Baldwin, Gabriel Byrne, Benicio del Toro, Kevin Pollak and Kevin Spacey. They're five criminals who think nothing of stealing, lying, assaulting and, on occasion when deemed necessary, dispatching anyone for any reason. You've got Keaton (Byrne), a crooked ex-cop with a vicious reputation. There's Fenster (del Toro), a wild card who speaks in a dialect no one can understand. McManus and Hockney (Baldwin and Pollak) hate each other and display explosive, hair-trigger tempers. And the mysterious Kint (Spacey), hobbled by cerebral palsy, seems to possess some knowledge but no physical ability. Put these volatile personalities together for three capers of increasing size, complexity and danger, and there's bound to be trouble—lots of it. This one became a cult hit because of its extremely convoluted plot, surprisingly amusing banter among the five principals, and its sudden and shocking revelation. [Trivia note: Oscar-winning screenwriter Christopher McQuarrie started out working in a detective agency. He said his experiences there inspired much of the movie's plot] [Caution: violence and constant rough language] **[W]**

Walking Tall
1973 – Phil Karlson

Here's Joe Don Baker again, this time in a heroic but tragic role as real-life Sheriff Buford Pusser in a raw tale about small-town corruption in Tennessee. Pusser is a former pro wrestler who returns to his roots and attempts to establish a lumber business with his father (Noah Beery Jr.) His plans are interrupted when he runs afoul of the crooked owners of a local gambling and prostitution den. Nearly beaten to death, Pusser recovers and takes personal revenge on his attackers. The action leads to his arrest and a trial, where he's acquitted after suddenly and dramatically bearing his wounds to the jury. He then begins a campaign for sheriff in an attempt to fight the county's rampant corruption. He wins, but his effort proves extremely costly, both to him and his wife Pauline (Elizabeth Hartman). New York Times critic Judith Crist described *Death Wish*, released the following year, as an "urban version of *Walking Tall.*" That's appropriate – except in this case it's the good citizens of the town who finally step up and finish what Pusser had struggled so hard to achieve. A rough and tough tale but an unforgettable one. [Trivia note: *Walking Tall* was associated with one of the most successful publicity campaigns in Hollywood history. Its simple tagline, "When was the last time you stood up and applauded the movie?" attracted such crowds that the movie grossed 80 times its production budget] [Caution: violence and constant rough language] **[W]**

The Whole Nine Yards
2000 – Jonathan Lynn

Who's the nasty in this black comedy? Actually, there are several. Most prominent is Sophie Oseransky (Rosanna Arquette), the scheming and unfaithful wife of "Oz" Oseransky (Matthew Perry, late of the hit TV series Friends), a henpecked dentist. Sophie hates Oz and wants him killed. Then there's Janni Gogolak (Kevin Pollak) and his various henchmen. Gogolak is a mob boss hunting for errant hitman Jimmy "The Tulip" Tudeski (Bruce Willis), who's in hiding and turns out to be Oz's next-door neighbor. On the so-called good side are Jill St. Claire (Amanda Peet in another sensational role), Oz's receptionist and an aspiring assassin; Cynthia Tudeski (Natasha Henstrich), Jimmy's estranged wife, looking to acquire his concealed $10-million fortune; and (possibly) Frankie "Figs" Figueroa (Michael Clarke Duncan), another Gogolak henchman but secretly allied with Jimmy. That's the cast. As for the plot ... well, it would require great lengths to explain it, and I think doing so would spoil much of the guilty fun. Plus, if you've watched some of the other titles in this category, you might find this one a source of comic relief – particularly two scenes; one in which Jill meets Jimmy, and he begins to instruct her in the rules of the hit game as if they were discussing legitimate tradecraft, and another where Jill, about to complete her first assignment, distracts her target using a rather ... um, notable device. [Caution: language, violence and sexuality] **[W]**

31. A Naughty Boy – Who Made Good

Terrence Steven McQueen, born March 24, 1930, and died November 7, 1980, of mesothelioma, enjoyed a nearly 15-year run as one of the most popular stars in American movies and, for a short time, became the highest-paid of them all. That was a meteoric rise from his beginnings. Deserted by his father before he was born, the young McQueen bounced around for years, living alternatively with his grandparents, an uncle, and his twice-married mother and two abusive stepfathers, before running away and living on the streets as a petty thief and gang member – beginning at age nine. After being institutionalized at a youth correctional facility, his full redemption came some years later during a stint in the U.S. Marines. Then came his interest and training in stage acting, where he showed immediate promise. It took nearly a decade before his breakthrough in films, however, co-starring in *The Magnificent Seven* in 1960, followed by *The Great Escape* three years later (both in PF5). A further series of hits established his stardom. Then, in the mid-1970s, after a strong performance in *The Towering Inferno* (also in PF5), he began a long hiatus from the big screen, spending much of his time traveling and racing motorcycles. When he re-emerged, in the last year of his life, he took on two roles based loosely on true stories, *Tom Horn* and *The Hunter* (neither on my lists). Both bombed at the box office. But McQueen's brief legacy remains strong, largely because of his riveting onscreen persona, which earned him the moniker "The King of Cool." Along with his laid-back rodeo star in *Junior Bonner* (another in PF5) and that aforementioned high-rise fireman in *The Towering Inferno*, as well as the original *Thomas Crown Affair*, elsewhere, here are seven more distinctive roles, chronologically…

266

Love With the Proper Stranger
1963 – as Rocky Papasano

McQueen made two movies scored by Elmer Bernstein that year: the superior wartime thriller *The Great Escape* and this one, a truly appealing romantic drama accompanied by Bernstein's lush orchestral music. Rocky Papasano is a musician (I'll mention more about that in a moment) who has romanced, and impregnated, Angela Rossini (Natalie Wood in one of her best performances). We learn this because Angela has tracked down Rocky at a musicians' union hall where he's busy lining up future gigs. Naturally, Rocky is stunned by the news and jumps immediately at Angela's suggestion that she abort the pregnancy. But when faced with the reality of the deed, he balks, pulling Angela out of the back-room location of the procedure and proposing to marry her. Thinking he's acting only out of sympathy, she declines, declaring that she wants to be wooed by someone "with bells and banjos." Her demand eventually turns into a literal performance by Rocky, leading to a happy ending. Directed by Robert Mulligan, who the previous year had done *To Kill a Mockingbird* (P25), it's a charming story, and the two leads seem just right in their roles. Wood later said this was her favorite film. [Viewing note: About Rocky's profession: Nowhere in the entire movie do we see McQueen playing an instrument – though he holds a banjo at the climax. A minor point but a curious one] [Trivia note: Watch for Brad Dexter, one of McQueen's fellow gunmen in *The Magnificent Seven* (also scored by Bernstein), in an uncredited cameo as a booking agent] [Caution: adult themes] **[B&W] [W]**

The Cincinnati Kid
1965 – in the title role

McQueen as card shark Eddie "The Kid" Stoner challenges Edward G. Robinson's Lancey "The Man" Howard in a high-stakes game of poker in New Orleans in the 1930s. Given the milieu and the characters involved, it's inevitable that corruption and crime will emerge, including blackmail. That happens to Stoner's friend Shooter (Karl Malden), who's forced to cheat in a card game to prevent shocking revelations about his wife Melba

(Ann-Margret at her most ravishing), who has been attempting to seduce the Kid and drive him away from Christian (Tuesday Weld), his girlfriend. The intrigue leads to the big game, in which six players dwindle down to two: the Kid and the Man. It's a tense standoff, and the multimillion-to-one ending is too good to give away. McQueen is fine as the Kid, but Robinson is outstanding, justifying the denouement for both men. The great actor agreed, writing in his autobiography that the "man on the screen, more than in any other picture I ever made, was Edward G. Robinson ... [I]t was symbolically the playing out of my whole gamble with life." Robinson also complimented McQueen, calling him "a stunner." Directed by Norman Jewison, who reunited with McQueen three years later in *The Thomas Crown Affair*, the edgy script is by veteran writers Terry Southern and Ring Lardner Jr., the latter of whom had been blacklisted in the 1950s. [Caution: adult themes] **[B&W] [W]**

Nevada Smith
1966 – as Max Sand

Here's a most unusual source for McQueen's title character: Max Sand/Nevada Smith was a *fictional* character within the Harold Robbins novel The Carpetbaggers, a thinly veiled portrait of tycoon Howard Hughes during his early Hollywood years. This movie purports to chronicle the *real* Sand's ordeal, which begins when his parents are murdered by a trio of outlaws. Therein begins the young man's decade-long quest to rain vengeance on the three killers, led by Frank Fitch (Karl Malden again, this time in a villainous role). Unfortunately, what also begins is a sequence of casting misjudgments that strain credibility at every corner. For example, the blue-eyed, 35-year-old McQueen is supposed to be the teenage son of a Native American mother (who's never shown). You've also got three beautiful, sophisticated actresses playing, in order, a Kiowa dance hall girl (Janet Margolin), the widow of one of the murderers (Joanna Moore) and a Cajun ... um, comfort woman (Suzanne Pleshette). And there are Fitch's two henchmen, Coe and Bowdre (Martin Landau and Arthur Kennedy), whom Sand tracks down and kills. It's a stretch for two

268

otherwise fine actors, and a game effort for McQueen and Malden – and weirdly fascinating overall – but calmer heads and better judgment should have prevailed with this one. The title? It's the alias Sand gives when trying to infiltrate Fitch's new outlaw gang. Shot entirely in California, Henry Hathaway directed. [Trivia notes: 1) Ten years earlier, Landau and McQueen became the only two aspirants accepted, out of thousands of applicants, into Lee Strasberg's legendary studio in New York. 2) And speaking of history – and miscasting – in the course of Sand's quest, his character and Pleshette's briefly become lovers. The problem is the two actors had been close platonic friends for a long time, and both found their intimate scenes awkward in the extreme] [Caution: violence] **[W]**

Bullitt
1968 – as SFPD Lieutenant Frank Bullitt
I'll make this one short. Two years before Gene Hackman electrified audiences by chasing down a would-be assassin across the streets of New York City in *The French Connection* (PF5), McQueen turned in a masterful chase sequence of his own – doing much of the driving himself – an 11-minute thrill road up and down the streets of San Francisco and some of the surrounding hills in this otherwise mundane crime drama directed by Peter Yates, in his debut. McQueen's *Magnificent Seven* colleague Robert Vaughn appears as a sleazy politician. [Trivia notes: 1) The bad guy driving the car Frank Bullitt is chasing is played by Bill Hickman, a stunt driver who actually did drive the fleeing vehicle. 2) Though Robert Vaughn considered running for political office in later years, his character in *Bullitt* dogged him because people linked him with the fictional persona. Yet he often called the movie his favorite] [Caution: violence and sexuality] **[W]**

Le Mans
1971 – as Frank Delaney
Possibly McQueen's most challenging and dangerous role because it involved his participating, though surreptitiously and

intermittently, in the real 24-hour race. It also presaged the climax of *Ford v Ferrari* (P25) some 48 years later, though the race outcome depicted in that movie had occurred four years earlier. By the time production began, McQueen was an experienced racer, driving competitively for nearly a decade. He even nearly won the 12 Hours of Sebring in 1969, losing to racing star Mario Andretti. In this highly troubled production, McQueen wanted to drive in Le Mans 1970 and film the race more as a documentary than a fictional drama. His insistence – and intransigence – cost McQueen dearly. John Sturges, his director on *The Magnificent Seven* and *The Great Escape*, and the original director here, quit before filming began. The large budget and scheduling overruns required him to forfeit his salary for and profit share of the movie. He also accidentally rolled a car after-hours, a mishap for which a crewmember accepted blame. And one of the stunt drivers lost a leg in a bad crash. The result? A hodgepodge, with some solid racing scenes but substandard melodrama – much like John Frankenheimer's *Grand Prix* (PF5) in 1966 without the slick editing and breathtaking Cinerama format. Furthermore, it was the last time McQueen ever drove a car competitively. [Caution: adult themes and intense racing scenes] **[W]**

On Any Sunday
1971 – as himself
Another quick one, not because there's anything wrong with this motorcycle-racing documentary directed and narrated by Bruce Brown (he of *The Endless Summer*) and featuring McQueen, who spent much of his adult life as an enthusiast. It's just that McQueen appears ever-so-briefly, intermittently and unprominently. In fact, you'll have to watch closely to spot him – though he did fund the production – merely one of the many filmed subjects riding happily or competitively – or both – on two wheels. The movie culminates in two amazing events. The first is the annual climb up a steep 600-foot hill near Salt Lake City called the Widow-Maker, for good reason. The second is a massive cross-desert race that draws up to 2,000 riders ... on any Sunday. The prize? A single trophy.

270

The Getaway
1972 – as Carter "Doc" McCoy

I could have easily placed this one, now in its 50th year, in the previous chapter. Directed by Sam Peckinpah, who notoriously used live ammunition in his shootout sequences – he liked to see real panic on his actors' faces – it's a brutal crime drama featuring McQueen as Doc, a convicted bank robber, and Ali McGraw as Carol, his wife. It begins when Doc is denied parole and Carol sacrifices her honor with Jack Beynon (Ben Johnson), a corrupt Texas businessman with political connections, to free him. Beynon arranges the release, under the condition that Doc perform a new robbery. The heist goes bad, however, setting off a chain of increasingly violent confrontations involving Doc and Rudy (an extremely menacing Al Lettieri), one of the other robbers, as they hunt each other during their ... getaway. Trouble also arises between Doc and Carol when he realizes what she did to secure his release. Another complication involves an outsider (Richard Bright) who steals the loot from the robbery, requiring Doc to chase him on a train. During it all, McQueen portrays an unyielding determination that makes Doc arguably his most arresting character. *The Getaway* is a wild, murderous ride, leading to a completely unexpected ending. Quincy Jones composed the surprisingly whimsical, jazzy harmonica score, featuring Toots Thielemans. [Trivia notes: 1) Two cast members from *The Godfather* (PF5), made the same year, appear here. Lettieri played the vicious rival mobster Sollozzo, and Bright became Michael's primary operative for assassinations. 2) Speaking of *The Godfather*, Ali McGraw was the wife of Robert Evans, an executive at Paramount involved in that movie's production. But then she began an affair with McQueen during *The Getaway*'s filming that ended her marriage – she eventually married McQueen] [Caution: sexuality, intense violence and constant nastiness] **[W]**

271

32. On a More Serious Note

Not often but sometimes, movies will successfully delve into the darkest and most disturbing subjects in an extremely mature manner, leaving us troubled by what we have seen but more aware of what has transpired in the real world when the end credits roll. These nine gripping dramas, all based on true events and all requiring a great deal of patience and fortitude to watch, do just that.

Amazing Grace
2006 – England – Michael Apted

Apted's vivid, star-studded dramatization begins with an older William Wilberforce (Ioan Gruffudd) and then flashes back 15 years to the time when, through a spiritual awakening, he begins his two-decade-long crusade to outlaw slavery in the British Empire. The year is 1782, and Wilberforce is a member of Parliament attempting to persuade his colleagues on the matter after being motivated by John Newton (Albert Finney), a former slave-ship owner who has dedicated his life to atoning for his past sins. Wilberforce's cause receives a boost when his close friend William Pitt (Benedict Cumberbatch) becomes Prime Minister, but it's a short-lived bit of optimism, and his abolition legislation is defeated. Flash forward, and an older and ill Wilberforce is about to give up his cause entirely. But encouraged by Barbara Spooner (Romola Garai), his soon-to-be wife, he renews his attempt, this time successfully winning Parliament's permanent ban of the slave trade. It's a solid portrayal of the effort, ably supported by screen stalwarts Michael Gambon, Ciarán Hinds, Toby Jones and Rufus Sewell. **[W]**

Conspiracy
2001 – England – Frank Pierson

January 20, 1942. The fortunes of war are beginning to turn against Adolph Hitler's Reich. The British Army is pushing back in North Africa, the Soviets are counterattacking on the Eastern Front, and the Americans have joined the battle. On that date, at a place called Wannsee on a lake outside Berlin, members of the German High Command met to craft a fateful plan, which the world will remember forever as "The Final Solution," the effort by the Nazis to exterminate all Jews and other groups they considered inferior from Europe. The film stars Kenneth Branagh, Colin Firth and Stanley Tucci as, respectively, Reinhard Heydrich (aide to Heinrich Himmler, dreaded chief of the notorious S.S.), Wilhelm Stuckart (a Nazi lawyer who helped write Germany's anti-Jewish laws) and Adolph Eichmann, who became Hitler's commander in charge of the Holocaust. *Conspiracy* re-creates with unerring accuracy much of what the participants said during that conference. How do we know? Because the Nazis conveniently transcribed their discussion. This excellent, made-for-TV production presents, in chillingly understated terms, the monstrous plan, which would have been carried out exactly if not for Germany's defeat. [Caution: adult themes]

The Garden of the Finzi-Continis
1970 – Italy – Vittorio de Sica

Watching the beginning of this dark drama about the fate of Italian Jews in World War II, you might not know what to expect because it seems so innocuous. But make no mistake; though the movie contains almost no violence and is set mostly against the backdrop of a beautiful estate – the "garden" of the title – it depicts a slow but relentless scourge descending on the principals. The garden is a universal metaphor for all people who cannot accept the reality of a tyranny enveloping them. Beginning in 1938, the story tracks the relationships and fates of two Jewish families living in Ferrara, Italy. There are the Finzi-Continis, the wealthy clan of the title, and a second, unnamed family. That family's son Giorgio (Lino Capolicchio) has been a friend since childhood of Micòl (Dominique Sanda, looking pert and pretty in an early role), the Finzi-Continis' only daughter. In fact, Giorgio has fallen into unrequited love with her, something he relates to Micòl's brother Alberto (Austrian actor Helmut Berger), another close friend. As the relationships are established, the story tracks them over the next five years, while Italy's growing fascism under Benito Mussolini exerts a subtle but ever-tightening grip on society – particularly Jewish society. At one point, Giorgio's father Beniamino (Romolo Valli) attempts to place a positive slant on their diminished freedoms. "We're not so badly off here," he tells his son after relating a litany of civil rights for Jews already withdrawn by the regime. Giorgio then counters with a bitter dose of reality. "We weren't the first to be persecuted," he says. "But we all kept quiet as long as we weren't hit." It's an age-old caution: When freedom is lost for others, inevitably it is lost for all. Based on Giorgio Bassani's novel, and winner of the Best Foreign Film Oscar, it's a quietly shattering portrait of one little corner of Europe at the time of the Holocaust, superbly presented by one of the world's great directors. [Caution: language, adult themes and sexuality] **[W]**

Gosnell
2018 – Nick Searcy
One of the most reprehensible aspects of modern life is the proliferation of abortion clinics run by people who, let's say it, care little about the work they do or the patients they are supposed to serve, and nothing about the unborn lives they extinguish. Kermit Gosnell was one such individual. Over the course of years, Gosnell and his so-called staff – comprising young adults with no formal medical training – performed abortions by drugging the pregnant women to induce labor and then killing the born-alive babies by clipping their spines. A particularly shocking case raised the attention of local authorities in Philadelphia, who dispatched investigators Wood and McGuire (Dean Cain and Sarah Jane Morris) to Gosnell's clinic, where they discovered the gut-wrenching horrors of the place, resulting in Gosnell's prosecution for multiple murders. A

courageous effort by the producers, cast and crew (director Searcy also plays Gosnell's defense attorney), who had to struggle for funding and distribution, the movie exposes how the process of abortion in America, once touted as "safe, legal and rare," in this case permitted that process to go horribly wrong. [Trivia notes: 1) The movie's full title is *Gosnell: The Trial of America's Biggest Serial Killer*. It's based on the fact that at the clinic hundreds of babies born alive were killed by Gosnell and his staff – one of whom confessed to killing at least 100 personally. 2) After his conviction, on four counts of murder, Kermit Gosnell was sentenced to life in prison without parole] [Caution: severe adult themes] **[W]**

Hotel Rwanda
2004 – co-written and directed by Terry George
The African nation of Rwanda in 1994 was the scene of a vicious, horrifying genocide against one of the country's major ethnic groups. The genocide was conducted by the Hutus, dark-skinned Africans who controlled the Rwandan government. Most of the victims were the lighter-skinned and smaller minority Tutsis. The Hutus regarded themselves as the superior race and the Tutsis as a subhuman species, whom they mocked openly on national media, calling them "cockroaches" and worse. When the genocide began, in April, the Hutus murdered Tutsis with ferocity – though counterattacks exacted a heavy toll on the Hutus as well. In this fact-based story, Don Cheadle stars as Paul Rusesabagina, proprietor of Hôtel des Mille Collines in Kigali, the country's capital. Rusesabagina is a Hutu, and his wife Tatiana (British actress Sophie Okonedo) is Tutsi. For a hundred days, and despite the disinterest and non-involvement of United Nations peacekeepers – including Colonel Oliver (Nick Nolte), their Canadian commander – Rusesabagina tirelessly struggled to protect his wife and children and, eventually, some 1200 refugees from the genocide, in which 800,000 Rwandans were killed. The versatile Cheadle is completely convincing as Rusesabagina, a man caught in the middle of a fight he abhors but forced to do anything and everything in his power, including risking his own life, to protect his family. [Caution: depictions of genocide] **[W]**

The Killing Fields
1984 – England – Roland Joffé

Another saga involving genocide, and another personal one, here occurring in the wake of the disaster that was the Vietnam War. The story chronicles the search for an individual amid the even larger catastrophe that befell the people of Cambodia. Perpetrated by a militant group called the Khmer Rouge ("Red Scarf"), a campaign of mass-murder began in 1975 against Cambodians suspected of being members of the country's educated class – to the point where even owning a pair of glasses could be incriminating. The penalty? Execution. Sidney Schanberg (Sam Waterston) had attempted to cover the Vietnam War for the New York Times from Phnom Penh, the Cambodian capital. He was assisted by Dith Pran (Haing S. Ngor, an actual survivor of the Khmer Rouge who had never acted before, in an Oscar-winning role), his friend and interpreter. When the genocide begins, Schanberg again attempts to provide coverage from the capital. But he quickly runs afoul of the Khmer Rouge, and Pran manages to get Schanberg and several colleagues out of dire trouble. Schanberg returns to New York, where he learns that Pran has been captured and has disappeared. From that point, the movie follows the twin fates of the two men, partly on Schanberg as he continues his career and wins a Pulitzer Prize for his reporting, but mostly – and wisely – on Pran while he struggles to survive as a prisoner, a forced laborer and, eventually, an escapee. Based on Schanberg's book The Death and Life of Dith Pran and filmed in Thailand, it's a slightly romanticized version of the real story. But it's vivid enough to provide a glimpse of the horrors suffered by the ordinary people of Cambodia caught up in a monstrous moment in history. [Caution: depiction of genocide] **[W]**

Romero
1989 – John Duigan

Sometimes, a movie can lack the sheen of a Hollywood production yet still be worthwhile, and *Romero* is one such example. Raúl Juliá stars, in an understated performance, as Oscar Arnulfo Romero, the pacifist Catholic archbishop who tried to bring peace to his war-torn country of El Salvador in the 1970s. It was a daunting and ultimately costly effort, given the two factions in the matter: a Marxist guerrilla insurgency and a brutal regime. At first reluctant to become directly involved, Romero grows increasingly – though passively – resistant to the government's harsh suppression of dissent. He does so by practicing his faith more and more openly, which eventually requires him to sacrifice his own life, occurring at the most sacred moment of the Catholic mass. It's an earnest, painful-to-watch ordeal of a humble man's courageous resistance to dictatorship. Produced by the Paulist Fathers, a Catholic organization, it's directed with sympathy and care by Duigan, an Australian best known for light comedies. Richard Jordan co-stars in a brief but sincere performance as Father Rutilio Grande, an ill-fated friend of Romero's. [Caution: adult themes and violence] **[W]**

Spotlight
2015 – co-written and directed by Tom McCarthy

My three compilations feature only a few titles about the craft of journalism – a career that occupied me for four decades. One reason is not many movies have dealt with the subject. From my perspective, few have ever done the honest, dogged members of the profession justice. *Spotlight* is one of the most satisfying exceptions. Based on a true story, it concerns a terrible scandal within the Catholic Archdiocese of Boston in the late 1990s and early 2000s. The archdiocese, headed by Cardinal Bernard Francis Law, permitted nearly 100 priests, all guilty of sexually molesting innocent children, to be reassigned to escape criminal punishment while his archdiocese quietly settled many of the cases as civil matters. Only the determined work of several Boston Globe reporters, most of them Catholic, finally exposed the scandal and provided the surviving victims (more than a few eventually committed suicide) a sense of justice. The excellent cast is headed by Michael Keaton (who had won Best Actor the previous year for the unsavory *Birdman* – not on this list) as Walter Robinson, longtime editor of Spotlight, the Globe's special investigations unit. Mark Ruffalo, Rachel McAdams and Stanley Tucci also turn in fine performances as, respectively, lead reporters Mike Rezendes and Sacha Pfeiffer, and victims' attorney Mitchel Garabedian. It's as well-honed a tale based on real events in the newspaper business as you're likely to see. [Caution: explicit language and adult content] **[W]**

Unplanned

2019 – co-written and co-directed by Cary Solomon and Chuck Konzelman

Another abortion theme, but a more personal story based a real individual's testimony. I use the word deliberately, because given the enormous public controversy (another word used deliberately) surrounding the issue, I offer this recommendation based on the power of that testimony. As far as its veracity, you should watch it and draw your own conclusions. Based on the memoir of the same name by Abby Johnson (here played by Ashley Bratcher), a woman who had two abortions, went to work for Planned Parenthood but eventually became a fierce advocate against that organization and the procedure. She did so because, as Abby claims in her narration, during her stint as a manager of an abortion clinic she was urged to "double" the number of procedures performed. As I mentioned, the movie is based on Abby Johnson's testimony. You might choose to disregard it. But there is no denying that she once worked for Planned Parenthood and, based on her experiences there, quit the organization, publicly opposed it and began working for a group that helps abortion workers find alternative employment. [Caution: adult themes, including graphic depiction of abortion] **[W]**

33. On the Big, Big Screen

It might seem surprising to consider, because the format still seems so modern and up-to-date, but IMAX – short for "Maximum Image" – has been in use for nearly half a century now. It's the big, big-screen equivalent of VistaVision, which was introduced by Paramount in the 1950s. That format used 35-millimeter film run sideways through a camera with a special aperture and mechanism. The effect created a widescreen image without as much loss of sharpness as occurred with CinemaScope and other anamorphic formats, which used the conventional photographic and projection processes but compressed or expanded the image optically. The IMAX process operates the same way as VistaVision but uses 70mm film, yielding an image three times larger than conventional 70mm.

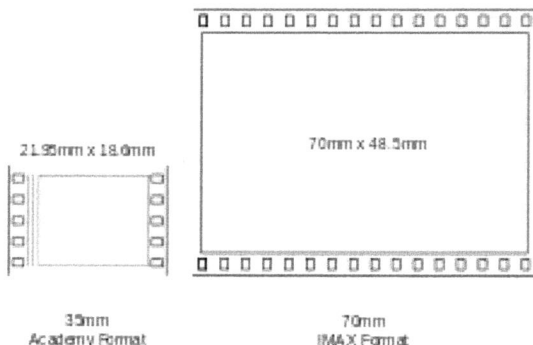

21.95mm x 18.6mm   70mm x 48.5mm

35mm
Academy Format

70mm
IMAX Format

Founded by Canadians Roman Kroitor and Graeme Ferguson (both of whom I once interviewed for an article), IMAX has been used in hundreds of films. Here are seven documentaries, the work of talented and brave IMAX filmmakers and technicians, that I've found particularly memorable – with their running times listed. [Viewing notes: 1) Some of these features are available on video, but needless to say even the largest home screen cannot convey the dramatic impact of the real thing. That's why I'm not including links to clips here. If you're interested in any of these titles, by all means seek them out in the proper format. 2) I included running times because in IMAX's early days the horizontal film-projection platters had a limited capacity. It took years before technicians could invent a way to handle the enormous film reels for full-length features]

To Fly!
1976 – Jim Freeman and Greg MacGillivray
The premiere film at the opening of the Smithsonian Institution's National Air & Space Museum in Washington, D.C., it remains glorious and unforgettable, now some 46 years since its first showing, particularly the view of Niagara Falls from directly above and featuring a lovely score by Bernardo Segall. **[W] [27 minutes]**

Hail Columbia
1982 – Graeme Ferguson
Watching the launch of the first space shuttle, on a screen that shows the spacecraft nearly half its real size, is an awesome experience. The later tragedy of Columbia notwithstanding (it disintegrated over the western United States during re-entry on February 1, 2003), this is a glorious tribute to the shuttle program. **[W] [37 minutes]**

Grand Canyon: The Hidden Secrets
1984 – Kieth Merrill
Re-creating the 19th-century expedition of John Wesley Powell, director Kieth (no misspelling) Merrill installed the massive camera on a raft heading along the rampaging Colorado River to give audiences a thrilling glimpse of the rapids close-up and nearly full-size. **[W] [34 minutes]**

Niagara: Miracles, Myths and Magic
1986 – Kieth Merrill
Merrill's second IMAX feature again brings the mighty falls into overwhelming view, this time up close. **[W] [41 minutes]**

Fires of Kuwait
1992 – David Douglas
In March 1991, U.S. and allied forces entered the Middle Eastern country of Kuwait to eject the invading army of Iraqi dictator Saddam Hussein. During that army's retreat, they set fire to every Kuwaiti oil-production rig, creating clouds of smoke that could be seen from space. The movie documents the heroic efforts by "hellfighters" from all over the world to douse the flames. **[W] [36 minutes]**

Titanica
1992 – Stephen Low
Five years before director James Cameron took his camera crew two miles down to the wreck of the Titanic, which sank in frigid waters on April 14, 1912, a team of Russians visited the site and filmed the lost ship in IMAX. This was one of the first feature-length films to use the big format. **[W] [95 minutes full-length or 40 minutes in general release]**

Everest
1998 – David Breashears
There's a special poignancy to this one, which documents the tragedy of the 1996 climbing season. Breashears, an experienced climber, and his crew of Nepalese Sherpas, lugged the heavy IMAX cameras to the top of the world's highest mountain, intending yet another triumphant documentary in the format. Instead, they witnessed the worst tragedy in the mountain's brief 45-year history of successful ascents, when eight climbers died in one day. Much of the film focuses on that event. [Caution: adult themes] **[W] [45 minutes]**

34. Only in the (early) Sixties!

In recent history, no decade embodied social upheaval more than the 1960s. From the Space Race and the Cold War to the Beatles and the Rolling Stones; from the assassinations of John F. Kennedy, Robert F. Kennedy and Martin Luther King Jr. to the civil rights movement and the Vietnam War; not to mention the beginning of the sexual revolution, America by 1970 scarcely resembled the nation it had constituted only 10 years before. It was our consummate decade of change. Yet Hollywood, far from being a cultural precursor and groundbreaker, lagged well behind the upheavals – at least for the first half of the decade. Back then, much of its output consisted of comedies with slyly couched and suggestive plotlines but absolutely nothing overt or explicit – even cuss words were minimal. Given the nature of so many of today's graphic stories and language, these 11 throwbacks seem positively demure. It isn't to say they're not entertaining. It's just that they demonstrate how Hollywood in the early '60s reflected the sensibilities of an era rapidly receding into history.

Pillow Talk
1959 – Michael Gordon

I'm beginning with this title, made just before the '60s, because it helped give birth to the genre called, ludicrously, sex comedies – most, like this one, produced at Universal Studios – which enjoyed their brief heyday in the ensuing years. It's likewise fitting because it starts off with a peppy theme song sung by Doris Day, something that also characterized much of its ilk. It co-stars Day, Rock Hudson and Tony Randall in the first of three outings for the trio. It's also yet another variation of the storyline in *The Shop Around the Corner* (PF5). Day and Hudson share what back then was called a party line, meaning two unrelated users had the same telephone number – an inconvenience related to exploding demand for phone service amid limited capacity. That party line causes frequent conflicts between the two strangers. Simultaneously, the same two have met and begun a mutual attraction, unaware each is the source of the other's daily antagonism. Predictably, both aspects of the relationship surface, creating even more conflict but, of course, an eventual romantic resolution. Yes, it sounds silly, but don't sell it short. For one thing, the script won the Best Original Screenplay Oscar, and the movie received four more nominations, including one for Day as Best Actress. The roles also led to a close friendship between Day and Hudson that lasted the rest of their lives. In the years since, Hudson's rather unconventional private life has been widely reported, but back then the press-liaison people at Universal Studios worked overtime to keep what would have been an explosive scandal well hidden, allowing him to maintain a successful career as a romantic lead. [Trivia note: Rock Hudson became one of the first celebrities to disclose he had contracted the disease now known as AIDS. He died of it in 1985 at age 59. Doris Day, meanwhile, was married four times, including to an abusive spouse and another who badly mismanaged her fortune. She spent much of her private life promoting animal welfare and died in 2019 at age 97] **[W]**

Lover Come Back
1961 – Delbert Mann

A perfect example to begin the decade proper, a flyweight sex comedy again featuring Rock Hudson and Doris Day, with Tony Randall playing Hudson's buddy and providing comic relief. The plot? Two advertising professionals begin as (what else?) antagonists. But through a series of predictable misunderstandings, they end up together. Really, that's it. But in the early sixties with Hudson and Day it was enough, including Day once again singing the title song. [Trivia note: Two future cast members in popular sixties TV shows landed bit parts here: Donna Douglas, much better known as Ellie Mae Clampett in The Beverly Hillbillies; and Ted Bessell, costarring with Marlo Thomas in That Girl] **[W]**

Boys' Night Out
1962 – Michael Gordon

Kim Novak in her second role in a tale of infidelity within a couple of years (see *Strangers When We Meet*), but this time co-starring with James Garner in a comedy. As the story begins, three married suburban New York guys, played by Howard Duff, Howard Morris and Tony Randall, bemoan the loss of their freedom and the single life. Then their fondest wish seems to come true when a beautiful woman (Novak) agrees to spend one evening a week with each of them. The truth is, however, the woman is a graduate student working on her thesis about the sexual fantasies of married men. Her initial hunch is correct. The three really don't want to engage in actual affairs; what they crave is attention and company, which she willingly provides as part of her research. Meanwhile, the trio's friend (Garner) is shocked by the woman's behavior. Will the three marriages collapse? Will the only single man among them eventually link up with the supposed kept woman? C'mon, it's an easy guess and a diverting couple of hours. The wives are played by Janet Blair, Anne Jeffries and Patti Paige, who (instead of Doris Day this time) sings the theme song. **[W]**

Sunday in New York
1963 – Peter Tewksbury

Rod Taylor and Jane Fonda co-star in an innocuous story about love at first sight between a young man and young woman who accidentally meet on a … Sunday in New York. Eileen (Fonda) is the adult but virginal younger sister of Adam (Cliff Robertson), an airline pilot enjoying the single life in Manhattan. The victim of a misunderstanding, Eileen heads out onto the streets looking for Adam (who isn't where he said he was going to be). There, she bumps into Mike (Taylor) and, well, one thing leads to another, all of it revolving around Eileen's … um, uninitiated status. Based on Norman Krasna's Broadway play, it seems stagey at times but never dull, and the three principals work well together. Bobby Darin does the theme-song honors. **[W]**

The Thrill of It All
1963 – Norman Jewison

Here's Doris Day in the first of two domestic comedies paired with James Garner that year – the same year he also did *The Great Escape* (PF5). He's an obstetrician; she's his wife who achieves sudden fame and fortune as a star in soap commercials. It's a standard storyline for the time. When a wife begins to outshine her husband, she engenders jealousy in him and conflict between them. But it's a comedy, so it ends up happily – according to the prevailing social mores – with her abandoning her new career and returning to run the household and raise her children. Most notable scene: Garner accidentally drives his Chevy convertible into the household's newly built swimming pool and sinks to the bottom. Larry Gelbart wrote the basic story, while Carl Reiner did the script and appears in some of the bits on TV surrounding Day's soap commercials – but perhaps a bit too frequently. It's Jewison's second directing credit; four years later he would helm *In the Heat of the Night* (PF5), which won Best Picture. For unexplained reasons, Day didn't sing the movie's requisitely peppy theme song. That gig went to the Johnny Mann Singers. [Trivia notes: 1) Among the cast members are Reginald Owen, who played Scrooge in my favorite version of *A Christmas Carol* the year before he played Colonel Boom in *Mary Poppins* (both in PF5); and Kym Karath as Day and Garner's young daughter. Two years later she became the youngest Von Trapp child in *The Sound of Music* (PF5 again). 2) Reiner and Gelbart, respectively, created two of the most famous and successful TV series of the '60s and '70s: The Dick Van Dyke Show and M*A*S*H] **[W]**

Move Over, Darling
1963 – Michael Gordon

Another Day–Garner sex comedy but with a tragic association. A remake of *My Favorite Wife* (P25), the 1940 Cary Grant–Irene Dunne vehicle about a wife who had been presumed dead in a shipwreck turning up alive after seven years and causing complications for her remarried husband. Originally, the remake was to be titled "Something's Got to Give" starring Marilyn

Monroe and Dean Martin. But she died during the shoot, so Day replaced Monroe, Garner replaced Martin, and the movie was retitled. Day resumed her role here of performing the theme song, perhaps appropriately a bit more serious than usual. **[W]**

Wives and Lovers
1963 – John Rich

Here's an iffy entrée and a bit of a departure from the others, though it's definitely about sex and marriage and, technically, it's considered a comedy. Based on the semiautobiographical play "The First Wife" by Jay Presson Allen, it concerns Bill and Bertie Austin (Van Johnson and Janet Leigh). They're a married couple living in a rundown Manhattan tenement with their precocious seven-year-old daughter (Claire Wilcox). Bill is a struggling writer while Bertie works as a dental hygienist to support them. Suddenly their fortunes rise when Bill's agent Lucinda (a glamorous Martha Hyer) sells his first novel as a major property. Soon the Austins are living in a mansion in Connecticut, and Bill finds himself the toast of the town with a Broadway play in prospect based on his novel. But instead of happiness and marital bliss, the success creates a crisis between the spouses involving infidelity and separation. The question is whether Bill and Bertie can reconcile, given that both have strayed. A common dilemma, even for the era, and an ending that wraps things up too abruptly (running well under 2 hours, the movie could have used another scene or two), but Allen's script is passably sophisticated. Good supporting performances by Shelley Winters and Ray Walston as the Austins' next-door neighbors. There is a theme song associated with *Wives and Lovers*. Sung by Jack Jones, it became a hit in its day – but it earned its popularity separately and wasn't heard in the movie. [Trivia note: As with her better-known counterparts Robert Towne and William Goldman, moviemakers often called on Allen to improve or rewrite problematic scripts. Her best uncredited work was rewriting Carroll Ballard's superb *Never Cry Wolf* (PF5)] [Caution: adult themes] **[B&W]**

The Brass Bottle
1964 – Harry Keller

Here's an entrée with a pair of twists. For one, Tony Randall plays the romantic lead instead of second banana, and for another there's literal magic involved. Harold Ventimore (Randall) is a struggling architect who buys an antique vessel containing a genie imprisoned for three millennia by the legendary Turkish sultan Suleiman the Magnificent. The genie, Fakrash al-Amash (singer–actor Burl Ives in a delightful performance), quickly places himself and his powers at Ventimore's disposal – naturally with unintended consequences and frequent silliness. That's particularly true in the case of Ventimore's pursuit of Sylvia Kenton (Barbara Eden in her debut). Despite all the complications, it's all in fun – it's the early sixties, after all – so it ends happily. The movie is something of a precursor to the popular TV series I Dream of Jeannie, which began the following year and starred Eden as a (female) genie freed from a … brass bottle. **[W]**

Send Me No Flowers
1964 – Norman Jewison

Rock Hudson and Doris Day, once more directed by Jewison, and the two of them again paired with Tony Randall – back in his supporting role – in my favorite of the trio's collaborations. Hudson plays George Kimble, married man and hypochondriac who, in a predictable case of misunderstanding, becomes convinced he's about to expire. Therefore, with the help of his best friend and neighbor (Randall) he seeks a replacement mate for his wife (Day) in the form of the tall and strapping TV Western star Clint Walker. Implausible throughout, it's also perfectly innocuous and entertaining. Day once again performs the title number, composed by Burt Bacharach. [Trivia note: This one, like so many, many other movies produced by Universal, was shot mostly on its back lot, which today – as far as I know – is still featured on the studio tour. The house where the Kimbles live would become the exterior in the 1970s of the residence of Robert Young, playing a TV doctor named Marcus Welby] **[W]**

287

How to Murder Your Wife
1965 – Richard Quine

Despite the title this is, mostly, a clever and innocuous sex comedy. It harbors a problem, however. A bit too much of its humor derives at the expense of a particular female cast member. Jack Lemmon stars as Stanley Ford, a successful newspaper cartoonist living free and loose as a Manhattan bachelor – until he gets drunk one night at a bachelor party and marries a knockout of a dame (gorgeous Italian star Virna Lisi) he encounters there. Soon his well-ordered life is in ruin, and he's made a laughingstock by his buddies. So, he kills off his new bride – but only in the pages of his comic strip. The vicarious deed, however, results in Ford being arrested for murder because Mrs. Ford, seeing her demise in print, flees the scene. It's a complication requiring Ford to defend himself in court, which he does and successfully, but not before the spectacle humiliates Edna Mayoff (Claire Trevor), the wife of his lawyer, as well as the rest of the women in the room. Edna takes the big fall, but the derision heaped upon wives in general renders a wrong note in an otherwise breezy tale. Eventually, Mr. and Mrs. Ford make up and live, we presume, happily ever after. Lisi's first appearance – rising out of a cake – will prove heart-pounding for male viewers. Likewise, her medication-induced dance at a second party. Written by George Axelrod, who had collaborated with Quine on the delightful *Bell, Book and Candle* (PF5) seven years earlier, and Neal Hefti contributed the sexy score. [Trivia notes: 1) Virna Lisi's career eventually spanned 50 years and included more than 100 movies, almost all of them in Italy. She died in 2014 at age 78. 2) Lisi's appearance here, her first in an American film after a decade of experience overseas, proved momentarily frightening for Lemmon when her husband turned up unexpectedly on the set. Seeing his wife completely undressed and covered only by a bedsheet for a particular scene, Lisi's husband exploded in rage and chased Lemmon outside and down the street] [Caution: mild sexuality] **[W]**

Strange Bedfellows

1965 – produced, co-written and directed by Melvin Frank

Closing out the bunch, here's a romantic comedy starring Rock Hudson but without Doris Day – or a theme song. Instead, Rock pairs with Gina Lollobrigida in a tale about a tempestuous relationship between Carter Harrison, a straightlaced American salesman, and Toni Vincente, a hot-headed Italian radical. They meet, "once upon a time," as the opening narration declares, in London where Carter, on his first visit to the city, is promptly (though accidentally) smeared with paint in the puss by Toni as she scrawls protest slogans along a wall. Apologetic, she invites him to her apartment to clean him up, and … well, those two gorgeous individuals lock in a passionate embrace, which leads to a quickie … um, union. Soon, however, Carter and Toni realize their fundamentally different personalities are leading to constant conflict. "They agree on nothing," the narrator again intones. "Politics, polygamy, peanut butter, Pushkin – you name it." Toni finally chases Carter out of the house, and he leaves England to resume his business travels. Seven years later, he returns to undo their hasty marriage, but despite their differences, the sudden close proximity ignites another round of instant and intense passion – until the next round of fiery disagreements. Actually, that's where the movie really starts, and though often silly and predictable it's also pleasantly diverting, due largely to the two stars – particularly Lollobrigida, appearing here at the peak of her allure and remarkably skilled at comedy. *Mama mia, che bomba!* [Caution: mild sexuality] **[W]**

An early '60s postscript:

It doesn't fit into the category of light "sex comedies" from the first half of the decade, but the Beatles' debut movie did appear in that time period and it's too good to leave out. Likewise, the homage to the four most famous Liverpudlians made nearly a decade and a half later.

A Hard Day's Night (and) I Wanna Hold Your Hand
1964 – England – Richard Lester, and 1978 – co-written and directed by Robert Zemeckis

The first and best of the five movies made by the Beatles as a group. What's it about? Nothing in particular. The boys (John Lennon, Paul McCartney, George Harrison and Ringo Starr) perform a dozen of their hits at the time – including the popular theme song – while running around the streets of London to escape their rabid fans while romancing lovely young women. You'll have a good time watching them do both – and, yes, Harrison really does trip and fall on his face in the opening shot. **[B&W] [W]**

*　　*　　*

I Wanna Hold Your Hand makes a perfect double bill with *A Hard Day's Night*, and it belongs here even though it wasn't made in the '60s because it's also about the Beatles in their heyday. The story takes place in early 1964, and the "Fab Four," as they were called, were scheduled to appear on The Ed Sullivan Show on CBS television. The prospect of encountering the Beatles prompts a group of New Jersey teens (including Marc McClure, Bob Di Cicco, Eddie Deezen, Nancy Allen and Wendy Jo Sperber) to plan a ruse that might place them in close proximity to their newfound idols. Naturally, their plan runs amok, but not before yielding some delightfully unexpected surprises. It's a fun romp about the early days of the world's most famous rock 'n' roll band. Gary Arnold's Washington Post review called the movie "inconsistent but zestful" and "a showcase for fresh, young talent," which fits it well. [Trivia note: McClure and Sperber played brother and sister in all three of Zemeckis's *Back to the Future* movies (parts I and III in PF5), while Di Cicco, Deezen and Allen all landed roles in Steven Spielberg's bomb of a World War II comedy, *1941*, the following year] [Caution: mild sexuality and a little bit of rough language] **[W]**

35. Originals versus Remakes

These days, it's difficult to keep track of how many remakes of earlier titles are appearing as updated versions on screens large and small. In prior years, they were rare, but occasionally directors would remake their own movies, or they would move up to directing from originally working on the crew. Cecil B. DeMille, for example, returned after 30 years with the spectacular 1956 version of *The Ten Commandments*. Likewise, William Wyler moved up three years later to direct the definitive version of *Ben-Hur* (both in <u>PF5</u>). Other, more modest examples include Frank Capra's *Lady for a Day* and *Pocketful of Miracles*, and Leo McCarey's *Love Affair* and *An Affair to Remember* (all below). Whether the products of different directorial eyes – sometimes even in different countries – or the same individual, it can be interesting to compare the outcomes – such as with these dozen pairs (24 titles). Let's see how they match up.

Dr. Jekyll and Mr. Hyde (vs.) Dr. Jekyll and Mr. Hyde
1931 and 1941 – Rouben Mamoulian and Victor Fleming

A difficult choice here, given that both are classy productions with high-caliber casts. In the first, it's Fredric March in an Oscar-winning role as cinema's most famous man with a split personality. In the remake, it's the inimitable Spencer Tracy. Their co-stars, respectively, are Miriam Hopkins, one of the best-known dramatic actresses of the early talkies period, and the immortal Ingrid Bergman. Speaking of immortal, the source material is Robert Lewis Stevenson's 1886 short novel <u>The Strange Case of Dr. Jekyll and Mr. Hyde</u>. It's the story of a mild-mannered English physician and scientist who seeks the source of the darkest human passions. He develops a potion that can transform him, not only emotionally into a man with no inhibitions but also physically into a repellant yet hypnotic figure. And the transformation is literal. In fact, March's devolution into Hyde shocked audiences with its realistic depiction. And Hopkins's character's attempted seduction of Jekyll was more explicit than the Hollywood censors would permit only a few years later.

*   *   *

There's nothing wrong with Fleming's version of the story a decade later, working again with Tracy four years after his Oscar-winning performance in *Captains Courageous* (PF5), and for the only time with Bergman. The movie, technically superior and following the 1931 version almost moment by moment, tones down the more shocking and explicit elements of the earlier work.

*   *   *

[Trivia notes: 1) The moviemakers achieved that first 1931 transformation via an ingenious use of makeup and camera filters, which made March's skin appear to change colors spontaneously. They used camera dissolves and edits for the later ones. The technique was so successful that Fleming employed it with Tracy in '41. 2) Others had attempted to produce this story for the screen several times earlier, most notably in 1920 starring John Barrymore. 3) In the other temporal direction, there have been two, let's say modern interpretations of the story, both titled *The Nutty Professor* (neither on my lists). The first, in 1963, starred Jerry Lewis, who also directed – and whose alter ego actually resembled Fredric March as Hyde. The second, in 1996, put comedian Eddie Murphy in the role. 4) March and Hopkins co-starred two years later, in decidedly different guises, in the sophisticated Ernst Lubitsch comedy *Design for Living*] [Caution: dated but still-scary material, and sexuality in the 1931 version] [B&W]

Phil' Favorite? As mentioned, this is a difficult call. But I'll give the slight edge to the earlier version because of its less-restrained approach to Stevenson's sensational tale.

Dracula (vs.) Dracula
1931 and 1979 – Todd Browning and John Badham

Three landmark horror films in that year of early talkies: *Dr. Jekyll...* above, James Whale's *Frankenstein* (PF5) and this one,

292

based on the 1924 stage play, which in turn was based on Bram Stoker's 1897 novel about a vampire in human form. Count Dracula (Bela Lugosi) avoids the light, drinks human blood and makes no reflection in mirrors. The role became such a sensation for Lugosi that he was never remembered for anything else, save his bit part in *Plan 9 from Outer Space* (not on my lists), which many critics consider the worst mainstream movie ever made. Yet Lugosi appeared in more than a hundred more films, going back 20 years from *Dracula* and for nearly 30 years afterward, including a small but distinctive part in *Ninotchka* and reprising his role as the Count in *Bud Abbott and Lou Costello Meet Frankenstein* (both in PF5). Even for the time period, it's a clumsy attempt. The sets are bargain-basement, the "bat" is obviously a puppet on strings, the other effects are nonexistent (most of the time the complex things happen off-camera) and the acting is amateurish at best. That goes particularly for Lugosi, whose entire persona consists of hard stares and frowns. Nevertheless, it was groundbreaking in its day and worth a look for both horror and classic movie buffs. [Trivia note: Despite the movie's limitations, the role affected Lugosi for the rest of his life. He would often dress as Dracula in public and repeat the vampire's mannerisms – and when he died, he insisted on being buried in the costume] [B&W]

*   *   *

Badham's version, 48 years later, brings Stoker's novel to the screen once again, but with far more flair and panache than its predecessor, and with the emphasis on the love story – yes, love story – between the Count from Transylvania and a young but assertive Englishwoman. As Gary Arnold put it in his Washington Post review, "There has never been a more beautifully visualized horror movie," and I agree. The fine cast includes Frank Langella, reprising his stage role as the Count and giving the screen performance of his career; Laurence Olivier as Professor van Helsing; and Kate Nelligan as the vampire's love interest, Lucy. John Williams contributed the powerful orchestral score, and sharp ears will detect its similarities to some of his themes in *Star Wars, Superman* and even *Close Encounters of the Third Kind* (all in PF5). [Trivia note: Because this focuses on the romance between the Count and Lucy, it more closely resembles the hit play from the 1920s by Hamilton Deane and John L. Balderston] [Caution: bloody violence and frightening scenes] **[W]**

Phil' Favorite? As affectionately remembered as the 1931 *Dracula* is, Badham and Langella created a far superior movie and an even more memorable performance. Count me in for the '79 version.

The Girl with the Dragon Tattoo (vs.) The Girl with the Dragon Tattoo

2009 (Sweden) and 2011 – Niels Arden Oplev and David Fincher

Known as *Män Som Hatar Kvinnor* ("Men Who Hate Women") in its home country, and based on the international best-seller by Stieg Larsson, the movie chronicles the attempt by an investigative journalist and the title character to uncover a serial killer among one of Sweden's premier corporate families, one with past connections to Nazi Germany and infected with virulent anti-Semitism. Noomi Rapace is Lisbeth Salander, a young woman with a troubled past but an exceptional ability with computers. She teams with Mikhael Blomkvist (Michael Nyqvist), who's just lost a costly defamation suit, faces imprisonment and needs to replenish his assets. That predicament leads him to Heinrick Vanger (Sven-Bertil Taube), patriarch of the family, who has been tormented for 40 years by the disappearance and presumed murder of his beloved niece. It's a dark, dark tale, with moments of shocking violence and images of gruesome brutality, and where everyone is either nursing a tormented past or trying to hide an evil present. It will engross you or drive you away quickly. [Caution: violence and sexuality, both intense] **[W]**

*   *   *

In the American version, Daniel Craig – interrupting his run as James Bond – takes over the more passive role of Blomkvist while newcomer Rooney Mara plays Salander in a sensational performance. It's a more streamlined version of the story, and despite its shocking but intermittent episodes of gruesome violence, it's a somewhat milder adaptation. The main attraction of Fincher's remake, however, is the extraordinary work of the production crew. In the story, Blomkvist and Salander attempt to solve the murder mystery by sifting through hundreds of photographs and many more documents. Because this is fiction, each one of those objects had to be researched and acquired or manufacturered outright. There were similar sequences in the original, but they're much more extensive here, and the result is stunning, all the more so because 1) if you don't realize that what you're watching has been created, you probably won't appreciate the enormous work required to create the illusion; and 2) as far as I know, no critic has mentioned this aspect of the movie. The stellar supporting cast includes Christopher Plummer as the patriarch, Steven Berkoff as his lawyer, Joely Richardson as a family member harboring a terrible secret, Stellan Skarsgård as another sibling harboring an even worse secret, and Robin Wright as Blomkvist's business partner and lover. The bleak Scandanavian winter landscapes induce shivers, as does the chilling, percussive, Oscar-winning score by Trent Reznor and Atticus Ross. [Trivia notes: 1) Mara's punk street urchin character notwithstanding, she comes from upper-class, all-American roots. Her paternal great-grandfather was Tim Mara, founder of the New York Giants football team, while her mother's grandfather was the legendary Art Rooney Sr., founder of the Pittsburgh Steelers – hence her name. 2) Mara had worked with Fincher four years earlier on *The Social Network*, in a minor role far removed from Lisbeth. You can see her brief performance in the movie's opening scene] [Caution: violence and sexuality, likewise both intense] **[W]**

Phil' Favorite? The Swedish version moves along and provides constant interest, but *The Girl with the Dragon Tattoo*, version 2011, is as gripping as gripping can be, with a superior cast in every respect. This one adds Fincher to my list of directors – including John Boorman, Alan Parker, James Mangold and the Coen brothers – whose work I generally don't like but who has created one single, terrific movie.

Goodbye Charlie (vs.) Switch
1964 and 1991 – Vincente Minnelli, and written and directed by Blake Edwards

The "Charlie" in the title is none other than petite and oh-so-feminine Debbie Reynolds. Yes, you read it right; she's playing a man – a murdered cad of a man named Charlie Sorel who, via either bad karma or divine retribution, has been reincarnated as a woman. But the plot, based on a play by George Axelrod, contains a surprising amount of wit and insight into the virtues and vices of both sexes – at least, from the era's perspective. The movie begins at a wild, sixties-style party aboard a yacht where Charlie has secreted away the wife of the yacht owner and is in the process of seducing her. Suddenly, the cuckolded husband (Walter Matthau, in a subpar performance as an expatriate Hungarian movie producer) bursts in and fires six shots at Charlie, who's trying to escape through a porthole, and it's into the drink and ... goodbye. That is, until a naked woman, wearing an overcoat provided by a Good Samaritan (Pat Boone), shows up at Charlie's beach house where his best friend George Tracy (Tony Curtis) is staying after delivering the eulogy at the sparsely attended funeral. The woman seems to have suffered amnesia, and George doesn't know what to make of her – until she awakens, screaming, in the middle of the night and shocks the both of them into an unbelievable reality: *she* is Charlie! What happens next turns those infamous five stages of grief upside down, as Charlie at first ignores the denial, anger, bargaining and depression phases while immediately accepting his fate with a vengeance, exploiting his history of carousing for all it's worth – including the pursuit of Boone, who happens to be filthy rich. But then it's Charlie's turn to be surprised, again, as those inevitable stages return and begin working on his long-forgotten conscience. "I was a fink and a hustler for 30 years and now suddenly I'm an ingenue?" asks Reynolds as Charlie. "I don't know how to handle it." The plot eventually runs off the rails, as comedies of this vintage often do. But until then it's reasonably entertaining. One other complaint: Reynolds overacts quite a bit in her early Charlie guise. [Trivia note: That dark-haired woman sitting with Debbie-as-Charlie at

296

lunch in the restaurant went on to change her name and became Ellen Burstyn. [Caution: mild sexuality] **[W]**

*   *   *

In *Switch*, also based on Axelrod's play, the movie features Ellen Barkin and Jimmy Smits (of TV's L.A. Law) as the two leads – except that in this version they end up sleeping together, and she ends up pregnant. The first movie is a breezy, slightly naughty comedy from the early 60s. This one's quite a bit naughtier, and foul-mouthed, but Barkin turns in her best performance ever in a challenging role. She's completely convincing as a former man now trapped in a woman's body. As nasty as her character is, you can't help pulling for her. [Caution: language and sexuality] **[W]**

Phil' Favorite? Despite its rough edges, I'm inclined to go with *Goodbye Charlie*, though I'd give Barkin's performance the edge. The thing about Blake Edwards, may he rest in peace, is that he was always capable of producing sparkling comedies, such as *Operation Petticoat, The Return of the Pink Panther* and *Victor/Victoria* (all in PF5), as well as some excellent adult romances and dramas, including *Breakfast at Tiffany's* (P25), and *Days of Wine and Roses* and *Experiment in Terror* (elsewhere). But he also produced some of the most despicable, tasteless or lifeless duds, such as *Blind Date, S.O.B., That's Life* and, most especially, *10* (none here). He veered into that territory again with *Switch*, but Barkin's all-out effort saved the movie.

Invasion of the Body Snatchers (vs.) Invasion of the Body Snatchers
1956 and 1978 – Don Siegel and Philip Kaufman

This low-budget depiction of an earthly invasion of an alien species is also thoughtful, often witty and at times decidedly frightening. Kevin McCarthy and Dana Wynter co-star as former lovers suddenly confronted with increasingly strange behavior in their town that turns out to be a lethal alien … invasion. The production was particularly difficult for the cast. In Wynter's case, it involved being completely encased in a mold of liquid plastic, which would eventually represent her alien duplicate. The

297

claustrophobia-inducing contraption required her to breathe through a straw while the liquid dried. McCarthy, frequently required to run at top speed from the alien threat, often reached physical exhaustion – a dangerous situation because his runs involved weaving his way through automobile traffic. [Trivia notes: 1) The movie introduced the term "pod people" into the lexicon, which has come to mean essentially brainless individuals. 2) This being the 1950s, Allied Artists, the movie's distributor, worried about censorship of the "nude" replicas of the cast. So, the crew disguised certain parts of the pod people with foaming bubbles – an effect that also made their emergence more frightening] [Caution: creepy scenes] **[B&W] [W]**

* * *

If Siegel harbored any resentment about his movie being remade, he must have kept it to himself, because he appears in Kaufman's atmospheric and witty update in a bit role as a cab driver. Set in San Francisco, the story begins, as did the original, with otherwise normal people beginning to act strangely. One of them is Geoffrey (Art Hindle), the live-in partner of Elizabeth (Brooke Adams), the latter of whom works with Matthew Bennell (Donald Sutherland) at the Public Health Department. It turns out Geoffrey's behavior is more than strange, and what happens to him – and many others – makes for a tale of gripping suspense. It might even give you the same feeling about falling asleep that *Psycho* (elsewhere) and *Jaws* (PF5) did, respectively, with taking showers and swimming in the ocean. Jeff Goldblum and Veronica Cartwright play besieged friends of the protagonists, and Leonard Nimoy (the immortal Mr. Spock of the Star Trek TV series and movies) appears as a best-selling pop-psychologist. [Caution: non-sexual nudity and creepy scenes] **[W]**

Phil' Favorite? The 1956 version is considered the classic, but I prefer Kaufman's rendition, which I found richer, witty and more entertaining.

Lady for a Day (vs.) Pocketful of Miracles
1933 and 1961 – both by Frank Capra

You could call *Lady for a Day* the first of two bookends for Capra, because it and *Pocketful of Miracles* marked, respectively, the beginning and end – in the latter case, literally – of his extraordinary four-decade career. It's a slightly rough-around-the-edges but endearing comedy about "Apple Annie" (May Robson), a poor street hustler in New York City whose daughter (Jean Parker) has been raised in Europe, is engaged to a nobleman (Barry Norton) and believes her mother is a wealthy socialite. The ruse had been working, but when the daughter cables her mother that she, her fiancé and her prospective father-in-law (the wonderful Walter Connolly) will be sailing to America, it throws Annie into a panic. Desperate, she pleads for help from one of her regular customers, Dave "the Dude" (Warren William), a gangster who believes Annie's apples bring him good luck. From there, it's a mad scramble to create the illusion that Annie is indeed the fantasy woman she has pretended to be. And as happens often in Capra's comedies, fate intervenes to guarantee a happy ending. Written by Robert Riskin and based on a short story by Damon Runyon – appearing in Cosmopolitan magazine, of all places, four years earlier – it's fine fun. [Trivia note: *Lady for a Day* garnered nominations for Best Picture, and Best Actress for Robson. Capra also received one for Best Director, a distinction that created the most embarrassing moment of his career. At the Oscar ceremony in 1934, host Will Rogers, announcing the winner, said "Come up and get it, Frank," to which Capra sprung from his seat and ran to the podium – only to discover Rogers had meant Frank Lloyd, the director of *Cavalcade* (not on my lists). Capra's low point was short-lived, however. The next year he won – both Best Director and Best Picture – for *It Happened One Night* (PF5)] **[B&W]**

*   *   *

Flash forward 28 years and Bette Davis plays Apple Annie in *Pocketful of Miracles*. Glenn Ford plays Dave, and a host of more-familiar names occupies the main roles, including Ann-Margret as the daughter; Peter Falk as Dave's prime henchman; Hope Lange as Queenie, his girlfriend, and Thomas Mitchell in his last performance as a drunk who must masquerade as a judge and Annie's escort. It's exactly the same story – and set in the same time period, the Prohibition era – but in widescreen and color, skillfully photographed by Robert Bronner. The theme song, by Jimmy Van Heusen and Sammy Kahn, later was performed by Frank Sinatra and became a hit. A troubled production – Ford and Davis, among others, bickered constantly – it was mostly ignored by the motion picture academy and barely broke even at the box office. Yet it turned out surprisingly well, a respectable valediction for Capra. Along with Mitchell, look for Ellen Corby, a cast member in Capra's immortal *It's a Wonderful Life* (<u>PF5</u>), as one of Annie's street-hustling comrades. [<u>Trivia notes</u>: 1) There's a melancholy note connected with the production involving Davis. She accepted the role after Jean Arthur, Shirley Booth, Helen Hayes and Katharine Hepburn had turned it down, all thinking it already had been done well in *Lady for a Day* and that Capra, who hadn't scored a hit in 15 years (after *It's a Wonderful Life* – see <u>PF5</u>), had, as they say in show biz, lost his edge. Davis, meanwhile, was hurting financially and needed the role for that reason. 2) Speaking of Sinatra; he was Capra's original pick for Dave the Dude, but he left the production over creative differences with the director] **[W]**

Phil' Favorite? There's no doubt *Lady for a Day* is the better rendition of the story, coming as it did just as Capra was emerging as the father of screwball comedy. Likewise, *Pocketful of Miracles* shows diminishment in his directorial gifts. Its dialogue, as well as its more-complex staging, are somewhat clumsily delivered. Nevertheless, I've retained a soft spot for it. So, in this one instance, I'm declaring a draw.

Love Affair (vs.) An Affair to Remember
1939 and 1957 – both by Leo McCarey
Sometimes, veteran directors will return to their earlier works to update them decades later. Two examples coming immediately to mind are Cecile B. DeMille redoing *The Ten Commandments* (<u>PF5</u>) after 30 years and, on a much smaller scale, Frank Capra repeating

Lady for a Day and *Pocketful of Miracles* (neither on my lists) after a similar interval. McCarey makes another interesting example. In *Love Affair* – one more product from what's known as Hollywood's best year – he takes a sparkling screenplay by Delmer Daves and playwright Donald Ogden Stewart, casts Charles Boyer and Irene Dunne at their peaks, treads lightly on the limitations of censorship and produces a surprisingly enduring screen romance. Boyer plays Michel Marnet, a French painter with a naughty reputation, while Dunne is Terry McKay, an American singer and music teacher. Though both are attached to others, the couple quickly falls in love on a trans-Atlantic voyage. Not knowing what will happen when they reach New York, their destination, they agree to meet in six months atop the Empire State Building if they want to resume their relationship. I won't reveal more, except that this story has become a famous tear-jerker, and … well, I'll explain in the summation. [<u>Trivia note</u>: It wasn't nearly the same situation, because he was traveling with his wife at the time, but McCarey conceived the story while crossing the Atlantic on an ocean liner himself] **[B&W]**

*   *   *

In the remake, instead of Boyer and Dunne in black & white, he casts Cary Grant and Deborah Kerr in color and widescreen, and with stereophonic sound, as the (temporarily) ill-fated lovers who meet on their trans-Atlantic voyage. This version, a nearly shot-by-shot duplication of the earlier feature, seems to have found a permanent place in popular culture, particularly its use of New York City's Empire State Building as the couple's intended rendezvous location – which likewise was in the original. And when Nora Ephron made *Sleepless in Seattle* (<u>P25</u>) in 1993, she once again employed the Manhattan landmark. Charming and beguiling with a tear-jerking denouement, it remains a romantic classic. **[W]**

<u>Phil' Favorite?</u> I like the 1939 version better, and my reason relates to the censorship issue. At the time, the story was considered inappropriate because it supposedly dealt with adultery – even though neither Boyer's nor Dunne's character was married.

301

McCarey overcame the objection by employing Donald Ogden Stewart to insert as much comedy as possible, particularly in the repartee between the two stars. In the Grant–Kerr update, adultery as a theme had become much more common in movies and less of a censorship concern. So, McCarey had his new couple play the story more for drama – and consequently it lost much of its original sparkle.

The Man Who Never Was (vs.) Operation Mincemeat
1956 and 2021 – both in England – Ronald Neame and John Madden

Maybe more than any other conflict in history, World War II featured elaborate deceptions intended to fool the enemy and save Allied lives. The United States and Great Britain, for example, went to extreme lengths to prevent the Imperial Japanese military and the German Third Reich from learning that they had broken both codes used for exchanging highly sensitive wartime information. The Allies under General Dwight Eisenhower successfully persuaded Hitler that the invasion of France would take place at Pas-de-Calais, instead of the real location at Normandy, a feint that greatly improved the odds for the event known as D-Day. And a year earlier, British Intelligence conducted another effective deception, involving where the Allies would strike next following their victories in North Africa. Here are two renditions of that effort, called Operation Mincemeat in both movies, and both based on The Man Who Never Was, the chronicle by one of the chief participants, Royal Navy Lieutenant Commander Ewan Montagu.

*   *   *

The Man Who Never Was, the movie, begins on an empty beach at sunrise. A body floats in on the gentle surf, and soon a local fisherman discovers it and summons the authorities. That beach is near the town of Huelva, Spain, and the time is April 1943. Unbeknownst to the body's discoverers – including the town's officials, the higher Spanish authorities and the Nazi spies who have infested neutral Spain – the body was delivered to that destination via submarine. The dead man's hand is chained to a satchel, within which is a document that could determine the course of the war. We gradually learn all this as the story of Operation Mincemeat unfolds, and Montagu (here played by Clifton Webb in one of his best roles) does his best to create an elaborate but artificial identity for a vagrant who died of pneumonia – to make him … the man who never was. The plan seems to be working, according to German communications intercepted by British Intelligence. But there's a hitch: The Nazis dispatch Patrick O'Reilly (Stephen Boyd in an early role, and speaking in his natural Irish brogue) to England. He's an Irish Republican Army spy for Hitler, ordered to determine if the satchel-bearing body, identified as a Major William Martin of the Royal Marines, is a real person. Through skillful manipulation – and a very good bit of luck – O'Reilly is fooled. The Germans hastily redeploy forces to Greece – where the document discovered on "Martin" has revealed the Allied strike will take place – and away from Sicily, the real target. It's an earnest effort by all, and Neame, who got his start as a cinematographer in the 1920s, turns in some of his best work. [Trivia note: Given that the production of *The Man Who Never Was* took place only 13 years after the real events, it afforded Neame and his crew certain advantages. For example, the movie featured the real submarine, H.M.S. Seraph, that delivered the body of "William Martin" to the Spanish beach. Also, the movie features a brief role by the real Ewen Montagu] **[W]**

*   *   *

Flash forward 65 years, and the less romantically named *Operation Mincemeat* tells almost exactly the same story but with bigger production values, a more elaborate plot (the movie runs half-an-hour longer than its predecessor) and the always-excellent Colin Firth heading the cast as Montagu. Part of the elaboration is the addition – or, I should say, the reinsertion – of two characters involved in Mincemeat who weren't included in the first movie. There's Charles Cholmondeley (Matthew Macfadyen), a would-be Royal Air Force pilot washed out because of bad eyesight and excessive height. And there's Ian Fleming (Johnny Flynn) – yes, the creator of the most famous spy of all: Agent 007, James Bond.

303

Cholmondeley (pronounced "CHUM-lee") first proposed the idea of using a dead man disguised as a courier, and Fleming had previously included the idea in a long list of schemes he conceived to deceive the Germans. He also serves as the movie's narrator. It's an exquisitely detailed production, finely directed by Madden, who did the Oscar-winning *Shakespeare in Love* (PF5).

[Critic's note: Ian Fleming's character was probably considered nonessential in the 1956 version because he was five years away from international renown, even though his first James Bond novel, Casino Royale, had been published three years earlier. His rise to stardom occurred somewhat by accident. In answer to an interviewer's question in 1961, President John F. Kennedy declared he was "staying up reading James Bond." For Fleming, fame and fortune followed] [Caution: adult themes, two weird sex scenes and a gruesome forensic examination] **[W]**

* * *

[Operation Mincemeat trivia: 1) The real identity of "Major William Martin" remained classified for over half a century, while the man's body lay buried in a cemetery in Huelva under his fictitious name. Then, in 1998, the British government authorized an addendum to the gravesite. The words "Glyndwr Michael served as Major William Martin, RM" were carved at the bottom. Glyndwr Michael was a 34-year-old Welch vagrant who in despair had poisoned himself. 2) The effort's ruse produced an unexpected benefit the following year. A British officer had inadvertently left a set of genuine operational orders aboard a glider during the invasion of Holland. The Germans recovered the documents, but because of the ruse perpetrated by Operation Mincemeat, the High Command refused to believe the evidence. 3) Not portrayed in either movie, the underwear for Major Martin's corpse was donated by Oxford University, one of whose faculty members had died previously in a pedestrian accident and for reasons unknown had kept a large stash of the stuff]

Phil' Favorite? It's a close call, and I'd recommend either movie as a fairly accurate dramatization of Mincemeat – though both take their share of dramatic liberties. But I'll have to go with the

2021 version on the basis of the performances of Firth and Macfadyen; along with Kelly MacDonald playing Jean Leslie, a crucial feminine component of the ruse; and the dramatic, evocative score by Thomas Newman.

The Thing from Another World (vs.) The Thing
1951 and 1982 – Christian Nyby and John Carpenter

Several notable ... things about this early sci-fi tale. It was produced by Howard Hawks, so it carried his pedigree. Moreover, according to Hollywood lore, Hawks directed most of the movie. And Hawks co-wrote the script along with the legendary Ben Hecht (see *Wuthering Heights* elsewhere). It also debuted a young and hulking James Arness as the title character (the durable Marshal Matt Dillon in the long-running Gunsmoke TV series), wearing a costume that made him look like a human carrot. The story concerns a routine scientific mission to the North Pole suddenly confronted with evidence of a strange aircraft that has crashed into the ice, an aircraft that turns out to be a flying saucer. Further investigation reveals it was piloted by a rampaging, carnivorous alien – hence, Arness's character. From there, it's the standard battle for survival between the scientists and the creature. Pulpy and primitive by today's standards, but given the talents involved still entertaining. [Trivia note: Not exactly lexiconic, like "pod people" in the original *Invasion of the Body Snatchers*, the movie did inject the slogan, "Watch the skies!" into popular culture] [B&W]

*   *   *

Carpenter's remake of the 1951 story is his best and most coherent movie, except it's set at the opposite pole. It also deploys all the mechanical skills of makeup-effects wizard Rob Bottin, who excels at creating disgusting creatures and outdoes himself here. In the update, Carpenter dispenses with depicting the Thing's origin and instead has it arriving at an Antarctic research station in the form of a wayward sled dog, which is quickly befriended by the dozen members of the crew. Big mistake. Soon, the dog begins behaving strangely and then erupts into a ... well, you get the picture. From there and one by one, the alien (literally) invades the bodies of the 12 station members, gradually reducing their numbers in shocking ways. The cast includes Kurt Russell, Wilford Brimley, Richard Dysart (from TV's L.A. Law) and stalwart character actor Richard Masur. Harrowing and graphic at times, it's also a riveting story about hardened men in a desperate situation. [Caution: rough language and disgusting violence] **[W]**

Phil' Favorite? I've never been a fan of Carpenter's, but I'll go with his version here. For one thing, the casting is superior to the original's, and it's constantly fascinating to see how Bottin and his team can conjure ever more gruesome variations on the theme.

The Thomas Crown Affair (vs.) The Thomas Crown Affair

1968 and 1999 – Norman Jewison and John McTiernan

You might call the original *Thomas Crown Affair* the darker side of *A Man and a Woman* (PF5). It's similar to that romantic French crowd-pleaser because both are hip, stylish and atmospheric; both feature such romance inducers as a couple driving along a beach on a cloudy day; and both contain what became popular songs: the love theme from *A Man and a Woman* and "The Windmills of Your Mind," here. But this one isn't about an ordinary man and woman – glamorous though the French couple might have been. Nor is it quite as clever as the moviemakers think it is. Steve McQueen plays a millionaire businessman who fights boredom by betting excessively on golf shots and planning an intricate bank robbery. Faye Dunaway, at the peak of her appeal, plays Vicki Anderson, his love interest and rival, a determined insurance investigator who's sure that Crown is her man – in both senses of the phrase. Jewison's assured direction, Haskell Wexler's gorgeous cinematography and Michel Legrand's dreamy jazz score made the movie a hit – along with an exceptionally slick visual style consisting of frequent compositions of multiple images and shifting frame sizes. All that said, despite its sexy veneer, the movie harbors what's essentially a nasty soul. McQueen's Crown (his friends call him "Tommy") seems to feel

306

absolutely no concern for the henchmen he furtively hires, nor for the victims of the robbery or his large slate of employees who might face ruin if he's unmasked. It's an entertaining ride, but you might feel uncomfortably unsatisfied by the end. [Caution: violence and sexuality] **[W]**

*   *   *

In *The Thomas Crown Affair*, the 1999 remake, the crime in question shifts from a bank in Boston to an art museum in Manhattan. The stakes, predictably, are much higher (a $100-million Monet versus $2.5 million in cash), and though this Thomas Crown remains a multimillionaire businessman he's also an art collector of the highest order. Like his earlier namesake, Pierce Brosnan's Crown loves to take risks. Both personifications fly gliders, but this iteration has taken to racing – and swamping – an America's Cup-class catamaran sailboat in New York harbor. His nemesis/romantic interest this time is insurance investigator Catherine Banning (Rene Russo) – though Faye Dunaway appears briefly but periodically as Crown's psychiatrist. And while nudity had begun appearing in mainstream movies back in the late '60s, the coupling between McQueen and Dunaway was demure compared to the (literal) Brosnan–Russo tango. Alas, because the moviemakers attempt a few one-upmanships with the original, the remake plot contains a few blatant implausibilities. Example: There's a skillful forgery of the stolen painting, but it's created in, shall we say, record time and in a deliberate attempt at tormenting Banning, who likewise discovers its whereabouts in record time. And there's no explanation whatsoever of how "Tommy" manages to steal a second painting. Still, *Crown* '99 preserves a lot of screenwriter Alan Trustman's crisp original dialogue, it maintains a basically breezy tone throughout – allowing recovery of the Monet in a neat homage to the famous assassination scene in *Foreign Correspondent* (PF5) – and director McTiernan forgoes Jewison's penchant for split-screen gimmicks and opts for good, old-fashioned, solid camera work. Bill Conti supplied the clickety jazz score. [Trivia notes: 1) The two movies share one other connection: At the ball in the remake, the first song played by the band, and then twice later on in different arrangements –

307

including a vocal – is "The Windmills of Your Mind," the theme song from the original. 2) McQueen was a competent golfer, which shows during his scene in the sand trap, but Brosnan needed to take lessons just to pretend to be playing, and it's evident from his cringeworthy swing. 3) Set in Manhattan as it is, *Crown '99* joins the sad legacy of movies that display the ill-fated twin towers of the World Trade Center] [Caution: language and, as mentioned, more explicit sexuality than the original] **[W]**

Phil' Favorite? The first *Thomas Crown Affair* was groundbreaking in terms of its style and amoral audacity, and McQueen overall is a far more appealing and grounded screen presence than Brosnan – not to mention a much, much better golfer. But the second version is, for me, simply more fun.

Top Gun (vs.) Top Gun: Maverick
1986 and 2022 – Tony Scott and Joseph Kosinski
Okay, technically this is an original and a sequel. But given the time between the two (36 years) and the similarities of the stories, it wouldn't be too much of a stretch to place them in this category. Both, however, star Tom Cruise, which *is* unusual for a remake. Still, indulge me for the moment.

*   *   *

During the early years of the Vietnam War, American carrier-based fighter pilots experienced a savage series of defeats at the hands of North Vietnamese, Chinese and, occasionally, Russian air forces in the skies over Southeast Asia. The reason? In the 1960s, the U.S. Navy brass decided that aerial dogfights – close combat among aircraft using large-caliber machine guns – had become obsolete, and the only weapons pilots would need in the future were air-to-air missiles. Except the enemy air forces did not abandon the guns. After a long series of tragic losses, the Navy reconsidered and 1) began refitting its fighter aircraft with guns, and 2) established the Miramar flight school, near San Diego, to train its new pilots in the latest air-superiority techniques; nicknamed Top Gun. Here, Tom Cruise's Pete "Maverick" Mitchell, so-named because of his tendency to bend the rules, is a hotshot version of one of those pilots. He rides in on his Kawasaki Ninja motorbike full of bluster and reeking of confidence. That's when his painfully real education begins, amid some thrilling aerial scenes. Kelly McGillis, hot off her smashing debut in *Witness* (PF5) the previous year, plays an aeronautical scientist who becomes his love interest. Tom Skerritt is arresting as Mike "Viper" Metcalf, Top Gun's seasoned commander. Also distinctive are Val Kilmer as Tom "Ice Man" Kazanski, a rival hotshot pilot, and Anthony Edwards as Nick "Goose" Bradshaw, Maverick's radio man riding in the back seat of the cockpit. Tony Scott directed; "Highway to the Danger Zone," the throbbing theme song by Kenny Loggins, became a Top-40 hit; and the movie soared at the box office. [Trivia notes: 1) Much of the aerial footage was real – though detailed miniatures were used for certain scenes – the ones requiring the most dangerous maneuvers. Art Scholl, following the action in his camera biplane, at one point crashed into the ocean and was killed. Neither Scholl nor his plane was ever recovered. *Top Gun* is dedicated to him. 2) The principal actor/pilots all rode in real F-14 Tomcat fighters during the filming, and most vomited frequently during the radical maneuvers. Cruise was no exception, though he claimed to love the adrenalin rush from the experiences. 3) If you once owned a collection of VHS tapes, instead of renting them from the video store, credit *Top Gun* for starting the process. Originally, the studios priced their tapes so high that only the stores could afford more than a few of them. But the producers struck a deal with Pepsi to insert a commercial for the soft drink before the movie began. It allowed them to drop the price dramatically. Customers responded with enthusiasm, and the home-video market soon exploded] [Caution: language and sexuality] **[W]**

*   *   *

Along with my placing a sequel in the category, instead of a true remake, here's another technicality: *Top Gun: Maverick* was completed and ready for release in 2020, but movie exhibition and distribution went haywire that year due to the COVID outbreak and the public's extreme reluctance to gather in large groups indoors – mask mandates notwithstanding. So, the producers wisely held back the release until moviegoers were ready to return. And return they did! In the movie's opening weekend, Memorial Day 2022, it breached $300 million at the box office.

*   *   *

In *Top Gun: Maverick*, after a surprise introduction, which might or might not permanently begin the movie, the title character, who has refused promotion after promotion so he can keep flying, is ordered to return to Miramar some 36 years later. Maverick's job is to train a group of Top Gun graduates for the most difficult mission of their lives. No more details, however. Suffice it to say that, as in *Top Gun*, the melodrama is standard, and the mission is pretext for some of the most astounding aerial maneuvers ever seen on the big screen. Also as in *Top Gun*, much of the flying is real; in this case in F-18 Superhornets, while the "enemy" aircraft are actually F-22 Raptors, the world's pre-eminent fighters. In a genuine dogfight, the Raptors would eat the Hornets alive. But this is fiction, and it's electrifying to see what director Kosinski and the Navy pilots have achieved. There's even a scene where Cruise, a pilot in private life, takes Jennifer Connelly (Maverick's love interest) for a ride in a vintage P-51 Mustang. The only other returning cast member is Val Kilmer, again playing "Ice Man" but now an admiral and a close friend to Maverick. It's a game effort by Kilmer, who has been fighting throat cancer for several years and can no longer speak. Tony Scott died in 2012, and the movie is dedicated to him. [Viewing note: About the mission? Whether an homage or unrelated, its parameters are humorously similar to those specified in a beloved blockbuster some 45 years earlier. If you catch the reference, my guess is you'll laugh out loud in recognition] [Mild caution: language, a brief and tasteful sex scene, and intense aerial sequences] [Trivia note: Kilmer was able to speak in his scene with Cruise via computer-generated recreations of his voice from past performances created by the electronics company Sonantic, which the actor later wrote, "masterfully restored my voice in a way I've never thought possible"] **[W]**

Phil' Favorite? Given the eye-popping aerobatics of *Maverick*, I'll award it the edge. But both movies, filmed entirely in the U.S.A., deserve great credit, not only to their production crews but also to the brave men and women of the U.S. Navy, and in particular at Miramar and aboard the carriers U.S.S. Abraham Lincoln and U.S.S. Theodore Roosevelt, who did the heavy lifting to create those dazzling sequences. As *Maverick* director Kosinski commented in an interview, "Every day they showed us why they are who they are – they are the best of the best."

West Side Story (vs.) West Side Story
1961 and 2021 – Robert Wise and Jerome Robbins, and Steven Spielberg

Based on the smash-hit Broadway musical of the late 1950s, with lyrics by Steven Sondheim and music by Leonard Bernstein, Wise and Robbins mounted a sprawling movie version that won Best Picture and Supporting Actor and Actress awards for George Chakiris and Rita Moreno, as well as seven other Oscars. Despite its flaws, and there are several, the movie became a huge crowd-pleaser and one of the most honored by the motion picture academy. Among those accolades were for Robbins's spectacular choreography, arguably the best ever in a motion picture – except anything done by Fred Astaire and Ginger Rogers, and Gene Kelly (Robbins could receive only an honorary Oscar because choreography has never been an official category). Then there was Daniel Fapp's impeccable cinematography, as crisp as you're likely to see in widescreen – shot on 70 millimeter film. The story takes Shakespeare's tragic romance "Romeo and Juliet" and places the two lovers (Richard Beymer as Tony and Natalie Wood as Maria) in contemporary New York City. Instead of the Montagues and Capulets, the rival factions are the Sharks, a gang of Puerto Rican immigrants, and the Jets, a mix of native-born street toughs. Ernest Lehman, who would work with director Wise four years later in *The Sound of Music* (PF5), another Best Picture winner, adapted the play for the screen. It's a throbbing, vibrant musical, with a long list of unforgettable numbers, including "Something's Coming" and "Maria" by Tony;

"America" by Moreno's character Anita; and "Tonight," "One Hand, One Heart" and "Somewhere," by Tony and Maria. There are several others, such as the hilarious "Gee, Officer Krupke" performed by the Jets. All will leave you either exhilarated or shattered. The flaws? Much of the acting is wooden, made even less appealing by the contrast with the musical numbers. Likewise, quite a bit of the dialogue. And because the two lead actors were not singers, their voices had to be dubbed – James Howard Bryant for Beymer and Marni Nixon for Wood. The contrasts between their speaking and singing voices are noticeable. Still, it's one of the finest and most popular screen musicals ever made, and its excellence after six decades remains undimmed. [Trivia note: Regarding dubbed voices, here are two neat little tidbits. Tucker Smith, one of the Jets, sang for Russ Tamblyn's character Riff in "When You're a Jet," even though Smith also sang for himself in that scene. And Moreno was a strong singer, but Betty Wand had to dub her in the electrifying "A Boy Like That" because the song's key was too low for her. In the annals of musical cinema, there are many more such examples] [Caution: violence and mild sexuality] **[W]**

*   *   *

I was more curious than eager to see Spielberg's 60th anniversary remake. As it turned out, any hopes that he would create a fresh and exciting update to the musical remained unfulfilled. I found the new *West Side Story* inferior to its predecessor in almost every way, a major miss by a director whose work I deeply admire. Four main points. First, the choreography by Justin Peck can't hold a candle to that of Jerome Robbins in the '61 version. Example: In the glorious prologue of the original, there's a moment when three of the Sharks, led by George Chakiris, do an exuberant high kick with arms extended during their dance. It's an iconic image, expressing hope and longing by dynamic but troubled young men. There's nothing comparable here – not one similar frame you would want to freeze and savor. Likewise, the women's dances. Peck seems to crowd the performers together into an indiscriminate mass, whereas Robbins kept them separate and distinct, even during the synchronous moves. A related second

312

point: Spielberg's puzzling framing of much of the dancing. He often shoots the performers only from the waist up, cutting out their legs and feet. Or, he places them in compositions so wide you can hardly make out their moves; sequences that must have Fred Astaire turning over in his grave. Third, Ansel Elgort, who plays Tony, has a lovely singing voice – and it's his own on screen. But in every one of his numbers he fails to project the emotions his character is supposedly feeling. Whether it's Spielberg's direction or his own limitations, he always seems so inhibited, like he's enjoying himself but never overwhelmed by passion. I don't recall him even once reaching out with his arms. Rachel Zegler as Maria, meanwhile, sings beautifully and acts convincingly in her screen debut. But she, too, often seems restrained. Despite their dubbed singing voices, Richard Beymer and Natalie Wood generated real sparks. Fourth is Janusz Kamiński's cinematography; stark and featuring his habitual harshly contrasted look. It makes the late '50s urban decay environment appear even more grungy. In the praise column, kudos to Rita Moreno, the only member of the '61 cast to re-appear (though Chakiris and Tamblyn, at this writing, are still with us). Here, she's the fictional widow of "Doc," the drugstore owner played by Ned Glass in the original. At age 89, she's sharp and commanding (she's also listed as one of the movie's executive producers), and her soft, solo version of "Somewhere" near the end conveys poignancy and hopefulness. Mike Faist does a nice turn as Riff, leader of the Jets. His wise-guy take on the character seems just right. The same for Josh Andrés Rivera as Chino, Maria's shy but lethal suitor. And along with a few of Spielberg's visual touches, which once again prove his mastery of the medium, Tony Kushner's screenplay clarifies and deepens some of the themes written by Arthur Laurents in the original stage production and in Ernest Lehman's 1961 script. [Caution: language, violence and sexuality] **[W]**

Phil' Favorite? I suspect *West Side Story* 2021 will be politely received and fade away, while *West Side Story* 1961 will continue to be revered by posterity. There's a prominent image in

Spielberg's prologue, which film historians might choose as the symbol of his taking on one of the great works of stage and screen – it's a wrecking ball.

36. Out There

Even more than historical epics, the genre that requires the most effort in special effects – and imagination – is science fiction. Sci-fi movies, as they're called, often need groundbreaking visuals and huge expenditures to fulfill the writer's or moviemaker's concept. But sometimes, as you'll see with several of these 10 titles, cleverness and ingenuity can create convincing illusions and compelling stories even on meager production budgets.

Android
1982 – Aaron Lipstadt

Let's start with a low-budget wonder (under $1 million at the time), produced by Roger Corman's New World Pictures. Though the studio was notorious for squeezing every last dollar, it also functioned as the proving ground for several major moviemakers, including Francis Ford Coppola and James Cameron. The story takes place in the year 2036 at a space station inhabited by a (what else?) obsessed scientist named Dr. Daniel (German actor Klaus Kinsky) along with his troupe of … androids. Or, at least, Daniel appears to be a scientist. His most recently created android is Max 404 (Don Keith Opper in a most convincing though uncredited performance), who's been endowed with innate curiosity and whose behavior is becoming more and more human-like. In fact, Max is in the process of creating his own android, an alluring female prototype named Cassandra One (Kendra Kirchner). While this is going on, the station's relative peace and quiet are disrupted by the arrival of a spaceship carrying criminals in disguise, pushing things in a messy direction in a hurry. But it's all surprisingly fascinating to watch. [Trivia note: Typical of productions at New World back then, *Android* was shot in 20 days, and it recycled many of its props from earlier titles] [Caution: female android sexuality] **[W]**

Arrival
2016 – Denis Villeneuve
From entertaining schlock to top dollar and high quality – and in my view the best of the bunch. This melancholy but mesmerizing tale involves language expert Louise Banks (Amy Adams in one of her best performances), called upon to make contact with a pair of aliens who have … arrived on Earth in one of 12 giant, seemingly taco-shaped, gravity-defying spacecraft. Banks is recruited – actually, she's ordered into service – by Colonel Weber (Forrest Whitaker), who's running the military surveillance of this particular craft. She'll be working with Ian Donnelly (Jeremy Renner), a physicist tasked with analyzing the aliens' technical capabilities. Her main task becomes deciphering their extremely complex visual communications, fascinating creations by Canadian artist Martine Bertrand. Impeccably conceived and executed, the plot is better discovered than revealed. You might almost believe it's based on a real incident – though the ending is contrived, a bit confusing and, in one instance, inconsistent with the rest of the narrative. Max Richter composed the haunting, appropriately otherworldly score. Also, consider what you might think of encountering a couple of seven-legged, underwater elephants nicknamed "Abbott and Costello." [Trivia note: Adams and Renner had co-starred three years earlier in the distinctly unfunny but overpraised comedy–drama *American Hustle* (not on my lists)] **[W]**

The Brother from Another Planet
1984 – written and directed by John Sayles
Film and TV veteran Joe Morton in his first starring role is a mute an unnamed alien with dark skin and very long toenails who hides out in Harlem while two other, menacing humanoid aliens (Sayles and David Strathairn) are hunting him. The local residents are more than happy to shelter the … brother because his special abilities include healing the sick and repairing appliances. A strange tale in any genre, it's nevertheless captivating, fitfully funny and among Sayles's best work. [Caution: (alien) sexuality] **[W]**

Enemy Mine
1985 – Wolfgang Petersen

A decent-sized budget but an often-recycled storyline derived from sources such as Star Trek TV episodes and, particularly, the recurring enmity between the Federation and the Klingon and Romulan empires. Dennis Quaid and Louis Gossett Jr. play Willis and Jeriba, enemy combatants in an interstellar war who become marooned for three years on a desolate planet and must cooperate to survive. Jeriba is a Drac, a lizard-like alien race at war with humans near the end of the 21st century. After three years of exile, the two beings become close friends, all the more so when Willis learns that Jeriba is pregnant – the Dracs reproduce asexually. Knowing he might not survive giving birth, "Jerry" – as Willis now calls him – persuades his friend to learn as much about Drac society and traditions as possible so he can stand in for him at the right-of-passage ceremony for his offspring. As mentioned, a recycled plot but a compelling movie, well-acted by the two leads. [Caution: battle violence] **[W]**

The Man Who Fell to Earth
1976 – Nicolas Roeg

Rock-music legend David Bowie stars as an alien from a dying planet in this, arguably, the most laid-back of sci-fi movies. Bowie's character poses as Mr. Thomas Jerome Newman, a soft-spoken individual who seems to be an Englishman and who possesses extremely lucrative technical information, which he exploits to generate needed cash. We eventually learn that Newman is raising the money to build spacecraft to transport water back to his unnamed and arid home planet. In the meantime, he partakes of some of the pleasures of human flesh – including intensive TV-watching – with the assistance of Mary-Lou (Candy Clark), a young woman who initiates him in said pleasures. Eventually, Newman's secret identity is revealed, and he's captured. From there, the movie takes a morose turn from which it doesn't recover. The change nearly spoils the story, but enough good material remains to justify a look and a place on this list. [Caution: explicit sexuality] **[W]**

The Martian
2015 – Ridley Scott

Along with returning to and permanently colonizing the Moon, humans for many years have yearned to explore the Red Planet, the other, relatively nearby solar system body that potentially could accommodate humans. That said, traveling to Mars, and remaining there, present enormous challenges and extreme dangers, each of which must be overcome to prevent any mission from producing fatalities – space and Mars as well as our Moon have a thousand ways to kill the careless, the unprepared and the unlucky. Here's a lavishly produced tale about a Mars expedition facing such hazards, conducted in the year 2035. Matt Damon plays Mark Watney, an astronaut and would-be ... Martian colonist who's accidentally deserted and must fend for himself until he can be rescued. A daunting task, because that rescue could be at least four years away. Based on Andy Weir's best-selling novel of the same name, the movie presents excellent effects portraying the Martian surface, Watney's survival activities and his eventual rescue via returning spacecraft. Those achievements aside, two problems with the story and one technical inaccuracy bothered me. First, as soon as Watney realizes he has been abandoned, he should have altered the configuration of his site so that mission controllers monitoring reconnaissance satellites could notice he's still alive. That's what eventually happens but acting more quickly would have bought him precious time. Second, the spacecraft that slingshots around Earth to rescue Watney exposes its crew to a doubling and potentially fatal dose of space radiation. Yet there's no mention of the hazard. And third, the Martian atmosphere is so thin that the fierce sandstorm depicted early on would be impossible. But those are quibbles. All-in-all, it's a fine addition to the sci-fi genre, and Damon is riveting in his quest to stay alive. [Caution: language] [W]

Stowaway
2021 – co-written and directed by Joe Penna
Another survival tale with excellent effects portraying a Mars mission. It's a variation of the plot of the original *Alien* (PF5), in which the seven-person crew of the space freighter Nostromo is confronted by an unwanted and deadly passenger. Here, the passenger (Shamier Anderson) is likewise unwanted and potentially deadly, but his addition to the three-person crew (Toni Collette, Anna Kendrick and Daniel Dae Kim) is, improbably, accidental. The potentially deadly aspect derives from the fact that the spacecraft, dubbed MTS-42, wasn't designed to support four humans during a two-year round trip to the Red Planet. Therefore, the crew must attempt several risky actions to overcome their rapidly deteriorating situation. Despite the contrived premise, *Stowaway* turns out to be a surprisingly gripping survival drama. [Caution: graphic medical procedures] **[W]**

THX1138
1967 – written and directed by George Lucas
Not to be confused with Lucas's first big-screen effort in 1971 starring Robert Duvall and Candy Clark. For one thing, the 1971 movie was indeed titled *THX1138*. This one's full title is *Electronic Labyrinth: THX1138 4EB* and was Lucas's University of Southern California student film. Given the lack of resources available, it's not only quite impressive; it's also better than the full-length version. In my three compilations, I've only recommended one other student film. That was Martin Brest's spectacular 1977 musical *Hot Tomorrows* (PF5).

When Worlds Collide
1951 – produced by George Pal
Pal creates state-of-the-art effects for the '50s in this apocalyptic tale that's fanciful but makes an engrossing drama. Bellus, a rogue star with an orbiting planet named Zyra, has invaded our solar system and in eight months will collide with Earth. In a mad dash, scientists and engineers want to develop a Noah's Ark-like rocket

that will ferry a small group of lottery-chosen humans, along with a basic assortment of farm animals, to the surviving alien planet. There, they will – if successful – attempt to restart civilization. Skeptical governments reject the plan, but a group of wealthy businessmen agree to finance the project, an arrangement that causes inevitable conflicts of interest and schemes by certain individuals determined to ride the rocket to survival. [Trivia notes: 1) The massive computer shown in the movie was real. Developed by General Electric at a cost of $125,000, the device contained much, much less memory and processing power than even the least powerful of today's smartphones. 2) The escape rocket was designed by famed concept artist Chesley Bonestell]

The X-Files
1998 – Rob Bowman
Based on the TV series (and filmed in between the fifth and sixth seasons), with David Duchovny and Gillian Anderson reprising their roles as Scully and Mulder, it turns out to be an absorbing sci-fi mystery. Beginning with twin prologues set, respectively, during the last ice age and then jumping to contemporary times, the story quickly propels the two leads into tracking down what could be an alien virus infecting the human population and causing (what else?) bizarre changes in behavior and sudden death. And that isn't all. The virus seems to be spreading uncontrolled and has apparently created a huge conspiracy involving high levels of the government as well as an enormous alien facility that has been constructed in Antarctica. And so on, as Scully and Mulder move from one close call to another in their attempt to unravel what's been happening to the unsuspecting human population. Atmospheric and gripping, the movie makes a solid jump from the small screen. [Trivia note: If the location of the final scene looks familiar, it's because it was filmed in Tunisia in the same area that portrayed the planet Tatooine in the original *Star Wars* (PF5). In fact, the place has been renamed Foum Tatouine in honor of the movie] [Caution: violence] [W]

37. Ring Trilogy (Plus one)

You might have noticed in a previous chapter (28) that I listed a quintet of titles portraying or located in Pittsburgh, my birthplace. Here, I'm featuring four related to the opposite end of the Keystone State; specifically, Philadelphia, the City of Brotherly Love, a metropolis known for the Liberty Bell, great cheesesteaks, terrifically outspoken people and some of the worst political leadership in the country. Three of the movies concern the sport of boxing, all products of writer/star Sylvester Stallone. There have been better examples of the genre, particularly *Cinderella Man* and *Creed* (PF5), and *The Fighter* (P25), but I credit Stallone for creating this popular cinematic dynasty, and these aren't half bad. Meanwhile, the fourth entrée stands at the top of its genre: basketball.

Rocky
1976 – John V. Avildsen

Stallone's breakthrough role won Best Picture and set him on a course to be a movie action hero for nearly half a century. Here, in a simple story, he plays Rocky Balboa, a low-rated, semi-pro boxer in Philadelphia also working as an enforcer for a loan shark. Through an improbable twist of fate, he gets a shot at the heavyweight title currently held by Apollo Creed (Carl Weathers in a tremendously appealing performance of his own). At the same time, he finds romance with Adrian (Talia Shire) the plain-Jane sister of his best friend Paulie (Burt Young). *Rocky* contains every dramatic, romantic and boxing-movie cliché ever used, but it wins you over, nevertheless. And Stallone's physical performance is impressive. John G. Avildsen directed, and Bill Conti did the rousing and now-famous fanfare. [Trivia notes: 1) The scene where Rocky arranges for him and Adrian to skate in an empty ice rink – which has become an audience favorite –

happened by accident. Originally, the rink was supposed to be full of skaters, but budgetary concerns forced the hiring of only a few extras. So, Stallone reworked the scene to feature only the two leads. 2) Lack of funds also required many of the exterior training scenes to be shot without obtaining permits from the city. Director Avildsen and a small crew quietly filmed Stallone in the streets, let's say, unofficially. 3) The story behind the movie has become Hollywood legend. Stallone, a struggling actor with little money and no car rejected the first offer for his script, which would have ended his poverty immediately. Instead, Stallone insisted that he play the title character, an enormous risk at the time but one that paid off handsomely, to say the least] [Caution: boxing violence and rough language] **[W]**

Rocky III
1982 – written and directed by Sylvester Stallone
Skipping over the clumsy and unresolved sequel, Stallone directs himself as Rocky Balboa fights and loses a match against the intimidating "Clubber" Lang (Laurence Turead, better known as "Mr. T"). When the chance for a rematch arises, Apollo Creed befriends Rocky and agrees to train him – under the condition that if he wins, he must also give Apollo a rematch, but one-on-one and in private. [Caution: boxing violence and rough language] **[W]**

Rocky IV
1985 – written and directed by Sylvester Stallone
After his friend and former rival Apollo Creed is killed in the ring by the monster Russian Ivan Drago (Dolph Lundgren), Rocky meets the Russian to avenge the loss. [Trivia note: Lundgren, an engineering student who was nevertheless a big bruiser, hit Stallone so hard once during filming that he put him in hospital for four days] [Caution: boxing violence and rough language] **[W]**

Hustle

2022 – Jeremiah Zagar

If there's anything I've learned in my years as a movie fan and sometime critic, it's that you should never assume a non-favorite actor or moviemaker can't suddenly produce something first-rate and memorable. *Hustle* is one such example. I've never been a fan of Adam Sandler or his previous performances. But here he jumps to near legendary status as Stanley Sugarman; former player, veteran scout and would-be coach for the Philadelphia 76ers basketball team. Stanley finds himself in a near-desperate situation when Sixers owner and Stanley's patron Rex Merrick (Robert Duvall) dies, leaving the team in the hands of Merrick's son Vince (Ben Foster), with whom Stanley immediately clashes. Tired of life on the road, Stanley nevertheless complies with Vince's order that he travel to Spain to seek talented new players for the team. Failing at his mission, a forlorn Stanley looks for a local pick-up court where he can "shoot some hoops" before returning home. There, he spots what appears to be a phenomenally talented young adult named Bo Cruz (current Utah Jazz player Juancho Hernangómez). Therein begins a long, long slog as Stanley attempts to prepare Bo for a tryout with the Sixers. I'll reveal no more, except to say that the two actors work extremely well together, that the movie features over two-dozen current and former National Basketball Association players in cameo roles (including Julius "Dr. J" Irving along with fellow stars Charles Barkley, Shaquille O'Neal and Allen Iverson), and that the training sequences – filmed along some of the same Philadelphia streets – are as thrilling as anything shown in the *Rocky* trilogy. It's a terrific story about the game of basketball; in my view the best ever made. [Caution: nearly constant rough language] **[W]**

38. Royal Rascals

Quite a few movies over the years have dealt with the challenges facing, and foibles of, members of the world's monarchies and the aristocracies. Here are eight, a mix of dramas and comedies, that do so notably.

Downton Abbey: A New Era
2022 – Simon Curtis

I might have placed this one in my final chapter, called Second (and Third) Acts, because it's the superb sequel to the film version of *Downton Abbey* (P25) and a further expansion of the captivating British TV series. But it's here as a fine film in its own right, dealing with the theme of aristocracy – though it's best if you hold at least a basic familiarity with the series and its vivid characters. This story begins in 1928 with the romance between Tom Branson (Alan Leech) and Lucy Smith (Tuppence Middleton) having blossomed into love and marriage. Meanwhile, Violet Crawley (the great Maggie Smith), the family matriarch, receives a bit of astounding news. She's been bequeathed a lavish French seaside villa by a former suitor who might be her son Robert Crawley's real father, an immense complication that throws the family into turmoil. Both major plot developments continue threads that emerged in the previous installments of the Crawley clan. The new and completely unexpected development here starts with the pitch by a Hollywood director to shoot a movie on the Downton estate and inside the mansion. It's a delightful twist because of what it appropriates from *Singin' in the Rain* (PF5) when the movie crew confronts the sudden reality that their production must become a "talkie." Any fan of what's been called everybody's favorite musical will savor the parallels – particularly the one involving the movie-within-the-movie's female star. Other plotlines either expand on or resolve issues that have beset members of the large cast all along. And despite a sad, but not unexpected, departure of one of the principals, *A New Era* wraps things up most enjoyably. [Caution: adult themes and mild sexuality] **[W]**

Hero

2002 – China – co-written and directed by Zhang Yimou

A masterfully told, expansive historical tale of intrigue, attempted assassination and ... heroism in China at a time when Europe and the Middle East were experiencing Christianity's first growing pains. Starring Jet Li as a wandering warrior whose character is called Nameless, *Hero* was at the time the country's most expensive production, its biggest-grossing film and a nominee for a Best Foreign Film Oscar. The plot is sophisticated and complex. A paranoid king (Chen Daoming) allows no one to approach him because of recent and near-successful attempts on his life. But Nameless arrives at the palace and claims to have killed the king's would-be assassins. In a long sequence reminiscent of Kurosawa's *Rashômon*, Nameless describes his deeds on the king's behalf, which we see portrayed but which the king doubts. The king then relates his own version of events, in which he accuses Nameless of plotting to kill him – which we also see. The same with Nameless's response to the king. And so on. This being a tale of ancient feudal times, and given the characters involved, you'll realize at some point it isn't going to end happily. But it's all beautifully photographed, meticulously staged and engrossing to watch. Once again, Zhang has shown himself to be a consummate perfectionist and among the world's finest directors. [Trivia note: How much of a perfectionist? Two examples. For a duel taking place against a backdrop of autumn leaves, Zhang had his crew gather and sort thousands and thousands of leaves to spread on the ground in carefully graduated shades from foreground to background. And he took weeks to shoot a scene set against a pristine lake because he insisted that the water's surface be absolutely still and would only call "action" when it was] [Caution: violence] **[W]**

325

Love and Death
1976 – written and directed by Woody Allen

Consider this dilemma. You're an up-and-coming movie writer–director, and you've contracted to write a murder mystery–comedy, but you're suffering from writer's block. What to do? If you're Woody Allen and in your creative angst you notice a classic Russian novel on your bookshelf and begin reading, soon, *voilà*! You put the partial script aside and instead crank out a comedic take on the Russian aristocracy in the days of Napoléon. Then you head to, of all places, Hungary to begin shooting. There, your food paranoia prevents you from partaking of the local cuisine – a good thing, because most of your cast and crew contracts dysentery from it. Eventually, you create the fitfully funny tale about Boris Grushenko, a schnook who's conscripted into the Russian Army to fight Bonaparte and accidentally triumphs in battle. Boris then briefly marries his cousin (Diane Keaton, in one of eight onscreen collaborations with Allen) and must face death repeatedly, though ultimately unsuccessfully. Whatever happens, remember this is a comedy, one that Gary Arnold called "funny with remarkable and delightful consistency." [Trivia note: Allen had such a bad experience filming in Hungary, with those food-borne illnesses and with a non-English-speaking crew, that he didn't try shooting abroad again for 20 years] [Caution: adult themes, mild sexuality and comic violence] **[W]**

The Mouse That Roared
1959 – Jack Arnold

Peter Sellers plays multiple roles (including the Duchess) in this charming farce about Fenwick, a tiny and fictional European duchy that declares war on the United States – and wins. Fenwick's nobles had decided to wage war because the country's failing wine industry was throwing their economy into bankruptcy. They figured they could attack New York City (via crossbows and suits of armor), surrender and then receive foreign aid from a forgiving America. What they hadn't planned on, however, was inadvertently capturing the Q Bomb, a superweapon under development by Dr. Kokintz (David Kossoff), a scientist working in Manhattan. They take him and his daughter Helen (Jean Seberg) back to Fenwick, forcing America to negotiate return of the hostages and the bomb. Naturally, complications ensue, all gently funny and endearing. Filmed entirely in England, the crew compiled background shots of Manhattan for certain scenes. Director Arnold is best remembered for his twin pulp sci-fi hits earlier in the decade, *It Came from Outer Space* (PF5) and *The Creature from the Black Lagoon* (P25).

Outlaw King
2018 – Scotland – co-written and directed by David Mackenzie
I would've loved to have seen Angus Macfadyen star in this tale of Robert the Bruce, the legendary king of Scotland who fought for his country's independence from England in the early 14th century. That's because he did such a terrific job in that role in Mel Gibson's Oscar-winning *Braveheart* (PF5). Instead, here we've got Chris Pine, otherwise known as Captain James T. Kirk in the latest iteration of the Star Trek movies, trying his hand at the Bruce. A somewhat clumsy telling of the legend, but amid stunning panoramas of the country's landscape. The story begins near where *Braveheart* ends, with the Scottish defeat at Stirling. After a slow and lengthy background sequence, which fills in the political intrigues involved, the Bruce plans a new rebellion against the British crown. It fails initially, and the king's soldiers relentless hunt the Bruce and his new bride, Elizabeth de Burgh (feisty newcomer Florence Pugh), as … outlaws. The resulting battles are huge and intense, and despite Pine's usual roles in Hollywood blockbusters, he's surprisingly effective here. As with all such dramas – *Braveheart* included – *The Outlaw King* takes liberties with history. Nevertheless, it's engrossing. [Critic's note: Actually, Macfadyen *did* star as Robert the Bruce, the next year in a movie of the same name. But as of this writing I haven't yet seen it] [Trivia note: Two years earlier, Pine had worked for director Mackenzie in the contemporary American western *Hell or High Water* (not here)] [Caution: violence and sexuality] **[W]**

The Private Lives of Elizabeth and Essex
1939 – Michael Curtiz

Remember the beginning of the great TV series Hill Street Blues, when two of the main characters (police captain Frank Furillo and public defender Joyce Davenport) appeared at first to be antagonists but actually were secret lovers? Here's a tragic twist on that arrangement, preceding Hill Street by four decades – and historically by four centuries – and meeting the couple quite late in their relationship. The inimitable Bette Davis is 63-year-old Elizabeth, queen of England, and Errol Flynn is the 32-year-old Earl of Essex, commander of the Royal Navy. As Essex returns to the queen's court after defeating the Spanish fleet, he's anticipating praise from his monarch, and some love ... in private. Instead, Elizabeth berates him for failing to capture the enemy's treasure. Insulted and furious, Essex storms away. Therein begin misunderstandings and treachery aplenty that lead, inevitably, to an execution. It's entertaining period drama, looking grand in Technicolor and with Flynn as dashing as ever. He's supported by his frequent romantic co-star Olivia De Havilland (the same year she played Melanie Wilkes in Gone With the Wind – see PF5). In this case, however, she's a fly in the romantic ointment. Both were working together for the fifth of seven times with Curtiz, in a glorious Technicolor production. [Historical note: Elizabeth and Essex indeed were lovers, though they were also cousins, and closely related ones at that, but the movie ignores that aspect] [Trivia notes: 1) Davis and Flynn were playing lovers, but the two great actors disdained each other and barely spoke between takes. In the scene where Elizabeth slaps Essex, during one take Davis delivered a real blow to Flynn's face, momentarily stunning him. 2) I mentioned the characters' ages because Davis and Flynn were both in their early 30s here – with Davis undergoing severe makeup applications to portray the aging monarch]

The Queen
2006 – England – Stephen Frears

In this case it's the contemporary Elizabeth – Elizabeth II of England – as played by Helen Mirren in an Oscar-winning role.

The story involves ... the queen as she's forced to deal with the sudden and shocking death of her world-famous daughter-in-law, Princess Diana, in 1997. She's joined in her travails by her husband Prince Philip (the usually reliable but miscast James Cromwell), her son and Diana's widower Prince Charles (Alex Jennings), and newly elected Prime Minister Tony Blair (Michel Sheen, who so closely resembles Blair that he has played him several times). The queen's dilemma is twofold. Does she accede to Diana's family's request that her funeral be private or acknowledge the widespread public grieving and cries (which she terms "hysteria") for a state funeral? And, will she personally attend that funeral and address the public? We follow this process via Mirren's fine and thoughtful performance. Written by Peter Morgan, the movie seems a rough draft of his exquisite British TV series The Crown, which he created and produced starting in 2016 and, at this writing, about to begin its fifth season. [Caution: language and adult themes] **[W]**

A Royal Affair
2012 – Denmark – co-written and directed by Nikolaj Arcel

As was common for European nobility down the centuries – in this case the 18th – English Princess Caroline Matilda (Swedish actress Alicia Vikander) has been betrothed by her family to Christian VII (Mikkel Følsgaard), the King of Denmark. Accepting her fate, she arrives at the royal court only to find: 1) many of the beloved books she has brought along are banned, 2) her husband is ... shall we say, not *compos mentis* and 3) though Caroline quickly bears Christian a child, he soon thereafter abandons any intimate interest in her. That's when Johann Friedrich Struensee (Mads Mikkelsen), a German doctor, is summoned to help the king overcome his affliction. The two men become fast friends, but the doctor also falls in love, and begins an affair with, the king's wife. It's a sophisticated story, involving politics and philosophy as well as an affair of the heart. It received an Oscar nomination for Best Foreign Film. And the three principals perform well, particularly the versatile Mikkelsen, who played the villain Le Chiffre in Daniel Craig's first outing as James Bond in *Casino Royale* (<u>PF5</u>). Sophisticated or not, the movie depicts a period in history when people tended to lose their heads over political disagreements, and *A Royal Affair* is no exception. [<u>Trivia note</u>: Call it an unfortunate linguistic coincidence, but the name Struensee in Danish is similar to the Italian pejorative meaning piece of … um, excrement] [<u>Caution</u>: sexuality] **[W]**

39. School Days

Not really "dear old Golden Rule days" as far as Hollywood is concerned, most of its dramas and even comedies about youth in school have tended to focus on aberrant or dishonorable behavior, though a few managed to maintain good spirits and produce happy endings. Or, in the case of dramas, some effectively probed the issues of the day. These nine constitute among the best in those respects.

Blackboard Jungle
1955 – written and directed by Richard Brooks

Let's start off with an exploration of some of the darkest recesses of public education, and featuring a cast sprinkled with actors who would go on to prominent careers on the stage and TV, and in the movies – none more so than Sidney Poitier but also several other famous or recognizable names. It's the story of Richard Dadier (Glenn Ford, who was already a star), a World War II veteran newly hired to teach at an inner-city school populated by, let's say, a bunch of misguided youth. As one of his colleagues puts it, the school is "the garbage can of the educational system." Dadier's class contains two of the worst delinquents, Gregory Miller and Artie West (Poitier and Vic Morrow, both playing teens but both in their late 20s), neither of whom shows the slightest respect for him, precipitating a series of tense encounters. Worse, at one point they physically attack Dadier and a fellow teacher on the street. The situation grows worse and worse, leading to a showdown in the classroom. Based on Evan Hunter's autobiographical novel, in turn based on his own brief experience as a teacher in New York City's South Bronx, it's a somewhat clumsy but rough and raw depiction of inner-city life in the 1950s. [Trivia notes: 1) Though most of the young cast had no history as troubled youths, Poitier was the exception. A Bahamian by birth, his family sent him to America in his teens to escape his delinquent associates and begin a new life. 2) The movie has been credited with introducing Rock 'n' Roll music into the popular culture, beginning – and ending – with "Rock Around the Clock" by Bill Haley and His Comets. It's the same opening song used by George Lucas nearly 20 years later for *American Graffiti* (PF5). 3) The suggestion for the theme song originated with Glenn Ford's son Peter, a fan of Bill Haley, who played the record for director Brooks. 4) About those future well-knowns? I already mentioned Vic Morrow, who starred in the TV series Combat in the '60s. Among the others is Paul Mazursky, later distinguishing himself as a director. There's Anne Francis, who co-starred the following year with Walter Pigeon in the sci-fi classic *Forbidden Planet* (PF5). There's Richard Kiley, who immortalized the character of Don Quixote in the Broadway musical "Man of La Mancha." And there's Jameel Farah, better known as Jamie Farr, likewise immortal as the cross-dressing Corporal Max Klinger in the TV series M*A*S*H] [Caution: adult themes, tough talk and violence] **[B&W]**

Dear Evan Hansen
2021 – Stephen Chbosky
From the historic to the contemporary, and from classroom reality to group delusion. Based on the Tony Award-winning musical, it stars Ben Platt, who had played the lead onstage several years earlier. Evan is a high school misfit whose self-help letter creates a major misunderstanding and, eventually, a crisis of conscience. The misunderstanding stems initially from the parents of Connor Murphy (Colton Ryan), a classmate. They mistakenly believe that Evan and their son – who has committed suicide – were close friends. At the same time, Evan is attracted to Connor's sister Zoe (Kaitlyn Dever). Not wanting to add to the family's grief, and looking for opportunities to pursue a relationship with Zoe, Evan concocts a tale about his relationship with Connor – much of it expressed in song and, occasionally, dance. The subterfuge grows by leaps and bounds, stretching across the entire community. Of course, it can't last indefinitely, and Evan is finally forced to

confess, at great cost to all concerned. A box office failure, the movie nevertheless has its moments, particularly the dance numbers, well-choreographed by Danny Mefford, who also did the stage play. Julianne Moore and Amy Adams contribute star power as, respectively, Evan's and Connor's mothers. [Trivia note: Ben Platt at age 27 received criticism for playing a high school senior in the movie. Ironic, because that's also the age of Sidney Poitier and Vic Morrow as high-school delinquents in *Blackboard Jungle*] [Caution: language, adult themes and sexuality] **[W]**

Lean on Me
1989 – John G. Avildsen
Back to the blackboard jungle, this time from the principal's point of view. Morgan Freeman plays Joe Louis Clark, a dedicated educator tasked with bringing a once excellent but now unruly Paterson, New Jersey, high school under control. That he does, but not without abundant controversy, which also dogged the real-life Clark for most of his career. It begins on the first day of school, when Clark summons the entire student body for an assembly and promptly expels a bunch of known drug dealers and other troublemakers. He orders all of the building's exterior doors to be chained during school hours. He even disciplines teachers for not complying with his reforms. The result is a community divided between those supporting Clark's actions, which are resulting in improved test scores, and those who consider his policies unduly harsh. It's a thoughtful – though toned down – depiction of one man's efforts to break the tragic cycle of failure and despair besetting so many inner-city schools, and Freeman, as always, is superb. Look for Michael Imperioli, one of the lead characters in TV's The Sopranos, in a minor role. [Caution: language] **[W]**

My Bodyguard
1980 – Tony Bill
Ricky Linderman (Adam Baldwin in his debut), ostensibly tough and uncaring, is in reality a troubled soul – he's been harboring a

terrible secret. Ricky inhabits a local high school in Chicago where the other students give him a wide berth, partly because of his size (he's considerably larger and seems older than the other kids) and partly because of a rumor that he once had killed someone. Eventually, he meets and befriends schoolmate Clifford Peache (Chris Makepeace), a smart but slight youngster who has become the bullying target of Melvin Moody (Matt Dillon) and his gang. Clifford likewise is an outcast because he's chauffeured to school every day in a limousine, the result of his father (Martin Mull) being the manager of a downtown hotel. The spectacle naturally draws the interest and suspicion of the other students. When Clifford brings Ricky home with him one afternoon and introduces him to his grandmother (the multi-talented Ruth Gordon, 84 years old in a lovely performance), she eventually coaxes out much of what Ricky has been hiding. From there the story, unfolding in its own sweet time, delivers some surprisingly touching and funny moments. Director Tony Bill, a also a sometime actor, does well in his own debut. [Trivia note: Among the minor cast members is George Wendt, forever loved as Norm Peterson, the laconic bar patron and regular on TV's Cheers] [Caution: schoolyard language and fighting] **[W]**

Pretty in Pink
1986 – Howard Deutsch

Moving ahead nearly three decades after *Blackboard Jungle* but within a lighter dramatic framework, here's another movie cast sprinkled with well-known actors at or near the beginning of their careers. It's about teen romantic angst, in a plot written by John Hughes that mirrors what has occurred in real life countless times. Andie Walsh (Molly Ringwald, at the height of her popularity) has a crush on classmate Blane McDonough (teen heartthrob at the time Andrew McCarthy). Her best friend "Duckie" Dale (an appealing John Cryer) also loves her but is too shy to speak up. In addition, Blane is part of what used to be called the "preppies" (rich kids) at school, while Andie lives with her working-class father (Harry Dean Stanton) and is embarrassed by her status. At stake is the upcoming senior prom, and the question is whether

Andie will go with Blane or Duckie. Some mildly tense moments, but all ends well – for both Andie and Duckie – in this basically sweet-tempered story with a soundtrack containing some of the most popular songs of the day. [Trivia note: The rest of the future well-knowns in the cast? Margaret Colin, Gina Gershon, James Spader and Kristy Swanson, now TV and screen veterans all; comedian Andrew Dice Clay, and Annie Potts, already well known from *Ghostbusters* (PF5) who likewise has compiled a lengthy TV and screen career] [Caution: language and mild sexuality] **[W]**

School Daze
1988 – written and directed by Spike Lee
Moving temporarily out of high school, here's arguably Lee's best film – and a musical, no less – about the goings on at Mission, a fictional black college. The basic plot concerns "Dap" Dunlap (Laurence Fishburne), a campus activist pushing his various causes during homecoming weekend. Dap is opposed by "Dean Big Brother Almighty" Eaves (Giancarlo Esposito), a politico and fraternity bigwig, as well as Harold McPherson (blues musician and actor Joe Seneca), Mission's president. There's also "Half-Pint" (Lee), Dap's cousin, a freshman and fraternity pledge trying to edge his way into campus society. That's all pretext to what's really bubbling in Mission's society: deep-in-the-bone issues such as skin color, hair thickness (the "nappies" versus the "wanna-be's") and economic status. Though the conflicts are generally treated lightly and humorously with songs (Bill Lee, the director's father, composed the music) and well-staged dances, there's no doubt about their resonance. Lee drives the point home hard at the fade-out, with an unexpected and direct plea for unity by Dap to the African American community, and with an affirmation by the entire cast. [Trivia note: Lee housed the nappy and wanna-be girls separately during filming to encourage their onscreen tension] [Caution: language and sexuality] **[W]**

Sixteen Candles

1984 – written and directed by John Hughes

You might be too young to remember, but back in the 1980s Hughes practically owned the teen genre, beginning with this slightly raunchy but breezy wish-fulfillment hit comedy starring Molly Ringwald and Anthony Michael Hall. The title refers to the 16th birthday of Samantha Baker (Ringwald), a high school sophomore and daughter of a suburban Chicago family – all of whom have forgotten the day because they're busy preparing for the marriage of Sam's older sister Ginny (Blanche Baker). But that's only the beginning of a long string of amusing misfortunes befalling her, most of them involving her teen insecurity, but others perpetrated by the vivid characters comprising her family and friends. Among them are Ted (Hall), an annoying freshman in pursuit of her; Mike (Justin Henry), her annoying and potty-mouthed little brother, and Long Duk Dong (Gedde Watanabe) a foreign-exchange student being hosted by Sam's grandparents. There's also Sam's seemingly fruitless pursuit of Jake Ryan (Michael Shoeffling), the most popular senior boy. But fear not; it all ends well, and along the way Hughes infuses almost everyone in the cast with good humor and appealing, even touching moments, particularly Paul Dooley as Sam's father, and Hall in what could have been a thankless role. As Gary Arnold wrote in his Washington Post review, the ensemble contributes "to an amiably hectic illusion of the eccentric human society in which Samantha circulates." He added that "Hughes keeps his feet on the ground while indulging comic exaggerations, perhaps because he views both suburban settings and family circles as rich, comfortable, reassuring hotbeds of wackiness." [Trivia note: I credit Hughes with giving Paul Dooley and Carlin Glynn, as Sam's mother, good scenes that humanize their roles. But he did so because both actors demanded that he elevate their characters from the stereotypical parents he had originally conceived] [Caution: language and sexuality] **[W]**

Summer School
1987 – Carl Reiner
For all you slackers out there, those who agonized through each day of high school classes, here's one for you. And for you dedicated followers of the indefatigable TV series NCIS, here's a chance to see Mark Harmon way back in a most leisurely comedy. Harmon stars as Freddy Shoop, a high-school gym teacher forced to instruct a ... summer school remedial English class for (what else?) a motley group of students who couldn't pass the subject during the regular semester. "Motley" is the operative term. It's a deliberately exaggerated assortment, all of whom resent being there almost as much as Shoop does. His solution? Remember what the Delta House gang did in *Animal House* when things looked darkest? Here, instead of a road trip, Shoop organizes a series of field trips – to the zoo, to the beach and so on. It's all fun, until ... well, the plot's too gossamer to take seriously, so maybe just ride along until the happy ending arrives – including Shoop finding romance with Robin Bishop, the teacher next door (Kirstie Alley, the same year she began her outstanding run as Rebecca Howe in TV's Cheers). [Trivia note: Harmon's all pleasant appeal here, but that isn't exactly why Reiner cast him. The director had just seen him play serial killer Ted Bundy in a TV miniseries and somehow thought Harmon could make the transition to a friendly schoolteacher. Turns out, he was right] [Caution: language, deliberately fake gore and mild sexuality] [W]

To Sir, With Love
1967 – England – written and directed by James Clavell
Now let's end by coming full circle. Twelve years after playing a street tough in *Blackboard Jungle,* and the same year his stunning performance owned the Oscar-winner *In the Heat of the Night* (PF5), Sidney Poitier returns to the classroom in a tremendously appealing role. Poitier, who died early this year, plays Mark Thackeray, an immigrant engineer taking on a teaching job in London's East End until he can find a position in his field. Not quite the situation of Glenn Ford's Richard Dadier, but Poitier's Thackeray is a similar character – well-educated but tough-

minded. Those traits come in handy because his students are all rejects from other schools. We also find Thackeray resembling Dadier in his fits of frustration when the kids either fail to cooperate or engage in outright rebellion. And the classroom dynamics somewhat mirror *Blackboard Jungle*'s, with Thackeray's persistence winning most of them over, but one holdout continuing to cause trouble. Another similarity to this movie's predecessor: it features several future notables in British cinema in debut roles, including the big-voiced singer known as Lulu (Lulu Kennedy-Cairns), whose rendition of the theme song became the biggest hit in America that year. [Trivia notes: 1) The field-trip montage in mid-movie was an improvisation. The British Museum revoked permission for the production to film inside the building, so the cast acted out the scenes and the crew snapped still photos that were edited together with Lulu's theme song as background. 2) As I mentioned in the *Blackboard Jungle* capsule, Poitier had experienced a troubled and impoverished youth of his own, giving him more in common with the classroom characters than the actors playing them] **[W]**

40. Still More Oscars

In six years, as of this writing, we'll reach the century mark of the Academy Awards. Looking back on the previous nine decades, it's been interesting to observe the wide variety of movies winning Hollywood's highest honor. Among my favorites in the first two compilations, which I listed both in specific categories and intermittently throughout the texts, were 53 Best Pictures. Along with the following seven honorees (not including a worthwhile add-on), and eight others elsewhere, my Oscar-winning favorites rise to 68 out of the current total of 94. That means, despite my energetic quibbles with some of the motion picture academy's selections, I've generally supported them more than two out of three times. All things considered, they've compiled a pretty fair record. Adding to my list, in chronological order...

Grand Hotel
1932 – Edmund Goulding

Call this the first all-star movie, because the five principal players had achieved fame by then, particularly John Barrymore and Greta Garbo, both of whom had emerged from the silent era to an appreciative public. Arguably more important, the basic plot formed the foundation for uncounted titles that followed – on television as well as in the movies. Likewise the subplots. Consider these characters. An impoverished nobleman (Barrymore) fighting to hide his reduced status. An accountant facing mortality (John's older brother Lionel Barrymore) splurging in his last days. A tycoon (Wallace Beery) looking to close one more big deal. A social-climber (a young and striking Joan Crawford) seeking opportunities. And an aging Russian ballerina (Garbo) considering suicide. Their fates all clash, mostly tragically, during their stay at Berlin's ... Grand Hotel where, ironically, one of the other guests (Lewis Stone) laments, "Always the same. People come. People go. Nothing ever happens."

Apparently, audiences didn't agree because they made the movie a smash hit. Now 90 years old and dated in many ways, the performances by the principals – particularly Barrymore and Garbo – remain solid. [Trivia note: *Grand Hotel* still holds the distinction of being the only Best Picture winner to receive a single Oscar – in fact, it wasn't even nominated in any other category] [B&W]

The Great Ziegfeld
1936 – Robert Z. Leonard

William Powell portrays the legendary showman Florenz Ziegfeld Jr., whose productions dazzled theater audiences by their sheer scale and complexity – and expositions of female flesh. The movie tracks Ziegfeld's early life, successes and failures followed by his eventual rise to prominence as America's premier impresario during the 1920s and early '30s. Its centerpiece number, literally, is done to Irving Berlin's "A Pretty Girl Is Like a Melody." Sung by Dennis Morgan in an uncredited role, the 8-minute extravaganza took weeks to shoot, involved nearly 200 singers, dancers and models, and would cost $4 million today. Even at its 3 hours-plus running time, like *Grand Hotel* its appeal has faded somewhat over the decades. But there's no denying the expense and effort the production required, and despite the lack of an Oscar nomination, Powell gives a smashing performance as Ziegfeld. [Trivia note: A number of the 30 women who played (uncredited) Ziegfeld Girls in the movie went on to distinguished careers in show business. Or they became well known for other reasons. The two most notable were Susan Fleming, called "the girl with the million-dollar legs," who became the wife of Harpo Marx; and Pat Ryan (real name Thelma Catherine Ryan) who became First Lady Pat Nixon, wife of President Richard Nixon] [B&W]

My Fair Lady
1964 – George Cukor

Slightly controversial in its day because of the "voice" issue – Marni Nixon dubbing most of Audrey Hepburn's singing, while

Julie Andrews, a superior songstress who starred in the musical on Broadway, wasn't cast – it's nevertheless deeply enjoyable, with a slate of lovely tunes by lyricist Alan J. Lerner and composer Frederick Lowe. Based on George Bernard Shaw's play "Pygmalion," it's the story of language professor Henry Higgins (Rex Harrison, reprising his Broadway role) who bets he can convert street urchin Eliza Doolittle (Hepburn) into his ... fair lady while eventually competing for her affections with suitor Freddy Eynsford-Hill (Jeremy Brett). Winner of seven other Oscars, including Best Director for Cukor and Best Actor for Harrison (Audrey wasn't even nominated), the score includes unforgettable numbers such as Eliza's "I Could Have Danced All Night," Freddy's "On the Street Where You Live" and Henry's sublime recitation, "I've Grown Accustomed to Her Face." Beautifully performed and staged – when Audrey isn't "singing" or playing the urchin, she's captivating – it's one of Cukor's crowning achievements in a four-decade career. [Viewing note: Dubbing is a practice as old as the talkies themselves. Usually, it's unobtrusive – for example, "On the Street Where You Live" features Don Shirley dubbing Jeremy Brett, who could sing fairly well, with nary a peep from the critics. But when a voice as familiar as Hepburn's has been supplanted (she was likewise a decent singer, and you can hear her occasionally), despite Nixon's beautiful renditions it's grating every time you hear it] [Trivia note: Here's a backstage moment worth repeating. When Audrey first appeared on the set as Eliza in her ballgown, she stunned the entire cast and crew into sighs and momentary silence, followed by prolonged applause and cheers at her beauty] [W]

Guess Who's Coming to Dinner
1967 – produced and directed by Stanley Kramer

I'm including this one because I consider it a profile in courage – or, it could be argued, a profile in stubbornness. The Oscar-winning script by William Rose was written specifically for the great Spencer Tracy, whose health was so poor at the time that Columbia Pictures, worried about the actor, required director Kramer and co-star Katharine Hepburn to defer taking their salaries until Tracy could complete his scenes. And complete them he did, in a fine performance capping a legendary career. You could call *Guess Who's Coming to Dinner* the first woke movie. It concerns Matt and Kristina Drayton (Tracy and Hepburn), a liberal Los Angeles couple whose young-adult daughter Joanna (Hepburn's real-life niece Katharine Houghton) arrives home from a trip with her new, African-American fiancé, Dr. John Wade Prentiss (Sidney Poitier). Taken aback by Joanna's sudden announcement – but trying to hold onto their liberal sensibilities – the Drayton's are hit with a second surprise: John declares to Matt that he will not marry his daughter unless he approves. The challenge sets off a string of arguments and discussions leading to Matt's final monologue delivered to the combined families, including John's parents (ably played by Roy E. Glenn and Beah Richards). It was the last scene Tracy ever performed. He died two-and-a-half weeks later. Not a Best Picture-winner (that honor went to *In the Heat of the Night*, also starring Poitier), it's considered a groundbreaker. In the year of the movie's release, prohibitions against interracial-marriage were finally struck down by the U.S. Supreme Court. The so-called anti-miscegenation laws had still prevailed in more than a dozen states. [Trivia notes: 1) At one point, John's father tells him that by marrying Joanna he would be breaking the law in certain areas. That's because the scene was filmed before the Supreme Court decision and wasn't reshot to correct the record. 2) In case you weren't aware, Tracy and Hepburn, who did nine movies together, had conducted a three-decade-long love affair. Those tears Hepburn showed during Tracy's final monologue were real] [And a critic's note: Nominating Tracy for a Best Actor Oscar (his ninth) that year was understandable, given his lengthy career, failing health and near-universal admiration in Hollywood. But doing so robbed Poitier of a more worthy choice> His terrific performance as Virgil Tibbs dominated *In the Heat of the Night* and stood head and shoulders above everyone else. Not to diminish Tracy – whose body of work I deeply admire – the fact that Poitier wasn't even nominated is yet another example of poor judgment by the members of the motion picture academy] **[W]**

Oliver!

1968 – Carol Reed

People either loved or hated this one, produced BIG from the stage version, with vast, elaborately choreographed numbers in a musical interpretation of the Charles Dickens novel <u>Oliver Twist</u>. The title character (played by nine-year-old Mark Lester) is trapped in a miserable life in a 19th-century London orphanage, followed by a brief but even nastier turn at an undertaker's. From there it's a temporary life of crime under the tutelage of master thief Fagin (Ron Moody, reprising his stage role in a show-stealing, Oscar-nominated performance), and once again under threat, this time from the evil Bill Sikes (Oliver Reed – an established dramatic actor and the director's nephew). More menaces follow, including the demise of one of Oliver's protectors, but a happy resolution – of course – emerges for the young protagonist. The musical numbers? As with *My Fair Lady*, the best are the solos; "Where Is Love?" by Oliver; "As Long As He Needs Me" by Nancy, (Shani Wallis), Oliver's sometime protector; and the witty "Reviewing the Situation" by Fagin. As for the rest – and there are a lot of them – I'm reminded of something TIME magazine critic Richard Schickel wrote about *The Wiz* (<u>P25</u>). He described the ensemble numbers as "elaborate as D-Day." I admit, it's one of the weakest Oscar-winners I've listed, though it won six in all, including an honorary Oscar for choreographer Onna White. It's the type of screen musical that my old friend theater critic Hap Erstein complained overwhelmed the intimacy of the stage production. Still, it offers some moments to enjoy, particularly Moody as Fagin – though his Semitic background in the novel is downplayed. [<u>Trivia note</u>: Here's another case of dubbing that caused no critical outcry. Mark Lester's solos were sung by Kathe Green, who was music supervisor Johnny Green's daughter] [<u>Caution</u>: violent threats against children] **[W]**

Kramer vs. Kramer
1979 – written and directed by Robert Benton

Benton, creator of the wry L.A. detective story *The Late Show* and the poignant, Depression-era drama *Places in the Heart* (both in PF5), here creates his only Best Picture-winner with Dustin Hoffman and Meryl Streep (in her co-starring debut) as Ted and Joanna … Kramer, a couple caught in a suddenly collapsed marriage. The drama begins at the end of what otherwise would be a normal workday for Ted, a successful New York advertising copywriter. He returns home with news of a well-deserved promotion only to learn that Joanna is leaving him and their six-year-old son Billy (eight-year-old Justin Henry, who also played Samantha's obnoxious younger brother in *Sixteen Candles* five years later). The resulting trauma for both father and son – including some heartrending early conflicts – eventually results in a tight and heartwarming bonding between the two. But that's when the real drama begins. Joanna reappears as suddenly as she had left, now demanding custody of her son – hence a courtroom battle and the reason for the movie's title. Beautifully shot by Nestor Almendros, the cast features a strong performance by Jane Alexander as an eventually supportive neighbor, and an appealing debut by JoBeth Williams as one of Ted's co-workers and a humorous one-night stand. The movie also won Oscars for Benton's direction and script, and for Hoffman's and Streep's performances. Technically, this should have tied *Kramer vs. Kramer* with *It Happened One Night* (PF5) 45 years earlier, except that Streep won Best Supporting Actress while Claudette Colbert won the top actress honor. Personally, I thought Hoffman frequently overacted while Streep maintained her dignity in a distinctly unsympathetic role. That quibble aside, I liked Gary Arnold's take on the movie in his Washington Post review. He wrote that it "rakes up complicated emotions about profoundly important relationships. Moreover, it implies that these relationships may require a certain heroic effort to preserve or sustain in a middle-class culture that subjects people to a great deal of centrifugal, status-seeking, family-breaking pressure." [Trivia notes: 1) Despite Streep's relative inexperience – by that time Hoffman had been starring in movies for a dozen years and nominated for three Academy Awards – she displayed enough confidence to resist Hoffman's frequent off-camera verbal challenges and on-camera abuse (including a real slap and a suddenly thrown wine glass) and land the first of her three Oscars. She also insisted on rewriting her courtroom monologue, which writer–director Benton permitted and later praised. 2) Justin Henry remains the youngest individual ever to be nominated for an Oscar] [Caution: adult themes and sexuality] [W]

Argo
2012 – Ben Affleck
Badly outclassed that year by Steven Spielberg's *Lincoln* (PF5), it's nevertheless an entertaining re-creation of one of the worst foreign-policy disasters in American history. In November 1979, a mob of (supposed) Iranian students overwhelmed the guards at the U.S. Embassy in Tehran and took 52 staff members hostage in an impasse that lasted 444 days. The ostensible motivation for the takeover was President Jimmy Carter's allowing the deposed Shah of Iran to seek cancer treatment in the United States. At one point, Carter dispatched a special-forces mission to surprise the captors and rescue the trapped Americans. It failed, resulting in the deaths of eight of the servicemen. Meanwhile, six other staff members had escaped the takeover and eventually hid inside the nearby residence of the Canadian ambassador. There they remained for over 80 days, until CIA operatives could execute an elaborate ruse to exfiltrate them – as they say in the covert community – out of Iran. *Argo* tells that story, though with a great deal of dramatic license. Yes, it's entertaining, but in more of a feel-good way for the hostages than a sense of a meticulous re-creation. Even President Carter, commenting on the movie to the cable TV network CNN, said it neglected the courageous and primary roles the Canadians performed in facilitating the rescue, particularly Ken Taylor (played in the movie by Victor Garber), the ambassador at the time, whom Carter called "the main hero." Director Affleck also stars as CIA operative and mastermind Tony

Mendez, with John Goodman, Alan Arkin and Bryan Cranston in strong supporting roles as, respectively, a Hollywood makeup artist and a producer participating in the ruse, and Mendez's CIA supervisor. [Trivia note: Though they shared not one scene together in either movie, Arkin and Cranston also had appeared in *Little Miss Sunshine* (PF5) six years earlier] [Caution: language] **[W]**

Nomadland
2020 – written and directed by Chloé Zhao
Zhao has developed a reputation for screen stories that take their own time developing but that tend to stay with you in a haunting way. Her previous feature, *The Rider* (P25), dealt with the difficult lives of Lakota Sioux rodeo performers and featured two real riders, and she shot the entire film on the Pine Ridge Reservation in South Dakota. Here, it's a slow-starting tale as well, but one that surprisingly holds your interest despite its pace. The versatile Frances McDormand – who also produced – stars in an Oscar-winning role as a character known only as Fern. She's a lonely widow whose Nevada hometown becomes deserted after its single employer shuts down, forcing her to wander across the Southwest in her van, picking up odd jobs and fitfully interacting with friends, family and strangers – all of whom, except for co-star David Strathairn, are fellow nomads or locals the film crew encountered along the way. Zhao's film portrays Fern's odyssey by following McDormand, for real, in a van over four months and seven states. At several places, *Nomadland* risks sinking into boredom, but it never does. Among Hollywood's 94 Best Pictures to date, it's a unique and quiet gem. [Trivia note: So low-key was this production, and so in-character was McDormand, that almost no one she encountered realized she was an acclaimed actress (three acting Oscars to date). Local people would genuinely commiserate with her fictional widowhood (she's married to director Joel Coen) and on several occasions would offer her jobs] [Caution: bodily functions and sexuality] **[W]**

41. Talent Down Under

Here's a trio of Australian directors who have gained international acclaim and made some of the most interesting and mature dramas in cinema over five decades beginning in the 1970s, including these nine early titles, three each – plus an extra – listed alphabetically by the directors' names.

High Tide
1987 – Australia – Gillian Armstrong
Armstrong, who gave us the sublime *My Brilliant Career*, the gripping *Mrs. Soffel* and the beguiling *Little Women* (all in <u>PF5</u>), here directs this gossamer story about a love triangle – albeit a most unusual one – taking place in an idyllic but working-class village on the country's southeast coast. Orphaned fifteen-year-old Ally (Aussie TV star Claudia Karvan at the beginning of her career) lives with her hardworking grandmother Bet (Jan Adele) in the Down Under equivalent of a mobile home park. There, she helps Bet serve customers in her ice cream truck, engages in a tentative teen romance and dreams about her future, which might possibly be as a surfer like her dead father. Into their marginal but stable existence drops Lillie (Judy Davis), who's been fired as a backup singer for an (inept) Elvis Presley impersonator and is stranded with a conked-out car. It's a fateful encounter, because all three characters are connected – deeply. Not one of Armstrong's major titles, but if you're willing to stick with it (and ignore the groan-inducing music performance at the opening), you'll find a surprisingly moving drama about longing and redemption. Davis is great, as always, and the relatively unknown Adele is downright arresting in a difficult role. [<u>Caution</u>: sexuality] **[W]**

The Last Days of Chez Nous
1992 – Australia – Gillian Armstrong

Once again, Armstrong demonstrates why she is one of the world's finest directors. Here she assembles a multi-national cast in what, under less-talented hands, would have slipped into dreary domestic drama. Instead, she and her cast create a penetrating tale of – as the publicity materials proclaim – "love, trust, betrayal and lust." Of course, that's an oversimplification. More accurately, it's a sharp multi-character study with vivid performances all around. Vicki (New Zealander Kerry Fox) visits her older sister Beth (fellow Kiwi Lisa Harrow) and Annie (Aussie actress Miranda Otto), Beth's teenage daughter from a former marriage. Arriving at Beth's home in Sydney's vintage Glebe neighborhood, Vicki discovers Beth is now married again, this time to J.P., a Frenchman (the late, great – and Swiss – Bruno Ganz). Forced to take a long trip into the Outback with her estranged father (veteran Aussie actor Bill Hunter), Beth must leave Annie with Vicki and J.P. A large miscalculation on several levels, as we see unfolding in the twin storylines. Given the personalities involved, you can guess what's coming, but it's surprisingly satisfying to watch. [Caution: adult themes and sexuality] [W]

Starstruck
1982 –Gillian Armstrong

You'll find several movies with this title, so be sure to choose the right one. A look at Aussie teens in the early '80s, this effort by Armstrong – a few years after her smashing international debut with *My Brilliant Career* – is a wry and bouncy musical about two kids looking to make a splash. Jackie (the vivacious Jo Kennedy) is a singer, and her cousin Angus (Ross O'Donovan) fancies himself her publicity agent and impresario. Together, they scheme to draw a crowd by having Jackie walk a tightrope semi-nude (she's actually wearing an exaggerated, flesh-colored costume) in downtown Sydney. That's probably all you need to know. If it sounds intriguing, seek it out. If not, move on. Just remember how talented Gillian Armstrong is – particularly her ability to elicit appealing and distinctive performances from even the minor players. [Caution: sexuality and some real nudity] **[W]**

Don's Party
1976 – Australia – Bruce Beresford

Here's an early effort by the versatile director of the Oscar-winning *Driving Miss Daisy* (PF5) as well as the gripping military courtroom drama *Breaker Morant*, the hard-edged murder mystery *Double Jeopardy* and the captivating biography *Mao's Last Dancer* (all in P25). *Don's Party* creates an intriguing social dynamic involving a group of friends and acquaintances gathering for an election-night party in late 1969 at the home of … Don (John Hargreaves) and his wife Kath (Jeanie Drynan) to watch the national returns. The eight partygoers – and their hosts – become less and less inhibited, and more argumentative, as the evening wears on and several uncouplings and recouplings unfold. Based on the play of the same name by David Williamson and shot within the confines of a real house in northwestern Sydney, it's part marital drama and part lustful encounters with a bit of political discourse and even some slapstick thrown in. All told, an engaging glimpse of suburban life Down Under in that era, and Drynan as Kath makes an appealing anchor to the chaos around her. [Caution: plentiful sexuality] **[W]**

The Getting of Wisdom (and) Puberty Blues
1978 and 1981 – Australia – Bruce Beresford

Beresford, best known in America for directing *Driving Miss Daisy*, the 1989 Oscar winner, turned out two appealing coming-of-age movies in his home country about a decade earlier. *The Getting of Wisdom* is based on the turn-of-the-20th-century novel by Henry Handel Richardson (actually the pseudonym of Ethel Florence Lindesay Richardson) about a teenager's experiences in a boarding school in Victorian-era Australia. The girl, named Laura Tweedle Rambotham (Susannah Fowle), is precocious and rebellious, and she runs afoul of both her teachers and her more prim and conventional schoolmates. But her independent spirit is likely to charm you. [Trivia note: H.G. Wells, who was considered

349

well ahead of his time politically and socially, called the source novel for *The Getting of Wisdom* "magnificent."] [Caution: mild sexual content and adult themes] **[W]**

*   *   *

In *Puberty Blues*, two teens girls (Nell Schofield and Jad Capelja) love to surf but must fight against the stereotypes of the era that confine girls to the beach casting admiring glances at their boyfriends catching the waves. What's distinctive is the movie's frank but sympathetic portrayal of the awkwardness of teen sex. [Caution: rough language and explicit sexuality] **[W]**

Gallipoli
1981 – Australia – co-written and directed by Peter Weir
Weir's inclusion creates a problem here. Justifiably praised for his exotic political thriller *The Year of Living Dangerously*, his superb police drama *Witness* and his terrific seafaring drama *Master and Commander: The Far Side of the World* (all in PF5), there's no doubt he's one of Australia's top filmmakers. But his three earlier works don't live up to the later achievements – though I'm not implying they're poorly made. On the contrary, *Gallipoli* for example, beautifully photographed by Russell Boyd, who also shot two of Weir's three exceptional titles, is a massive, first-rate production. Mel Gibson (star of *The Year of Living Dangerously*) plays a young Aussie soldier involved in the titular battle, one of his country's bloodiest and most tragic engagements during World War I. That tragedy serving as background, the movie fairly drips with earnestness and, as Gary Arnold pinpointed in his Washington Post review, "solemnity." So much so, he added, "that the entire presentation is robbed of human interest and historical resonance." I'd characterize *Gallipoli* as a failed attempt to focus tightly on two individuals (Gibson's character and a comrade in arms played by fellow Aussie Mark Lee) caught within the maelstrom of battle. It doesn't compare to William Wellman's electrifying World War I silent drama *Wings*, Samuel Fuller's similar approach in *The Big Red One* (both in PF5), or Oliver Stone's shattering *Platoon*, or even to Weir's own triumph in *Master and Commander*. In trying to paint the bigger picture, he

neglects to allow the humanity of his characters to emerge. The result is strangely unaffecting. [Trivia note: Like Akira Kurosawa's *Kagemusha* the previous year, *Gallipoli*'s production team faced a shortage of skilled horsemen for the cavalry scenes. They solved the problem the same way: by hiring skilled equestriennes and dressing them as soldiers on horseback] [Caution: wartime violence] [W]

The Last Wave
1977 – Australia – co-written and directed by Peter Weir

Weir's ostensibly mystical tale involves David Burton (Richard Chamberlain), a tax attorney drafted by Sydney's legal-aid organization to defend a group of Aborigines involved in a downtown bar fight that resulted in a drowning death. At the same time, two parallel phenomena develop. In one, the city is subjected to a series of strange meteorological events, including exceptionally heavy rainfall, massive hailstones and even frogs dropping from the sky. In the other, Burton begins experiencing extremely bizarre dreams connected to both his legal case and the unusual weather. In those dreams, he's frequently visited by one of the jailed defendants, Chris Lee (David Gulpilil, until his untimely death in 2021 Australia's best-known Aboriginal actor). Eventually, Burton comes to believe he's mystically connected not only to the accused men but also to the spirits of his country's past. To tell the truth, despite its dazzling images, the more the story progresses the sillier it seems – though Gulpilil's presence anchors the drama and keeps it from going completely off the rails. Cinematographer Russell Boyd shot this one as well. [Trivia note: Here's a weird (and mystical?) twist for you. Though set in Sydney, the production had to be relocated to Adelaide, a city 700 miles west, because Sydney's weather was unusually rainy at the time] [Caution: violence] [W]

Picnic at Hanging Rock
1975 – Australia – Peter Weir

Going back farther, Weir's genuinely spooky second film is based on a real incident, involving a group of schoolgirls on a

351

Valentine's Day outing at the turn of the 20th century. The girls, accompanied by two of their teachers, go ... picnicking near the school at a landmark called ... Hanging Rock, about 60 miles northwest of Melbourne. At some point during the afternoon, three of the girls and one of the teachers disappear. Though one girl and the teacher are eventually found – the teacher apparently having died in a fall – the other two remained missing despite extensive searches. Their whereabouts are unknown to this day. It's a strange, almost dreamy tale, and though there's no overtly scary material, the spookiness pervades the story. [Trivia note: Part of that dreamy feeling was encouraged by cinematographer Russell Boyd, who draped thin gauze over his camera lenses to give each scene a slightly blurred look] [Caution: adult themes and mild sexuality] [W]

And a Peter Weir postscript

In one respect, Weir resembles Martin Brest, whom I covered in a previous chapter. Another acclaimed director, Brest made only six films in Hollywood before suddenly retiring. Weir directed 13, which garnered 29 Oscar nominations with six wins for him as director, writer or producer. But he has made only two movies since the turn of the century: *Master and Commander* and the following title. At this writing, Weir is, effectively, retired.

The Way Back
2010 – co-written, produced and directed by Weir
Not an Australian production (Weir's international fame meant he could easily find funding elsewhere), he shot the movie in Bulgaria, Morocco and India. It was "inspired" by (translation: loosely based on) the chronicle of Slavomir Rawicz, a Soviet political prisoner in Siberia in 1941 who claimed to have escaped and walked to freedom in India, some 4,000 miles away. In this story, Rawicz's character is represented by Janusz Wieszczek (Jim Sturgess). He's joined in his odyssey by an American (Ed Harris), two Russians (played by Mark Strong and Colin Farrell), and four others. After a frightening escape, the group begins its grueling push south, almost immediately losing one of its members to the

frigid conditions and, soon thereafter, taking on a young, orphaned girl (Saoirse Ronan, who was 16 at the time). From there, the trek takes them through various landscapes, each presenting severe hazards that gradually attrit the group, each loss occurring in a unique way. It's absorbing but heavy-going throughout, so much so that the characters' final triumph seems strangely anticlimactic. [Caution: wartime violence and adult themes] **[W]**

42. Teeth

Two of the manliest stars in cinema history, in terms of their physicality – and ever since I was a boy two of my personal favorites – also shared the characteristic of a big, wide, toothy grin. The men, one born Burton Stephen Lancaster in 1913 and the other Issur Danielovitch in 1916; one in New York City and one in upstate New York, became world-famous as Burt Lancaster and Kirk Douglas. Separately or together (in seven films over the years), they lit up the screen for five decades beginning in the 1940s. Burt, who spent his young manhood as a circus performer, died of a heart attack at age 80. And Kirk, who endured crippling poverty in his youth and began acting in his teens, died in 2020 after surpassing the century mark by nearly four years. I've already picked 26 favorites (out of their combined 167 film roles and seven Oscar nominations) in the first two compilations and elsewhere in this one. Here are a dozen more opportunities to enjoy this tremendously appealing pair of actors, including twice when they co-starred. In chronological order...

Champion
1949 – Kirk as Michael "Midge" Kelly
In this taut and tragic boxing drama, directed by Mark Robson with a screenplay by the superlative Carl Foreman, Midge Kelly makes his way to the top of the fight game by brutalizing his opponents – almost gleefully. He's also not much of a human being outside of the ring, particularly – and time after time – in his relationships with women. The thing about Kirk, for the entirety of his career, is that he could play two widely divergent personalities, sometimes within the same film. His aforementioned wide, toothy grin could charm the pants off of anyone. But there always was something extremely dark lurking within him, something no actor can create without harboring such

a trait for real to some degree. Possibly his difficult childhood and young manhood planted the darkness inside him. Whatever its origin, when the dark side emerges, and he clenches that prominent jaw of his, few actors can match Kirk's portrayal of menace – on prominent display here. [Caution: adult themes and boxing violence] **[B&W]**

Mister 880

1950 – Burt as Secret Service Agent Steve Buchanan

Call this a fact-based drama that retains a twinkle. Burt's Buchanan is a U.S. Treasury agent on the trail of Edmund Gwenn's title character, a lovable counterfeiter in this predecessor to *Catch Me If You Can* (PF5) but on a much, much smaller scale. Directed by Edmund Goulding with a script by Robert Riskin, and in turn inspired by St. Clair McElway's article in The New Yorker magazine, the title refers to Emerich Juettner, the U.S. Treasury's case number. Except in the movie Gwenn is William "Skipper" Miller, an impoverished elderly "antique" dealer living in New York. For 10 years, Skipper aka Mister 880 has eluded the department's best efforts to identify him. One reason is he prints only one-dollar bills, currency that's least likely to be inspected by its recipients. Also, he passes the bills one at a time, usually buying necessities. Mainly, however, Skipper's counterfeits are "ridiculously inept," as the movie's narrator explains. That ineptitude has prolonged the search because the Treasury agents keep looking among established forgers, while Skipper frequently – and literally – passes right under their noses. Finally, headquarters assigns Agent Buchanan to the case to give it a fresh perspective – and Buchanan promptly walks into an encounter with Skipper! I won't reveal more, because the story's too sweet and sentimental to spoil. Likewise, the ending, which mimics the real outcome. [Trivia notes: 1) There's a scene where Skipper (Gwenn) is walking down a street, and in nearby parade a band is playing "The National Emblem March." It's the same tune played three years earlier during Santa's appearance in the Macy's Thanksgiving Day Parade in *Miracle on 34th Street* (PF5) – with Gwenn as Kris Kringle appearing as Macy's Santa. 2)

Speaking of *Miracle...*, both that movie and this one feature Gwenn in climactic courtroom scenes. 3) When 20th Century-Fox purchased the rights to real-life counterfeiter Juettner's story, the studio paid him much more money than he'd ever printed] **[B&W]**

The Big Sky
1952 – Kirk as Jim Deakins
The first of two movies where the guys don buckskins and, in turn, play frontiersmen in the early 19th century. Kirk, working with director Howard Hawks trying to repeat his success four years earlier chronicling the beginning of the Chisholm Trail in *Red River* (PF5), here attempts a huge production in Wyoming depicting the expansion of the fur trade up the Missouri River in the 1830s. I meant "up" literally. Kirk's Deakins and a crew of nearly three-dozen fellow trappers take a 62-foot keelboat (constructed on location for the movie) upriver from St. Louis to the Missouri's headwaters in Montana. There they seek to trade with the Blackfoot tribe of that area. As an offering of good will, they're bring along Teal Eye (Native American fashion model Elizabeth Threatt in her only movie role), the daughter of a chief whom one of the trappers has rescued from a rival tribe. That's the plan, but another trading company attempts to block the expedition from reaching the Blackfoot, and striking a deal, by kidnapping Teal Eye and setting the keelboat on fire. Other dangers emerge as well. Somewhat dated, particularly in its portrayal of Native Americans – though real members of the Blackfoot and Crow tribes played many of the extras – it's an authentic-looking portrayal of frontier life. [One quibble: The scenery along the river (Wyoming's Snake, standing in for the Missouri) is so consistently gorgeous it's a shame Hawks didn't film in Technicolor] **[B&W]**

The Kentuckian
1955 – Burt as Elias "Big Eli" Wakefield (and directed by Burt)
A rough-hewn but engaging early American tale, with Burt directing Burt playing a ... Kentuckian yearning to head to Texas,

back in the days when traveling meant on foot or horseback, or if you were lucky via stagecoach or riverboat. Big Eli's aim? To begin a new life with his young son "Little Eli" (Donald MacDonald) far away from towns or people. Except their odyssey leads to encounters with people, including a crooked sheriff (veteran character actor Rhys Williams) who jails him, two brothers (longstanding journeymen players Douglas Spencer and Paul Wexler) trying to avenge a family feud, and some family troubles with Eli's older brother Zack (John McIntire, yet another veteran actor). Then there are Hannah and Susie (Diane Foster and Diana Lynn), two young women who end up vying to be Big Eli's bride. And there's a brutal confrontation with tavern-owner Stan Bodine (Walter Matthau in his debut), an expert with a bullwhip. Lots of fussin' and fightin' – for both Eli's – with some romancin' and shootin' and even some singin' thrown in. Filmed almost entirely in Kentucky, amid some of its most gorgeous rustic locales, it's an entertaining, early widescreen portrayal of frontier America. Bernard Herrmann supplied a score punctuated by those minor-key phrases so familiar in his work for Alfred Hitchcock. [Trivia notes: 1) That massive "Texas" steamboat Eli and company so eagerly await is the Gordon C. Greene, previously featured in *Gone with the Wind* (PF5). 2) To prepare for the climactic scene, in which Eli must run down one of the Frome brothers (an uncredited Paul Wexler), with whom the Wakefields have been feudin' for years, before the man could reload and fire his flintlock rifle at him, Burt rehearsed by having Wexler reload repeatedly while he ran away from him at full sprint, until Burt knew exactly how far away he could be for Eli to overcome his enemy before getting shot. It ended up being a heart-pounding moment. 3) Lancaster ended up hating directing so much that he attempted it only once more, for *The Midnight Man* (not here) nearly 20 years later] **[W]**

Gunfight at the O.K. Corral
1957 – Burt as Wyatt Earp and Kirk as 'Doc' Holliday
John Sturges directs the boys in this re-creation of the famous 1881 shootout in Tombstone, Arizona, and the movie became one of the

357

biggest hits of that year. Burt's Marshal Earp and Kirk's gunfighter Holliday make an imposing pair, taking on all comers in this rambling and convoluted historical re-creation, climaxing with the thrilling … gunfight at the … O.K. Corral. Richard Coe, film critic for The Washington Post at the time, appropriately called the movie "bloodthirsty, empty-headed and good fun." The cast features two actors destined for popularity on television in the 1960s: Martin Milner, co-star of Route 66; and DeForest Kelley, forever known as Dr. Leonard "Bones" McCoy in the original Star Trek; both of them playing Wyatt's brothers. Novelist Leon Uris wrote the screenplay, and Dimitri Tiomkin contributed the rousing score, with the popular theme song performed by Frankie Laine. [Trivia note: As you should know by now, movies are filmed in small intervals called shots and then pieced together in the editing room. Kirk's role as the tubercular Doc presented a particular challenge for the moviemakers because his character coughed so frequently, thereby complicating the editing process. Kirk addressed that challenge by rehearsing and memorizing how many times he would cough and when in each scene, and then repeating those coughs precisely during multiple takes] [Caution: gunfighting and other violence] [W]

The Vikings
1958 – Kirk as Einar
Kirk and Tony Curtis are rival sons of the horrible King Ragnar (Ernest Borgnine – who was actually younger than Kirk), both lusting after the beautiful Princess Morgana (Janet Leigh – Curtis's real-life wife) in this scenic epic directed by Richard Fleischer and filmed in Norway. But talk about convoluted plots! So many twists and turns you'd think this was a three-hour extravaganza instead of a standard-length feature. Suffice it to say that Kirk is playing the bad brother here, while Curtis is the hero and blessed by the gods. He needs to be, falling into mortal danger repeatedly during his quest to win the heart of the woman he loves while continually fighting his brother and other enemies. It's entertaining silliness, but Kirk is as fierce as ever. [Trivia note: Kirk and Curtis would face each other in mortal combat again two

years later, but in different circumstances, in the superb epic *Spartacus* (PF5)] [Caution: violence and mild sexuality] **[W]**

Elmer Gantry
1960 – Burt in the title role

Burt won his only Best Actor Oscar (in four nominations) as the traveling evangelist, loosely based on a short story by Sinclair Lewis. The usually prim and terminally pretty Shirley Jones won Best Supporting Actress as Lulu, an alcoholic prostitute. And the enchanting Jean Simmons, the same year she co-starred with Kirk in *Spartacus*, here plays a revivalist with electrifying passion. But there's backstory and intrigue and hidden agendas galore as the literal love triangle unfolds, leading inevitably to tragedy. I admit, I've got problems with this one, a thinly veiled – and unfair, I think – attack on evangelist Billy Graham, whose real character in no way resembled Gantry's. In fact, Graham was an early ally of Dr. Martin Luther King – just as Burt was, attending the "I have a dream" speech in Washington and touting the event via national television appearances. Whatever Burt's motivation for playing Gantry, you can't deny the energy and power of his performance. It's his most uninhibited role. [Trivia note: Here's a weird connection with a later movie in an entirely different genre. Two cast members, character actors Edward Andrews and Max Showalter, appeared together 24 years later in the John Hughes teen comedy *Sixteen Candles*, playing Molly Ringwald's two grandfathers] [Caution: adult themes] **[W]**

Strangers When We Meet
1960 – Kirk as Larry Coe

The same year he shined in his unforgettable title role in *Spartacus*, Kirk played it contemporary and straight, co-starring with Kim Novak in this uneven but appealing drama directed by Richard Quine about infidelity in suburban California. Larry Coe is an architect who becomes bored with his career and his wife (Barbara Rush) – particularly when he meets Maggie Gault, his spectacularly attractive neighbor who's trapped in a loveless marriage. They begin a passionate and temporarily discreet affair that creates more unhappiness than it solves. Written by Evan Hunter and based on his novel of the same name, it's a fairly straightforward tale of marital distress enhanced by the charisma of the two stars. Walter Matthau appears in a thankless role as a sleazy neighbor, and George Duning did the sultry score. [Trivia note: Here's another example of a screen romance where the two leads didn't get along off-camera. Problems began when Novak, involved with director Quine at the time, suggested how Kirk should play certain scenes – not a particularly wise move] [Caution: adult themes] **[W]**

Cast a Giant Shadow
1966 – Kirk as General 'Mickey' Marcus

Based on the real general who commanded Israel's defense forces during the country's first war with the Arabs after its creation in 1948, Kirk plays one of that country's national heroes, an American World War II veteran who had helped surviving European Jews recover from the Holocaust. Recruited by the Haganah, parent organization of today's Israeli Defense Forces, Marcus wages war against Arab interests intent on preventing Israel's establishment as a new and permanent nation. He also helps train the young nation's first corps of fighting men. Marcus was a heroic but tragic figure, and he's passionately played by Kirk, whose European Jewish roots were largely unknown but ran deep. The movie features strong supporting roles by Angie Dickinson and Senta Berger as, respectively, Marcus's wife and a Haganah colleague, with cameos by Yul Brynner as another fellow Haganah member, Frank Sinatra as a self-sacrificing American pilot, and John Wayne as General Mike Randolph, Marcus's friend and former commander. Shot almost entirely in Israel, with that nation's soldiers playing fighters on both sides, it's a gripping wartime drama set at a critical time in that country's history. [Trivia note: *Cast a Giant Shadow* marks the second of three times – in three consecutive years – when Kirk co-starred with John Wayne. The first was in the World War II epic *In Harm's Way* (PF5), and the third was in the western actioner *The*

360

War Wagon (not here)] [Caution: adult themes and wartime violence] **[W]**

The Swimmer
1968 – Burt as Ned Merrill
The slightest and oddest of the bunch, and perhaps of this whole compilation, it's based on a John Cheever short story about a middle-aged man's regrets, delusions and despair. Ned Merrill is a Connecticut resident indeed facing middle age and deciding, suddenly during a party, to "swim" home by diving into a series of pools in his neighbors' back yards. Each one brings him a different but not necessarily satisfying experience and leading to a rather shocking conclusion. This strange but fascinating little movie – chock-full as it is with cringeworthy '60s moments – was written and directed by the married team of Eleanor and Frank Perry, and filmed on location in Westport, Connecticut, the Perrys' home town. Despite its many shortcomings, through it all, Burt is mesmerizing, an immensely sympathetic figure. Marvin Hamlisch did the sweetly melancholy score – his debut work. [Trivia notes: 1) Notwithstanding that Burt often said he considered *The Swimmer* his favorite film, he clashed with director Perry on a daily basis, to the point where producer Sam Spiegel finally replaced him with an uncredited Sydney Pollack. 2) Spiegel likewise eventually quit the troubled production, removing his name from the credits. 3) Burt worked out daily to maintain his 55-year-old physique during the shoot. He also practiced swimming constantly, under the supervision of former Olympian Robert Horn] [Caution: adult themes and sexuality] **[W]**

The Gypsy Moths
1969 – Burt as Mike Rettig
In his 56th year, and the fifth and final time working with director John Frankenheimer, Burt plays aging professional skydiver Mike Rettig, who with his comrades Joe Browdy (Gene Hackman) and Malcolm Webson (Scott Wilson) travels from town to town putting on air shows for the locals. Together, they're the … Gypsy

Moths, "men drawn to the flame of danger," as the movie's publicity declares. Of course, neither Burt nor Hackman nor Wilson actually performed the movie's dangerous freefall stunts – though Burt actually did a bit of parasailing, riding a chute while being towed by an automobile. Those chores were handled by a team of seven expert amateur skydivers, who jumped a collective 1300 times during the shoot. They also did the aerial cinematography above the various Kansas locations. That left the principals free to engage in some rather standard melodrama, including romancing local women played by Bonnie Bedelia, Sheree North and Deborah Kerr – reuniting with Burt 16 years after their smoldering scenes in *From Here to Eternity* (PF5). The stuff on the ground aside, the aerial footage is thrilling and groundbreaking – though audiences at the time largely rejected both. [Caution: language and sexuality, some of it involving Kerr, of all people] **[W]**

Tough Guys
1986 – Burt as Harry and Kirk as Archie
Here the boys play a pair of aging ex-cons who try for one last caper, and they do it mostly for laughs, which is partly why there's no need to describe the plot. The other reason is that the plot, to put it kindly, is rather far-fetched. Moreover, the rest of the production team here, particularly the director and writers (who shall remain nameless), turn in lame efforts all around, hamstringing the performances of Eli Wallach, Charles Durning, Dana Carvey and Alexis Smith, who appear in supporting roles. That includes the otherwise excellent and versatile composer James Newton Howard. Those limitations aside, Burt and Kirk carry off their roles well, with tongues planted firmly in cheeks and with considerable spring in their steps. It's a passable swansong for the duo. [Trivia note: In a bit of tragedy, Adolph Caesar was supposed to play the boys' nemesis, but he died suddenly of a heart attack and was replaced by Wallach as a nearsighted hitman] [Caution: violence] **[W]**

43. That Melancholy Dane

If I asked you which dramatic work begins with, "Who's there?" would you remember "Hamlet," William Shakespeare's longest and most famous play? Written in 1600, over the intervening four centuries and change, the Bard's work has been studied endlessly in classrooms around the globe, particularly the immortal soliloquy, which begins with, "To be, or not to be…" Along with countless stage performances, "Hamlet" has appeared, at last count, an amazing 50 times in various guises on the silver screen. That includes Jack Benny's humorous and repeatedly abortive portrayals in *To Be or Not to Be* (PF5), and Arnold Schwarzenegger's brief and awkward parody in *The Last Action Hero* (not on this list). But here are the four versions I've found most notable – all, naturally, bearing the play's title.

Hamlet (1948)
Laurence Olivier

Yes, *Shakespeare in Love* (PF5) did win Best Picture for 1998, and a marvelously entertaining movie it is, revolving around the young Elizabethan's creation of "Romeo and Juliet." But Olivier's straightforward though abridged telling of "Hamlet" (he cut out nearly half the dialogue) with himself in both the title role and as the king – Hamlet's deceased father – still marks the only time one of Shakespeare's works captured the motion picture academy's top screen honor. Dated, and crudely produced compared to the more recent trio, it nevertheless bears inclusion for the chance to see the great Olivier in one of his few self-directed onscreen roles, as well as several future stars in early appearances – including horror-movie stalwarts Peter Cushing and Christopher Lee, but most prominently a young and stunning Jean Simmons as Ophelia. [B&W]

Hamlet (1964)
John Gielgud

Here's a great example of cinema serendipity. The same year as they were filming *Becket* (P25), Richard Burton and Peter O'Toole became friends and ... um, drinking buddies. Reportedly, during one of their carousings, they hatched a plan in which they would both, though separately, play Hamlet on stage. They would seek Laurence Olivier or John Gielgud as their director and perform on Broadway or London's West End. To decide, they flipped a coin, and Burton won Broadway and Gielgud. This movie is the film record of Burton's performance, which I saw in high school and to this day regard as one of his best. But there's more. In preproduction, Burton expressed to Gielgud his disdain for elaborate costumes – with which he had just been burdened in *Becket*. So they agreed to let the cast wear, essentially, street clothes or what we now would call business casual, with minimal stage props. Burton wore a dark V-neck sweater and slacks, and the rest of the players dressed similarly. The result is surprisingly captivating. You find yourself concentrating on Shakespeare's words, which Burton delivers subtly but commandingly and with a surprising amount of wit. It's an excellent introduction to the Bard for all ages – and listen for Gielgud's voice in a cameo as the king's ghost. **[B&W]**

Hamlet (1990)
Franco Zeffirelli

Another unusual presentation of the play because so many of its scenes are set outdoors, using the grounds of three Scottish castles, and because the movie stars Mel Gibson in the title role and Glenn Close as Gertrude, Hamlet's mother – two popular screen actors not known for classical stage performances. Zeffirelli applied the same approach he used for *Romeo and Juliet* (P25), streamlining the dialogue and making it more accessible to younger audiences. Alan Bates, Ian Holm, Paul Scofield and Helena Bonham Carter appear in supporting roles. **[W]**

Hamlet (1996)
Kenneth Branagh

Call this the *Gone with the Wind* (PF5) version of the play. Branagh had directed and starred in the magnificent presentation of *Henry V* (also in PF5) seven years earlier, which I consider the best movie rendition ever of a Shakespeare play. He repeated the dual tasks in 1993 with *Much Ado About Nothing* (P25), a delightful romp. Here, he goes all-out, again starring in the title role and directing while presenting the full, unabridged, four-hour version on lushly decorated sets with a huge cast. He's assisted by, among others, Julie Christie, Kate Winslet, Robin Williams, Gérard Depardieu, Jack Lemmon, Billy Crystal, Michael Keaton, Charlton Heston, Richard Attenborough, Judi Dench, Derek Jacobi (the onscreen narrator in *Henry V*) and John Gielgud (who directed the Burton version). The result is overwhelming, and everyone is excellent – except, unfortunately, Branagh, who often seems unenergetic and even exhausted. Maybe he should have stepped back from directing this one. [Caution: sexuality and violence] **[W]**

Phil's Favorite "Hamlet" soliloquy

Of the four performances above – Olivier, Burton, Gibson and Branagh – whom do I think rendered the best version? Interesting question. On stage and on film, two challenges seem perennially to defeat even the best actors. One is playing Jesus. The role seems so intimidating that most portrayals come off as silly. To my mind, the only exceptions were Robert Powell in Zeffirelli's TV miniseries *Jesus of Nazareth* and Jim Caviezel in Gibson's *The Passion of the Christ* (P25). Both managed to humanize the character in appealing and extremely sympathetic ways. The other involves those four minutes of "Hamlet," in which the title character contemplates suicide. Lord Olivier begins, after the camera sweeps up a high stone staircase, speaking out over the ocean from a rocky promontory. A good start, but he quickly switches to a voice-over monologue and lapses into somnolence. Burton starts out energetically enough but then falls into uncomfortable anxiety. Surprising, but Gibson, descending into the crypt containing the king's sarcophagus, delivers the words most affectingly. He makes you believe he's actually weighing the drastic action aloud to himself. And Branagh, strolling slowly in a room that belongs more to Louis Quatorze than Elsinore, recites the full, unclipped version. But "recites" is the operative term; in short, he is unconvincing. Among the four, believe it or not I'll go with Mel.

44. 'The Horror, The Horror'

Those words, uttered by Colonel Kurtz, Marlon Brando's notorious character, at the end of *Apocalypse Now!* (P25), inadvertently reflected how many moviegoers reacted to the ordeal of watching Francis Ford Coppola's overblown but fitfully brilliant Vietnam War epic. It's doubtful that's what Coppola had intended. But often, moviemakers deliberately want to frighten or even horrify audiences at what they're presenting. These nine titles often do just that.

Dragonslayer
1981 – co-written and directed by Matthew Robbins

Starting with the original screen version of Sir Arthur Conan Doyle's *The Lost World* in 1925 (not on this list), in *King Kong* in 1933 and *Mighty Joe Young* in 1949 (both in PF5) and in hundreds of features since, moviemakers often employed stop-motion animation to make artificial creatures come alive. The enduring problem with the technique was it never looked completely real, because the movements usually appeared quite jerky. Then in the 1970s, moviemakers began experimenting with an improved process called "go-motion." It worked by moving the camera slightly during each film frame's exposure. The idea was to supply a little bit of blur in the image to mimic the way a real person, animal or object in motion would be captured. In 1993, *Jurassic Park* consigned both techniques to obsolescence with its advanced computer-generated images – or CGI. But go-motion reached its pinnacle with *Dragonslayer*, a sometimes thrilling fantasy about medieval wizards and knights and, well, dragons. In this case, the creature is a combination of full-size mechanical devices and go-motion miniatures, and it's often sensational. The cast features Sir Ralph Richardson in one of his last roles as a sorcerer, Peter MacNicol as his apprentice, and Pittsburgh native Caitlin Clarke in her movie debut as a village virgin masquerading as a boy (see the movie and it'll be explained). Derek Vanlint's moody cinematography well-captures the Scottish and Welsh countryside locations. The wrong notes are the Matthew Robbins/Hal Barwood script that ridicules Catholicism gratuitously, and Alex North's tinny and grating score – a far cry from his wonderful suite for *Spartacus* (PF5). [Caution: some gruesome scary scenes and one brief bit of underwater nudity – male and female] **[W]**

The Exorcist
1973 – William Friedkin

Two years before *Jaws* (PF5) became a colossal hit by scaring the bejeebers out of moviegoers, after first generating laughs, this one went entirely for terror. Based on William Peter Blatty's best-seller of the same name, it's the story of a young girl (Linda Blair) who begins acting strangely and continues to get worse. When repeated medical exams draw blanks, the girl's distraught mother (Ellen Burstyn) calls in two priests (Jason Miller and Max Von Sydow) to ... exorcise the demon she believes has possessed her daughter. Shot in the Georgetown section of Washington, D.C., it's a dark, dark tale that has been known to drive the emotionally fragile to nearly fainting. Nevertheless, the movie became a huge hit that year and remains one of the highest-grossing R-rated releases ever. [Trivia note: As emotionally punishing as *The Exorcist* turned out to be for audiences, it was physically much worse for the cast. Miller was hit full in the face with projectile vomit. The 44-year-old Von Sydow endured painful daily makeup applications to appear much older. Burstyn permanently injured her spine after being jerked too violently in the harness she was wearing for a scene. Blair likewise suffered injuries from harnesses as well as wearing extremely uncomfortable prosthetics and nearly freezing on the refrigerated set. And Mercedes McCambridge, providing the voice of the demon possessing Blair's character, went to unprecedented lengths to create vocal stress – including being bound to a chair and gagged] [Caution: extremely foul language and shocking, scary scenes] **[W]**

The Fly
1986 – co-written and directed David Cronenberg
An intriguing premise that eventually falls into disgusting excess. Jeff Goldblum stars as Seth Brundle, a research scientist who believes he can create a real version of the Transporter, the device made familiar by the Star Trek series – except he calls it a "telepod." After a gruesome failure or two, and the promise of success, Brundle decides he'll try to transport himself. It works – except he doesn't realize when he entered the machine a housefly entered it as well. So, when the teleportation occurs, the machine combines his genetic material with the fly's. Watching after that will depend on how strong a stomach you have. Geena Davis, who eventually coupled with Goldblum for a while in real life, plays a journalist and Brundle's love interest. Howard Shore composed the appropriately foreboding score. [Caution: sexuality and grotesque violence] **[W]**

Interview with the Vampire
1994 – Neil Jordan
Tom Cruise gets top billing (and the singular image on the poster) in this horror story written by Ann Rice and based on her best-seller, but Brad Pitt does the heavy lifting. He's surprisingly effective as Louis de Pointe du Lac, who in an … interview claims to be a reluctant 200-year-old vampire living in present-day San Francisco. Narrating to Daniel Molloy (Christian Slater), a justifiably frightened reporter, Louis explains he was involuntarily introduced to the … um, life of the undead in late 18th-century New Orleans by Lestat de Lioncourt (Cruise), a much-older vampire who bit him and relegated him to bloodlust and a nocturnal existence. The same happens with Claudia (Kirsten Dunst), a little girl whose parents had died in a plague epidemic. Except Claudia, at least temporarily, enjoys her conversion and becomes an enthusiastic predator. Eventually, Louis and Claudia turn on Lestat, and the battle through the

centuries – and across the Atlantic – is on, with increasingly gruesome consequences. Lavishly produced and excessively violent, Pitt remains the surprisingly human anchor. [Trivia note: As with *The Exorcist*, *Interview with the Vampire* contained physical challenges for the cast. In order to achieve the appearance of veins throbbing during the transformations, Pitt, Cruise and Dunst had to hang upside down for half-hours at a time, allowing blood to flood their faces so the makeup artists could locate their veins and paint their skin precisely] [Caution: violence and sexuality] **[W]**

The Omen
1976 – Richard Donner

Call this one the male equivalent of *The Exorcist*. Instead of a young girl being possessed by a demon, here it's a little boy named Damian (six-year-old Harvey Spencer Stephens) – except he might actually *be* a demon in human form. Based on David Seltzer's novel, Gregory Peck and Lee Remick star as the boy's adoptive parents, who begin to believe they've got a monster in their house. State-of-the-art mechanical effects provide many of the scares, and Jerry Goldsmith's ominous, throbbing score, complete with screeching choir, won him his only Oscar in 18 nominations – despite his distinctive, timeless work for *Chinatown* and his magnificent suite for *Patton* (both in PF5). Not for the emotionally fragile, and panned by a lot of critics, the movie was a big enough hit to spawn three sequels and a remake (none here). [Caution: violence and frightening scenes] **[W]**

Poltergeist
1982 – Tobe Hooper

According to Hollywood lore, Steven Spielberg, who's credited as the movie's producer, actually directed. It's plausible. All of the scenes have a Spielbergian feel, and nothing Hooper had done before (he's best-known for doing *The Texas Chainsaw Massacre* – most definitely not on my lists) resembles anything here – and see if you can find any footage of him actually directing. Craig T. Nelson and JoBeth Williams co-star as a couple recently settled into a new suburban tract that apparently was built over an old graveyard, something that has made the deceased occupants a bit restless. Some genuine scares, particularly an early encounter between the couple's young daughter (Heather O'Rourke) and one of the "TV people," as she calls them. Jerry Goldsmith's orchestral score, featuring a children's choir, is often more pleasing to the ear than his Oscar-winning suite for *The Omen*. [Trivia note: Two years earlier, Nelson and Williams had appeared together – though not romantically linked – in the silly Richard Pryor–Gene Wilder comedy *Stir Crazy* (not here)] [Caution: adult themes and scary scenes, including children in jeopardy] **[W]**

Predator
1987 – John McTiernan
Some movies, regardless of their initial quality, will spawn what are called franchises – remakes and sequels that span decades such as *Star Trek*, *Star Wars*, *Alien*, *The Terminator* and, of course, the biggest of them all, the James Bond series, which has hit the half-century mark (the best six of the Bonds in PF5). *Predator* is another one, with the latest installment out this year – though I've included none of the others. Arnold Schwarzenegger co-stars with, of all people, Jesse Ventura, the former wrestler and governor of Minnesota; and Carl Weathers, late of the *Rocky* series (another franchise). They're part of a Special Forces unit operating a covert mission in Central America when they encounter an alien being (played by 7-foot, 2-inch Kevin Peter Hall) who seems to behave like a … predator. That is, the creature kills and devours humans. It's also packing powerful weapons and some sort of invisibility cloak. When it takes out one of the group, the battle is on, with the Predator hunting down the commandos one by one. Naturally, it comes down to team-leader Dutch (Arnold) and the creature, face-to-face in a battle of brawn and brains. As preposterous as it all seems, it's genuinely gripping. [Trivia notes: 1) Even more than *The Exorcist* and *Interview with the Vampire*, Predator's production afflicted cast and crew alike. The location shoot, in a Mexican rainforest, featured snakes, scorpions, leech-infested water and oppressive heat and humidity. Everyone considered it a real survival exercise. 2) Achieving the Predator's

seemingly transparent nature was surprisingly easy, given the lack of computer-generated imagery (CGI) at the time. The costumers fitted Hall with a bright-red costume, to contrast with the colors of the rainforest and the sky. Then cinematographer Don McAlpine shot each scene twice; one with Hall against the desired background and another featuring only the background but with a slightly larger lens. Then the photo lab technicians matted out the Predator suit and, presto! Transparent alien!] [Caution: rough language, extreme violence and scary scenes] **[W]**

Psycho
1960 – Alfred Hitchcock

It might not be possible to go more horrifically into the human psyche than in this tale of perverse Oedipal attachment. *Psycho* became notorious in its day because of its frank (though not explicit) depiction of sex, because of its violence to a major character, and because … well, it's a plot giveaway I'll withhold. Janet Leigh co-stars with Anthony Perkins, who plays, let's say, a multiple role. Leigh's character Marion Crane meets Perkins's Norman Bates while on the lam from the law after stealing a large sum of cash from her employer. Bates is a strange young man who operates a forlorn motel off the beaten path. Their initial encounter leads to an increasingly shocking series of developments. Over the past six decades, many other moviemakers have attempted to match or top the raw fear delivered by this one. Some have succeeded. But kudos to Hitchcock – and his faithful composer Bernard Herrmann for his singularly creepy, stringed score –to invent what has come to be called the "slasher" movie genre. *Psycho* is its granddaddy. [Trivia notes: 1) Much has been written about the production, but here's something you might not know: It became Hitchcock's biggest moneymaker personally. Why? Because Paramount executives held so little confidence in the movie's potential that they offered the director a large percentage of the gross instead of his standard fee. Hitchcock accepted, and the box-office receipts rolled in by the bushel. 2) As he had done with key objects in *Spellbound* and *Dial 'M' for Murder* (both in P25), Hitchcock used a giant shower head to create the effect he wanted for that infamous scene] [Caution: sexuality and extremely scary scenes] **[B&W] [W]**

Them!

1954 – Gordon Douglas

This 1950s-vintage sci-fi offering doesn't feature guys in rubber suits pretending to be monsters, as did many other titles of the period. But it used something equivalent: Its giant creatures (and they really were giants) were cable-controlled marionettes. The plot, which unfolds like a detective story, involves strange happenings in the desert that include some pretty gruesome (but off-camera) killings. It turns out that radiation from atomic-bomb testing – a big theme in the early '50s – has produced a strain of enormous ants marauding across the countryside. The cast features James Whitmore as the local sheriff attempting to investigate the murders, and Edmund Gwenn (always remembered as Kris Kringle in *Miracle on 34th Street* – see PF5) as the scientist who figures out what sort of creatures have been causing all the trouble. Also, two future TV stars appear in bit parts: James Arness (late of *The Thing from Another World* but eventually to become Marshal Matt Dillon of Gunsmoke) and Fess Parker (Davey Crockett in the Disney series of the same name). Technically amateurish by today's standards, it's nevertheless involving, often exciting and the only one of the bunch you can watch with the kids. **[B&W]**

45. They're History

Dramas and biographies depicting real people can be challenging, particularly when the subjects are familiar. And truth be told, Hollywood's tendency to streamline, fudge and outright fabricate is legendary. Still, even the most tenuous connection to history can produce terrific movies – witness *The Right Stuff* (PF5), Philip Kaufman's unforgettable epic about test pilots and the original Mercury astronauts loosely based on Tom Wolfe's exceptional history of the early space program. I admit it; none of these dozen profiles rises to that level. But they're all good enough to entertain you and present at least a partially true glimpse of the past.

Against the Ice
2022 – Iceland and Denmark – Peter Flinth

Let's start with the best of the bunch. As recently as the early 20th century, most of the globe's polar regions had not yet been explored extensively. For example, the northern expanses of Greenland, a territory of Denmark, were largely unknown. Consequently, the area came under dispute between Denmark and the United States. That's because late-19th-century explorer Robert Peary, who had traveled to that part of the world, reported that Greenland was actually two islands separated by a channel, which he promptly named after himself – and claimed the new island for America. To settle the issue, the Danish government in 1906 dispatched a small research party to map Greenland's north shore and determine whether a channel indeed separated Greenland from a second island. Two years later, the party was declared lost, and Denmark sent a new expedition to solve the mystery of the Peary Channel. It was led by Ejnar [EYE-nar] Mikkelsen (Nikolaj Coster-Waldau), an experienced explorer in his own right. Commanding the small research vessel Alabama, Mikkelsen reached eastern Greenland in 1909 and set off overland with Iver Iversen (English actor Joe Cole), his ship's mechanic, to find any documents left by his predecessors. The movie chronicles the pair's efforts and is based on Mikkelsen's memoir, Two Against the Ice. A long introduction, I know, but it's important to understand the context of one of the most extraordinary adventure chronicles ever produced. It's also important to know that Mikkelsen isn't the real hero; it's Iversen, a last-minute addition to the Alabama's crew and someone who had never been to the Arctic before. Beyond that, I'll leave it to you to follow the pair's harrowing, sometimes terrifying and ultimately interminable ordeal. Except for two obviously computer-generated polar bears, it's a chilling masterpiece. [Trivia notes: 1) The movie doesn't mention it directly, but Mikkelsen's expedition wasn't initially – or entirely – funded by the Danish government. The owner of the U.K. Daily Mail newspaper offered to commission it in exchange for exclusive rights to the story. Mikkelsen balked, writing later, "As a Dane I did not like the idea of an Englishman paying for the expedition and of his money acquiring the rights to what three Danes had given their lives to achieve." His government finally authorized half the money, and Mikkelsen himself put up the rest. 2) The hut where Mikkelsen and Iversen spent nearly two years in isolation remains standing today and was restored in 2016 by the Greenland government] [Caution: language and some intense survival scenes. **[W]**

Ali

2001 – co-written and directed by Michael Mann
In this compressed biopic, the always reliable Will Smith does a fair impression of Muhammad Ali, considered by some (including yours truly) to be the greatest boxer of all time. By compressed, I mean the movie focuses on 10 years in Ali's life, from his invincible defenses of the heavyweight title in the mid-1960s to one of his most famous championship bouts, against the young George Foreman (real-life boxer Charles Shufford), who was as feared as anyone who ever entered the ring. Foreman had easily defeated Joe Frazier (champion boxer James Toney) to win the title, and he bragged about how quickly he would take down

the aging Ali in a match to be held in Kinshasa, Zaire (later the Democratic Republic of the Congo). Smith, who trained heavily for months and gained weight for the movie, never quite matched the real physicality of Ali, who was just as tall as Foreman and whom Foreman outweighed by only 4 pounds. In retrospect, it was a tough sell for Smith, a charismatic movie star who nevertheless could not mirror Ali, one of the world's most famous and identifiable personalities. But Smith performed as well as anyone else could have in the role. Less persuasive was Jon Voight, attempting to portray sports commentator Howard Cosell and doing what could kindly be called a caricature. [Trivia note: Though George Foreman is portrayed as an arrogant bully – and he was at the time – he eventually embraced Christianity and became a beloved figure both in and out of the ring. He regained the heavyweight title an astounding 20 years later at age 45 – and he and Ali eventually became close friends. Of his former foe, Foreman once said, "I am not closer to anyone else in this life than I am to Muhammad Ali"] [Caution: language, violence – including boxing violence – and sexuality] [W]

Chaplin
1992 – produced and directed by Richard Attenborough
In this, my third compilation, *Chaplin* sits on the most precarious basis – I almost placed it in the What Went Wrong? category in the Epilogue, because it began with so much promise but ended up leaving me scratching my head about what I'd just seen. Still, Robert Downey Jr. sometimes plays the legendary comedian and filmmaker very well in this biographical drama, directed by Attenborough, co-written by William Goldman and graced by a large slate of stars. It's a surprisingly masterful performance – again, some of the time. It begins, as so many biopics do, with an aging Chaplin discussing his past with the fictional editor of his memoirs, played by Anthony Hopkins (the year after Hopkins terrified audiences as Dr. Hannibal Lecter in *The Silence of the Lambs*). From there, naturally in flashback, we trace Chaplin's humble beginnings in 1890s England, where he's suddenly forced to enter the stage at age four. Gaining skills and popularity, he

heads to America in the early 20th century and meets pioneer comedic moviemaker Mack Sennett (Dan Aykroyd, in his second dramatic performance, following *Driving Miss Daisy* – see PF5). From there it's a meteoric rise, as Chaplin becomes world-famous for his inimitable character "The Little Tramp" – which Downey imitates to perfection. Instead of "meteoric," however, I could've used "mysterious," because therein lies the movie's major problem. Given our perspective a century later, no doubt Charles Chaplin was a comedic genius. His Little Tramp captivated audiences the world over for the entirety of the 1920s. But here, we see only fleeting moments of that genius, with no background or genuine insight into how the real man created it. Instead, we're given only fleeting references to the process Chaplin used to personify the character. Likewise, the movie glosses over several important aspects of his life – United Artists, for example, the first independent movie studio, which Chaplin created with his close friend Douglas Fairbanks (well-played by Kevin Kline) along with Mary Pickford (Maria Pitillo) and D.W. Griffith (not cast). You end up left with only a vague patchwork. So, why watch? Back to Downey. Despite the shortcomings, he manages to capture, in glimpses, a cinematic and cultural legend. He doesn't impersonate Chaplin as much as convey the man's essence. Downey's had a troubled personal life plagued by demons (as did Chaplin, for that matter). But here, his performance generated an Oscar nomination and a win of the British equivalent. It's an uneven but affectionate portrait of a man whose persona remains as recognizable as Muhammad Ali. Geraldine Chaplin, Charlie's daughter, plays his extremely troubled mother Hannah. [Trivia note: For well-reported reasons, Chaplin was exiled from America for many years. But in 1972 he was invited back to receive a special Oscar by the motion picture academy (which turns out to be one of the best sequences in the movie, because it contains scenes from the real Chaplin's performances). When he stepped onstage to receive it, the audience gave him the longest standing ovation in the event's history] [Caution: adult themes and sexuality] **[W]**

The Dig
2021 – England – Simon Stone

Though the movie portrays real people, the story is more about an episode than a particular character. Ralph Fiennes (pronounced RAFE FINE) stars as an amateur archaeologist who discovers one of the most important historical relics in British history, including a nearly intact Roman ship that had been secretly buried for well over a millennium under a mound in Suffolk. The story begins in early 1939, when landowner Edith Petty (Carey Mulligan) hires Basil Brown (Fiennes), an amateur archaeologist, to survey several ancient mounds on her property that are assumed to be Viking burial grounds. Through patient and sometimes hazardous effort, Brown discovers something much more dramatic, and the process is meticulously created and fascinating to watch – with some real drama and a surprise or two before the conclusion. [Caution: adult themes and sexuality] **[W]**

Dr. Ehrlich's Magic Bullet
1940 – William Dieterle

Edward G. Robinson, in his most serious and thoughtful role, portrays Paul Ehrlich, the co-discoverer of the treatment for syphilis. That might be interesting enough, including the heroic drama about the good doctor's quest for a cure, plus his groundbreaking research in the now-standard process of selective color staining. But the story behind the movie elevates it to compelling viewing. That's because the protagonist, Ehrlich, was a German Jew. Though Ehrlich had won the Nobel Prize for his research, in the 1930s, the Nazi regime attempted to remove all records pertaining to him. And here in the United States, Warner Bros. was reluctant to make and distribute the movie because 1) it dealt with a sexually transmitted disease and 2) Ehrlich's ethnic background would make the movie a tough sell in Germany, a major market. Fortunately, saner heads prevailed – though the movie makes almost no mention of Ehrlich's background. As for his effort, though opposed and ridiculed at times for his risky work – and early failures – he's finally exalted but at great cost. The movie also features actress and writer Ruth Gordon, playing

Ehrlich's wife, in the second of two notable roles that year and in this category (see *Abe Lincoln in Illinois*). [Trivia notes: 1) Robinson welcomed the opportunity to play Ehrlich, partly because he was likewise a Jew, and partly because he wanted to break away from the mobsters and thugs he had portrayed in earlier movies. 2) Salvarsan 606, the medication Ehrlich developed with Japanese researcher Sahachiro Hata, became the world's most prescribed drug for a decade, until the discovery of penicillin] **[B&W]**

Houdini
1953 – produced by George Pal

The life and times of the famous early 20th-century escape artist and his wife are fancifully but entertainingly portrayed, starring real-life husband and wife Tony Curtis and Janet Leigh. Harry Houdini began as a carnival performer in New York City, and he met his wife Bess in the audience at one of his performances. They quickly courted, married and began an onstage partnership. But money problems plagued the couple, forcing Harry to abandon the stage for a job as a lock tester. A fateful move, because it inspired him to conceive how he could escape from one of his employer's safes. That path in turn eventually led him to worldwide fame and fortune as an escape artist – but ultimately to tragedy. Along the way, Harry picked up a man named only "Otto" (the versatile British actor Torin Thatcher), who became his faithful assistant. As mentioned, it's a fanciful version of the real Houdini, but it's lovingly produced. George Pal, a pioneer in special effects, took the opposite approach here. Whenever possible, the illusions were done live and on-camera. Curtis, who in his younger years dabbled in amateur magic, performed many of the tricks himself, under the tutelage of legendary illusionist Joseph Dunninger. The result is a satisfying homage to one of the magic world's most influential figures – with an added touch of mystery. [Trivia note: Here's an odd little coincidence. The movie's producers originally wanted Burt Lancaster to play Houdini. He declined, instead heading abroad to do *The Crimson Pirate* (PF5) – in which Torin Thatcher co-starred]

Juarez
1939 – William Dieterle

A big-budget (for its day) historical epic featuring Paul Muni as Benito Juárez, the first popularly elected president of Mexico. In 1863, during the height of the American Civil War, French despot Napoléon III (Claude Rains) invades the country and installs archduke Maximilian von Habsburg of Austria (Brian Aherne) as Mexico's ruler in an attempt to depose Juarez and defeat his Republican Army. He does so, thereby kicking off a Mexican civil war, in which many Mexicans actually fought on France's side. Napoléon initiated the move in an attempt to take advantage of the chaos in the United States to exert control south of the border. The gain would be temporary, however. When our Civil War ended, America soon turned its attention to Napoléon's mischief and brought it to an end. In the meantime, however, it was a desperate battle, and Muni's performance as one of his country's greatest heroes is compelling. His co-stars Rains and Aherne, on the other hand, are passable at best as the story's villains, as is Bette Davis as Maximilian's scheming wife Carlota. Also featured are a young John Garfield as Mexican general and future president Porfirio Diaz, and Gilbert Roland (the only Mexican in the cast) as a colonel in Juarez's army. It's a cautionary tale for the ages. As Juarez tells Diaz, "When a monarch misrules, he changes the people; when a president misrules, the people change him."

[Biographical note: Throughout my compilations, I've praised certain actors for their versatility (such as the venerable Torin Thatcher in the previous title). But in the history of cinema, arguably no one personified the term more than Paul Muni, whom Warner Bros., in its publicity for *Juarez*, called "the foremost actor of the age." Consider that between 1932 and '39, Muni played, among other roles, a character based on gangster Al Capone in the original *Scarface*, an unjustly convicted felon in *I Am a Fugitive from a Chain Gang*, the famous French scientist in *The Story of Louis Pasteur*, a Chinese peasant in *The Good Earth*, an Oscar-winning performance as the French author in *The Life of Émile Zola* – which also won Best Picture – and, of course, Benito Juárez (none of the others on my lists). Earlier still, he even played seven different roles in the aptly named *Seven Faces*, one of Hollywood's lost films. Other than Russell Crowe, with *L.A. Confidential*, *The Insider*, *A Beautiful Mind*, *Cinderella Man* and *Master and Commander*, from 1997 through 2004 (and all in PF5), I can't recall another actor who ever compiled such widely varied credits within such a short timespan] [Trivia note: *Juarez* might be the most historically accurate drama Hollywood has ever produced. In researching the story, the production team acquired nearly 400 reference books for background information and created more than 7,000 sketches and blueprints for the sets and locations, including an entire Mexican village built on the Warner Bros. backlot] [B&W]

Mountains of the Moon
1990 – co-written and directed by Bob Rafelson

The name "Richard Burton" to movie buffs conjures the famous British actor who also consorted with and married Elizabeth Taylor. But in the mid-19th century, Captain Sir Richard Francis Burton meant the leader of a British expedition that set out from Egypt to find one of the most elusive geographical locations in the world: the source of the 4,000-mile-long Nile River. This is his story, well played by Patrick Bergin, as well as that of John Hanning Speke (Iain Glen), a fellow explorer with whom Burton would grudgingly share credit for the discovery. Engaged in their odyssey, Burton and Speke meet Mabruki (Delroy Lindo in a powerful performance), an escaped slave who becomes a source of courage, guidance and wisdom. They also encounter native tribes both friendly and decidedly unfriendly, attacks by several dangerous wild animals, the constant loss of men and materials, and an assortment of diseases, including malaria and indigenous fevers. It's a long, grueling slog but beautifully filmed by Roger Deakins amid some of Kenya's breathtaking scenery. Punctuated by terror-inducing moments, the saga culminates in the famous falling-out between the two explorers. Director Rafelson, whose credits otherwise include an eclectic mix of small comedies and dramas, distinguishes himself here on a much bigger project. He even manages to introduce humor in a few scenes, such as when

Burton, back in London, meets Dr. David Livingston (Bernard Hill). The two become fast friends, comparing respective wounds and after-effects from their travails in Africa. It's reminiscent of, and just as endearing as, the scene between Hooper and Quint in *Jaws* (PF5). [Caution: violence, including animal violence, and sexuality] **[W]**

The President's Lady
1953 – Henry Levin

Earlier, I offered a chapter about clumsy, big-budget epics in which Charlton Heston and Susan Hayward figured separately but prominently. Here, they co-star in a melodramatic, fanciful and dated – but also highly diverting – historical biography of Andrew Jackson and his wife Rachel Donaldson (one of the most appealing performances of Hayward's career), starting from their first meeting in Nashville, Tennessee, in 1789 and following their lives until his inauguration as seventh President of the United States in 1829. Along the way, they deal with marauding Indians, her nasty divorce from her first husband, the persistent scandal about their relationship and a personal tragedy or two. Heston plays Jackson as stubborn and temperamental, which probably does reflect the real character of "Old Hickory." But he's quite good, more so than his hard-edged circus boss Brad Braden the previous year in *The Greatest Show on Earth* or his pompous, post-exile Moses in *The Ten Commandments* three years later, or even his Oscar-winning title role in *Ben-Hur* in 1959 (all in PF5). Hayward has never been more alluring as the feisty Rachel (as I've mentioned previously, the phrase "heaving bosom" seems to have been coined for her) – that is, until the makeup artists begin to age her over the four decades of the story. It's based on Irving Stone's biographical novel, which was published the preceding year. **[B&W]**

The Story of Alexander Graham Bell
1939 – Irving Cummings

Along with *Juarez* (above) and *Young Mr. Lincoln* (next), another movie made in the year considered Hollywood's Best (see PF5).

Don Ameche stars in this well-mounted biography that tracks Bell's early life, including his work in teaching and helping the deaf, something that emerged from meeting his wife Mabel (Loretta Young), who had lost her hearing at an early age from a severe case of scarlet fever. But it mainly focuses on Bell's lengthy, hit-and-miss struggle to develop a working telephone, helped by his loyal assistant Thomas Watson (Henry Fonda). It includes the famous scene where Bell accidentally spills sulfuric acid on himself and yells, "Mr. Watson, come here, I want you" – which Watson, in another room, hears not through the air but via the primitive receiver the men have been struggling to build. Ameche's performance as Bell became so well-known at the time that many people began calling their telephone "the Ameche." [Historical note: In case you *didn't* know, Bell patented the first working telephone in 1876. He also founded American Telephone & Telegraph, AT&T, also known as Bell Telephone, for many years the world's biggest corporation. And he occupied a prominent place in the National Geographic Society, of which he served as president in the early 20th century] **[B&W]**

Young Mr. Lincoln (and) Abe Lincoln in Illinois
1939 and 1940 – John Ford and John Cromwell
Finishing the category, two respectable visions of one of our greatest presidents, the first starring Henry Fonda in the title role, working with John Ford the year before they did *The Grapes of Wrath* (P25). The story begins nearly three decades before the beginning of the Civil War, back when the ... young Abe Lincoln wasn't even practicing law yet. At the time, he owned a general store in Illinois and, to help a traveling family in need, in lieu of money he accepted a bunch of books – including a law book. Five years later, Abe begins his law practice in Springfield, the state capital. One of his first courtroom appearances (adapted from a much later case) involves a pair of brothers accused of murder, whom he defends while beginning his courtship of Mary Todd (Marjorie Weaver), who eventually becomes his wife. Fonda, wearing prosthetics to resemble Lincoln's famous face, and lifts in his shoes to match the great man's height, gives a convincing

though restrained performance. Not one of Fonda's, or Ford's, best efforts, it's nevertheless an absorbing look at a key episode in Lincoln's early life. **[B&W]**

*   *   *

Director Cromwell never achieved nearly the fame and status of Ford, but his *Abe Lincoln in Illinois* nevertheless carried an impressive pedigree. Based on Robert E. Sherwood's Pulitzer Prize-winning play of the same name, it stars Raymond Massey, reprising his Broadway role. Actress and writer Ruth Gordon, in her screen debut, co-stars as Mary Todd Lincoln. Larger in scope than John Ford's *Young Mr. Lincoln*, it begins with Abe leaving home for his first job, believe it or not conveying a boatload of pigs along the Ohio River to the Mississippi and then down to New Orleans. But fate intervenes and grounds the boat in New Salem, Illinois, where the pigs escape and Abe meets his first love, Ann Rutledge (Mary Howard). Abandoning his job on the river, he eventually begins a law practice and moves to Springfield, where he meets his longtime romantic and political rival Stephen Douglas (the always appealing Gene Lockhart). Defeating Douglas in love and politics – including the historic Lincoln–Douglas debates – Abe wins election as America's 16th president, and he and his new bride Mary Todd Lincoln depart for Washington and their rendezvous with destiny. This was considered by many to be Massey's signature role, one against which he would be measured for the remainder of his career. I would add that it remains arguably the best portrayal of Lincoln ever brought to the screen. [Trivia notes: 1) The role must have affected Massey profoundly. Not only did he continue to play Lincoln periodically on the stage, in film cameos and on television, but he also occasionally would dress as Lincoln in private life and affect some of the man's mannerisms. 2) In a bit of irony, Massey and Henry Fonda were both nominated for Best Actor Oscars in 1941, with Fonda nominated for *The Grapes of Wrath* (P25). They lost to James Stewart for *The Philadelphia Story* (PF5)] **[B&W]**

46. Tragedy Tomorrow...

The peppy song from the stage musical "A Funny Thing Happened on the Way to the Forum" (the lame movie version not here) contains the following partial lyrics:

Something familiar
Something peculiar
Something for everyone:
A comedy tonight!

Something appealing
Something appalling
Something for everyone:
A comedy tonight!

That about sums up this bunch of movie comedies, all of which basically tell us to put off our troubles and take time to laugh. But as has been attributed to various sources, including English actor Edmund Keane on his deathbed, dying is easy; comedy is hard. It's why so many would-be movie comedies don't cut it. But here are 18 that do, plus one that's iffy but worth mentioning.

At the Circus
1939 – produced by Mervyn Leroy
This lesser-known Marx Brothers vehicle sports some heavy hitters in the background, such as composer Franz Waxman; songwriters E.Y. Harburg and Harold Arlen (best known for their work on *The Wizard of Oz* (PF5), including the immortal "Somewhere Over the Rainbow"), who contributed "Lydia the Tattooed Lady," and the likewise immortal Buster Keaton as a consultant for the stunts. Meanwhile, the libretto has Groucho as J. Cheever Loophole, Chico as Antonio Pirelli and Harpo as a character called, simply, "Punchy," trying to save a circus from bankruptcy. Naturally, they do, but not before one of the wildest finales of all their movies, involving a gorilla swinging on a trapeze and perennial co-star Margaret Dumont being shot out of

a cannon. [Trivia note: In that finale, the ... um, cast member, Gibraltar the Gorilla, appears smaller than he did earlier in the movie. The reason? Track down Groucho's explanation, which he gave multiple times over the years in interviews] **[B&W]**

The Big Store
1941 – Charles Reisner
Here, the Marx Brothers wreak havoc on a department store, with Groucho as Wolf J. Flywheel and finally demonstrating his unique talent (versus Chico's piano playing and Harpo's ... harp artistry): he could ride a unicycle – though much of the time Groucho is being portrayed by a stunt double. Lucille Ball co-stars. But speaking of Chico, he and Harpo perform a delightful piano duet, the only one they ever did in their movies. **[B&W]**

Bruce Almighty
2003 – Jim Carrey as Bruce Nolan
I originally placed this one in my second compilation within the category "Characters Tormented." And indeed Carrey's Nolan is tormented, but only briefly. The rest of the story is done mostly for laughs, and as such it has its moments. As for the story, God (played by the venerable Morgan Freeman) grows tired of his constant duties as a deity and decides to take a vacation. In his absence, he bestows his omnipotence on Nolan, a failing TV news reporter whose life has been collapsing – and who has been so angry about it he has been complaining loudly to ... God. I must admit I'm no great fan of Carrey's. But here he gives maybe his finest performance as someone who suddenly personifies that sage caution, be careful what you wish for. The movie features two gems of brief scenes. The first, in a diner early on, Nolan seeks solace in a cup of coffee. It makes you realize just how precious that little pleasure can be at critical moments when you have no idea where your life is heading. The second involves his wreaking sweet revenge on a gang of street toughs, recalling Woody Allen's quip, "If life could only be like this!" in *Annie Hall* (PF5). [Trivia note: The town square used in this movie is the same outdoor set used in the *Back to the Future* (PF5) trilogy – including the infamous clock tower] [Caution: sexuality] **[W]**

Buck Privates
1941 – Arthur Lubin

Abbott and Costello join the Army in a wartime morale-building comedy, ably supported by the Andrews Sisters singing several of their most popular numbers of the time, including the sensational "Boogie-Woogie Bugle Boy" and the sentimental ballad, "Apple Blossom Time." As was usual with the comedy duo, much of their dialogue and antics were improvised. The effort paid off, however, because *Buck Privates* was one of the biggest hits of the year. [Trivia note: The movie might have been intended to use comedy to build public morale here in the States, but it had an unintended consequence. The Japanese Army got hold of a print and began showing it to troops to illustrate how inept the Americans were at war-fighting] **[B&W]**

The Cocoanuts
1929 – Robert Florey and Joseph Santley

A confluence of immortals, it was the Marx Brothers' first appearance in a movie, and a musical at that. Based on George S. Kaufman's hit play, it includes five (surprisingly forgettable) songs by Irving Berlin. Technically crude (it was an early "talky," and the boys were getting used to the new medium), with several dull stretches, it nevertheless delivers some good laughs and predictable mayhem. My favorite line: Chico appears and says, "I'm glad to see me." **[B&W]**

The Flying Deuces
1939 – A. Edward Sutherland

A remake and extension of a shorter feature they had made a few years earlier, Stan Laurel and Oliver Hardy join the French Foreign Legion. From there, it's pure and pleasant nonsense, and as always persistently witty and fitfully hilarious, including, as the title suggests, a scene with the boys trying to wrestle an airplane off the ground. [Trivia note: The movie features a rare connection with the Marx Brothers. In the scene where Stan strums a bedspring like a harp, it's actually Harpo dubbing Stan's playing] **[B&W]**

Grumpy Old Men
1993 – Donald Petrie
If Oscar Madison and Felix Unger had quit the big city and moved to small-town Minnesota, that's what you get with this one. Except their names are Max Goldman (Walter Matthau) and John Gustafson (Jack Lemmon). Old, old friends, they truly are grumpy old men interacting with each other, particularly when they begin vying for the affections of their new neighbor Ariel Truax (Ann-Margret, looking fabulous at 52). [Caution: language and mild sexuality] **[W]**

The Imposters
1998 – written and directed by Stanley Tucci
The multi-talented Tucci also co-stars with Oliver Platt in a wacky takeoff of *Some Like It Hot* (PF5) – including one of them appearing in drag. Instead of the Prohibition era in the 1920s, this story takes place during the Great Depression of the '30s. The two are unemployed actors and petty crooks whom fate requires to stow away on an ocean liner. Lots of strange characters, funny situations – much of it overacted – ably supported from other well-known actors and a surprise cameo appearance. [Trivia note: Tucci, Platt and fellow cast member Tony Shalhoub all studied acting together at Yale University's drama school] [Caution: sexuality] **[W]**

In & Out
1997 – Frank Oz
Kevin Kline and Tom Selleck ostensibly co-star in this romantic comedy about gayness and misunderstanding in a small Indiana town. But the movie's real attraction is Joan Cusack, who gives an endearing performance as a woman simply searching for a heterosexual mate – "Is everybody gay?" she plaintively asks at one point. The plot is set in motion when Cameron Drake (Matt Dillon), a graduate of the town's high school, wins a Best Actor Oscar in Hollywood for playing a gay soldier. Accepting his award, Drake cites as inspiration his English teacher Howard Brackett (Kline) and outs him. The problem is, Howard isn't gay

– at least, he claims not to be. Therein follows a long series of misunderstandings and surprises, leading to a comfortable conclusion for all. [Trivia note: The Oscar that Matt Dillion's character holds at the awards ceremony is actually Kline's, who had won it eight years earlier for *A Fish Called Wanda* (P25)] [Caution: mild sexuality] **[W]**

The In-Laws
1979 – Arthur Hiller
This silly and lamebrained but entertaining comedy features Alan Arkin and Peter Falk as would-be ... in-laws Sheldon Kornpett and Vince Ricardo. Sheldon's a nebbish of a Manhattan dentist, and Vince seems to be a government agent who's involved in something shady and dangerous. As the wedding of their daughter and son (Penny Peyser and Michael Lembeck) approaches, Vince asks Sheldon to do him a favor and accompany him briefly on a trip to "Scranton." That trip turns out to be an insertion into a dangerous though fictional country somewhere in Latin America, and Sheldon's growing suspicions about Vince prove true; he's indeed involved in covert activities for the CIA. From there, mayhem ensues, though because this is a comedy there's little worry involved and some decent funny moments. But the main attraction is watching the two actors at work. [Viewing note: Arkin is such a schnook here, but 12 years earlier in one of his first major roles he played the murderous character Roat, psychotically pursuing Audrey Hepburn in *Wait Until Dark* (PF5). Likewise, Falk was better known as the mild-mannered and rumpled-but-clever detective Columbo in his TV series of the same name, and as the lovable grandfather in *The Princess Bride* (PF5)] [Trivia note: Strange as it might seem, *The In-Laws* turned out to be one of Marlon Brando's favorite movies. He reportedly screened it at least 20 times and personally praised Arkin for his performance] [Caution: language and mild violence] **[W]**

It's a Mad Mad Mad Mad World
1963 – produced and directed by Stanley Kramer
In this compilation and the previous two, I've presented some 1500 favorites, either loves or likes. This is one of the few

exceptions, because I don't particularly care for it. I've included it for sentimental reasons – it was my dear late father's favorite movie. So, please indulge me a little. Kramer's only comedy ran nearly 4 hours when originally released and remains nearly 3 hours long in current versions. Its main attraction is its cast, including (in alphabetical order) Edie Adams, Eddie "Rochester" Anderson, Jack Benny, Jim Backus, Milton Berle, Joe E. Brown, Sid Caesar, Barrie Chase, Jimmy Durante, Paul Ford, Buddy Hackett, Buster Keaton, Don Knotts, Ethel Merman, ZaSu Pitts, Dorothy Provine, Mickey Rooney, Dick Shawn, Phil Silvers, Arnold Stang, Terry-Thomas, The Three Stooges and Jonathan Winters, all popular screen and television personalities in their day – and in the cases of Keaton and Rooney, long before and long after. What's it about? Remember the Hitchcockian term MacGuffin? It's here, it involves a large sum of money, and everyone is indeed after it, usually in automobiles and either in person or in the guise of the 80 stunt performers Kramer used in this extravaganza. Spencer Tracy pops in for a few scenes as well, as a police detective hunting the MacGuffin-hunters. I repeat, I don't care for it much, but it was a smash hit the year of its release. **[W]**

Miss Congeniality
2000 – Donald Petrie
Sandra Bullock tries slapstick comedy and proves reasonably adept at the genre in this hit-and-miss tale about an FBI agent trying to thwart a terror attack during a beauty pageant. Bullock is Agent Gracie Hart, forced by circumstances to infiltrate the Miss United States competition in San Antonio, for 25 years run by organizer Kathy Morningside (Candice Bergen), because someone known only as "The Citizen" has threatened to wreak havoc there. She's accompanied by fellow agent Eric Matthews (Benjamin Bratt) and is prepped in the ways of pageantry by veteran coach Victor Melling (Michael Caine in a scene-stealing role). There, masquerading as a bumbling Miss New Jersey, Agent Hart gets to know and befriend the other girls and keeps a sharp eye out – though in a couple of cases a bit too eagerly – for the would-be attacker. It's predictable but good fun. William Shatner

occupies space as the emcee Stanley Fields. [Trivia note: Four years later, Shatner and Bergen would co-star in the TV series Boston Legal] [Caution: language and sexuality] **[W]**

National Lampoon's Vacation
1983 – Harold Ramis

The beginning of the *Vacation* franchise stars Chevy Chase and Beverly D'Angelo as Clark and Ellen Griswald, Chicagoans who decide to take their son and daughter on a cross-country drive to visit the legendary Wally World (think Walt Disney) amusement park. Naturally, unintended consequences, naughty situations and mayhem ensue, including: a side trip to a St. Louis inner-city neighborhood;, a visit with Clark's "Cousin Eddie" (Randy Quaid, in what has become an iconic role), adding Ellen's Aunt Edna (Imogene Coca) and her mean dog Dinky as passengers; getting lost in a vast expanse of desert; and Clark having a brief fling with a supermodel (supermodel Christie Brinkley at her sexiest) he encounters on the road; and discovering that Wally World is closed for repairs. There's also the Wagon Queen Family Truckster (actually a modified 1980 Ford station wagon), the ... um, vehicle Clark buys for the trip, which seems to have been, as my late father used to say, shoved off the assembly line at the end of the day on a Friday. Some awkward and unnecessarily raunchy moments, but many genuine laughs. [Trivia notes: 1) Writer John Hughes based his script on a similarly eventful vacation he had shared with his family as a boy 25 years earlier. 2) Though her character receives a bit of cruel fate, Imogene Coca proved the most heroic of the cast members. She suffered a stroke during filming, and with the help of her husband spent weeks regaining her mobility and re-learning her lines before returning to the production and completing her appearance] [Caution: language and sexuality] **[W]**

No Time for Sergeants
1958 – Mervyn Leroy

In the early 1960s, Andy Griffith became one of the most beloved TV stars in America, based on the weekly series bearing his name.

He played Andy Taylor, the slow-talking, friendly sheriff of the small town of Mayberry, North Carolina. But in the years leading up to the show, Griffith had proven himself a versatile performer – in both drama and, once in a while, as a standup comedian. Here, he reprises his stage role as Will Stockdale, a strong-backed hick of a soldier from Georgia who makes his mark, so to speak, on the U.S. Air Force. He's joined by Nick Adams, another early '60s TV star, as Private Benjamin Whitledge, another Southerner who had wanted only to serve in the Army's infantry. Both actors shine in this fitfully hilarious service comedy based on Ira Levin's play, in turn based on Mac Hyman's semiautobiographical novel. [Trivia notes: 1) Speaking of the play, Griffith as Stockdale continues something his character did on stage: He "broke the fourth wall," as they say in show business, and occasionally addresses the audience. 2) And speaking of Griffith's TV series, one of the cast members here is Don Knotts, who also appeared in the stage version and who gained fame as Deputy Barney Fife of Mayberry] [B&W]

Planes, Trains and Automobiles
1987 – written and directed by John Hughes
Steve Martin and John Candy play Neal Page and Del Griffin, two strangers who meet and clash but are forced to cooperate trying to get home from New York to Chicago for Thanksgiving. Complications and setbacks occur aplenty, beginning when their flight is diverted to Wichita, Kansas, due to bad weather. That development gradually drains the two men of their money, their credit and their patience, which is where the trains and automobiles – and buses and trucks and even shoe leather – come in. Fear not, however. This is a comedy, and whatever befalls Neal and Del is usually hilarious, and it all leads – sooner or later – to a reasonably happy resolution. [Trivia note: As in *National Lampoon's Vacation*, Hughes based his script here on his own chaotic attempt to get home for the holidays one year] [Caution: language] [W]

392

The Russians Are Coming, the Russians Are Coming
1966 – Norman Jewison

Carl Reiner, Alan Arkin and Eva Marie Saint in a Cold War comedy with a simple but effective premise. The Cripynf (meaning "Octopus"), a Russian submarine, has become grounded off a fictional island near the New England coast (actually northern California). The boat's captain (played by Theodore Bikel) sends out a reconnaissance party headed by Yuri Rozanov (Arkin) to find or steal a boat to tow the Cripynf back to sea. In the process, the Russians encounter the family of Walt Whitaker (Reiner) on vacation, including his wife (Eva Marie Saint), their two young children and Alison, their nubile teen babysitter (Andrea Dromm). Naturally, Alison and one of the young Russians (John Phillip Law) meet, hormonal sparks fly and … well, from that connection, and others, all kinds of complications ensue, some of them tense, some innocuous and at least one a little too convenient. But all ends well, and peacefully. As in *The In-Laws*, Arkin in his debut displays a talent for comedy, and his interplay with Reiner's character (whom he calls "Whitaker Walt") is consistently funny. Likewise, the antics of Jonathan Winters, Ben Blue and Paul Ford as supporting players – particularly Blue's homage to Paul Revere at the fadeout. [Trivia notes: 1) Arkin, with a Russian family background, actually was fluent in the language, as were Bikel and Brian Keith, another cast member. 2) This was the third time Bikel played a naval officer. He was second in command of the German gunboat Louisa in *The African Queen* (PF5), and he played the original Captain von Trapp in the Broadway version of "The Sound of Music"] **[W]**

¡Three Amigos!
1986 – John Landis

Short and Martin and Chase, oh my! That's Martin and Steve and Chevy. The boys, all TV's Saturday Night Live alumni, don fancy western garb here as a trio of silent movie stars lured south of the border by the desperate residents of a small town harassed by the notorious El Guapo (Alfonso Arau). Think *The Magnificent Seven* (PF5) but done for laughs – or *Galaxy Quest* (also PF5) set in early

20th-century Mexico. You see, the desperate villagers are unaware that all of the onscreen bravado they see is a façade. Best moment: The boys, camping out in the desert, sing a ballad called "Blue Shadows on the Trail," accompanied by the local critters. Randy Newman composed that one and the other songs, and Elmer Bernstein supplied a suitably western score. It's pure silliness. [Caution: language and mild violence and sexuality] **[W]**

What Planet Are You From?
2000 – Mike Nichols
Here's the iffy entrée, an outrageous sex comedy from Nichols, with Gary Shandling as "Harold Anderson," an alien on the make. After extensive (and explicit) training, he has landed on Earth to mate with a human and return their offspring back to his dying planet. First problem: The ... um, necessary physical equipment is missing from his alien body, so his extraterrestrial colleagues have constructed an artificial device. Second problem: The device frequently malfunctions, either by ... moving into position, so to speak, at inappropriate times or by emitting mechanical noises. Despite the drawbacks, and several false starts, Harold finally meets his mate in Susan (Annette Bening). They procreate (like crazy, in maybe the movie's funniest scene), she conceives and gives birth, and they live happily ... well, not really. The story becomes increasingly ridiculous from then on, but it remains entertaining and surprisingly funny – though the movie failed with critics and bombed at the box office. Nichols, as usual, managed to attract a strong supporting cast, including Greg Kinnear, John Goodman, Linda Fiorentino, Ben Kingsley as the alien leader and Judy Greer in a scene-stealing performance as a ditzy airline stewardess who can't seem to concentrate on her assignation with Shandling's alien. [Caution: language, frequent sexuality and mild violence] **[W]**

47. Truman Show

From the amusing to the deeply tragic, focusing on a shocking and notorious event in the late 1950s and the efforts by one man to describe and explain it several years later. By "Truman," I don't mean Peter Weir's odd and overblown movie of 1998 (not here). I'm referring to Truman Capote, one of America's most famous authors of the mid-20th century and one of the oddest characters ever to attain celebrity. As for the event in question, it – and Capote – became the subject of these three titles. In chronological order...

In Cold Blood
1967 – written and directed by Richard Brooks

Based on Capote's riveting account, the movie is a stark, straightforward telling of the horrendous killing of a Kansas family in 1959 by two former prison inmates, Perry Smith (Robert Blake) and Dick Hickock (Scott Wilson). Falsely informed by a fellow inmate that farm owner Herbert Clutter (veteran character actor John McLiam) had hidden a large sum of cash on his property, the two made their way to the Clutter household where they proceeded to hold hostage and eventually murder Herbert, his wife and their two teenage children. The rapid discovery of the carnage prompted a nationwide manhunt eventually leading to Smith's and Hickock's arrest in Las Vegas, followed by their trial and execution. Brooks opted to tell the story mostly in flashback, with the perpetrators filling in much of the narration. Opting for as much realism as possible, he filmed some of the movie at the real Clutter farm, at the retail store where the killers attempted a scam en route to the farm, and in the courtroom where the two murderers were tried. He even cast six of the real jurors for the trial sequence. It's a raw, gripping account of a true horror story, the most chilling aspect of which is the matter-of-fact way Hickock, and particularly Smith, describe their deeds. [Trivia note: If you've ever desired to look directly into the eyes of men who have done evil, you can do so by viewing the movie's poster, which features the real eyes of Smith and Hickock] [Caution: intense violence] **[B&W] [W]**

Capote
2005 – Bennett Miller
Switching from the perpetrators to their chronicler, Philip Seymour Hoffman does a dead-on impersonation in the title role. He's well supported by Catherine Keener as Harper Lee, the author and Capote's lifelong friend, whom he basically betrayed in the process of producing In Cold Blood, his enhanced account of the murder of the Clutter family of Holcomb, Kansas, by former prison inmates Perry Smith and Dick Hickock (this time played by Clifton Collins Jr. and Mark Pellegrino). Supported by The New Yorker magazine, Capote and Lee travel to Holcomb where he begins teasing out the details – and creating some of his own – via interviews and certain inducements, including bribery. In a way, this examination of the dark side of human existence looks in two directions; into the souls of those two cold-blooded killers as well as the emotionless but brilliant writer who profiled them and the event in such a loosely factual way. Neither is savory, but the movie is riveting. [Caution: language and adult themes] **[W]**

Infamous
2006 – written and directed by Douglas McGrath
The second movie within a year portraying Capote's chronicle of the Clutter family murders, this one is based on George Plimpton's biography of the man. It stars Toby Jones in the title role and Sandra Bullock as Harper Lee, with Daniel Craig as Perry Smith. Jones's portrayal is more caricaturish than Philip Seymour Hoffman's, and less subtle, but it likewise conveys the enormous self-involvement of this particular celebrity. The surprise is Craig, the same year he triumphed as the latest Agent 007, James Bond, in the superlative *Casino Royale* (PF5). As convicted murderer

Smith, he plays a character who couldn't be further from his Bond persona in a performance Gary Arnold called "sensational." That performance, in which Smith and Capote form a strange and tenuous bond, provides the central narrative of the movie. It features a particularly shocking scene where Smith almost sexually accosts the author. As with the other two titles, it's rough to watch. It's also the most fictionalized version. Nevertheless, it's a mature bit of storytelling. The supporting cast includes Jeff Daniels as police investigator Alvin Dewey, and Peter Bogdanovich, Hope Davis, Gwyneth Paltrow, Isabella Rossellini and Sigourney Weaver as New York socialites and literati. [Caution: adult themes] **[W]**

48. Unlikely Heroes

As the old saying goes, some are born great, some achieve greatness and others have greatness thrust upon them. Seven of the characters (including two pairs) in this category don't quite achieve what you would call greatness. But to one degree or another, they do distinguish themselves. As for the last title, an ensemble performance portraying a real event, the term "greatness" applies not only to its caliber of cinematic achievement but also to the magnificent, collective heroism displayed.

The Defiant Ones
1958 – Sidney Poitier and Tony Curtis as Noah Cullen and John 'Joker' Jackson

This was producer–director Stanley Kramer's groundbreaking attempt at dealing, tangentially, with racial issues using the medium of the movies. Poitier's Cullen and Curtis's Jackson are escaped convicts and antagonists who are chained together and forced to cooperate to survive. They begin their ordeal after the prison truck conveying them crashes, and they manage to get away in the confusion and chaos. The mishap causes a half-hearted attempt by the authorities because, as one of them jokes, the two men will probably try to kill each other in their attempt to separate. There is some suspicion and anger between Cullen and Jackson, but that's quickly replaced by the realization they must work together to get away. And forced cooperation eventually turns into genuine friendship. There's terrific chemistry between the two stars, who performed most of their dangerous stunts and grueling physical challenges themselves, and who developed a lifelong friendship as a result of their shared experience. At first awkward and formulaic, the movie ends up as a surprisingly compelling story of male bonding – with the racial issue becoming secondary. Nominated for eight Oscars, and winning for its screenplay and cinematography, *The Defiant Ones* has become a minor classic. [Trivia notes: 1) The production featured a most unusual technical adviser: a real, escaped chain-gang prisoner whose identity was concealed. 2) In the opposite direction, one of the Oscar-winning screenwriters, Nedrick Young, had been blacklisted and forced to write under a pseudonym at the time. So, Kramer cast him as the prison truck driver in the opening scene and superimposed his fake name in the credits – so those in the know could see who the real co-writer was] **[B&W] [W]**

F/X
1986 – Bryan Brown and Brian Dennehy as Rollie Tyler and Leo McCarthy

Here's a most unlikely pair of heroes. Tyler is an effects specialist for low-budget movies who's hired by the U.S. Justice Department – or so he thinks – to stage the fake murder of Nick DeFranco (the great Jerry Orbach), a protected witness. McCarthy is a city detective on the trail of the same man whose murder Tyler has been hired to stage. Naturally, things go bad in a hurry, and Tyler becomes the man hunted by the feds. In the process of hiding out, his girlfriend Ellen (Diane Venora in a brief but vivid performance) is killed, and eventually Tyler and McCarthy team up for a slick bit of revenge on all of the bad guys. Diverting and surprising, *F/X* delivers a bit of guilt-free larceny against TPTB – the powers that be. [Trivia note: The movie's producer was none other than Dodi Fayed [Fay-ED], the Egyptian tycoon who was romantically involved with England's Princess Diana at the time of her tragic death 11 years later] [Caution: violence and sexuality] **[W]**

Iron Man
2008 – Robert Downey Jr. as Tony Stark

As you might know from reading my introductions, I'm not a big fan of effects-laden features based on comic books. Here's an exception. Downey in the title role plays the son of a wealthy defense contractor. Nearly mortally wounded in a surprise attack and imprisoned by terrorists in Afghanistan, Stark secretly co-creates a reactor-powered body suit that will make him invincible. Sound like a stretch? No doubt, as is most of the overblown plot. What gives the story heart, and provides frequent and genuine excitement, is the high caliber of Downey's performance. He transcends what is essentially comic-book pulp and turns it into an exciting story of a clever, resourceful, *humorous* superhero. Part of the credit also goes to Jon Favreau, who along with being a pretty fair actor has developed into a skilled director, particularly of big-budget productions. [Trivia notes: 1) Tony Stark/Iron Man is indeed based on a Marvel Comics character. The movie was the first adaptation of one of their products, a practice that as of this writing has become a $30 billion enterprise, now known as Marvel Comics Universe. 2) Favreau also directed, and co-starred with, Downey six years later in the delightful *Chef* (PF5)] [Caution: violence] **[W]**

A Man Called Ove
2015 – Sweden – Rolf Lassgård in the title role

Who knew serial attempted suicide could make such a gentle comedy and a charming story? But it did in this case. The Ove of the title, Ove Lindahl, is an aging widower forced into retirement, living in a townhouse community and suffering from deep depression. As a result, he repeatedly tries to kill himself. That's the basic plot, though Ove's goal of self-destruction is continually thwarted by circumstance. Good thing, because he eventually finds romance and purpose, including some spontaneous acts of heroism – hence its inclusion in this category. Given the frequent possibility of tragedy, it's remarkable that the movie doesn't descend into hopelessness. Instead, it becomes a touching testimony to the resilience of the human spirit. A Best Foreign Film Oscar nominee written and directed by Hannes Holm, it's an endearing little gem. [Caution: sexuality] **[W]**

Man in the Wilderness
1971 – Richard Harris as Zachary Bass

A member of a fur-trapping expedition across the American Northwest in the 1820s, Bass is badly injured from a bear attack. Presumed dead, he is buried and abandoned … in the wilderness by the group's leader (John Huston) and forced to survive alone. Eventually tracking down the men who abandoned him, Bass opts not for revenge but for seizing the opportunity to resume his life with his wife and young son. Harris, in one of his best performances, plays out the ordeal vividly, even though he's mostly silent and speaks very little. The story, based on the real-life experience of a trapper named Hugh Glass, was essentially remade in 2015 as *The Revenant* (not here) and starred Leonardo DiCaprio. [Trivia notes: 1) If some of the movie's landscape looks familiar, it's because certain scenes were filmed in the same locations in Spain as David Lean's *Doctor Zhivago* (PF5), six years earlier. 2) Director Richard C. Sarafian, who also acted, was an associate and friend of writer–director Robert Altman. He even married Altman's sister. The couple had five children, four of whom followed their father and became professionals in the movie business] [Caution: violence, including animal violence] [W]

Thirteen Lives

2022 – The entire ensemble

A last-minute addition, I now consider this the best title in my entire second and third volumes, excluded from my original Favorite 500 only because of the year of its release. Director Ron Howard, at age 69 and as of this writing into his seventh decade of acting and directing, has risen to the top of his profession. Filmmaking does not get any better than this; it's riveting. The movie, produced on a huge scale, re-creates one of the most incredible events in human history. On June 23, 2018, twelve boys from Pong Pha, a little town in northern Thailand, visited Tham Luang Nang Non (the Great Cave of the Sleeping Lady). A nearby tourist attraction, the boys often visited the cave, this time accompanied by Ekkaphon Chanthawong, their young soccer coach (Thai actor Teeradon Supapunpinyo). Soon thereafter, an unexpected monsoon downpour flooded the karstic cave's kilometers-long chamber, separating the group from the outside world. When the townspeople discovered the cave had flooded and the boys were missing, they quickly called in the local authorities, who soon summoned Thailand's equivalent of Navy SEALs to attempt a rescue. At the same time, thousands of Thais headed for Pong Pha to offer their help, and soon many more individuals from all over the world arrived, likewise rendering assistance. Meanwhile, the first attempt by the SEALs failed due to the extremely dangerous conditions, which eventually claimed two of them. Among the international arrivals, Richard Stanton and Jonathan Volanthen (Viggo Mortensen and Colin Farrell), a pair of experienced cave-rescue divers (the SEALs called them "the old men") from England, volunteered to navigate the cave's now-treacherous waters and locate the lost group—or their bodies. What happened next provides two hours of literal heart-stopping suspense and intense anguish. Yes, the outcome has been known since the incident attracted the attention of the entire world. But watching what was involved, how the rescue was accomplished – and what was required of the rescuers – becomes the stuff of cinematic legend. Howard's crew constructed a giant replica of the cave's interior inside an airplane hangar in Queensland, Australia. There, he thrust his actors and camera operators into the incredibly tight passages. Despite extensive safety precautions, Mortensen, Farrell and others later admitted experiencing panic attacks in the simulated environment, a taste of what the real divers encountered – for unbelievably longer periods. In these days of deep political divisions and a resumption of the Cold War, this story portrays the finest and noblest aspects of the human spirit, as thousands of former strangers spent a grueling, almost unbearable stretch of time attempting to save those thirteen lives. It's a particular tribute to the great people of Thailand and an unforgettable moviegoing experience. And speaking of the Thais, no description of the saga would be complete without extolling Chanthawong. Though mostly in the background, and not involved in the rescue, he kept his young charges calm and resolute through 12 days of isolation in darkness, without food or any hint of being rescued. Perhaps more than any character ever portrayed in the movies, this extraordinary young man personifies supreme grace and humility under pressure. [Trivia note (and a most stunning and terrifying one): Unnerving as it is to watch the divers, know that the real cave's waters were muddy, not clear; meaning the rescuers had to work their way through those long hours traversing the cavern essentially in total darkness] [Caution: extremely harrowing situations – be forewarned if you suffer from claustrophobia] **[W]**

49. Westward, Whoa!

Of all the great genres in Hollywood history, the western remains one of its most prolific, even heading into twelve decades of productions – witness the popularity of the TV series Yellowstone, starring Kevin Costner. Here are 10 selections that uphold that long and proud – though occasionally hokey – tradition.

Broken Arrow
1950 – Delmer Daves

Let's begin with a surprisingly enlightened story for the time, one that's loosely based on history. James Stewart, in his first significant western, plays Tom Jeffords, a tracker and U.S. Army scout who rescues and befriends a wounded young Native American boy. That boy grows up to become Cochise (Jeff Chandler), one of the leaders of the Apaches, at war with settlers and the Army in Arizona territory in the 1870s. Because of that friendship, Jeffords finds himself caught in the middle of a bloody battle involving Cochise, the Apache chief Geronimo (an uncredited Jay Silverheels), the Army and the settlers – including the villainous Ben Slade (Will Geer). Jeffords also becomes romantically involved with Sonseeahray (a nubile Debra Paget, in dark makeup and only 16 at the time), a young Apache woman. Given those components, the outcome could only be tragic. Yet the movie's ending is decidedly hopeful – the title derives from a Native American gesture, meaning "peace." [Trivia notes: 1) Stewart's onscreen romance with Paget – at age 42 – presages his two roles eight years later opposite Kim Novak, who was 26, in *Vertigo* and *Bell, Book and Candle* (both in PF5). 2) Two TV references, one for the 1950s and the other the '70s: You probably need to be my age to remember Jay Silverheels, best known for playing Tonto in the popular series, The Lone Ranger. And Geer became a beloved character, playing "Grandpa" Walton in ... The Waltons]

Broken Lance
1954 – Edward Dmytryk

Call this the distant precursor of the current hit TV series Yellowstone. It's also a precursor of the early '60s hit series Bonanza. And it's one of the first widescreen westerns. Spencer Tracy stars as Matt Devereaux, widower and patriarch of a ranch dynasty comprising three grown sons (played by Earl Holliman, Hugh O'Brian and Richard Widmark). A stern father, Devereaux often finds himself at odds with his offspring, to the point where they eventually turn against him. There's also his youngest son (Robert Wagner), born of his second wife (Katy Jurado), a Native American whose presence creates resentment among the nearby townspeople. The son engenders further resentment because he associates with his mother's family on the local reservation. And he elicits anger from his older brothers because he seems to be Matt's favorite. With so much bad blood building, violent conflict – and death – become inevitable. Tracy, as always, is rock-solid, and the supporting cast is first-rate. [Trivia note: Though the story is completely fictional, it does contain a connection with history. Chief Geronimo Kuth Le, grandson of *the* Geronimo, appears in a small role] **[W]**

Cat Ballou
1965 – Elliot Silverstein

Among the most unusual westerns ever produced, Jane Fonda stars in the title role as a daughter seeking to avenge the murder of her father. She thinks she's found the vehicle for revenge in the person of Kid Shelleen (Lee Marvin, in his only Oscar-winning role). It turns out, however, that the murderer is Tim Strawn – who happens to be Shelleen's twin brother (also played by Marvin). And though the Kid can be a fearsome gunslinger, he's hampered by his affinity for the bottle. Often awkwardly played and mostly for laughs (the scene with a drunken Shelleen atop his likewise drunken horse is considered a classic comic image), the movie also has its dramatic moments. Legendary stuntman Yakima Canutt directed the stunt sequences, and Nat King Cole and Stubby Kaye appear periodically as singing narrators. They also perform the movie's theme song. [Trivia note: A sad association with the movie concerns Cole, who unbeknownst to anyone at the time, reportedly even to himself, was dying of lung cancer during the production] **[W]**

Destry Rides Again
1939 – George Marshall

James Stewart and Marlene Dietrich try to foil crooked saloon-owner Brian Donlevy in this western with some comedic moments. Stewart, in the title role – an in his first western – is somewhat of a precursor to his character Ransom Stoddard in John Ford's iconic morality play, *The Man Who Shot Liberty Valance* (PF5), 23 years later. He starts off refusing to wear a sidearm but eventually shows he can be as lethal with a gun as anyone. Marlene is in fine form as Frenchy, the local barmaid, and she gets to belt out what became one of her signature songs, "The Boys in the Backroom." Not a sequel, it's based on an enormously popular novel of the time by Max Brand. Entertaining as it is, it's also interesting because it was directed by Marshall, a man whose career in Hollywood spanned six decades yet today is virtually unknown, except to the most avid and studious movie fans. [Trivia notes: 1) For the catfight between Marlene and co-star Una Merkel, the two actresses agreed to wing it – but under certain rules. That they did, but both carried bruises from the encounter for weeks. 2) There actually was a sequel to this one; *Destry*, in 1954, except it was nearly an exact remake of *Destry Rides Again*; it starred Audie Murphy, the highly decorated World War II veteran-turned-actor; it was strictly a drama – and it was also directed by Marshall] **[B&W]**

The Far Country
1954 – Anthony Mann

The fourth of the five westerns made by Mann that starred James Stewart, and though it's not nearly the best of them, it's got a lot going for it, particularly the awesome scenery of Alberta, Canada – beautifully shot in CinemaScope and Technicolor by William Daniels – substituting for the Yukon Territory. Here, Stewart's Jeff Webster is a rugged individualist hired to drive a herd of cattle and pack mules to the Gold Rush town of Dawson in the mid-19th century by saloon owner Ronda Castle (Ruth Roman). Along the way, he's harassed by a crooked sheriff (John McIntire) and several of his hired guns, as well as the assorted predators drawn to the prospectors and their bounty. It's a hard-edged story that pulls no punches, and Stewart is every bit as good as he was in *The Naked Spur*, playing a man willing to die if he can't be left alone. Walter Brennan plays his loyal sidekick, Corinne Calvet is a young French woman smitten with Webster, and Harry Morgan (Colonel Sherman Potter on the M*A*S*H television series) does a turn as a shifty cowhand. [Trivia note: By the time Stewart made this movie he had become comfortable in the saddle, and he rode the same horse in all five of his westerns with Mann. His sometime co-star and close friend Henry Fonda even painted a portrait of Stewart sitting on the horse, called Pie (which he calls by name in the movie), and Stewart had it framed and mounted in his living room – the portrait, not the horse] **[W]**

The Long Riders
1980 – Walter Hill

A rough-tempered but earnest telling of one of the most notorious episodes of post-Civil War American history, covering the relatively brief rampage of a gang of former Confederate soldiers from Missouri: the Millers, the Youngers and, best known, Frank and Jesse James. Somewhat of a gimmick, the cast features four sets of brothers: the Carradines, David, Keith and Robert; the Guests, Christopher and Nicholas; the Keaches, James and Stacy – who also produced the movie – and the Quaids, Randy and Dennis. One of the movie's distinctions is its frequent use of slow-motion to depict the most violent sequences. There's also a nasty, close-quarters knife duel between rivals Cole Younger (David Carradine) and Sam Starr (James Remar) for the affections of Starr's wife Belle (Pamela Reed), another notorious historical character. Ry Cooder provided the suitably twangy western score. [Trivia notes: 1) The Keach brothers came up with the idea of portraying the Jameses after playing Orville and Wilbur in a TV miniseries about the Wright Brothers. 2) Dennis Quaid and Pamela Reed appeared three years later in Philip Kaufman's space age epic *The Right Stuff* (PF5) as astronaut Gordon Cooper and his wife Trudy] [Caution: graphic violence, including that nasty barfight, and sexuality] **[W]**

Maverick
1994 – Richard Donner
Taking a break from the *Lethal Weapon* series, Donner and Mel Gibson here worked with James Garner and Jodie Foster on this big screen version of the popular TV series of the 1950s and early '60s, in which Garner had starred in the title role. It's more of a romp in period garb than a true western, with the principals having a grand old time, and with many friends and associates of the director and stars showing up in witty cameos. The plot, such as it is, involves Bret Maverick (Gibson) attempting to gather the funds needed to enter a high-stakes poker tournament aboard the sternwheel steamboat Lauren Belle. He's aided – but often hindered – by Zane Cooper (Garner) and Annabelle Bransford (Foster), two characters who might or might not be who they seem. Really, that's all you need to know, except that Gibson's *Lethal Weapon* co-star Danny Glover turns up in an improbable cameo, the versatile Alfred Molina provides the villainous role, the venerable James Coburn supplies an air of mischief as an associate of Garner's, and that despite the periodic and dangerous-looking predicaments, the only death, aside from the bad guys, is by natural causes. [Caution: mild sexuality and violence] **[W]**

North to Alaska
1960 – Henry Hathaway (and John Wayne)
As with *Cat Ballou* and *Maverick*, John Wayne appears in more of a frontier comedy than a western but containing many of the signature Wayne movie elements. Wayne plays Sam McCord, a

prospector in Alaska territory's great gold rush at the turn of the 20th century. Stewart Granger and popular singer Fabian play his partners, George and Billy Pratt. And the elegant but miscast French actress Capucine co-stars as Angel, a lady of ill repute. Throw in comedian–actor Ernie Kovacs as Frankie, the "slickest operator north of the Yukon," and you've got the makings of a diverting if lightweight tale of life on the grubby, mud-filled frontier – though the movie was shot mostly in California. Johnny Horton sang the popular theme song, but Fabian gets to perform a ballad as well. [Trivia note: Two tragic associations with the movie, both involving fatal highway crashes: Horton was killed before the movie was released, and Kovacs died in a separate incident two years later] **[W]**

Ride the High Country
1962 – co-written and directed by Sam Peckinpah
This might be the quintessential western, featuring two of the genre's most enduring presences, Joel McCrae, in his last significant role, and Randolph Scott, who appeared in 60 horse operas, more than anyone except John Wayne. They play, respectively, Steve Judd, an aging former marshal hired to guard a gold shipment, and Gil Westrum, an old friend whom Judd wants to ride through the … high country of California's Sierra Nevada range to help deliver the shipment. The men are joined on their journey by two others: Heck Longtree (minor player Ron Starr), an associate of Gil's who aims to steal the gold, and Elsa Knudsen (stage and TV actress Mariette Hartley in her debut), a runaway daughter who's secretly engaged to Billy Hammond (future TV star James Drury), one of the gold miners. From there, as you might expect, complications, double-crosses and showdowns ensue, all of them violent and most of them lethal. It's a raw portrayal of the American west in in the early 20th century, skillfully directed by Peckinpah, a graduate of TV in his second film. And it's a surprisingly touching swansong for McCrae and Scott, two of the best actors ever associated with the genre. [Trivia note: Though Hartley and Drury fought, literally, onscreen, they became friends in real life, and she appeared several times in his

popular western series The Virginian – as did several other members of the cast] [Caution: violence, including sexual violence] **[W]**

The Undefeated
1969—Andrew V. McLaglen

I've included plenty of John Wayne westerns in the three compilations, but I couldn't conclude without adding this one, a clunky favorite. Here, the Duke co-stars with Rock Hudson as, respectively, Union and Confederate officers just after the end of the Civil War who are forced to work together to fight the French, the Juaristas and some bad *banditos,* all in Mexico in a plot similar to *Major Dundee* (not on this list) but considerably more entertaining. The large cast features a host of familiar character actors as well as two members of the Los Angeles Rams football team, quarterback Roman Gabriel (here playing a Native American) and defensive lineman Merlin Olsen. [Trivia notes: 1) Despite their divergent personalities, Wayne and Hudson became good friends during the production. 2) At age 62, Wayne was becoming more vulnerable to injuries doing westerns. Here, he broke three ribs and injured his shoulder. And despite an unavoidable layoff to recover, he refused to stop filming his scenes, doing some with difficulty and in severe pain. 3) And as a closing, little-known tidbit about the iconic Wayne, he almost always wore lipstick on-camera. Not because of anything untoward but because his lips were unusually pale. Besides, who was going to ridicule him about such a thing?] [Caution: violence] **[W]**

50. Second (and Third) Acts

Earlier, I covered a dozen movies that were outright remakes of earlier titles. Here's a variation that quickly became popular in Hollywood: sequels. As the years went by, they grew more and more frequent, governed by the maxim that if such-and-such title made a good profit then duplicating it to some degree should succeed simply by name recognition. That's one reason why this category is my second lengthiest, with two dozen titles (three of them multiples) carrying on the names, or the spirit, of their predecessors. But most of them, with a few exemptions, are pale imitations. And because I've written at greater length elsewhere about almost all of the originals, I'll mention them (and where you can find them) and keep these capsules short and pithy.

Airplane II: The Sequel

1982 – Ken Finkelman (the directing trio's Airplane in P25)

In *Airplane II*, the original team of Zucker/Abrahams/Zucker – more about them momentarily – dropped out, as did Leslie Nielsen and a few others. But most of the original prime players are back, this time instead of riding, piloting or assisting a commercial airline flight in trouble they're riding, piloting or assisting a space shuttle to the moon – in trouble. And why not? Like its predecessor it's just an excuse for craziness, double-entendres, puns, sight gags and general nonsense, all done for laughs and, naturally, ending happily. [Trivia note: Regarding Zucker/Abrahams/Zucker: They chose not to do the sequel and even objected to its production. Artistic integrity? Over *Airplane*? Surely, *they* can't be serious] [Caution: no nudity but more crudity] [W]

The Bells of St. Mary's

1945 – Leo McCarey (McCarey's Going My Way in P25)

Ostensibly, Bing Crosby reprises his Oscar-winning role as Father O'Malley the previous year. Except McCarey, Crosby and cast actually completed this movie first. In it, O'Malley is delegated to the church of the title in an attempt to save it and its school from closure. He's assisted – and often resisted – in his efforts by Sister Mary Benedict (Ingrid Bergman). Like its predecessor, it's a sweet-tempered story, and despite the disagreements between the two principals, it ends happily. [Trivia note: *The Bells of St. Mary's* holds the distinction of being the first sequel ever nominated for a Best Picture Oscar, and like *Going My Way* it was the biggest box-office hit of the year] **[B&W]**

The Black Stallion Returns

1983 – Robert Dalva (Carroll Ballard's The Black Stallion in <u>PF5</u>)
A spotty but watchable sequel to the sublime original, this one takes place mostly in North Africa, where Alec Ramsey (Kelly Reno, star of the original, now four years older and a skilled and fearless rider but even less of an actor) has improbably pursued his beloved "Black." The horse has been kidnapped by a shadowy Arab figure who claims to be its rightful owner. Along the way, Alec meets a slimy villain (the terribly miscast Allen Garfield) and young Arab man named Raj (Italian-American actor Vincent Spano), who proves both worthy protector and trusted friend – though a rival rider. The wandering plot climaxes in a thrilling cross-desert race with Alec riding the Black, whom the Arabs call "Shêtân" (SHEE-tahn), and Raj atop his own horse against about a dozen others. Not nearly the caliber of its predecessor, which was directed by the great Carroll Ballard and photographed by the incomparable Caleb Deschanel, *The Black Stallion Returns* nevertheless should provide kid viewers with some exciting moments. [Caution: mild violence] **[W]**

Casino

1995 – Martin Scorsese
Not specifically a sequel; rather, a second attempt by Scorsese, writer Nicholas Pileggi and co-stars Robert De Niro and Joe Pesci to duplicate the success of *Goodfellas* (<u>PF5</u>) five years earlier. In fact, Casino couldn't be a sequel because they brought in perennial hood Frank Vincent (who was beaten to a pulp and buried alive in the previous movie) to play Pesci's brother and

comrade in crimes. With comedian Don Rickles in a rare dramatic role, and he's pretty good at it, applying his acerbic cabaret persona to a non-humorous medium. Some slick sequences, particularly when De Niro's character narrates the fine points of the casino business – this one in Las Vegas – but overall it lacks the humor and, odd as it might seem, the humanity of the predecessor. Also, Sharon Stone's hopelessly drug-addicted wife of De Niro is thoroughly unpleasant to watch. [Caution: rough language, sexuality and graphic violence] **[W]**

Cocoon: The Return
1988 – Daniel Petrie (Ron Howard's Cocoon in PF5)
The principal cast ... returns from the original, continuing the story about a group of senior citizens who have left the bounds of Earth to commune with aliens, now back to reconnect with a few old friends and settle some unfinished business, including retrieving one of the alien left-behinds who has been discovered and confined to a research hospital for testing. Not as fresh and appealing as the original, it does hit some sentimental highs. **[W]**

Creed 2
2018 – Stephen Caple Jr. (Ryan Coogler's Creed in PF5)
Michael B. Jordan, who has distinguished himself as a fine young actor, returns in the title role, again co-starring with Sylvester Stallone, who remains in fine form. This time, Jordan's Adonis Creed character engages in sort of a proxy rematch. "Donnie," the son of Apollo Creed, will be fighting Viktor Drago (Florian Munteanu), son of Ivan Drago (Dolph Lundgren), the man who killed his father in the ring before Stallone's Rocky Balboa dished him some justice, American style. [Caution: boxing violence and rough language] **[W]**

Escape from the Planet of the Apes
1971 – Don Taylor (Franklin Schaffner's Planet of the Apes in P25)
Like *Back to the Future Part III* (PF5), this one's a third act but better than its predecessor and would have made a fine sequel to the original. In a topsy-turvy plot, now it's the intelligent apes (Kim

Hunter and Roddy McDowall in heavy makeup) who tumble through time to confront our contemporary human civilization and are treated as freaks and outcasts. [Caution: violence] **[W]**

Evan Almighty
2007 – Tom Shadyak (Shadyak's Bruce Almighty)
Instead of Jim Carrey as the tormented, eponymous Bruce, this time it's Steve Carell as Evan in a witty, light-hearted and surprisingly endearing take on the legend of Noah – complete with long white beard and a real, full-size Ark, built to biblical specifications. Morgan Freeman reprises his role as the Almighty. **[W]**

The Expendables 2 (and 3)
2012 and 2014 – Simon West and Patrick Hughes (Sylvester Stallone's Expendables in PF5)
Credit Sylvester Stallone for being able to make fun of his previous tough-guy roles and for recruiting almost all of the popular action heroes of the time, both of which he initiated in the first installment (PF5) and continues with these two sequels. The movies don't use plotting so much as formula, so I'll skip describing what's essentially the same story repeated. Instead, consider the casting. Participating in the extreme mayhem, punctuated by frequent wisecracks (such as Stallone saying, while gruesomely dispatching a bad guy, "Rest in pieces"), are such action luminaries as Jean-Claude Van Damme, Wesley Snipes, Mel Gibson, Harrison Ford, Arnold Schwarzenegger, Bruce Willis, Jet Li and Chuck Norris, accompanied by Stallone's frequent co-star Dolph Lundgren and even TV's Kelsey Grammer. The mayhem? Let's say it naturally involves the excessive use of heavy-duty firearms and explosives, the spectacular dispatching of all kinds of transport and, of course, causing the violent end of hordes of bad guys. Don't take any of it seriously, and you'll be in for a rollicking good time. [Viewing note: As of this writing, there was an *Expendables 4* in production. But the sequel has been bouncing around for seven years, Stallone's role will be limited

and my guess is it live up to the original trilogy] [Caution: rough language and outrageous violence] **[W]**

Faraway, So Close!
1993 – Germany – co-written and directed by Wim Wenders (Wenders' Wings of Desire in P25)
A genuine sequel – after all, the original ended with the title card, "To be continued…" – but this one's in English and features a guest appearance by former Soviet Union premier Mikhail Gorbachev. Once again, it features two angels passively but sympathetically observing the lives of Berliners. Again, one of the angels desires to become human, which occurs, bringing with it the unintended consequences and dire choices associated with such transformations. And again, Bruno Ganz, Peter Falk and Otto Sander reprise their roles – and their divine (or mortal) statuses. Dreamy, surprising and intelligent, it's sophisticated fantasy at its best. Along with Gorbachev, Willem Dafoe and Nastassja Kinski appear in cameos. [Caution: adult themes, violence and sexuality] **[B&W, with color sequences] [W]**

Father's Little Dividend
1951 – Vincente Minnelli (Minnelli's Father of the Bride in P25)
Continuing Spencer Tracy's domestic odyssey, previously as the father of the bride, and here, one year later, the expectant grandfather of his daughter Liz Taylor's child in an irresistibly sweet follow-up. Uncomplicated and simply entertaining. **[B&W]**

Ghostbusters II
1989 – Ivan Reitman (Reitman's Ghostbusters in PF5)
The boys – and Sigourney – return to save Manhattan again. As the tag line says, "The superstars of the supernatural are back." If you recall, in the final battle in the original, the Ghostbusters (Dan Aykroyd, Ernie Hudson, Bill Murray and Harold Ramis) had to battle a giant Stay Puft Marshmallow Man. This time, in a twist, they enlist the help of one of New York's landmarks to come to the city's aid. Clumsier than its predecessor, it's still entertaining. [Caution: language and slightly scary scenes] **[W]**

415

Grumpier Old Men
1995 – Howard Deutsch (Donald Petrie's Grumpy Old Men elsewhere)
Matthau and Lemmon reprise their roles, joined again by Ann-Margret and adding Sophia Loren, who's still dazzling at 61. Burgess Meredith and Ann Morgan Guilbert add some naughty byplay as, respectively, Lemmon's father and Sophia's mother. [Caution: language] **[W]**

Hot Shots! (and) Hot Shots! Part Deux
1991 and 1993 – both co-written and directed by Jim Abrahams
I'm including both installments in this category because, technically, they're merely carrying on the silliness of the *Airplane!* franchise and are the products of one of its creators. This one takes aim at *Top Gun*, the Tom Cruise vehicle featuring … hot-shot Navy fighter pilots. Charlie Sheen stars as "Topper" Harley in the pilot role. As for the plot, well, if you accept that not much will make sense, that every scene is constructed to reach a punchline, and that it's all a sendup of other movies, you'll probably enjoy it just as much as if you knew what to expect. The supporting cast includes Lloyd Bridges (father of Beau and Jeff, veteran of the *Airplane!* movies and switched to comedy instead of drama late in his career) as a looney admiral, Cary Elwes as an aerial rival and Valeria Golino as Topper's therapist and love interest – a woman whose … um, talents include being able to launch an olive out of her navel into her mouth. [Caution: language and mild sexuality] **[W]**

* * *

The sequel resumes Charlie Sheen's character Topper Harley, but instead of his being a Navy pilot, this time he's a Rambo clone sent to stage an assault on Saddam Hussein's headquarters. It's the same drill as the earlier movie: throwing in everything – including the kitchen sink – if it will possibly get a laugh. It works, fitfully, but it works, particularly a witty scene that features Sheen the younger parodying his Chris Taylor character from *Platoon*, meeting up with Martin Sheen reprising his Captain Willard role from *Apocalypse Now* (both in P25). [Caution: language, mild sexuality and cartoon violence – including a running tab of the body count] **[W]**

Indiana Jones and the Last Crusade
1989 – Steven Spielberg (Spielberg's Raiders of the Lost Ark in PF5)

In this third installment of the franchise, Sean Connery joins Harrison Ford, Denholm Elliott and John Rhys-Davies as Dr. Henry Jones, Indiana's estranged father and, surprising, his romantic rival. I rate this one higher than the second installment, the distasteful and forced *Indiana Jones and the Temple of Doom* (not on my lists) – plus we get to see how Indie got that scar on his chin and why he hates snakes. But it's often forced and implausible. As the Monty Pythons attempted in one of their film outings, the Joneses are after the legendary Holy Grail. How they find it and what happens as a result might leave you giggling at its silliness, particularly the final scene with the holy relic and its guardian. [Caution: violence] **[W]**

Lethal Weapon 2 (and 3 – and 4)
1989 and 1992 and 1998 – all by Richard Donner (Donner's Lethal Weapon in P25)

Another combination of a franchise. Mel Gibson and Danny Glover are joined by Joe Pesci and, eventually, Rene Russo and Chris Rock, to create the most popular cop-action series Hollywood ever produced – though it's chock-full of increasingly excessive and implausible violence and mayhem and is decidedly not for the genteel-minded. [Caution: sexuality and graphic violence] **[W]**

Mary Poppins Returns
2018 – Rob Marshall (Robert Stevenson's Mary Poppins in PF5)

A risky proposition after 54 years, given that its predecessor became the Disney Studio's biggest hit and achieved immortality due to the fabulous performances of Julie Andrews in her Oscar-winning title role, and Dick Van Dyke as Bert, the chimney sweep, plus the unforgettable songs of the Sherman brothers. Here, the

417

two Banks children, grown up and facing hardships during the Great Depression, again need salvation from Mary (this time played – and impersonated well – by Emily Blunt). She's aided in her efforts by Jack (Lin-Manuel Miranda), a charming lamplighter. The movie's most memorable aspect, however, is the return appearance by Van Dyke, 93 years young and playing Dawes Jr. – son of the ancient banker he had played, in a dual role, in the original. The great Angela Lansbury – who died in 2022 at age 96 – turns in a lovely cameo as the "Balloon Lady," here at 93. Rob Marshall, who did the Oscar-winning *Chicago* (not here) in 2002, directed. [Slight caution: a couple of scenes of children in danger] **[W]**

National Lampoon's Christmas Vacation
1989 – Jeremiah S. Chechik (Harold Ramis's National Lampoon's Vacation elsewhere)
An often clumsy and crude continuation of the saga of the Griswald family also contains a few genuinely touching moments – emphasis on "a few" – and some genuinely funny moments as well, most of them provided by Randy Quaid as the good-hearted but misbegotten "Cousin" Eddie. [Caution: language and sexuality] **[W]**

The Odd Couple II
1998 – Howard Deutsch (Gene Saks's The Odd Couple in PF5)
I admit I had my doubts when I learned that Walter Matthau and Jack Lemmon were returning as Oscar Madison and Felix Unger, their unforgettably incompatible duo from three decades earlier. But reunite they do, and it's a diverting reunion, written – as was the original – by Neil Simon. After 17 years of noncommunication, the duo must travel to California for the wedding of Oscar's son (Jonathan Silverman) to Felix's daughter (Lisa Waltz). Naturally, the journey runs amok, requiring them to think fast to extricate themselves from a series of scrapes – potentially dangerous but none really serious – to arrive at the wedding. Working together for the 10th and last time, Matthau and Lemmon display effortless

timing together, and they put on a pleasing valedictory show. [Caution: language] **[W]**

One Special Night
1999 – Roger Young
Like *Casino*, this made-for-TV Christmas story technically isn't a sequel. But it does unite Julie Andrews and James Garner romantically for the third time following 1964's *The Americanization of Emily* and 1982's *Victor/Victoria* (both in PF5). In a convenient contrivance, the two stars play Robert Woodward and Catherine Howard, two strangers marooned during a blizzard and forced to take refuge in a wooded cabin near the road. Strangers, they live in the same community but have traveled in separate circles. They're brought together again at the local hospital, where she's a pediatric cardiologist, and he's dealing with his grandchild's damaged heart at birth. Then, through the inevitable misdirections and fateful interventions, they finally get together. Predictable, yes, and sometimes feeling like just another Hallmark movie (though it was produced for CBS), it's elevated by the enduring appeal of the two stars. **[W]**

Queen and Country
2014 – England – written, produced and directed by John Boorman (Boorman's Hope and Glory in PF5)
An iffy continuation of Bill Rowan's story after Boorman's wonderful, fictionalized autobiography 27 years earlier. In this one, Rowan (Callum Turner) has grown into a young man and is preparing to join his British Army comrades in combat in Korea in 1952, the year of Queen Elizabeth II's coronation. He shares his coming-of-age adventures with his friend Percy (American actor Caleb Landry Jones), he romances a mysterious young woman (Tamsin Egerton) and develops a friendship with another (Aimee-Ffion Edwards). Told straightforwardly, the movie lacks the magic and sense of wonder of the original. It's as if Bill Rowan has grown up dull. One bright spot: Vanessa Kirby, smashing in her role as Princess Margaret in the magnificent British TV series The Crown, supplies some crackle as Bill's older sister, Dawn. And

David Hayman reprises his role as Bill's father, Clive. [Caution: sexuality] **[W]**

The Second Best Exotic Marigold Hotel
2015 – John Madden (Madden's The Best Exotic Marigold Hotel in P25)

Continuing the story of a group of elderly expatriate Brits attempting to begin new lives in Jaipur, India, with the original cast members, minus Tom Wilkinson (whose character died in the original), plus Richard Gere, Tamsin Grieg and David Strathairn, picking up pretty much where they left off. Except this time the story focuses more on the impending marriage of hotelier Sonny (Kev Patel) to Sunaina (Tina Desai), while Maggie Smith takes over narrating duties from Judi Dench. Several new subplots and conflicts, but all ends well at the wedding, featuring a lively ensemble dance number. Almost as beguiling as the original, everyone seems to be enjoying the reprise. Thomas Newman once again supplied the … exotic score. [Caution: mild sexuality] **[W]**

Son of Paleface
1952 – Frank Tashlin

Maybe put aside your high-falootin' tastes for a spell and enjoy this second bit of pure silliness from one of America's immortal funny men, Leslie Towns "Bob" Hope. Here, in the same year as *Road to Bali* but sans Hope and Lamour, he plays Junior Potter, a Harvard grad who heads west to the town of Sawbuck Pass to claim a stolen inheritance. There, he meets a singing cowboy (legendary singing cowboy Roy Rogers) and a buxom dancehall girl (the buxom Jane Russell), and … well, how could you resist a movie whose credits include, "Trigger, Smartest Horse in the Movies," and "8 Beautiful Girlies (count 'em)," and a song titled, "There's a Cloud in My Valley of Sunshine"? Why is the movie in this category? Its predecessor, *The Paleface*, a 1948 feature directed by Norman Z. McLeod, also starred Hope and Russell. But it's, excuse the pun, a pale precursor. Though successful at the box office, the first movie hasn't aged well, isn't on this list and is worth no further mention.

Epilogue: What Went Wrong?

Consider this a teaser for part of my possible next compilation, in which I'm contemplating adding 501 more titles to the 1500 already covered. The difference is I won't necessarily be recommending any of the new entrées. Some I'll actually be panning as a matter of useful information, such as these 20. Each was written and/or directed by a person of distinction and accomplishment, someone whose other work I have praised, sometimes profusely – and I'll mention those movies as we go along (all reviewed in PF5 unless otherwise noted). I'm also including, at the end, a gigantic production by a novice director that involves arguably the most popular movie character of all time. Whatever, this group illustrates a point made long ago by my late friend, mentor and screenwriting teacher Sheldon Tromberg. Shelly used to say that every movie is a miracle; meaning it's such a daunting task, with so many potential pitfalls, that merely completing a production can be considered miraculous. Nevertheless, each of these is a bona fide dud, whether artistically or financially, though most still offer some entertainment value. But given the talent involved, they all should've known better.

1941

1979 – Steven Spielberg

In 1979, Spielberg was the hottest director in Hollywood, following his box-office blockbuster *Jaws* in 1975 and his dazzling science fiction tale *Close Encounters of the Third Kind* two years later. At the time, the public probably would have bought tickets to his next movie sight unseen. When it was announced that Spielberg would be doing a special-effects-laden, World War II-era comedy with an all-star cast – including, among many others, the wildly popular John Belushi and Dan Aykroyd from NBC's

Saturday Night Live – the stage seemed set for blockbuster number three. But in this case, boy, were the expectations ever misplaced! The production suffered from many problems, including drugs – lots of them – for just about everybody involved. The result is much more sad than funny, considering the enormous waste of talent and resources. Example: A miniature beachside Ferris wheel sequence cost an astounding (at the time) $2 million to shoot – because it didn't work the first time and had to be completely rebuilt and shot again. Still, some of the effects sequences – back in the days before CGI – really are dazzling; likewise some of the comedy. Plus, there's a witty send-up of *Jaws* at the beginning, and the peppy martial score by John Williams is the best of all. But pay close attention to the dialog, because as Gary Arnold wrote about *1941* at the time, "a bad movie tattles on itself," and you can hear just as many pejoratives, screams, moans and complaints from the cast as you're likely to utter yourself – particularly if you watch the closing credits. There's also a scene in which General Stillwell (Robert Stack), who headed Pacific Coast defenses when the war began, watches *Dumbo* in a theater – *Dumbo* was released in 1941. As he sits there, moved to tears by a sad sequence in the cartoon, it makes you think, "Please, let's just keep watching *this*!" Over the years, Steven Spielberg has built, and in many cases justifiably, a gigantic reputation. He is, at this point, the most successful commercial director of all time. He or his movies have been nominated for Academy Awards in each of the past six decades – a singular achievement. With *1941*, however, surprisingly soon after those first two blockbusters, Spielberg hit the bottom of his career, and for the worst of reasons: He vastly overestimated his audience's capacity to accept crudity and nonsense. [Caution: sexuality, constant demeaning treatment of women and occasional profanity] **[W]**

Avatar
2009 – written, produced and directed by James Cameron
You might be surprised at my including one of the biggest-grossing movies of all time (approaching an astounding $3 billion

at last count) in this category. Cameron's long-awaited follow-up to the Oscar-winning *Titanic* also turned out to be – until its budget was blown away by *No Time to Die* – the most expensive movie ever made. That was to be expected. If there was anything the director had shown in his 25-year career as a major director – whose smash hits included the first two *Terminator* movies, *Aliens* and, especially, *The Abyss* as well as *Titanic* – it was an awesome capacity for technical preparation. In *The Abyss*, Cameron used the largest water tank in the world to create an underwater environment. And in *Titanic*, his crew built a nearly full-sized replica of the ill-fated ocean liner and decorated its interior to perfection. As the director once said of his movies, "all the money is on the screen," meaning he spared no expense to entertain audiences. *Avatar* was no exception. Cameron's science-fiction tale of Pandora, a distant, idyllic world threatened by economic interests seeking its precious (fictional) mineral would become his most ambitious production to date. *Avatar* would be a hybrid, a movie that bridged the gap between computer-generated, animated characters and real actors, something that required Cameron to wait 10 years for technology to catch up with his ambition and four years to create. And, true to form, Cameron again spared no expense in realizing his vision. He hired language experts to create a complete dialect for the Pandorans. He transported his cast to Hawai`i to familiarize them with the tropical rainforest environment. He commissioned the finest scenic artists he could find to depict the planet's lush landscapes. And so on. I must admit, the result is visually stunning. Every scene – every shot – has been exquisitely rendered. For his efforts, bordering on obsession, Cameron succeeded in providing a captivating vision of a fantasy world, as impeccably finished as Walt Disney's classically animated masterpiece *Pinocchio*.

* * *

So, what's my beef? It's something that began early on with Cameron, going back to the original *Terminator*. Despite his overwhelming visual sense, and his unparalleled ability to stage action, Cameron's stories have often lacked sophistication, subtlety and, that most essential element of the best movies, surprise. Boiled down to basics, the story of *Avatar* has been told a thousand times – parts of it by Cameron himself in his earlier features – and often, very often, better by others. An example? One critic correctly noted *Avatar* is, at its core, *Dances with Wolves* in outer space. Another likewise asked, appropriately, if there was a single moment in Avatar where you didn't know what was going to happen next. I take nothing away from Cameron's dedication to his craft. But once a moviemaker completes his work, and projects the result on the screen, he becomes subject to the judgment of the ultimate authority: the viewer. As an avid member of that group, I recall the words of Shakespeare's Hamlet; "The play's the thing." Look it up. [Caution: computer-animated violence] **[W] [3D]**

Beat the Devil
1953 – co-written and directed by John Huston
From the massive in scale to the minuscule – though the story does share something with *Avatar*. Two years after Huston and Humphrey Bogart returned from filming *The African Queen*, and 12 years after *The Maltese Falcon*, they collaborated again, this time on a story I defy you to explain. There's good reason for that. Huston, working with Truman Capote as his screenwriting collaborator, handed newly written script pages to the cast each day. The group, including Jennifer Jones, Gina Lollobrigida (in her first English role – playing Bogie's wife), Robert Morley and Peter Lorre, tried their best. But the result was a mess. Don't believe me? Watch for yourself. The producers at one point failed to renew the copyright, so the movie has been in the public domain for some time. The connection with *Avatar*? The plot concerns an attempt to exploit a valuable mineral – in this case uranium – from a primitive land. **[B&W]**

Black Sunday
1977 – John Frankenheimer
Robert Shaw, Bruce Dern and Marthe Keller in a suspense yarn involving European terrorists plotting to explode a bomb during the Super Bowl in Miami. Frankenheimer, who skillfully helmed

two classic thrillers, *The Train* and *The Manchurian Candidate* (P25), here presents a movie that's so inflated, tiresome, predictable and often laughable that you can't believe it's the product of a top-of-the-line director. Likewise the screenplay, co-written by Ernest Lehman, who once was capable of *North by Northwest* and *The Sound of Music*. A small example: Law enforcement, alerted to the possibility of a terror attack, sets up security checkpoints at all entrances to the football stadium. They're screening everyone, but somehow they allow the chief terrorist (Dern) to slip by. As Gary Arnold wrote in The Washington Post, that moment is "a scream" for the audience because, from the obvious expression on his face, "he might as well be wearing a sign around his neck labelled 'Psycho.'" And a large example: Today, CGI would make the task of staging a lighter-than-air vehicle attacking a Super Bowl crowd a relative snap. Back then, however, it presented a logistical nightmare – which, unfortunately, Frankenheimer and his crew couldn't overcome. The sequence involves some quick edits, forced perspectives and, ludicrously, a mockup of a portion of the Goodyear Blimp supposedly threatening the crowd. Boy, does it not work! [Caution: violence] **[W]**

Blame it on Rio
1984 – Stanley Donen

Guys, how could you do this? The director of *Singin' in the Rain* and *Charade*, two of my top favorites; Larry Gelbart, the writer and creator of MASH, one of my TV favorites; as well as the venerable Michael Caine, here stoop to a sex comedy with an enormous ick factor. Two American dads (Caine and Joseph Bologna) take their teenage daughters (19-year-old Michelle Johnson, and Demi Moore at age 22 but looking considerably younger) on vacation to Rio de Janeiro without their wives. Soon, Johnson's character confesses a sexual attraction to Caine's and ends up seducing him. The so-called comedy stems from the misunderstandings and misdirections that occur when Bologna's character finds out about his daughter's misbehavior, but not that Caine is the guilty party. Except it's unfunny as well as uncomfortable and consistently awkward. I think Gary Arnold explained it best in his Washington

Post review when he called the movie "atrocious" and "the pits," adding, "Donen's failure to derive much sensual stimulation from the setting itself may betray a fundamental embarrassment about it all." Ironic, maybe, but a half-century earlier, the RKO studio released *Flying Down to Rio*, a rather risqué movie for its day. Along with introducing two dancers named Astaire and Rogers, the whole thing was fun. One reason: All of the sexual interplay was between adults. [Caution: inappropriate sexuality] **[W]**

Bobby Deerfield
1977 – Sydney Pollack
Back to adult drama, but maybe the biggest stinker of the bunch, from Pollack of all people, who gave us the gorgeous *Out of Africa* and the irresistible *Tootsie*, plus Al Pacino, who needs no further description, in the title role. Here, he plays an emotionally distant Grand Prix racecar driver who falls in love with a free-spirited but terminally ill cancer patient (Marthe Keller, again with her distinct lisp. Example: "Wisks, Deewfield. You like taking wisks?") The basic idea is that Keller's character is supposed to elicit the necessary emotions Deerfield has kept buried. Fine. In capable hands, that's the makings of solid melodrama. But here? The most powerful actor of his generation is consistently dull and uninteresting. And I won't even get into Pacino attempting a Mae West impersonation. Using one of Gary Arnold's reviews again, he called *Bobby Deerfield* the "landmark embarrassment of [Pacino's] career," writing that here, he "resembles an expensive, coddled property rather than an imaginatively engaged actor." Yep. [Caution: sexuality and (a few) intense racing scenes] **[W]**

The Bourne Ultimatum
2007 – Paul Greengrass
When Robert Ludlum's fictional CIA super-assassin exploded onto the screen in 2002 in *The Bourne Identity*, with Matt Damon in the title role, it represented what I considered a step up even from the James Bond series in sophisticated storytelling. Bourne, nearly dying in a botched mission, and anguished over the loss of his … identity to traumatic amnesia, proved an exceptionally

compelling character. Then, two years later, Greengrass took over from Doug Liman's capable hands to direct an even better installment, *The Bourne Supremacy*, which like *The Godfather Part II* broadened and deepened the original story and characters. And now? Alas, Greengrass and his cast and crew took a step too far, without seriously considering in what new and satisfying direction they could take Bourne and his dilemma. The result, to put it kindly, is repetitive as heck. Every part of the plot already was done – more skillfully and engagingly – in the first two movies. Here, Bourne continues to be pursued by shadowy operatives from his home agency, one by one dispatching them in narrow escapes while his current superior, Pamela Landy (Joan Allen, reprising her role from the first sequel), continues to try to reel him in. It's big and complex and showy, of course, but ... ultimately pointless. They should have stopped with *Supremacy*. Its ending, like *Godfather II*, was quietly shattering. [Caution: violence] **[W]**

The Boys from Brazil
1978 – Franklin J. Schaffner
Remember, in the Introduction to my original compilation when I mentioned how common it is that moviegoers differ in their reactions, and I specifically mentioned sometimes sitting side-by-side through the same movie with Gary Arnold and ending up with opposite reactions? We didn't screen this one at the same time, but we did react oppositely. Gary, in his Post review, called *The Boys from Brazil* "admirably crafted and surprisingly effective." And as usual, he made a strong case. On the other hand, I didn't buy it, for one of the reasons Gary praised it. He wrote that the story was a "synthesis of accumulating suspense, detective work, pseudoscientific speculation and historical wish-fulfillment." Based on Ira Levin's novel, Gregory Peck and Laurence Olivier star in this tale about an attempt to produce multiple clones of Adolph Hitler – hence the title. But Schaffner, who gave us the magnificent *Patton*, here attempts to duplicate Levin's extremely intricate plot. The movie begins with so many disparate introductory sequences that you begin to think he's

using discarded parts from other plots. And they're all vague, overly mysterious and bordering on dramatic carelessness – the kinds of things that tend to unsuspend disbelief. Example: How could an amateur, ragtag Nazi hunter in Paraguay (Steve Gutenberg in an early role) afford to make a call to Vienna, where Olivier's character is based, and be placed on hold interminably without being cut off by the international operator? Such lapses, and the excessive mélange, really never let up, keeping things confusing and at times annoying. And, composer Jerry Goldsmith, who did the immortal *Patton* score, here creates a weird mélange of his own, fusing a Viennese waltz theme with harsh and strident string phrases resembling his work for *The Omen*. Plus, Olivier as a frail Nazi hunter, à la Simon Wiesenthal or even his Van Helsing character in *Dracula*? That I can accept. But Peck in heavy makeup as a Nazi villain? Unh-uh. [Caution: violence] **[W]**

The Chase
1966 – Arthur Penn
Imagine a movie that featured a Southern potboiler drama à la William Faulkner whose adaptation was written by Lillian Hellman based on a play by Horton Foote – who two years earlier had adapted *To Kill a Mockingbird* for the screen. Imagine also that it starred Marlon Brando and Robert Duvall six years before *The Godfather*, and Robert Redford and Jane Fonda one year before they charmed audiences as newlyweds in *Barefoot in the Park*. What if it featured solid supporting players E.G. Marshall, James Fox, Janice Rule, Clifton James, Martha Hyer and Angie Dickinson? What if the great John Barry composed the music, and Maurice Binder – who did some of the best of the James Bond movies – created the title sequence? And what if the whole thing was produced by Sam Spiegel, among whose credits were *On the Waterfront* (P25), *The Bridge on the River Kwai* and *Lawrence of Arabia*, Oscar-winners all? Wouldn't that get you anticipating you were about to see something amazing? Amazing, yes, but alas not in the way you think. *The Chase* contains all of those ingredients and still turns out to be a colossal dud. Every scene – and nearly

428

every shot – seems either overblown or devoid of energy. There's not a single moment that feels emotionally true, and every one of those talented actors appears absolutely ridiculous. There's Redford, for example, playing of all things a loser of a character named Bubber (not a misspelling), an escaped convict with a longstanding score to settle with several of the characters. There's Fonda, who is utterly unconvincing as Bubber's white-trash wife. There's Duvall as a shy, creepily resentful wuss. And then there's Brando, playing a redneck sheriff – a role that would win Rod Steiger an Oscar the very next year in *In the Heat of the Night* – with so little energy he can't even speak his lines without slurring or mumbling them. Why watch at all? Because here is perhaps *the* textbook lesson in how even the best moviemaking talents can go awry, and they do so without exception. There's plenty of blame to spread around, but most of it must fall on director Penn, who four years earlier had helmed *The Miracle Worker* (P25) and two years later would do *Bonnie and Clyde* (elsewhere) – both of which produced acting Oscars – so you'd think he would have been capable of better. I have to confess the movie remains somewhat of a guilty pleasure for its portrayal of what passed for steamy behavior in the '60s. [Trivia note: Penn shot the fight scenes at a slower camera speed, so Brando gets bombarded with real punches, but they're much gentler than they appear] **[W]**

The Cheap Detective
1978 – written by Neil Simon

Gary Arnold and I did agree about this one, and I can convey my reaction by describing one image. If you think Peter Falk, in the title role and standing in his office pointing a gun at an old-fashioned telephone mouthpiece is funny, then this is the comedy for you. Otherwise…? And yet it's Neil Simon, who over the years generated some of the wittiest and most popular stage-to-screen comedies of the 20th century, such as *The Odd Couple*, *Barefoot in the Park* and *The Goodbye Girl*, not to mention his semi-autobiographical trilogy beginning with *Brighton Beach Memoirs* (P25). Here, after a slick opening sequence, and a funny – if you can call them funny – series of murders, and despite the impressive supporting cast, the comedy gets weaker and weaker, to the point where you feel worn out at the end, as though the sheer effort of trying to laugh at what's been presented was an exertion. Gary explained the problem in his Washington Post review. He wrote that the movie reminds you "how narrow the margin for error is in parody. There's a reason why the best [Sid] Caesar (one of the cast members here) or Carol Burnett film spoofs were quarter-hour distillations." I agree. One of the best parodies I've seen, *Dead Men Don't Wear Plaid*, generates good laughs for about two-thirds of its running time before petering out. This one doesn't sustain its humor for even a fraction of that. Plus, never forget the admonition of English stage actor Edmund Kean, who said on his deathbed, "Dying is easy; comedy is hard." [Caution: language and mild sexuality] **[W]**

Congo
1995 – Frank Marshall

In *The Chase*, I described how gathering even the best talent and ingredients in a movie's production cannot guarantee success. Well, *Congo* follows in that dubious tradition. It's based on a novel by Michael Crichton (*Jurassic Park*), with an adaptation by John Patrick Shanley (*Moonstruck*). Jerry Goldsmith (*Patton*) provided the score. Allen Daviau (*The Color Purple* and *Empire of the Sun*) did the cinematography. Legendary makeup-effects artist Stan Winston (*The Terminator* and *Aliens*) applied his special skills. And director Marshall and his wife, producer Kathleen Kennedy, worked with Steven Spielberg on several of his greatest hits. The result? A colossal, laughable, jaw-dropping dud. I won't even go into the plot, except to say it involves, no surprise, an expedition into the ... Congo region of Africa by a group of individuals with diverging motivations; a young, female, sign-language-trained mountain gorilla looking to return home; a lost diamond mine thought to belong to King Solomon that's guarded by murderous primates, and an active volcano. Short version: None of it works. And about the cast and their performances? Suffice it to say that two veteran character actors – Joe Pantoliano and Delroy Lindo – chose to be uncredited. That might have been the wisest course

430

for all concerned. Two others, Ernie Hudson and Laura Linney, try gamely to overcome their miscasting (he as a soldier of fortune and she a former CIA special operator), but to no avail. [Caution: excessive gore, both human and animal] **[W]**

The Deep
1976 – Peter Yates
Four aspects make this one, based on Peter Benchley's follow-up novel to Jaws, worth watching: 1) Jacqueline Bisset frequently … um, displays her perfect form, 2) the principals (Bisset, Nick Nolte and Robert Shaw) actually work convincingly underwater, 3) the underwater photography, by Al Giddings and Stan Waterman, is gorgeous, and 4) John Barry composed another sexy, silky score. Otherwise, the director of the delightful *Breaking Away* gives us lame thriller fare, involving a pair of lost treasures found by a newlywed couple (Nolte and Bisset) on a sunken derelict off the Bermuda coast. Worse, the movie distastefully treats all of its black characters as villains, including their exclusively leering at Bisset. As Gary correctly pointed out in his Post review, "since Bisset's bosom has been the main photogenic attraction for the first 15 minutes of the movie, it's quite hypocritical to single out the black characters for getting lustful." Didn't anyone associated with the production think of that? [Caution: sexuality and violence] **[W]**

Exorcist II: The Heretic
1977 – John Boorman
In my capsule on *Hope and Glory*, I commented that Boorman was one of a handful of directors who had made one of my very favorites but whose other works I disdained – this one, for example. Richard Burton stars in the sequel in one of the worst turkeys of all time. It's astoundingly bad for a mainstream production. In fact, words finally fail me, so I'll rely on Gary's dead-on condemnation, derived from personal experience at an early screening. "I've never heard an audience reject a movie as vocally and resoundingly as the packed house (where he attended). In fact, the crowd was so unified in its ridicule of [the]

endless parade of inexplicable, hysterical or unintentionally funny spectacles that the effect was almost the same as being at a good comedy with a receptive audience." More pertinent, Gary speculated that *Exorcist II* seemed "to have evolved out of delusions of cinematic grandeur shared by Boorman and writer William Goodhart. It's obvious that they wanted to contrive a metaphysical thriller that would be astonishing and spiritually inspiring, but their thought processes [were] so muddled that the movie degenerates almost instantly into a confounded shambles." I'll add that Boorman, in an interview following the movie's disastrous response, could barely answer questions about it – words seem to have failed him, too. [Caution: a few intensely scary scenes] **[W]**

The Fury
1976 – Brian De Palma
Legendary New Yorker critic Pauline Kael went bananas for this one, which co-stars Kirk Douglas and Amy Irving. In my view, however, De Palma's follow-up to *Carrie* is an astounding clunker despite its technical razzle-dazzle, without a single affecting moment, and an ending that another critic described as "*Zabriskie Point* (not on my lists) on a personal level," referring to that movie's explosive climax. Given the perspective of nearly half a century, I stand by my assertion. The moviemaking techniques De Palma employed so well in *Carrie*, in which Irving played a crucial role, work not at all here. As yet another critic put it, watching *The Fury*, mostly you find yourself enduring the many dull stretches, waiting for the big set pieces to develop – and they're likewise disappointing. That's no way to do things on the screen. Audiences can be patient and tolerant if the dramatic payoffs are good enough, but those qualities aren't unlimited. Here, they're tested beyond their limits. Along with gushing over the movie, Pauline Kael also loved the John Williams score. As you should know by now, I consider him among the very best – and certainly the best-known and most popular – of film composers. Here? He's shockingly ordinary. No? Replay in your head the themes for *Jaws*, *Star Wars* and *Raiders of the Lost Ark*. Now, try it with the

theme from this one – even after you've just heard it. [Caution: violence] **[W]**

The Godfather Part III
1990 – co-written and directed by Francis Ford Coppola
I can tell you what went wrong with this, the last installment of the saga, in one word: Pacino. Eighteen years earlier, the unknown actor exploded onto the scene with an astounding performance as Michael Corleone, son of Vito, *the* Godfather. Working with Marlon Brando in the title role, Pacino stood toe-to-toe with the acknowledged finest actor of his generation. Then, in *The Godfather Part II*, he deepened and darkened Michael's character; he became unforgettable. But here? It's as though the actor had forgotten everything that constituted his character's personality. The ice in his veins, that chilling stare, that clenched jaw, the menace in his eyes, the constant potential for ferocious outbursts – all gone. Instead, it's as though Michael Corleone had taken an anger-management class from an inept instructor. He's no longer threatening, but at the same time he's no longer interesting. Worst case: Michael replaces his chauffeur to take his ex-wife Kay (Diane Keaton, who's likewise uninteresting) on a brief tour of Sicily. You'd think Michael had never, ever been a "cold-hearted bastard," as he was called in the original movie by his sister Connie (Talia Coppola Shire), and with good reason. Speaking of Connie, for some reason she's always dressed in black and wearing heavy, dark makeup, looking ridiculously like a Dragon Lady. Who on earth thought of that ensemble? Then there's Michael's daughter Mary (played by Sophia Coppola, the director's daughter), who's supposed to be the heart and soul of the movie and the source of Michael's greatest tragedy. Meaning no disrespect to Ms. Coppola, who went on to become an award-winning writer–director, but her presence sucks the air out of every scene she inhabits, particularly when she and Andy Garcia (as Vincent, Michael's heir-apparent) supposedly engage in romantic byplay. I could go on and on, but along with Pacino's non-performance, here's what's wrong with *Part III* in a nutshell. It has to do with Nino Rota's immortal trumpet fanfare, played at

433

the opening of all three installments. In *Part I*, it's self-contained, followed by that understated but riveting first scene. In *Part II*, it's followed by a brief orchestral flourish that instantly enriches the sense of anticipation for what's coming. But in *Part III*, the original brief fanfare returns. It's as though Coppola had nothing further to say. He should have taken that idea to heart before muddying the waters with this enormous letdown. [Caution: violence, language and sexuality] **[W]**

The Great Race
1965 – co-written and directed by Blake Edwards

In a previous category, I mentioned *It's a Mad Mad Mad Mad World* as my late father's favorite movie, explaining that I included it for sentimental reasons even though I didn't particularly care for it. Well, I'd rather sit through all of its 3 hours again than repeat this one. Like *IaMMMMW*, *The Great Race* is an epic-scale comedy. It stars Jack Lemmon, Tony Curtis and Natalie Wood. With that cast, direction by Edwards and a score by Henry Mancini, it should've been a delight. It isn't. It's astoundingly awkward and unfunny. Trying to figure out … what went wrong, I'm reminded of Lemmon and Curtis in *Some Like It Hot*, considered by many (including yours truly) to be the best comedy of all time, a brilliant achievement by writer–director Billy Wilder and his collaborator I.A.L. "Izzy" Diamond. That movie is consistently hilarious, surprising and unforgettable because Wilder and Diamond never forgot the most essential element of good comedy: the humor derives from the situations and the characters' reactions to them. Think about it. In *Some Like It Hot*, we laugh at the predicaments that Jerry and Joe continually bring upon themselves. We aren't laughing at how they're acting – it's how they're *re*acting. Here, Edwards has Lemmon, whose character is "Professor Fate," hamming it up so much that he's basically imitating Snidely Whiplash, the cartoon character in the beloved Rocky and Bullwinkle TV series. Edwards should have known better. It's something that, unless you're the Marx Brothers, never works. An erratic moviemaker occasionally capable of brilliance, he shows only excess here. In the process he fails his actors – and us. **[W]**

Marathon Man
1976 – John Schlesinger

Schlesinger had directed Dustin Hoffman seven years earlier the Oscar-winning but detestable *Midnight Cowboy* (not on this list). He also had done *Far from the Madding Crowd*, a sumptuous version of the Thomas Hardy novel, a decade earlier; and the subtly witty *Cold Comfort Farm* (both in P25) two decades later. Here, in between, Schlesinger and Hoffman tackle William Goldman's novel of the same name, with Roy Scheider as Hoffman's older brother, a CIA operative; Marthe Keller as a woman of mystery; and Laurence Olivier in a rare villainous role, one that garnered him an Oscar nomination. His role also gave the question, "Is it safe?" a chilling meaning in our cultural lexicon. The movie's problem is simple: At bottom, it makes no sense, and it wastes tons of time on matters having little or nothing to do with the story. Example: In the first scene after the opening credits, two individuals engage in a traffic dispute that instantly escalates into road rage and then, effectively, mortal combat. What does it have to do with the plot? To this day, I couldn't tell you. And the title? Well, Hoffman's character runs all the time, something which allows him to escape pursuing bad guys in one sequence. Other than that? Goldman was a legendary screenwriter and script doctor who once said, describing Hollywood, "Nobody knows anything." In this case, he seems to have applied it to himself. [Technical note: *Marathon Man* first displayed the use of Garrett Brown's Steadicam, a soon-to-become standard device allowing smooth shots of characters in motion – in this case, Hoffman's jogging] [Caution: violence and sexuality] **[W]**

Outbreak
1995 – Wolfgang Petersen

In 1994, writer Richard Preston published his best-seller The Hot Zone, about an ... outbreak of the deadly Ebola virus that nearly spread across America. Immediately, moviemakers began plotting how to bring Preston's riveting nonfiction tale to the screen. As often happens in such cases, particularly when they attempt to outhustle one another, the corporate negotiations result in a movie that has little resemblance to the source material. So it is with *Outbreak*, a lame and often laughable drama featuring Dustin Hoffman again, along with Rene Russo and Cuba Gooding Jr. (more about him momentarily). Petersen, who had risen to international prominence 13 years earlier with *Das Boot*, his powerful epic about German U-boats in World War II; and directed *Clear and Present Danger* (P25), based on a Tom Clancy thriller, the year before this one. But that sure directorial hand seems to have vanished here. Every scene and every performance seems clumsy and forced, so an event that should make moviegoers nervous at the possibilities instead provokes a combination of boredom and laughs. It's particularly the case because Petersen and his writers, who shall remain nameless, have interjected a military conspiracy into what should have been a straight drama about fighting a deadly epidemic. It becomes rather silly. As for Gooding, he seems to be the ultimate jack-of-all-trades. There's nothing he can't do, including piloting a helicopter. So, good man to have around. [Caution: violence] **[W]**

Quantum of Solace (and) No Time to Die
2008 and 2021 – Marc Forster and Cary Joji Fukunaga

If you recall in PF5, I praised *Casino Royale* to the heavens. The 2006 debut of Daniel Craig as James Bond, Agent 007 of Her Majesty's Secret Service, gave the Bond franchise, then 44 years old, a fresh new look and feel. Every moment of the movie, from the tense, black&white prologue that exploded into a dazzling, animated credit sequence underlain by a smashing new theme song, "You Know My Name" by Chris Cornell, through the stunning action scenes and harrowing encounters with the bad guys, to the inevitable confrontation between Bond and the character known as Mr. White – with Bond indeed answering the title song in a way that drew audience cheers – showed an elegance, wit and rough-hewn determination missing from the series for many years. The effect was altogether thrilling and satisfying. So…

Despite my eager anticipation for the next installment of the saga of 007, with Craig reprising his role, the whole thing blew up for me from the beginning, as we joined Bond in the midst of transporting White to a rendezvous with "M" (Judi Dench) and what figured to be a serious debriefing. It's a complex, hugely staged vehicular chase scene – but one in which the edits are so quick and numerous that you can't possibly follow it. Instead of leaving you breathless, it leaves you exhausted. Worse, from there, despite a solid supporting cast (Dench, Olga Kurylenko, Mathieu Amalric, Giancarlo Giannini, Gemma Arterton and Jeffrey Wright), *Quantum of Solace* descends into utter confusion. In fact, if you can resist checking Wikipedia for the plot summary, I'll bet you can't give a coherent description. For that matter, how about figuring out what the title means? There's no mention of it within the story. All of it a shame, because what had begun so promisingly with Craig quickly wore out its welcome. [<u>Caution</u>: violence and sexuality] **[W]**

*   *   *

In that same vein, I'm closing with the 25th installment in Bond's six-decade saga, which also marked Daniel Craig's exit from the series. No one worked harder at the role, and at least in his debut in *Casino Royale*, Craig matched the raw energy, menace and sex appeal of Sean Connery at his best as Bond. Over those decades, the productions got more and more expensive, with *No Time to Die* rumored to have cost a whopping $300 million. Among its distinctions is the production's effort to carry off stupendous action sequences as realistically as possible – i.e., with minimal CGI. Okay, okay, it does that and then some. But the movie also does something highly objectionable, something none of the other Bond episodes ever did: It puts young girls in jeopardy – not once but twice. It's a plot device that leaves a bad taste in your mouth, to the point where you want to renounce viewing anything further from the franchise. Less offensive but also a negative: As with *Quantum of Solace*, the plot is so convoluted it defies comprehension. Which brings me to my gripe about most of the series. Ever since *You Only Live Twice*, itself well over half-a-century old now, those increasingly expensive productions, with *Casino Royale* the only exception, have failed to match the entertainment value of the first five – from *Dr. No* to *You Only Live*

Twice. And like so many of the entrées in this category, the fault lies with the scripts. In their efforts to create bigger and bigger villains and fiendish plots, the writers left solid dramatics and common sense behind. Yes, the Bond brand has made billions (an estimated $7 billion to date). But from artistic and cinematic standpoints, the series became a case of diminishing returns. I hope someone someday can conceive a fresh, new and crowd-pleasing persona and assignment for 007. Otherwise, a better title for this one requires removing the word, "No." [<u>Caution</u>: sexuality and violence – including children in peril] **[W]**

An Appreciation and an Appeal

My trilogy of favorites comprises some 1500 titles, with many more mentions sprinkled among them. In those capsule commentaries, I've praised – and occasionally criticized – the work of directors, producers, actors, composers and other professionals. But I can't close down without also expressing appreciation to the legion of other, indispensable participants in the amazing process of creating these treasures of our cultural legacy.

Here's one small example. In every movie you've ever seen, when a character walks across a surface – a wooden floor, a forest path, a concrete sidewalk –you can hear their footsteps. Except those aren't the sounds the actors are making. In movie production, attempting to capture footsteps properly would lay on an extra and burdensome layer of complication for the audio recordists. Can you imagine a situation where a director has called "cut" to end a scene because the actors have performed perfectly, only to hear the recordist announce that the scene must be redone because the footsteps were too soft?

Almost from the beginning of the "talkies," moviemakers realized that the audio elements could be produced separately from the cinematography. Hence, the foley artist emerged. It's a person who re-creates, exactly, the sound of the footsteps – or other noises – supposedly emanating from the actor. Back to the beginning? Yes. In every Fred Astaire and Ginger Rogers movie, for example, you've never heard their real tap-dancing. Instead, the actors, or their supporting dancers, recorded the taps separately in a studio, in sync with the filmed performances. That's why the taps sound so clear.

I remember the first time I began to notice the artistry behind the non-music soundtracks of movies. It was 1976, and I was watching the Academy Awards. At that ceremony, *Jaws* won an Oscar for Best Sound. I had watched Verna Fields win for her brilliant editing of the movie, and John Williams for his now-classic score. But best sound? It was just a trio of guys chasing a shark in the ocean. Other than holding a microphone in the general direction of the action, what else was involved? That's when I began studying the subtle and intricate work of recordist John Carter and the rest of the movie's audio team, and how truly challenging it was for them to capture just the right sounds at just the right moments.

I got to the point where, when the movie's 30th anniversary DVD was released in 2005, I actually noticed that some of those original, Oscar-winning sounds were missing from the disk's audio tracks: a tin can and a license plate being tossed onto a floor; the shark ramming the hull of the Orca, attempting to attack Brody, Hooper and Quint; and the sound of the pistol Brody fires at the shark. All vivid and memorable on the screen, but muted and ordinary in the re-mixed DVD.

So distinctive was the artistry of the audio team.

Here are two other examples, both involving famed makeup artist Stan Winston and his crew. In *Aliens,* the movie introduced the alien queen, a larger, nastier, four-armed version of the original monster. To develop the concept, Winston's team built a full-size mockup of the queen out of steel rods and foam rubber, with two crewmembers hiding inside to work all of the arms. Eventually, the men were replaced by hydraulic controls, but those controls required more than a dozen operators.

A few years later, in the original *Jurassic Park,* the technology had advanced to where Winston and company could render a complete, mechanical T-Rex without first building such a crude mock-up. This time, the crew needed to fabricate and attach the animal's skin as well as design, build and execute the controlling mechanisms. In both cases, though, their creations worked perfectly, and audiences screamed and recoiled with delight.

I can give you hundreds more such cases, from the location scouts, set designers, costumers and hair stylists to the sketch artists and modelers who create the initial concepts and the craftsmen who build the objects that impress and delight us. And don't forget the brave stunt people who risk their lives to bring us vicarious excitement and protect the safety of the actors and actresses we long to see. Their collective work is on the screen as well.

To all of them, my sincere thanks for the memories!

*   *   *

As far as my appeal, .it concerns the best possible venue for watching the movies I have listed, in all three compilations. That's in a movie theater, on a big screen, in the company of dozens, hundreds or even thousands of like-minded fans. Yes, movies had their beginnings on tiny screens called Nickelodeons. And yes, it took decades before the theaters installed ever-larger screens. But eventually the communal experience of moviegoing firmly established itself in our culture. People still go to the movies, but not nearly in the numbers of the past. That's a shame. Speaking from personal experience, I've spent some of the best and most memorable times of my life in movie theaters. Don't let such a precious part of our culture slip away. Whenever you can, make the effort to see an intriguing attraction on that big screen, in the company of moviegoers. In particular, consider this whenever a classic or a favorite is being revived. Help keep the practice alive.

And one more thing. Over the course of the 20th century, what were popularly known as movie palaces became among the grandest and most beautiful buildings in the country, places where legions of fans gained memories to last a lifetime. Some of those palaces remain standing, and some show movies to this day. Whenever you can, patronize them. Support them. Fight for them. They represent a precious and irreplaceable part of our cultural heritage. And if they can be preserved, I have no doubt they will delight and entertain audiences for many generations to come.

Recommended Books

Building on the format of my previous two compilations, here now are 50 – count 'em, 50! – worthwhile reads related to the titles reviewed above.

Against the Ice
Ejnar Mikkelsen

An updated version published in conjunction with the movie of the same name, it's Mikkelsen's own account of his grueling two-and-a-half years in Greenland, first leading the rescue mission looking for traces of the lost Denmark Expedition of 1907, then waiting for a rescue himself, along with his ship's mechanic Iver Iversen, both trying to hang onto their sanity, as portrayed in Peter Flinth's often-electrifying drama.

An American Tragedy
Theodore Dreiser

Dreiser's landmark 1925 novel, based on a true incident and resulting criminal trial, describes in excruciating detail an ambitious young man's rise and fall, brought about entirely by the choices he made for himself. The story has been adapted repeatedly over the decades, but arguably never better than in George Stevens's *A Place in the Sun*.

The Best Exotic Marigold Hotel
Deborah Moggach

The source of the original movie of the same name, which generated the sequel listed elsewhere, Moggach's novel is a bit different from, and darker than, either story, which chronicles the escape of several elderly Brits to would-be cheap and pleasant retirement in India, where they are quickly hit with the reality of their situations – and its eventual unexpected benefits and pleasures.

The Big Year: A Tale of Man, Nature and Fowl Obsession
Mark Obmascik
Updated as a companion to the movie *The Big Year*, Obmascik's book chronicles the trio battling to hold the 1998 record as they venture into deserts, swamps, Arctic terrain and other avian habitats while logging over 200,000 miles for the bragging rights of becoming the world's best birder.

The Blackboard Jungle
Evan Hunter
Hunter's semi-autobiographical novel served as the basis for the hard-hitting movie of the same name, a portrayal of a new teacher's ordeal in an inner-city school in the 1950s – though unlike his fictional protagonist, who persevered, Hunter quit teaching after only a few months.

The Body
Stephen King
Originally a short story, King's novella became the basis for *Stand By Me*, Rob Reiner's tale of five boys lured by the possibility of viewing their first dead body.

Born on the Fourth of July
Ron Kovic
The basis for Oliver Stone's powerful but highly opinionated movie of the same name, the book chronicles Kovic's blunt, shattering memoir of his youth, his enlistment in the Army and his service during the Vietnam War, including his tragic injury and its aftermath, and his personal perspectives on the system that pursued the war and the factors that eventually turned much of America against the military and political establishments.

Cold Mountain
Charles Frazier
Frazier's 1997 debut novel became one of the fastest-rising best-sellers of all time. It depicts the desperate odyssey of a wounded Civil War soldier as he tries to reach his lover amid the collapse of the Confederacy, while she tries to keep body and soul together while awaiting his return.

Dangerous Liaisons
Choderlos de Laclos (translated by Helen Constantine)
Military warfare is always a dangerous occupation. But as de Laclos illustrates in his early 19th-century novel, written in the form of correspondence among the key players, romantic pursuits can be just as treacherous and deadly, with an equal amount of unintended consequences.

The Death and Life of Dith Pran
Sydney H. Schanberg
The real-life chronicle of a survivor of Cambodia's notorious genocide at the hands of the Khmer Rouge in the mid-1970s, by the New York Times reporter, whose story became the inspiration for the film *The Killing Fields*.

The Dig
John Preston
Preston's meticulous novel served as the basis for the movie starring Ralph Fiennes and Carey Mulligan, and depicting the real … dig that yielded one of the biggest archaeological finds in British history.

Dodsworth
Sinclair Lewis
Lewis's satirical novel takes aim at the social mores of America and Europe in the 1920s, as the Sam Dodsworth of the title retires from the automobile business at age 50 and takes a long-desired transatlantic cruise to Europe with his wife, setting in motion a series of severe challenges to his marriage and his self-image.

Dracula
Bram Stoker
Along with Mary Shelley's <u>Frankenstein</u>, Stoker's chilling novel is the most famous tale of horror from the 19th century, describing as it does the world of the Transylvanian count who sleeps by day and ravages by night – and attacks the social values of his time.

The Exorcist
William Peter Blatty
From 19th-century horror to more modern times, Blatty's tale about demonic possession in Georgetown has scared the bejeebers out of readers and movie audiences alike, from a half-century ago to this day.

Fahrenheit 451
Ray Bradbury
Originally published in 1953, Bradbury's novel concerns a totalitarian future where forbidden books are burned (the title refers to the ignition temperature of paper), and a secret group of brave individuals preserves literary history by memorizing entire texts and then teaching the younger generation to remember them. Chilling yet ultimately hopeful.

The Films in My Life
François Truffaut
Apart from being an exceptional moviemaker, Truffaut was a fine writer, and his love of the film medium, which could be described as a benign obsession – he lived and breathed almost nothing but movies – permeates this loving take on the medium. Containing more than a hundred of his reviews and essays, it's a classic that should be owned by every cinephile on the planet.

Flags of Our Fathers
James Bradley (with Ron Powers)
Consider this one of my highest recommendations. Perhaps the most iconic photo in our country's history captured the moment, in February 1945, during the terrible battle of Iwo Jima when U.S.

Marines raised the Stars and Stripes on Mount Suribachi, high above the beaches where they had recently stormed and fought for every inch of the island. John Bradley was one of those men, and his son James's account of his father's experience – based not on his father's words (he never spoke of his ordeal) but on his letters and personal photos – powerfully conveys that desperate struggle, as well as a poignant look at what happened to the men afterward.

The Garden of the Finzi-Continis
Giorgio Bassani (translated by William Weaver)

Superbly adapted by Vittorio de Sica, Bassini's dark tale of two fictionalized Italian Jewish families delivers an understated but shattering account of the scourge of the Holocaust descending on the country of Hitler's ally Benito Mussolini during the early years of World War II. In an interesting bit of literary trivia (for a change) Bassini wrote his novel in the home of the father of Judge Guido Calabresi, whose mother's family name was Finzi-Contini and who served from 1959 to 1994 as Dean of the Yale Law School.

The Getting of Wisdom and My Brilliant Career
(Henry Handel Richardson and Miles Franklin)

In the tradition of George Eliot and Isak Dinesen (Mary Ann Evans and Karen Blixen), two brilliant European novelists who wrote under male pseudonyms, here are two more – and if you search you can find both within a single volume. Richardson (Ethel Florence Lindesay Richardson) is linked to the 1978 movie encapsuled elsewhere, and the exquisite *My Brilliant Career* (see PF5), based on Franklin's novel (Stella Maria Sarah Miles Franklin), was made the following year by Gillian Armstrong. Each portrays the life of a distinctive, determined, appealing female protagonist growing up in Australia in the early 20th century, and each is a worthwhile read particularly for young women seeking perspective on earlier times as well as an entertaining read.

The Great Santini
Pat Conroy
Conroy's semi-autobiographical novel chronicles the difficult, often fiery relationship between an ambitious and exemplary young man and his strict disciplinarian father, an ill-fated military flier.

The Harder They Fall
Budd Schulberg
The source of the 1954 movie of the same name starring Humphrey Bogart, it's Schulberg's hard-hitting but fictional expose of corruption in professional boxing. Heavyweight champion Gene Tunney once called it "the best book on fighting that I have read."

Hawaii
James A. Michener
First published in 1959, Michener's chronicle of the millennium-long Polynesian history of the Hawai'ian Islands, which collided with the zealous faith of Christian missionaries arriving in the 19th century, makes for an epic drama.

Hillbilly Elegy
J.D. Vance
Vance's extraordinary odyssey from deep poverty in rural Kentucky to a successful career, first in the military, then as a lawyer and finally as a politician with national aspirations, all due to the stern but steady guidance of his maternal grandmother.

Hitchcock/Truffaut
François Truffaut
In this groundbreaking volume, Truffaut spent 50 hours interviewing the renowned director about every facet of his work over his half-century career. It's one of the most penetrating looks at the creative cinematic process.

The Hot Zone
Richard Preston

Too bad the producers of *Outbreak* couldn't match Preston's storytelling ability. His non-fiction chronicle reads like the best of suspense novels, from its bone-chilling opening sequence to its methodical but equally scary description of the extreme dangers of dealing with a new and highly infectious organism.

The Iliad and The Odyssey

Enjoy *Troy* as a laughable epic, but then consider exploring these two classics of the Western world, together in a single concise volume, penned by the Shakespeare of his day. Whether legend or history, Homer's Iliad creates one of the most captivating stories of all time. Centering on the abduction of Helen, a Greek princess of surpassing beauty, by Paris, a Trojan prince and her lover, it also celebrates a group of great warriors; Ajax, Achilles and Hector as well as a quartet of fascinatingly complex kings: Agamemnon, Priam, Menelaus and Odysseus. It's a grand tale for the ages. As is The Odyssey, which furthers the story of Odysseus and creates the model for all vast journeys – odysseys. It's a rendering of the king's decade-long return to Greece after the Trojan War, including encounters (as depicted on the cover image) with the beautiful but deadly Sirens, the various Greek gods of sea and sky, and several enemy forces. These two works deserve a place in every home library.

In Cold Blood
Truman Capote

Capote's account of the 1959 murder of a Holcomb, Kansas, farming family actually helped create a new literary genre: the non-fiction novel. An exceptionally well-written reconstruction of the murders, the manhunt and eventual capture of the killers, and their trial and execution, it's a landmark work, made more so by the fact that the ordeal extracted such an emotional cost from Capote that In Cold Blood became his last book.

Like Water for Chocolate
Laura Esquivel

Esquivel's best-seller chronicling the saga of Tita, her sisters and her suitors in a series of chapters linked to the months of the year and including the recipes for the dishes served in the movie.

The Long Walk
Slavomir Rawicz

In 1941, when World War II was still in its early days, and China was allied with the United States against Japan, author Rawicz claimed that he and six other fellow prisoners escaped a Soviet labor camp in Yakutsk, Siberia, and walked nearly 4,000 miles to British India. A best-seller in its day, the Rawicz's account has periodically been challenged by historians and other experts for its accuracy. Nevertheless, it's a gripping account, as also portrayed in Peter Weir's *The Way Back*.

Madam Bovary
Gustave Flaubert

Flaubert's tragic, mid-19th-century novel has been called the story of the original desperate housewife, a woman trapped in an unhappy marriage who seeks satisfaction and happiness elsewhere, both sexually and via profligate spending. It might be why the novel has been one of the most adapted works in all of cinema. In this movie compilation, Emma's story is portrayed with some strange and comic twists in *Gemma Bovery*.

The Man-Eaters of Tsavo: And Other East African Adventures
John Henry Patterson

Patterson, an engineer working for the British Army, is assigned to build a railroad bridge in Kenya in 1898. Little does he know on arrival that among his duties will be to track down and kill two huge and voracious male lions who have been savagely attacking the construction workers – or that the hunt for the predators will take nine months and cost 130 lives. Still in print after a century, it's a riveting account of the incident that became the basis for *The Ghost and the Darkness*.

The Man Who Never Was (and) Operation Mincemeat
Ewen Montagu (and) Ben Macintyre

Few books enjoy the privilege of inspiring more than one movie, and even fewer the distinction of serving as the source of two excellent screen stories, but Montagu's autobiographical chronicle of his participation in one of the biggest and most crucial deceptions of World War II fits that description. Likewise, Macintyre's painstakingly detailed, skillfully written account of the operation.

The Martian
Andy Weir

Weir's best-seller chronicles the desperate and painstaking efforts by astronaut Mark Watney to survive after a tragic accident results in his being marooned on the Red Planet with no chance of rescue for perhaps four years. It's a meticulous speculation about how human life could gain a foothold on our nearest planetary neighbor.

No Time for Sergeants
Mac Hyman

Hyman's witty, semiautobiographical novel differs from the movie – and from Ira Levin's play – by telling the story of Air Force Private Will Stockdale from the protagonist's point of view.

North Dallas Forty
Peter Gent

Gent, a former wide receiver for the Dallas Cowboys in the 1960s under coach Tom Landry and quarterback Don Meredith, condensed and dramatized his career in this best-selling novel, one of the most penetrating looks at pro football ever published.

Oliver Twist
Charles Dickens

Original title <u>Oliver Twist, or the Parish Boy's Progress</u>, Dickens' second novel was published, as were many of his later works, in newspaper installments over a period of two years beginning in 1837. It's considered one of the first social novels. The author used the story to expose the cruel conditions to which 19th-century London's poor were subjected by following a young waif's journey from an orphanage to the streets and thievery, and finally to redemption via the kindness of an adoptive father.

One Flew Over the Cuckoo's Nest
Ken Kesey

Kesey's counterculture best-seller depicts the tragic collision of wills between free-spirit prison inmate Randle P. McMurphy and strict disciplinarian Nurse Ratched in a minimum-security mental institution in Oregon in the 1960s. The novel became the source of the Oscar-winning movie starring Jack Nicholson and Louise Fletcher.

Pentimento: A Book of Portraits
Lillian Hellman

The source of the movie *Julia*, the book traces various episodes and acquaintances in the author's life. The title in Italian literally means repentance but is used metaphorically in the work to describe the artistic phenomenon where a visible trace of an earlier painting shows beneath a layer or layers of paint on a canvas. Particularly when poor artists could ill afford supplies, they frequently began a work then became dissatisfied – repented, so to speak – and painted over an image rather than striking a fresh canvas.

Pride and Prejudice
Jane Austen

Not featured among my list of movies in this compilation, I nevertheless recommend it for two reasons: It's the inspiration for Helen Fielding's novel <u>Bridget Jones's Diary</u> (not here), subsequently made into the 2001 movie of the same name – which I did include elsewhere. Also, it's one of the finest and most entertaining reads of the 19th century, so it's worth considering in any event.

Primary Colors
"Anonymous"
The novel, whose author was eventually unmasked as political writer Joe Klein, is a delicious, biting, thinly veiled insider's description of life behind the scenes with Bill and Hillary Clinton during the 1992 presidential campaign.

The Railway Man
Eric Lomax
Lomax, a British soldier serving in Singapore at the outbreak of World War II, is taken prisoner by the Japanese and transported up the Malay Peninsula to a site near the border with Thailand. There, he and his surviving comrades are forced to build a new railway line for their captors, similar to the plotline in *The Bridge on the River Kwai* (PF5) – except this story focuses on the ordinary soldiers, and of course Lomax in particular. Considerably different from the movie, Lomax's account presents a harrowing story with a most unexpected resolution.

The Red Shoes
Hans Christian Andersen
Andersen's beloved children's story that became the basis for the classic film.

A River Runs Through It
Norman Maclean
Journalist Maclean spent several frustrating years attempting to find a publisher for his lovely novella. Eventually, he turned to the University of Chicago Press, which reaped the benefits of its rapid popularity.

The Russia House
John Le Carré

Le Carré's absorbing 12th novel explores the closing days of the Cold War, with Russian and British spies attempting to wring every last bit of intelligence out of one another, and with an ordinary bookseller caught in the middle and fighting to save the lives of his love and her children.

The Strange Case of Dr. Jekyll and Mr. Hyde
Robert Lewis Stevenson

Along with Bram Stoker's Dracula (above) and Mary Shelley's Frankenstein (see PF5) Stevenson's dark tale of a scientist's experimentation with a literal split personality marks yet another example of the formidable imaginations of 19th-century novelists. And, as with those other two classics, *Dr. Jekyll and Mr. Hyde* remains a frequent source of cinematic adaptation.

Surely You're Joking, Mr. Feynman! and What Do You Care What Other People Think?
Richard P. Feynman

For further reading if you've sampled the part of Feynman's story portrayed in *Infinity*, you might want to sample these two works; subtitled, respectively, "Adventures of a Curious Character" and "Further Adventures of a Curious Character," the two memoirs describe the life and work of one of the most brilliant, literate and accessible physicists of the 20th century. One reviewer praised Feynman's work as "buzzing with energy, anecdote and life," adding that he "almost makes you want to become a physicist."

The Three Musketeers
Alexandre Dumas

Dumas's classic action novel is among the most frequently adapted to the screen. The story of D'Artagnan, a 17th-century French swordsman who, with his comrades Athos, Porthos and Aramis, fight for the honor of the Queen against the advances of the evil Cardinal Richelieu, has captivated readers for generations.

The Water Is Wide
Pat Conroy

The autobiographical novel that became the 1974 movie *Conrack* chronicles Conroy's year of teaching black children on a small, isolated island off the South Carolina coast. Quite a bit more detailed than the story in the movie, the book covers the environmental degradation threatening the idyllic life of the island's residents. A fine early work by a gifted American writer.

Alphabetical List of Titles

D

H

Q

R

S

T

W

X

Y

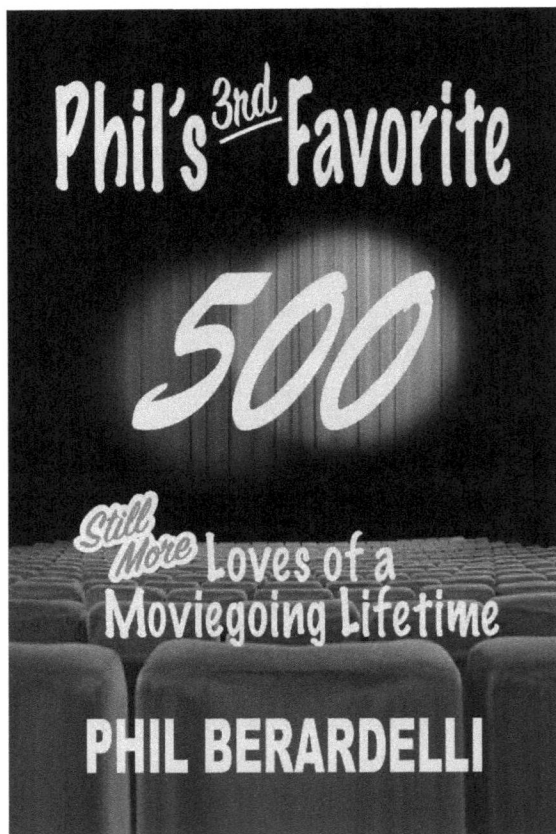

If you have enjoyed browsing through this compilation, please consider buying the ebook edition as well. Along with all of the content within these pages, I've included hundreds of links to movie clips and featurettes plus other references related to the capsule reviews. It's an inexpensive ($6.99) but fascinating and valuable addition to your moviegoing library.

www.ingramcontent.com/pod-product-compliance
Lightning Source LLC
Chambersburg PA
CBHW060234100426
42742CB00011B/1529